D1030764

FORBIDDEN NEIGHBORS

A Study of Prejudice in Housing

FORBIDDEN

HARPER & BROTHERS

by *CHARLES ABRAMS*

NEIGHBORS

New York

To Ruth

C O N T E N T S

PREFACE

THOUGH I had often sensed the close link between the housing problem and the growth of prejudice in American communities, the more serious aspects of the relationship became clearer to me in 1946 after Roger N. Baldwin, then director of the American Civil Liberties Union, and Walter White, of the National Association for the Advancement of Colored People, had asked me to prepare a pamphlet on race bias in housing.[1] In gathering the facts for the pamphlet I was surprised at the nature of the assumptions which had worked their way into popular thinking. Homeowners, home-builders, and mortgage-lenders seemed convinced that people should live only with their own kind, that the presence of a single minority family destroys property values and undermines social prestige and status. National and local real estate organizations were accepting these assumptions as gospel, as were popular magazines, college texts, and technical journals. They were being taught in many colleges as fact, translated into policy, and even the federal government, now the main influence in homebuilding, was making racial exclusion and neighborhood homogeneity its official position.

A major change had taken place in American neighborhoods, with vast implications for America's social and political structures, but these implications had not even been explored. What was known as the slum problem had become largely a *minority* slum problem and the most serious aspects of the housing problem appeared to be the problem of housing those minorities, who were now mostly non-whites.

[1] Charles Abrams, *Race Bias in Housing,* sponsored jointly by the American Civil Liberties Union, the National Association for the Advancement of Colored People, and the American Council on Race Relations. New York, July, 1947.

While minorities had made substantial gains economically, these gains were threatened on the housing front. As the focus of racial conflict widened with the movement of nonwhites to the North, discrimination, a word generally associated with the South, began to evidence itself in northern cities and in their expanding suburbs. The discrimination took form in the creation of segregated patterns in new and old neighborhoods, in the withholding of housing which minorities needed, and in their wholesale displacement from areas in which they had already settled. Discrimination was reinforced by social sanctions and by violence which erupted in city after city.

The most serious danger, however, lay in the political sphere. In the transition from a private to a welfare economy, private housing operations were now being implemented by public power, public credit, and public subsidy. And there was the danger that the prejudices of the private market would not only be adopted and supported by the government but be backed by its coercive power. From 1935 to 1950, in fact, prejudice and public power were already well advanced toward an alliance which was challenging the fundamental values of the American system.

Considerable progress has been made in the last few years in alerting officials to their ethical responsibilities and to the dangers implicit in the support of private prejudices. Favorable judicial decisions, successful demonstrations of interracial cooperation, and economic progress achieved by minorities are other positive factors. But the fight is far from won and the dangers far from eliminated. They loom larger with the weakening of institutional protections which have occurred in other sectors of the political process.

At such a time the need for exposing the facts and pressing for the exertion of ethical responsibility by official agencies becomes paramount. It is with this in view that I have written this book, neither concealing the frustrations nor underestimating the hopes.

I am indebted to a number of people who helped make this a better book: Lloyd Rodwin, for his painstaking reading of the manuscript and his valuable criticism; Alexander L. Crosby, for his editorial revisions; Hortense W. Gabel, of the National Committee Against Discrimination in Housing, for pressing me to write it, as well as for her comments; Esther S. Rosenzweig, for her continued assistance in the many details and for her valuable suggestions; Rhoda Dupler, for her research on some of the background chapters and other sections; Elliot Cohen, for his criticism of various articles on the subject which appeared in *Commentary;* Shirley Adelson Siegel, G. D. N. Worswick; Frank S. Horne and Corienne R. Morrow of the Racial Relations Service of the Housing and Home Finance Agency, for reviewing the manuscript; Blanche M. Koffler, for some of the background material in Chapter X; the Anti-Defamation League, the American Jewish Congress, and the American Jewish Committee, for affording me access to their files; finally, to my students at the New School for Social Research, the University of Pennsylvania, the City College of New York, and the Massachusetts Institute of Technology, all of whom graciously served as sounding boards for many of the ideas here expressed. The title *Forbidden Neighbors* is also the title of a brouchure issued by the New York State Committee on Discrimination in Housing, and I am indebted to the Committee for allowing me to use the title in the same cause.

New York City
January, 1955

I

RENASCENCE AND REACTION

WHILE race, color, and religious frictions have been common throughout history, these frictions have assumed a new emphasis in the world's cities.

Increasing industrialization and the inability of rural areas to support their populations intensified urban migration. The newcomers to the cities were often different in color, background, race, religion, or social status. There was no housing for them and none could be built at costs they could afford. Squatting, slums, and overcrowding became common. Simultaneously the competition for sites and housing, coupled with the differences between the newer and older residents, brought tensions and demands for the newcomers' exclusion or segregation. Patterns differed throughout the world. Sometimes segregation was effected by voluntary agreement between residents, sometimes by compulsion.[1]

The need for city rebuilding after World War II, the growing housing shortage, and the general assumption of national responsibility for mass welfare brought a sharp increase in the powers of governments. This in turn led to an effort to employ the expanded public powers toward segregating the new minorities. It also posed the critical question of whether official sanction would now be lent to the isolation and segregation of people who were different, and

---

[1] Examples of the voluntary agreement are the private racial restrictive covenants in the United States and Kenya, Africa. In Holland, voluntary segregation is being effected through Catholic and Protestant cooperative housing developments. In South Africa, racial zoning is official policy. Housing programs in Tanganyika provide for future separation of natives from Europeans. In Southern Rhodesia, Asians insist on the right to homes in the European area, but Moslems shun Hindus as neighbors and vice versa.

thereby reverse a tendency toward tolerance for diversity and an impartial use of public power which had been the most promising aspects of nineteenth-century political and social development.

In this context the spotlight turned upon the United States which for more than 150 years after its founding had remained the world's beacon of liberty and its haven of tolerance. To the victims of religious, economic, and political oppression who sought its refuge, the new nation had always offered a Bill of Rights which declared people equal, regardless of race or color. Its immigration doors were open and the same opportunities, privileges, and protections were offered to newcomers as to those already there; despite the differences in their origins, they could secure land, speak freely, and protest; they could move at will, work or quit their jobs, raise their children without fear.

There was, of course, bias and strife during the adjustment process. But as the immigrant bettered his lot, he was free to move up the social or economic scale. No ghetto hemmed him in when he chose to leave it. His children could mix with those of the landowner, teacher, artist, writer, or trader. Prejudice and discrimination remained personalized and did not corrupt the underlying political morality. America came as near to providing a social and economic utopia as any nation since the dawn of history.

That the country could remain unaffected by the disruptive forces at play made its demonstrated principles the more remarkable. There was the anomaly of slavery; the mass influx of peoples of different nationalities, races, and backgrounds; the rise of industrialism and its subordination of the old rural economy; the corruptive influences of some who sought to pervert the governmental processes. All these obstacles this unique country overcame. And though in 1954 new pressures pull at its great democratic foundations, and conflicts between groups erupt in its cities, it still stands with enough of its old reserves to continue as an example of tolerance for the world.

To understand the force of these reserves and the contrast they offer to policies elsewhere, the impact upon this country of four world revolutions must be examined.

The first was a political revolution, the concepts and inspirations of which still exert their moral influence upon American institutions and people. It asserted the rights of the individual over the state, guaranteeing him the right of privacy, security against forfeiture of his property, and civil and political protection. Where beliefs differed, men could nevertheless practice them freely. They were not handicapped by their diversity. If uniformity existed at any point in the pattern it was uniformity in the faith that underlay it—a faith in man's ability to form a society offering equal access to its opportunities and a guarantee of natural or fundamental rights.

Reinforcing these general principles came the second revolution—a revolution in land.[2] Land in the eighteenth century had been the dominant form of wealth, the great arcade into opportunity. "The United States," said Madison in 1787, "have a precious advantage also in the actual distribution of property, particularly the landed property; and in the universal hope of acquiring property." The latter "peculiarity" constituted one of the "happiest contrasts in their situation to that of the old world." The majority of the nation were "freeholders, or the heirs, or aspirants to Freeholds."[3]

The popular view was that government lands represented sterilized wealth that should be handed over to individual exploitation without delay. The aim, not always fulfilled, was to put small holdings into the hands of the rank and file. The English system of great landholdings could not take root in this country, nor could its feudal tenures, entailments, quit-rents, and restraints against alienation.

Most of the public land was thereafter sold in small parcels on easy terms and even the larger tracts that had been turned over to speculators were subsequently divided into small holdings. The nature of the landed operations made for individualized development, the operations remaining personal, small-scale, and localized. Subsistence was available through self-help, and specialization had not yet arrived to subordinate men to bureaucratic routines. As federal lands were parcelled out, the dominating theme became profit rather than prestige, turnover rather than engrossment. No matter how riotous the speculation, how regrettable the methods of disposal, one thing seemed certain: ownership of land was unaffected by caste, ancestry, race, or religion. No dead hand prevented property from

[2] For a more extended exposition, see Charles Abrams, *Revolution in Land.* New York, Harper & Brothers, 1939.

[3] *The Records of the Federal Convention of 1787,* (Max Farrand, ed.). New Haven, Yale University Press, 1911, vol. III, p. 451.

being sold. If land ownership was also a way of life to some, it was not the prestige of large-scale ownership and accumulation that was the main aim of tenure, but fluidity of choice in holding, buying, selling, or moving on to other opportunities.

In 1861, Lincoln could still describe America as a nation where no worker was permanently fixed to a condition of life.

> The prudent, penniless beginner in the world labors for wages a while, saves a surplus with which to buy tools or land for himself, then labors on his own account another while, and at length hires another new beginner to help him. This is the just and generous and prosperous system which opens the way to all . . . gives hope to all, and consequent energy and progress and improvement of condition to all.[4]

Suburban snobbism had not yet emerged, urban mobbism had not materialized as feared.

The Civil War marked the end of the southern landholding class as a major political force in America, shifted the Negro's status from slave to minority, and conferred upon the Negro minority the freedom to own land and property. The Fourteenth Amendment and an accompanying statute declared that "all citizens shall have the same right in every state and territory as is enjoyed by White citizens thereof to inherit, purchase, lease, sell, hold and convey real and personal property." The Civil War victory also endowed the Negro with a new right he never had as a slave—the freedom to move without his master's permission. This indeed was his primary freedom. With the increasing call for labor in the North, the Negro did move, slowly at first, and more recently by the millions.

With the dawn of the twentieth century the new industrial system superimposed itself upon the old pattern with an unremitting momentum. Its new entrepreneurs were no paragons of Christian virtue, striving to bring equality and happiness to men. Indeed theirs was a struggle for inequality. To make more money they imported cheap contract labor and broke the backs of native labor seeking a better wage. Under the overruling drives that marked the period they watered stocks, exploited the public, ruthlessly wiped out opposition. Yet oddly their stark ruthlessness worked to the benefit of minorities. The pattern made for a hiring of labor in a free market and tended to keep the competition open on the basis of skill not skull, talent not

[4] Message to Congress.

pigment, toil and moil not breed or creed. America, in fact, developed into a nation of minorities and the Negro who moved to the North was no better or worse off than other migrants. Bias existed, but it was localized and contained. Racial or anti-alien agitation, when it erupted, exhausted itself in harmless episodes. The Jewish, Negro, or Catholic immigrant who was kept out of certain trades by biased employers might be held back for a time but would soon find his direction.

The institutional pattern erected during the old land economy survived to afford its protection in the new industrial era. The function of government was to assure full freedom of opportunity both in agriculture and industry. Its role was that of custodian of the democratic morals: to keep the channels of opportunity open and to see that free enterprise remained truly free—a cash transaction in the open market, something not to be subordinated to monopolistic practices or inequities imposed on the basis of color, race, or religion. Any discriminatory deviation in the state's activities was made subject to check by the constitution, the Civil Rights Acts, and the public policy.

There were setbacks and some incursions upon rights almost from the beginning. There were the early Alien and Sedition Laws and the more recent local exclusion devices. But federal and state governments were drawn steadily toward imposing their higher constitutional standards upon private enterprise when the latter threatened to forsake the cash-nexus for the racial-nexus. Hotels and restaurants were forbidden by northern states to discriminate though they were private businesses. Courts, though refusing to outlaw segregation in schools, nevertheless insisted upon equivalence; they refused to enforce contracts that were against public policy. Public policy increasingly reflected a concern for the ideals which had symbolized the nation's founding. The free enterprise society, regulated by democratic government against abuse, soon produced one of the great historical demonstrations of a democratically tolerant society. Though ghettos appeared on urban horizons, they were voluntary. Though there was anti-alien antagonism and violence, they were not long lasting.

Soon one could see within a single city block the newly evolving pattern of the Jewish tradesman, the Italian barber, the Chinese laundryman, the German restaurant keeper, and the Negro superintendent. Any of them could live with his own countrymen or not, as he chose, and few in the cities considered it an assault on neighborhood dignity if the servant or tradesman moved into the same general area with those he served. Distances between home and work place were measured by furlongs and limited by the horse's endurance, so that employee and employer, mistress and servant, tradesman and customer, lived in the same neighborhoods, albeit in sharply different houses. Minorities in fact had to live nearby to serve their financial betters, launder their collars and cuffs, bake their bread, trim their sideburns. Their presence undermined neither the social status of their more fortunate neighbors nor the value of their Victorian mansions. Indeed, it was fashionable for the mansion folk to have their Negro housekeepers live in the house across the alley, if not within the houses themselves. The type of structure was more reliable than the type of neighbors in gauging wealth and status. In the smaller cities, too, old and young, Catholic and Protestant, Negro and white, well-born and humble, all lived in the same general area without loss of face or position.

These three revolutions—political, land and industrial—were worldwide, but they had affected the different countries of the world with varying impacts. In Russia, Italy, and Germany the political revolution had won few lasting reforms for the individual, and the state retained the dominant controls. The land revolution which had swept through the United States, France, Belgium, Holland, and Scandinavia came later in Germany, only recently in such countries as India and Mexico, and not at all in some South American countries where latifundia still persist. In England, though land remained in relatively few hands, corrective measures were taken only after the turn of the century to redistribute ownership or to bring it under greater public control.[5] In Russia, the state had taken over all the land, and concentration of land ownership was merged with concentration of political controls to effect one of the strongest consolidations of power in world history.

Later in the twentieth century another revolution began to make its influence felt—a welfare revolution. The welfare revolution in the

[5] The first dramatic effort came with Lloyd George's budget in the early part of this century and the trend is still under way. See also: Expert Committee on Compensation and Betterment, *Final Report* (popularly known as the Uthwatt Report) London, H.M. Stationery Office, 1942; *Town and Country Planning 1943-1951*, London, H.M. Stationery Office, 1951.

United States was ushered in during the administration of President Franklin D. Roosevelt. The general welfare clause of the Constitution, after continued evasion of the issue by the Supreme Court, was finally construed as an independent and a substantive power authorizing direct federal expenditure and legislation in the general welfare.[6] The federal government was no longer to be limited or its functions circumscribed by the specific powers once granted it by the states. Now it could lend and spend, regulate and condemn land, insure risks, build housing or other public works in the general interest. Its aims were partly humanitarian and partly economic. The revolution affected minorities profoundly.

The curtailment of European immigration in the 1920's had created a void in the labor market. Negro sharecroppers left their rural slums and farms where they had been earning 75 cents a day for the cities. Here, though their wages were still half those of whites, they could improve their living standards. The depression set them back, but as the New Deal primed the recovery and the war boom accelerated it, they resumed their northward move. The sharp demand for labor now opened up new jobs, while high employment kept them steadily at work. White Okies and Arkies, driven from their farms by drought and dust storms, took unskilled, semiskilled, and skilled jobs in industry. Mexicans pushed up from the Rio Grande, and Puerto Ricans migrated from their hard-pressed island in the Caribbean.

One of the most difficult problems for the new minorities was housing. The Negroes, Puerto Ricans, and Mexicans were identifiable by their color. The assimilative processes which had functioned so effectively in neighborhoods for most white European immigrants worked sluggishly for the new migrants. Social differences were highlighted more sharply as they moved into the cities; older settlers resented intrusion by the newcomers. Housing shortages added to the difficulties and sparked tensions.

Simultaneously the New Deal's interest in housing produced some thorny problems for them. Occupancy policies and the conditions for urban settlement were now increasingly influenced by public agencies and public policy. An odd tendency soon developed. While nonwhites were able to move into some publicly owned housing

[6] *Steward Machine Co. v Davis*, 301 U.S. 548.

projects built under a small public housing appropriation, other housing agencies sponsoring vast new neighborhoods were actively encouraging private bias and advocating social and racial discrimination.

In the process there was danger that a serious mutation of the democratic pattern might be occurring almost unnoticed: the right to move where one pleased was steadily being impaired by social and economic sanctions privately executed and publicly endorsed. Race hatred seemed to have become the stock-in-trade of land-hucksters, realtors, "civic associations," and suburban journalists. New all-white neighborhoods were creating segregated schools and community life. The racial issue was becoming centered around the home, the most emotional possession of the American family and mass interest in bias was being generated as millions of homeowners were falling easy prey to opportunism or bigotry. Bombings and arson were employed to dislodge Negroes and other minorities who had moved into white neighborhoods and scores of lives were lost in race riots in Detroit, Chicago, and elsewhere.

The rioting and bombings were localized incidents. They were lawless and could be checked by police action. Bias remained a personal matter and might respond to the processes of education. Simultaneously, too, segregation in education and transportation were being struck at by the courts, and important legal and economic gains were being won. Despite the gains, however, a larger danger loomed— the democratic structure was being threatened at a crucial flank.

The danger lay in the open use of public powers to effect discrimination. Public powers were reinforcing discriminatory practices in housing and preventing minorities from moving into areas as they pleased. By 1940 the freehold economy which had opened land to all began to be modified by a rigid and constricting system of restrictions.

In many cities, land for homes could no longer be bought by minority families. Government agencies advocated covenants under which Negroes, Mexicans, Orientals, and other minorities were being forcibly confined to ghettos. Up to 1948, racial covenants were not only enforced by courts but were being written into government manuals and urged upon developers by the Federal Housing Administration. Neighborhoods, and sometimes whole cities, were proscribed against the minorities. In the very years we were signing our treaties and our declarations of nondiscrimination, the FHA was deploring the presence of "unharmonious racial groups" and even prescribing the form of racial covenant to keep such groups in their place. When the racial restrictions were removed fifteen years after they were written, government-aided segregation continued in the field. A Supreme Court decision barring enforcement of the covenants, rendered in 1948 in the renascent atmosphere of the postwar period, did not stop discriminatory practices nor persuade government housing agencies to challenge segregation.

Some cities banned the new migrants from land and homes, forcing them into the slums of the old city centers. Many later faced ouster on the claim that their homes were needed for public works, parks, and urban redevelopment and slum clearance schemes. The right to move in these cases was being supplanted by the obligation to move or the compulsion to stay.

Thus, resting on the premise that the right to property and to equality were no longer parallel natural rights but conflicting rights to be resolved in favor of property, race antagonism had begun to recruit the crucial and powerful instruments of political control. Administrators and legislatures were sanctioning encroachments upon the human being's right to live where he chose. The closed city had begun to loom on the American horizon. With the ever-increasing role of federal and local governments in housing and with neighborhoods steadily expanding, an ominous issue wheeled into focus. Would private biases now be incorporated into the public ethic of America, causing the first major break in the American democratic structure and the first official reduction of the great American ideal?

II

THE WHITE MIGRATION

BY 1870 America was already a land of Scotch-Irish-English-German-Scandinavian hybrids, half-castes, and blends. These were no longer like their European forebears in manner or accent. Of every 1000 persons in the country, 292 were native-born whites of foreign or mixed parentage, 144 were foreign-born whites, 127 were Negroes, 1 was Chinese, and 1 was Indian.

The dual process of immigration and interfusion went on until 1924. Between 1870 and 1920 about 20 million additional immigrants had arrived, including Italians, Russians, Hungarians, Japanese, and Greeks. Before the barriers were finally lowered, Italy had sent us more than four and a half million; Austria-Hungary 4 million; Russia and Poland three and a quarter million. By 1945, 1 out of every 4 Americans was still either a foreign-born white or the child of foreign-born white parents. One of every 5 white Americans spoke some language other than English in his home.

The immigrants came for different reasons—land hunger and food hunger; insect plague and human plague; political persecution and pogroms; the lure of gold and the ballyhoo of steamship agents; over-population and starvation; crop failure and financial failure; displacement through mechanization or the competition of female and child labor.

Political Ferment

The grapes of wrath had an early harvest in America, and the hymn of hate was sung long before the Battle Hymn of the Republic. The ink had hardly dried on the Bill of Rights when the Alien and Sedition Acts gave President John Adams extraordinary powers to deport

10

"dangerous" aliens. Residential requirements for citizenship were extended to fourteen years. Political criticism was virtually made a crime. Some wanted to abolish naturalization altogether and deprive immigrants of political rights. Hostility to newcomers existed partly because many were for Jefferson and his ideas. When Jefferson won the election of 1800, the laws were repealed. The tide of bias, however, was not broken. For a few decades Jeffersonianism and a limited immigration kept the public temper banked safely down. But the coming of the Irish re-kindled the flame. The *bête noire* was not yet the Negro but the Catholic.

The Know-Nothing Party became a power in Pennsylvania, Massachusetts, Maryland, and in some parts of the South. It elected a governor in Massachusetts and controlled the state legislature in at least six other states. A hundred seats were claimed for it in Congress, and influential newspapers talked of a Know-Nothing President by 1856. The continued immigration of foreigners, many of whom joined the Army, coupled with the war against the South, soon helped divert enmities in another direction. Know-nothingism faded into nothing.

By the time the war ended, many of the immigrants had settled on the land. The atmosphere of racial equality made prejudice seem anomalous in the North. But in the West, anti-Chinese agitation was already in ferment. Nor was the North itself to continue long immune. As the land supply became exhausted and industry demanded labor to fill the mills, mines, and factories, a new crop of immigrants from south and east Europe began to pour into the cities. The settled workers began to charge the newcomers with lowering wages and raising taxes to maintain poorhouses and jails. Anti-Catholic sentiment rose again with the doubling of membership in the Catholic churches. A prominent writer in June, 1896, complained that we were getting "the less thrifty and prosperous members" of the European community,[1] many of them "unfit to be members of any decent community." Outstanding citizens asserted that the foreigners were coming in to destroy our government and divide our property. Even the *Encyclopedia of Social Reform,* one of the liberal tomes of the period (among its collaborators were Edward Bellamy, William

---

[1] F. A. Walker, "Restriction of Immigration," *Atlantic Monthly,* vol. LXXVII, no. CCCCLXIV, June, 1896.

Lloyd Garrison, A. T. Hadley, and Sidney Webb)[2] called immigration "morally dangerous." While conceding that many immigrants were friends of liberty, it said:

Too frequently the immigrant is a European peasant whose horizon has been narrow, whose moral and religious training has been meager or false, and whose ideas of life are low. Not a few belong to the pauper and criminal classes. Some countries of Europe deliberately, and other countries almost equally, send their discharged convicts to America, while fugitives from justice continually seek our shores.[3]

Other immigrants, it added, "mistake license for liberty in this country, and morally deteriorate."

Another writer told of the dangers of foreign population and how, in southern Wisconsin, a colony of 108 persons from one of the cantons of Switzerland grew to 1060 souls.

This Helvetian settlement, founded three years before Wisconsin became a state, has preserved its race, its language, its worship, and its customs in their integrity. Similar colonies are now being planted in the West. In some cases 100,000 or 200,000 acres in one block have been purchased by foreigners of one nationality and religion, thus building up States within a State, having different languages, different antecedents, different religions, different ideas and habits, preparing mutual jealousies and perpetuating race antipathies. In New England, conventions are held to which only French-Canadian Catholics are admitted. At such a convention in Nashua in 1888, attended by 80 priests, the following mottoes were displayed: "Our tongue, our nationality, and our religion." "Before everything else let us remain French." If our noble domain were tenfold larger than it is, it would still be too small to embrace with safety to our national future little Germanies here, little Scandinavias there, and little Irelands yonder.[4]

"Shall our clothing be made exclusively by those who are content to wallow as a hog in a sty?" it was asked.[5]

In 1887 political agitation found root with the formation in Iowa of the American Protective Association. Foreign-born citizens were eligible for membership if they would have no truck with Catholics. The A.P.A. thrived mainly on opposition to the Slavic, Italian, and other labor competitors from eastern and southern Europe. Reaching

[2] Edited by William D. Bliss. New York; Funk and Wagnalls, 1897.
[3] *Ibid*, p. 712.
[4] *Ibid*.
[5] *Ibid*.

peak strength in 1893–1894, it brought more demands for sharp restriction of immigration, precipitated rioting, and attained a powerful position in a few state legislatures. But again larger issues intervened on the American scene and the agitation was safely channeled into history.[6]

The year 1915 spawned the new K.K.K. nightshirt commandos who preached white supremacy, anti-Semitism, anti-Catholicism, and nativism. Meeting under the blaze of fiery crosses in the open country, its hooded members whipped, tarred, feathered, and lynched its victims in the name of "patriotism" and "the American way." Whites as well as Negroes came under the lash. The *New York World,* tabulating K.K.K. violence between October, 1920, and October, 1921, listed 4 killings, 1 mutilation, 1 with acid, 41 floggings, 27 tar and feather parties, 5 kidnappings, 43 persons warned to leave town or otherwise threatened, 14 communities threatened by warning posters, and 16 parades by masked men with warning placards.[7]

Ku Klux Klan violence spread terror throughout the country, particularly in the South. Estimates of membership in 1924 ran as high as six million. The Klan sought political power and achieved it in a number of states, electing a senator in Texas and playing important political roles in Arkansas, Connecticut, Oklahoma, Alabama, Georgia, and Oregon. The economic optimism of the 1920's slackened the move toward racism. Newspaper campaigns, a congressional investigation, and laws requiring unmasking caused the Klan's ranks to crack and prevented it from regaining its former strength. But the Klan movement never completely disappeared and as shown later reappeared on the scene with the rise of neighborhood tensions. Its crosses still occasionally burst into flame, its macabre meetings continue, its violence erupts sporadically.

With radio as a new medium for reaching a wide public, anti-Jewish agitation stirred in the 1940's when a Catholic priest named Father Charles Coughlin began a series of anti-Semitic broadcasts. After gaining a large audience he was finally curbed. Other "crusaders" rose and fell, each trying his hand at churning up racial and religious

[6] Carl Wittke, "Immigration Policy Prior to World War I," *Annals* of the American Academy of Political and Social Science, March, 1949, p. 11.

[7] Max Sylvius Handman, "Ku Klux Klan," *Encyclopaedia of the Social Sciences*. New York, The Macmillan Company, 1937, vol. 8, p. 607.

strife, but no major political footholds were gained—with one conspicuous exception.

This was the immigration policy written by Congress in 1924 and reaffirmed in 1952 by the McCarran-Walter Act. The policy assumes that certain people (Asians, Africans, and southern and eastern Europeans) are less desirable than others (northern and western Europeans, Latin-Americans, and Canadians). The 1952 law was enacted over the veto of President Truman. A few months after its passage the President's Commission on Immigration and Naturalization held hearings throughout the country, carefully analyzed the new law, and its report said:

The Commission believes that an outstanding characteristic of the United States is its great cultural diversity within an overriding national unity. The American story proves, if proof were needed, that such differences do not mean the existence of superior and inferior classes. . . .

The Commission believes that we cannot be true to the democratic faith of our own Declaration of Independence in the equality of all men, and at the same time pass immigration laws which discriminate among people because of national origin, race, color, or creed. We cannot continue to bask in the glory of an ancient and honorable tradition of providing haven to the oppressed, and belie that tradition by ignoble and ungenerous immigration laws. We cannot develop an effective foreign policy if our immigration laws negate our role of world leadership. We cannot defend civil rights in principle, and deny them in our immigration laws and practice. . . .[8]

The device for discriminating in the McCarran-Walter Act is the national origins quota system, first adopted by Congress in 1924. The 1952 law sets a small over-all quota of 154,000 immigrants a year from all countries outside the Western Hemisphere. This quota is divided by countries in the same ratio that people originating from these countries bore to the entire white population of the United States in 1920. The effect is to give about five sixths of the total quota to the northern and western European countries that now care little about migrating, while one sixth is left for the southern and eastern European states and all other nations which focus hopes on the United States. Thus Greece, which had supplied one sixth of 1 per cent of our

---

[8] *Whom We Shall Welcome,* Report of the President's Commission on Immigration and Naturalization. Washington, U.S. Government Printing Office, 1953, pp. *xiv–xv.*

white population in 1920, gets the same percentage of the 154,000 quota, or exactly 308 persons a year. But Great Britain may send 65,361 immigrants, Germany 25,814, Eire 17,756, the Netherlands 3136, and so on. The northern and western nations used only 17 per cent of their quotas from 1930 to 1944. Qualified applicants from the southern and eastern countries must wait years or even decades for their chance to migrate.

Because the McCarran-Walter Act gives quotas of 100 to some Asian countries for the first time and allows Japanese to become American citizens, its sponsors argued that the law is not discriminatory. The inconsequential gestures toward Asians are obliterated by a new stigma: the Asia-Pacific Triangle, defined by the new immigration law as including every country that lies wholly within the area north of the 25th parallel of south latitude and between the 60th and 165th meridians of east longitude. Every person born within this huge portion of the earth's surface is considered racially unfit for United States citizenship, save for a token quota of 100 persons a year for each country within the triangle and a few 100-person quotas for specific countries.

The stigma applies to the entire populations of India, Japan, China, the Philippines, Afghanistan, Pakistan, Burma, Ceylon, Thailand, Laos, Vietnam, Cambodia, Malaya, Korea, and the Pacific Islands. It also applies to some born outside of the triangle, for the son of a British scholar and his Indian wife, even though he were born in Cambridge, could not enter the United States under the liberal British quota of 65,361. He would be compelled to wait years for admission under the quota of 100 for India.

To keep out southern and eastern Europeans, the law ignored ancestry and relied on place of birth. To exclude Asians, the law ignored place of birth and relied on ancestry.

Immigrants from the British colony of Jamaica had been entering the United States at the rate of about 1,000 a year under the largely unused British quota. The McCarran-Walter Act arbitrarily limited the number to 100.

By insulting more than half of the world's population, the new immigration law encourages millions in Asia and eastern Europe to lend a sympathetic ear to Radio Moscow rather than to the Voice of America, according to one informed authority, a former acting director of the Census Bureau.[9]

The Great American Crucible

Newcomers are hated, feared, suspected, envied, rejected, or pitied. Rarely are they welcome. To the Mongols of Asia, westerners were foreign or evil. To the German today, a Sudetan refugee or a Polish D.P. is anathema. To many Europeans Americans are inferior too (though the American may not like to think so).

The Europeans who came here since 1830 were not exempt from the hostile emotions that stir in human beings when other human beings who are strange-looking approach en masse. Yet though fundamental cultural and racial characteristics have not been erased from all the immigrants who came here and though differences still exist among certain of them, they learned our language, adopted our social ritual, and despite initial opposition fully participate in the common social, economic, and political life. Many of varying nationalities and cultures have been blended, and though they may still retain a residuum of their cultural or racial identification, the special traits and habits which had distinguished them for centuries have been largely erased. If they are heterogeneous in some respects, they are homogeneous in their common loyalty and national interest, and to the general theme that underlies the American System. Americans have learned to work together in the same factories, support the same unions, live in the same neighborhoods; they have put their strength behind common causes; they have participated in organizations and movements of great number and diversity, and have generally demonstrated a remarkable capacity for meeting crises without veering into the dangerous waters of totalitarianism.

The racial conflicts, heightened by economic causes, social challenge, or by irrational elements, have been temporary; they have never attained a lasting foothold in the body politic or perverted the political mechanisms into an accepted tool for oppression of one group by another. The institutional pattern has remained saturated with the overlying ethic of human equality which was effectively in-

[9] See statement by Philip M. Hauser, Professor of Sociology, University of Chicago, *ibid,* p. 53.

voked whenever the fundamental rights of minorities were seriously threatened. Whether that ethic can be maintained against the onrush into our neighborhoods of millions of people different in color from the Europeans, and slower perhaps in the speed with which they can be assimilated, is the question that remains to be answered.

III

THE BLACK MIGRATION

WHEN in 1865 foreign immigration was in full swing and boatloads of Germans and Scandinavians were crowding into the port cities and then fanning out to the beckoning western lands, Negroes were on the move too. But it was more a shuffle than a migration, for they did not march toward the frontiers or port cities but drifted along southern roads as if to taste the strange savor of their new-found emancipation. As one Negro expressed it to a good master, "I must go. If I stay here, I'll never know I am free."[1]

The frontier seemed awesome and unfamiliar, for they were waifs caught between the rights of freedom and its problems and responsibilities. They roamed the South from camp to camp, moving on to nearby cities or flocking to military posts. A few built shacks, some bought or rented land; others returned to their former masters as free workers, and some moved North. But for most, the long journeys that the Europeans were making seemed out of the question. The Negroes were moving not to face freedom but to sense it. The opportunity for freedom gave them freedom of opportunity, but they seemed unable to grasp precisely where that opportunity lay.

One of their primary problems was shelter. Many could have remained in their old slave quarters, but that would have dulled the flavor of emancipation. Lacking funds to build homes or the skill to put them together, as the frontiersmen were doing, many lived under the sky, moved into deserted houses, caves, ruins, or improvised sheds on the banks of rivers and ravines. The descent of the freedmen upon Washington was so sudden that they crowded into little one-room shanties, twelve to a house, sleeping on the

[1] Henderson H. Donald, *The Negro Freedman*. New York, Henry Schuman, 1952, pp. 1–2.

18

earth floors and huddling together when the rains dripped through leaking roofs.[2] Elsewhere they occupied log cabins like those they had lived in as slaves. A door less than five feet high would give the only access to light; a room ten feet square with an earth floor was the living and sleeping quarters, and a fireplace would serve as kitchen. Sometimes there was an extra room for the old folk; sometimes, too, there were glass windows, but these were soon replaced by pieces of old clothing, quilting, or newspapers.

The freedom granted the slave had released the former master from the social responsibilities of slave ownership. He was now free to charge rent and to provide only the minimum facilities required by law and the market. Often the Negro's meager earnings were eaten up in rent and interest paid to landlords and money lenders who matched their wits against the Negro's inexperience.

Overcrowding, exposure, and low incomes brought the Reaper before the freedman could even sow. Smallpox epidemics destroyed great numbers and tuberculosis took thousands more. "The Negro children, without proper care or diet, died like flies, and for several years almost none were to be seen in some districts."[3] From one fourth to one third of the freedmen died during the first years of adjustment in some southern communities.[4]

In 1860, Negroes made up only 1.2 per cent of the total northern and western population, and it was still only 1.6 per cent in 1910. The urban Negro population in the South had meanwhile grown in the same period from 6.7 to 22 per cent of the regional population.

Many Negroes who migrated to the North made adjustments. Their number was too small to arouse opposition to them as neighbors or as competitors. Nor could racial segregation or prejudice thrive as a political institution in an atmosphere still filled with the smoke of

[2] *Ibid*, p. 51. By 1897 there were 333 alleys in Washington with 20,000 people living in or near them, 3 out of every 4 of them Negroes. Many of these alleys remain; many were within a stone's throw of the Capitol until a few years ago when they were torn down to make way for the new Senate Office Building.

[3] Donald, *op. cit.*, p. 154.

[4] Allan Nevins, *The Emergence of Modern America, 1865–1878*. New York, The Macmillan Co., 1935, pp. 12–13; also "Negro Mortality at the South," *The Nation*, vol 15, p. 106, August 15, 1872; *Compendium of the Tenth Census of the United States*, part I, pp. 402–403. Statistics are deceptive, for Negro deaths were often unreported. In some parts of the South today, health commissioners still turn a blind eye to vital statistics affecting Negroes.

civil conflict and the inspiration of a new Bill of Rights. Though the South was already segregating Negroes in schools, transportation, and in some of its neighborhoods, the northern climate after the Civil War seemed appropriate for acceptance of Negroes into mixed neighborhoods. In fact, when the federal Civil Rights Bill of 1875 was invalidated by the Supreme Court in 1884, most states in the Northeast and Middle West and some in the Far West enacted local laws guaranteeing nondiscriminating access to hotels, restaurants, and public places. These northerners, who had after all openly invited and even smuggled slaves across the border, had not yet been tested by an onrush of Negroes into their neighborhoods and competition for their jobs and dwellings. As for the millions of foreigners of diverse creeds and races pouring into the northern cities, color prejudice to them had been unknown. They were strangers as well, who did not even know the language. It was they rather than the Negroes who drew much of the animus.

In 1890, while the south and east European immigrations were in process, these immigrants were taking the menial jobs held by Negroes, but there were some jobs held by established Negroes for which the new immigrants could not even qualify. The Negroes were cooks, waiters, butlers, coachmen, footmen, and general household servants. "There was hardly a large hotel in any of the great Northern cities," writes Frank Julian Warne[5] of the latter part of the century, "where they were not employed almost exclusively as bell-boys, porters, waiters, and so on. They were our cabmen, janitors, office porters, bootblacks; virtually all our barber shops were run by negroes; and in a score and more different ways the black man was being fitted into a place in our industrial and social life which in course of time would have better adjusted him to his new and changed environment."

In Columbus, Ohio, Negroes in the twenty-five years prior to 1912 had even achieved political importance, serving with distinction in its City Council, on the Board of Education, and in important appointive positions. While Negroes were taking unskilled jobs in the buggy works, brickyards, lumber mills, and foundries, they also

[5] *The Immigration Invasion.* New York, Dodd Mead & Co., 1913, p. 174. Warne was census expert for the U.S. Census of 1910 and former Secretary of the New York State Immigration Commission.

held the better jobs as barbers, hack-drivers, draymen, hotel waiters, bartenders, hostlers, yardmen, and railroad clerks. They also latched onto political jobs. There was no professional or large middle class of Negro businessmen outside the barbers, saloonkeepers and restaurant operators, but the social and economic life of the times was such that white customers were having their moustaches trimmed by Negro barbers who exchanged tonsorial pleasantries, absorbed the culture, and established the contacts essential for leadership and understanding.[6]

In cities where the Negro migration was small and there was no competition for housing, jobs, or social position, the relationship between whites and Negroes was not unfriendly. The Negro was the servant who attended to the family's children, but he was also the building superintendent and postman. He was more privileged than the immigrant crop that later came up from the South, better educated, and suffering few of the handicaps of those reared in slavery or in the repressed environment of southern reconstruction. A respected Negro recalls several prosperous barber shops in Buffalo owned by colored people. While the majority of colored citizens were employed in domestic service, they lived in close proximity to their employers, who occupied the more exclusive sections. "The negro group mingled with the white with little evidence of race prejudice, and the narrator recollects attending parties as a child where German and negro citizens attended and German was spoken by both negro and white."[7] The same atmosphere prevailed in now turbulent Chicago.[8]

James Weldon Johnson recalls how in 1905 he was "delighted with San Francisco":

I encountered no bar against me in hotels, restaurants, theatres or other places of public accommodation and entertainment. We hired a furnished

---

[6] J. S. Himes, "Forty Years of Negro Life in Columbus, Ohio," *The Journal of Negro History*, vol. XXVII, no. 2, Washington, D.C., April, 1942, pp. 137–138. In Washington, D.C., the Negroes at the time of Emancipation operated many businesses and some even lived in commodious homes. They paid $650,000 in taxes.

[7] Niles Carpenter and Associates, *The University of Buffalo Studies*, vol. v, no. 4, June, 1927, Monographs in Sociology, no. 2: "Nationality, Color, and Economic Opportunity in the City of Buffalo," p. 156.

[8] The Chicago Commission on Race Relations. *The Negro in Chicago*, Chicago, University of Chicago Press, 1922, p. 109.

apartment in the business area, and took our meals wherever it was most convenient. I moved about with a sense of confidence and security, and entirely from under the cloud of doubt and apprehension that constantly hangs over an intelligent Negro in every Southern city and in a great many cities of the North.[9]

In New England cities where Negroes were already living, there was little social discrimination.[10] Negroes were also holding good jobs and were an integral part of the communities, while their children mixed with white children in schools. When W. E. B. Du-Bois entered high school, "The racial angle was more clearly defined against the Irish than against me. It was a matter of income and ancestry more than color."[11]

Living Patterns

The Negroes in the North more often clustered in small groups, but the patterns varied with the number. In some places there was no distinct Negro community before the turn of the century. A few families lived on one street, a larger cluster lived on another, and there were small scatterings throughout.[12] In Minneapolis, the Negroes were scattered throughout the city, and though the Negro population increased after the great migration the pattern was more or less the same in 1954. Chicago and Detroit had well-defined districts which grew more densely populated with the increasing migration.[13] Robert C. Weaver writes:

Prior to the movement of over 50,000 colored people to Chicago in the five-year period 1915–1920, Negroes lived in practically every section of the city. As in other northern communities, they were usually centered at the edge of areas inhabited by wealthy whites, for whom many of them worked as servants . . . as recently as 1910, in no area of Negro concen-

[9] *Along This Way, the Autobiography of James Weldon Johnson.* New York, The Viking Press, 1933, pp. 206–208.

[10] Gunnar Myrdal, *An American Dilemma.* New York, Harper & Brothers, 1944, vol. I, p. 601.

[11] W. E. B. DuBois, *Dusk of Dawn.* New York, Harcourt, Brace & Company, 1940, p. 14; see also, Robert A. Warner, *New Haven Negroes: A Social History.* New Haven, Yale University Press, 1940 (both cited in Myrdal, *loc. cit.*).

[12] Mary Louise Mark, "Negroes in Columbus," *Ohio State University Studies; Graduate School Series Contributions in Social Science,* no. 2. Columbus, Ohio State University Press, 1928.

[13] Charles S. Johnson, *Patterns of Negro Segregation.* New York, Harper & Brothers, 1943, p. 10.

tration were Negroes more than 61 per cent of the population; more than two-thirds of the colored people lived in sections less than 50 per cent Negro, and a third were in areas less than 10 per cent Negro.[14]

New York's Negro population in 1901 numbered 60,000. Negro settlements were scattered throughout the city, the chief center being in the area of West 53rd Street and the neighboring San Juan Hill district. There were also clusters near Washington Square and in Brooklyn. As the Negro population swelled, Negroes settled in the then depressed section of Harlem.

Curiously, the racial harmony that existed before the great migration is still found where Negro settlements are small and fixed. In New York City, as late as 1926, the writer recalls an experience involving a property purchased in West 8th Street, in the Washington Square section. There were nine houses on the plot occupied by Negroes, part of Clinton Court. The settlement was at least a century old and had been built on fill over Minetta Creek (which still flows beneath the Village Barn and the Eighth Street Playhouse erected on the plot). The Washington Square district was among the most fashionable sections of the city. When it was disclosed that Clinton Court would be demolished, the white political district leader protested because the Negroes were old residents and good Democrats. Instead of evicting these fine citizens, he asked, couldn't the Playhouse be built somewhere else?

One can tour Cambridge, Massachusetts, Providence, Rhode Island, and a dozen other New England cities and see Negro families still living in mixed neighborhoods with little hostility or competitive attitudes to disturb either prestige or home values. Negroes in some New England cities work in shops and even carry on their own businesses, serving whites as well as Negroes. They often belong to the same churches and attend the same schools. An occasional marriage with a white creates no panic and few are super-conscious of color.[15]

The Great Migrations

The great migration to the cities started in the South in about 1915 and accelerated as foreign immigration was curtailed in the

[14] Robert C. Weaver, *The Negro Ghetto*. New York, Harcourt, Brace & Company, 1948, p. 15.
[15] Myrdal, *loc. cit.*

1920's. Economic activity, spurred by wars and an expanding economy, brought demands for more labor. Between 1910 and 1940, the net northward flow of Negroes totaled 1,750,000. By 1940, 2,-439,201 Negroes lived in the North, east of the Mississippi, representing 19 per cent of the total Negro population in the country and 3.9 per cent of the total northern population.

The Negroes were mainly seeking factory jobs; Henry Ford's $5 minimum daily wage was more of a lure than the Klondike. Too often the migrants found themselves excluded from industry, though in domestic and service jobs they were usually preferred to European immigrants. The end of World War I marked a new redistribution of the Negro population in the North and West. Wages in the North were of course attractive, and conditions in the growing cities also seemed better to a people who in the South were visited by typhoid at twice the national rate and three times as often by pellagra and malaria.

Yet in the whole saga of American migration, no in-migrating group had faced such disadvantages. So many Negroes came in so few years that they taxed the absorptive capacities of the cities. Their dark skins made them conspicuous and discouraged assimilation. They were unequipped for their new frontier, for the South had given them little or no education. Often they knocked in vain at the doors of labor unions. Forced to accept low wages, they competed with whites for jobs; sometimes they scabbed, intensifying the wrath of white workers. Their low pay denied most of them the homes and amenities which might have won social acceptance by their neighbors. Indeed, they could hardly afford even the bare necessities of decent existence, to say nothing of elementary medical care. Too many of their children never opened their eyes to light, or they died in infancy—the infant death rate was often two or three times as great as that for whites. Crowded into ramshackle dwellings with others or forced to pay premium prices for tolerable shelter, the migrants spent on rent what should have been spent on food. Tuberculosis spread among them at a rate three to five times that of the local population as a whole.

When social reformers exposed slum conditions, and cities made efforts to improve housing conditions, the "improvement" took the form of higher standards for new buildings or the demolition of old ones, thus shortening the housing supply for Negroes and widening the breach between their shelter cost and their income. Even some from their own race who had been long established in the areas regarded the sudden influx as disturbing the neighborhood equilibrium.

When the antagonisms began they varied from place to place. In the Midwest the antagonism by the whites was intensified by propaganda spread by groups of dissident southerners.[16] Another writer says that the change became noticeable in Ohio about 1904 and 1905 with the first significant migration of southern rural Negroes, intensifying a decade later with the production boom of World War I.[17] With increasing antagonism after 1915, one after another of the privileges enjoyed in theatres, hotels, cafes, restaurants, public places, and even in certain employment opportunities were denied. Negroes in established enterprises began to feel the strictures as other groups began to replace them.

Warne, on the eve of World War I, noted the change in other cities:

Today, all these and many other positions have been wrested from the negro by the Slav and Italian. Our shoes are now blacked by the Greek and Italian; they wait upon us at table in our hotels and restaurants; we are shaved by the Italian barber; this newer immigrant is cooking our food and doing our household work, as the women of these races in ever increasing number join the men who preceded them. What has become of the type of negro they have supplanted is a serious question. As a general thing, not only has his economic status been lowered but he has also been removed from that close social intercourse with the white race which these occupations brought to him.[18]

The migrants came in great waves and no sooner had they secured jobs, found homes, established communities, placed their children in schools, and quieted the throbbing tensions, than another wave poured in, reviving old sores and renewing discord. They were unable to distribute themselves throughout the city, but had to enlarge existing concentrations. As their numbers increased they swelled out either into the adjoining sections or made inroads into new sections of established whites.

[16] Mark, *op. cit.,* p. 27.
[17] Himes, *op. cit.,* p. 139.
[18] *Op cit.,* p. 174.

White fears and resentments varied with the locale and with the number of Negroes. In the South where the Negro population was larger, the predominant fears were that the whites might lose supremacy, that class segregation would break down, bringing mixed marriages and social parity. Among the lower-income whites, job competition also played a part.[19] But once white supremacy was established, most southerners no longer feared loss of face simply because the Negro happened to live nearby. Thus, in cities like New Orleans they lived in the same blocks without challenging the white residents. Proximity of living quarters was frequently in fact a natural outgrowth of the former slave-quarters pattern. Various types of occupancy existed in the South—isolated Negro and white sections, mixed neighborhood occupancy, scatterings of Negro population in all-white areas. Occasional neighborhood tensions were more likely to be found where the Negroes were segregated than where they were an established part of the neighborhood.

As the Negroes moved from the farms to the southern cities in droves, however, opposition crystallized. The migrants were self-conscious and timid. The South had foregone serfdom but still expected servility. Southern attitudes soon filtered up to the North, widening the racial and social dichotomy.[20]

The measures taken to restrain the Negro's movements varied. Racial zoning was among the first. The supposition was that this was authorized by the "separate but equal" doctrine as well as by the best principles of safe and sound city development. Another device was the restrictive covenant written into deeds and providing against sale or rental to Negroes. Opposition also took the form of spontaneous gentlemen's understandings to maintain white supremacy and purity in neighborhoods. Simultaneously there was more organized opposition through Klan oppressions and "neighborhood improvement associations." Finally, there was violence, the most direct method of all.

The defense and war programs after 1940 brought a new wave of in-migration. Between 1940 and 1947 no less than 2,729,000 nonwhites migrated, mostly from rural to urban areas. About 1,200,-

[19] Ina Corinne Brown, *Race Relations in a Democracy*. New York, Harper & Brothers, 1949, p. 137.
[20] Myrdal, *op. cit.*, p. 183.

TABLE I. POPULATION, BY COLOR, FOR SELECTED CITIES OF 50,000 OR MORE: 1950 AND 1940

City	Total population			White			Nonwhite		
	1950	1940	Increase %	1950	1940	Increase %	1950	1940	Increase %
Total (all cities of 50,000 or more)	53,242,440	46,663,963	14.1	46,573,330	42,193,297	10.4	6,669,110	4,470,666	49.2
Akron, Ohio	274,605	244,791	12.2	250,727	232,482	7.8	23,878	12,309	94.0
Alameda, Calif.	64,430	36,256	77.7	58,104	35,125	65.4	6,326	1,131	459.3
Albany, N. Y.	134,995	130,577	3.4	129,114	127,564	1.2	5,881	3,013	95.2
Berkeley, Calif.	113,805	85,547	33.0	96,268	80,267	19.9	17,537	5,280	232.1
Buffalo, N. Y.	580,132	575,901	0.7	542,432	557,618	−2.7	37,700	18,283	106.2
Canton, Ohio	116,912	108,401	7.9	109,756	104,319	5.2	7,156	4,082	75.3
Chicago, Ill.	3,620,962	3,396,808	6.6	3,111,525	3,114,564	−0.1	509,437	282,244	80.5
Cincinnati, Ohio	503,998	455,610	10.6	425,313	399,853	6.4	78,685	55,757	41.1
Cleveland, Ohio	914,808	878,336	4.2	765,261	793,417	−3.5	149,547	84,919	76.1
Denver, Colo.	415,786	322,412	29.0	397,534	313,810	26.7	18,252	8,602	112.2
Detroit, Mich.	1,849,568	1,623,452	13.9	1,545,847	1,472,662	5.0	303,721	150,790	101.4
Flint, Mich.	163,143	151,543	7.7	149,100	144,858	2.9	14,043	6,685	110.1
Grand Rapids, Mich.	176,515	164,292	7.4	169,578	161,567	5.0	6,937	2,725	154.6
Los Angeles, Calif.	1,970,358	1,504,277	31.0	1,758,773	1,406,430	25.1	211,585	97,847	116.2
Milwaukee, Wis.	637,392	587,472	8.5	614,650	578,177	6.3	22,742	9,295	144.7
New York City	7,891,957	7,454,995	5.9	7,116,428	6,977,501	2.0	775,529	477,494	62.4
Philadelphia, Pa.	2,071,605	1,931,334	7.3	1,692,637	1,678,577	0.8	378,968	252,757	49.9
Portland, Ore.	373,628	305,394	22.3	360,388	299,707	20.2	13,240	5,687	132.8
St. Louis, Mo.	856,796	816,048	5.0	702,348	706,794	−0.6	154,448	109,254	41.4
San Francisco, Calif.	775,357	634,536	22.2	693,888	602,701	15.1	81,469	31,835	155.9
Washington, D. C.	802,178	663,091	21.0	518,147	474,326	9.2	284,031	188,765	50.5

SOURCE: *1950 Census of Population,* Advance Reports, U.S. Department of Commerce, Bureau of the Census, Series PC-14, No. 1, December 16, 1951, Table II, pp. 4–6.

000 moved between noncontiguous states. In 1940, 65 per cent of the total nonwhite population lived in nonfarm areas; seven years later the figure had risen to 77 per cent. As in previous waves, the Negroes had to hunt for housing. Finding restrictions tighter than ever, they crowded into the ghettos.

In 1950 a major shift in the Negro population was recorded for the previous decade. The nonwhite population had more than doubled in 30 standard metropolitan areas, Northwest, North-central and West. The nonwhite population in the metropolitan areas of the North (Northeast and North-central states combined) and of the West had increased by almost two million during the decade. In metropolitan areas of the West the percentage increase for nonwhites was 127.6 as compared with only 48.9 for whites. In Philadelphia the Negro population now represented almost 20 per cent of the total; in the Borough of Manhattan, New York City, it was more than 20 per cent, Chicago more than 14 per cent, Detroit more than 16 per cent, and Washington almost 35 per cent. Increases in Negro population ran as high as 300 per cent over 1940 figures in some cities.[21] Table I suggests the magnitude of the migration in the decade. From coast to coast black ghettos had sprung up, some small, some large. Curtailment of European immigration had helped make the Negro an indispensable part of America's working force in the steel mills, packing plants, mines, lumber camps, and other enterprises. He made his move and it was an important advance. But no homes were offered to enable the Negro to enjoy a normal life and to give his children and grandchildren the same chance to move up in the social scale which had been granted to those of other migrants before them.

[21] 1950 *Census of Population,* Advance Reports Series PC-14, no. 1. Washington, D.C., U.S. Department of Commerce, Bureau of the Census, December 16, 1951.

IV

THE FAR EASTERN INFLUX

Orientation without Orientals

THOUGH California was a latecomer to American settlement, she made up for lost time. By 1950 she ranked fifth in population. The wealth in her earth made her one of the great crop, gold, and oil producing centers of the world, and her climate made her a magnet for tourists and settlers. Soon settlers, tourist dollars, and industry poured across the country and California became a great industrial center as well.

The key to California's development was labor. For 100 years California absorbed wave after wave of immigrants—Chinese to mine her gold and build her railroads; Japanese, Filipinos, and Mexicans to work her soil; drought-driven Okies and Arkies ready to work at anything; croppers moving up to do the tough labor in her plants.

Situated on the western coast, her first foreign workers headed from the teeming Orient. Up to 1853 there were less than 100 Chinese—hard-working, mild-mannered, unobtrusive.[1] They sawed wood and drained lands. In a region where women were scarcer than gold, they also cooked the meals and laundered the clothes. The first Chinese were viewed as a "worthy integer of our population," and "the most desirable of our adopted citizens."[2] Governor John MacDougall in 1852 even recommended a system of land grants to induce their further immigration.[3]

[1] Joseph S. Roucek, "Chinese Americans," in Francis J. Brown and J.S. Roucek (eds.), *One America.* New York, Prentice-Hall, Inc., rev. ed., 1945, p. 316.

[2] *Daily Alta,* May 12, 1851.

[3] R. D. McKenzie, *Oriental Exclusion.* New York, American Group, Institute of Pacific Relations, 1927, p. 26.

29

The Chinese, it was felt, were adding a dignified element to the community. They were met by the mayor of San Francisco and a citizens committee and in an impressive ceremony were praised for their patriotism and hailed as the "best immigrants in California." "Whatever the white man scorned to do," said a Pacific coast editor, "the Chinaman took up; whatever the white men did, the Chinese could learn to do; he was a gap-filler, doing what no one else would do, or what remained undone, adapting himself to the white man's tastes, and slipping away, unprotestingly, to other tasks when the white man wanted his job."[4]

The Chinese were gentle and accommodating. Better still, they were cheap. But the hostility toward foreigners and strangers which had exhibited itself in the East soon appeared in the West. Some whites feared the prospect of a huge unassimilable vote which could not be reasoned with and might even be bought. "Know-Nothingism" was in ferment and had spread to the Pacific where California's gold was held to be "for Americans only." Skin color was receiving a new emphasis in the West, and soon the term "American" excluded not only Mediterranean natives, Chinese, South Sea islanders and Malayans, but South Americans, southern Europeans, and dark-skinned Frenchmen as well.[5]

The majority of white settlers were immigrants from the border states (Missouri, etc.) who were prone to be hostile to all but white Europeans. Southerners who brought their slaves with them became as intolerant of pigtails as of pigments. It was not long before the Chinese were singled out for special infamy. Governor Bingler charged them with being "contract coolies, avaricious, ignorant of moral obligations, incapable of being assimilated and dangerous to the welfare of the state." Simultaneously politicians, sensing the growing antiforeign feeling, began to use race antipathy as bait for miners' votes.[6]

As Chinese swarmed along the tracks of the Central Pacific Railroad and appeared in the cities, local and statewide anticoolie groups and associations organized for action. Mass meetings were called.

[4] *Pacific News,* cited in Mary Roberts Coolidge, *Chinese Immigration.* New York, Henry Holt and Co., 1909, p. 22.

[5] Lawrence Guy Brown, *Immigration.* New York, Longmans, Green and Co., 1933, p. 267; Coolidge, *op. cit.,* p. 29.

[6] Coolidge, *op. cit.,* p. 31.

Employers of Chinese labor were dubbed enemies of the state. Feared for his fertility, the Chinese, it was insisted, had to be fettered. Newspapers poured cavil upon them and mobs moved against them. To California labor there were now three great devils. Land monopoly and capitalist exploitation were two. The Chinese, once the most honorable candidates for citizenship, became the third.

In 1870 anti-Chinese demonstrations became common. Banners read "Women's Rights and no more Chinese chambermaids," "Our Women are Degraded by Coolie Labor," "No Servile Labor Shall Pollute our Land," "American Trade Needs no Coolie Labor," "We Want no Slaves or Aristocrats," and "The Coolie Labor System Leaves you no Alternative—Starvation or Disgrace."[7]

During the political campaign of 1871 an anti-Chinese outburst in Los Angeles resulted in 18 dead, several burned buildings, and considerable looting.[8]

The literature on Chinese immigration was the literature of abomination. The folklore had it that it was no crime to kill a Chinese.[9] The Chinese were not only "devoid of conscience" but "the lowest scale of humanity." "If he seems to conform to our ways it is only to get a better foothold for money-making. He professes friendship, of which sentiment he has not the remotest conception. He is cruel and unrelenting, only waiting the opportunity in which he may safely strike the object of his spite, cupidity or superstition."[10]

The Report of the Special Committee of the Board of Supervisors spiraled to a crescendo of obloquy reserved for no other section of the human race: "The beasts of the field, the vagrant dogs that the Pound-master gathers upon the streets to put to death by drowning,

[7] Elmer Clarence Sandmeyer, "The Anti-Chinese Movement in California." Urbana, University of Illinois Press, *Illinois Studies in the Social Sciences,* vol. 24, no. 3, 1939.

[8] *Ibid,* p. 48; for other diatribes, see Hon. Edwin R. Meade, "The Chinese Question," a paper read at the Annual Meeting of the Social Science Association of America. New York, Arthur and Bonnell, 1877, p. 14; *Report of the Special Committee of the Board of Supervisors of San Francisco on the Condition of the Chinese Quarter and the Chinese in San Francisco.* San Francisco, P.J. Thomas, Printer and Publisher, July, 1885, pp. 4, 5, 43; Jennett Blakeslee Frost, *California's Greatest Curse.* San Francisco, Joseph Winterburn & Co., 1879.

[9] Benjamin A. Botkin (ed.), *Treasury of American Folklore, Stories, Ballads and Traditions of the People.* New York, Crown Publishers, 1944, pp. 141–143.

[10] Meade, *op. cit.* p. 11.

are vastly better worthy of our commiseration than the whole Mongolian race when they seek to overrun our country and blast American welfare and progress with their miserable, contaminating presence."[11]

Chinese became the targets not only of social and economic but of legislative and judicial exactions. One early judicial opinion barred them from testifying against whites on the ground they were Indians. The reasoning was simple—in the days of Columbus all shores washed by Chinese waters were called the Indies, therefore all Asiatics were Indians. In any event (if this argument seemed too simple) testimony of Chinese was held to be against public policy. This made oppression easy. Outrages could be committed against a Chinese with impunity, since no Chinese could testify in behalf of another by law and few whites would, law or no law.[12]

Thereafter a whole catalogue of laws was enacted to starve them out of the country. "The Chinese Must Go" became the battle-cry. But if the Orientals ate little, they could stomach much; if they cowered they did not crawl. Soon they fought back valiantly in the courts.

Why their leaders should have turned to the courts in case after case remains arguable. Perhaps it was because the Chinese Unseen Power is not a personalized deity but an abstract right or bundle of laws and forces. Chinese literature and philosophy is imbued with the spirit of freedom, brotherhood, and mutual duties, emphasizing the need for individual obedience to the laws of this great impersonality and respect for heaven's decrees. The Supreme Court to the Chinese might have embodied this great impersonality which would respect the spirit of freedom and brotherhood.

The court did respect it. The Chinese won in case after case. It is a great tribute to them and to the court that some of these decisions stand out today as landmarks of a developing democratic tradition.[13]

The decisions, however, won advances in principle and not in fact. The Chinese who wanted to come in were subjected to special ex-

[11] *Op. cit.*, p. 43.
[12] Coolidge, *op. cit.*, p. 76.
[13] Some of these decisions became the precedents for the more recent ones granting the Negro equality in law.

clusion laws and those already here were inveighed against as though they were outside the pale of the human species.

The Chinese, insecure in his new environment, humiliated, identifiable, unfamiliar with the language, herded into his Chinatown ghetto. Shunned, exploited, reviled, and kept from the fruits of the soil he had helped to harvest, he soon became imprisoned in his ghetto. His withdrawal from the community, however, did not end the campaign against him. It put his poverty in sharper focus where he could be beleaguered more effectively than ever.

In the 1850's almost all San Francisco's Chinese had settled within the boundaries of Kearney and Stockton, Sacramento and Jackson Streets. Though the Chinese quarter expanded thereafter, by 1906 it covered no more than fifteen blocks. San Francisco housing had been designed largely for single men in search of fortune. The city was filled with hotels, lodging houses, and flop-houses, allotting minimal space to the human form. As the Chinese population grew in the 1860's, landlords cut the buildings into even smaller cubicles and packed the Orientals into them.

Soon there were blocks of buildings with rooms of 60 to 70 square feet lined with bunks shared by two to ten men. Repairs were neglected because the houses were generally run by shoestring lessees to whom gross rent and net profit were synonymous.

The primary tenants were transient men; the lessees were Chinese lodging-house keepers who like other landlords wished to make their stake and go home; the White agents charged all the lessee would bear; and the White owner discreetly avoided the premises. The Chinese who lived permanently in the quarter came, most of them, from regions where plumbing and a city sewage system were unknown, and were inert when their cellars and cesspools became saturated with filth. With every change of Health Officers the new appointees made the motions of cleaning up Chinatown, which consisted in a squad of men arriving in the quarter to whitewash and fumigate. But the Chinese soon learned "that only those were cleaned up who didn't pay up,"—in other words they paid the police to be left alone.[14]

Only when the bubonic plague threatened the oppressors as well as the oppressed was any real effort made at law enforcement.

The Chinese themselves were blamed for their wretched life. Their bunks were warmed by bodies in relays; many slept on floors as well; women and children were stowed without room, air, or privacy.

[14] Coolidge, *op. cit.,* p. 413.

But all this was considered congenital. Their herding together was called a "universal custom."

Chinatown, said a San Francisco legislative committee, is "the rankest outgrowth of human degradation that can be found upon this continent. Here it may truly be said that human beings exist under conditions (as regards their mode of life and the air they breathe) scarcely one degree above those under which the rats of our waterfront and other vermin live, breathe and have their being. And this order of things seems inseparable from the very nature of the race. . . . "[15]

In 1876 the California Legislature appointed a committee to investigate the Chinese and, with an eye on the forthcoming national election, distributed its 300-page report by the tens of thousands to editors, governors, and legislators. "In order to produce an anti-Chinese report the committee ignored, emasculated, or falsified most of the competent testimony, preferring in matters of religion the opinions of police officers to those of missionaries; on the subject of manufacture, the opinions of police officers to those of large manufacturers; and again on the subject of coolie slavery the opinions of city officials and policemen to those of persons who had lived for many years in China."[16]

Hatred was so rampant before the turn of the century that no officeholder or politician who valued the vote dared speak a good word for the Chinese. The Chinese became the villain of fiction, the hatchet-man and the wily conspirator of the Tong. Years later when the movies invaded the nation's nickelodeons, the Oriental was still the smuggler, the white slaver, and the murderer—until Charlie Chan transposed his role from destroyer of society to its savior.

A century after their emigration into America the coastal Chinese had spread throughout the country and there were 28 cities with established Chinatowns. Except in the largest cities, the Chinese are still few in number. In 1890 when their population was at its peak, they numbered only 107,488, and in 1950 there were only 117,629. Handicapped by racial and cultural differences, they moved

[15] *Report of the Special Committee, op. cit.,* p. 5.
[16] Sidney L. Gulick, *American Democracy and Asiatic Citizenship.* New York, Charles Scribner's Sons, 1918, pp. 34–35.

to the larger cities where they found work and trade in Chinese restaurants, laundries, and curio shops selling Orientalia. But though they have survived, the evidence is that no new Chinatowns will be created and some in existence will shrink or vanish.[17]

Far from wanting the Chinese to go, most cities now hold them in high esteem. They are looked upon as frugal, orderly, honest, and hard-working. Eastern cities boast about them. Busloads of sub-urbanites and hinterlanders come nightly to be reminded that humanity is not all of the same color and bone formation. None fear going into their streets at night. No one shrinks from their food. There is no dread of pollution by their blood or overrunning of our cities by their opium dens. They can move anywhere they please in New York City, though most still prefer to live in Chinatown where their shops are concentrated. A proposal to clear New York City's China-town section failed when the Chinese themselves decided that China-town, though crowded and substandard, was a thriving enterprise and should not be disturbed. In Los Angeles, a new Chinatown was built when the old one had to be torn down. The Chinese seemed to ac-climate to their new environment.

When the San Francisco local housing authority built a project for the Chinese it was still unthinkable for the city fathers to ease the overcrowding by expanding their living space beyond the ghetto. Resistance to Chinese as neighbors flared up again in 1951 in a San Francisco suburb where a Chinese named Sing Sheng had bought a house. But there was considerable protest by the San Francisco press and its citizens against the community's action.

In the main, the old-time fears have subsided in the cities and the Chinese are less unwelcome than in the earlier times. They may now be seen in white restaurants and some even live on streets once banned to them. Not even Chinese intervention in Korea or the shift into Communism by the home country was able to revive the old bitterness.

One of the reasons for the waning of anti-Chinese resentment was the influx of new scapegoat minorities. "The Chinese are tractable, patient, self-effacing, philosophical, self-respecting, and quite con-tent to remain as servants and laborers. Their intelligent leaders are

[17] Rose Hum Lee, "The Decline of Chinatowns in the United States," *The American Journal of Sociology,* March, 1949, pp. 422–432.

not insulted at the results of inevitable race differences, and no assimilation is required or desired." But the newest immigrants from the Orient "are sensitive to every discrimination, are ambitious to rise immediately above the status of laborers, are aggressive for recognition, and have gained an unenviable reputation for their disregard of contractual obligations."[18]

As their numbers and their competition were no longer challenging the whites, the antagonism against the Chinese had given way to a new antagonism against the Japanese.

The Japanese

No sooner had the oppressed Chinese headed homeward or eastward than budding California again began to feel the pinch for menial labor. Filipinos, Negroes, Hindus, Puerto Ricans, Mexicans, and Japanese were eagerly sought by California farmers. When the Japanese Government in 1884 authorized general emigration in response to the persistent demands of the Hawaiian sugar planters' association, Japanese started coming in to fill the labor gaps. Like the Chinese in their day, the Japanese too were welcomed. In 1887 a San Francisco doctor launched a local campaign in the municipal elections with the slogan "The Japs Must Go," but was considered a freak and got nowhere.

By 1890, however, labor agitation against the Japanese was already becoming more vocal. Shoemakers ousted Japanese workers from a shoe factory, San Francisco's Cooks and Waiters Union attacked a Japanese restaurant, and agitation was started to ban Japanese children from public schools. In 1900 symptoms of bubonic plague appeared in San Francisco and the mayor and the Board of Supervisors quarantined the Japanese as well as the Chinese quarters. The charge that it was a political quarantine fell on deaf ears.[19]

The new century saw mass meetings against Japanese, the San Francisco *Chronicle* launched a campaign to oust them, and the American Federation of Labor and the State Legislature resolved

[18] Robert Newton Lynch, "The Development of the Anti-Japanese Movement," *The Annals* of the American Academy of Political and Social Science, vol. XCIII, January, 1921, pp. 47–48.

[19] Raymond Leslie Buell, "The Development of the Anti-Japanese Agitation in the United States," *Political Science Quarterly*. New York, Ginn & Co., vol. 37, no. 4, December, 1922, p. 608.

that Congress prevent their further admission. A federal immigration act and "gentlemen's agreement" between the United States and Japan finally barred their entry.

Several factors heightened anti-Japanese agitation. One was the competition for dwellings after the San Francisco earthquake in 1906. To find new homes and business sites, thousands of Japanese whose homes had been destroyed ventured into the western sections of the city. This not only touched off violence but abuse of the legal processes. The school board resolved to segregate Japanese children in schools "for the purpose of relieving the congestion at present prevailing in our schools, but also for the higher end that our children should not be placed in any position where their youthful impressions may be affected by association with pupils of the Mongolian race."[20]

The total number of Japanese that ventured into California was, like the Chinese immigration, relatively small. By 1890 there were 2039 Japanese in the country; by 1900, 24,236; by 1910, 72,157. The greatest concentration was around Los Angeles County. Like most immigrants unfamiliar with customs and language, the Japanese generally lived together until social acceptance or economic success permitted them to spread out. Although some found work as domestics and as railroad laborers, most worked the soil, first as migratory workers and later as tenants and owners of small truck farms.

Coming from a country where land was scarce and intensively cultivated, they proved experts in growing vegetables, strawberries, asparagus, and sugar beets. When droughts in San Diego County drove many white farmers out, the Japanese, thanks to their cooperative associations and credit facilities, were able to survive. Among a representative group, 80.7 per cent were common laborers during their first five years in this country. Twenty years later only 46.1 per cent were laborers, the rest mainly owners, managers, or tradesmen.[21]

Working a few acres apiece, but operating close to the cities and to one another, they gave the impression of much larger numbers and more extensive ownership. Efficient in cultivating and irrigating, they were seen as competitors with less industrious whites. Hostility grew

[20] *Ibid*, pp. 621, 623.
[21] Edward K. Strong, *Japanese in California*. Stanford University Publications, University Series, Stanford University Press, vol. 1, no. 2, 1933, p. 116.

when the Japanese proved as productive indoors as outdoors. The appearance of picture brides at Pacific ports emphasized a new "yellow peril." California soon saw a challenge to the social and economic status of pure white American blood. The struggle for ethnic supremacy began to follow the familiar pattern.

The tendency of the Chinese city-dweller had been to remain in his Chinatown. But the Japanese were not satisfied with peasant culture and slum life. They sought to spread their living space and opportunities. The Japanese immigrant after the gentlemen's agreement of 1901 had higher social and cultural ambitions. He began to operate competitive groceries, hotels, dye works, and cleaning establishments. He also sought residence in the better sections of the city. The whites saw his presence as a threat to their own enterprises as well as to the standards of their neighborhoods. One author in 1921 put it bluntly:

> The real and very worst complaint—far from deserving the name "problem"—touching Santa Clara County, is the fact that in a few village sections the Japanese are slowly encroaching upon the choicest residential quarters and spoiling them. It is the same sort of aggravating nuisance evident in the Catskills where Jewish vacationists by their very presence drive away the gentiles; it is the kind of thing that happened when, at the opening of the Williamsburg bridge, the attractive, aristocratic Eastern District, Brooklyn, was turned into a bedroom for Yiddish New York. The only immediate, vital difference between the so-called encroachments of the Jews and of the Japanese in America lies in the fact that the former, nationally, are homeless, while the latter have a government back of them.[22]

The effort to improve oneself, normally viewed as a creditable trait, worked in reverse for the Japanese. Their success was considered an affront, their intrusion a challenge. They inherited the animus once aimed at the Chinese, fanned by the fear that they were pushing and clever. The stereotype was given added force by the expansionist foreign policy of the mother country. Nor was it modified for the American-born Japanese, for the convert or Christian, or for those who had abandoned all loyalties to Japan.

[22] Charles Roger Hicks, "The Japanese Problem in California," *The Journal of International Relations* (continuing the *Journal of Race Development*), vol. 11, no. 4, April, 1921, p. 606. (Mr. Hicks formerly taught in the First Commercial Middle School, Kyoto, Japan.)

The cries that the Japanese were putting the white farmers out of business or would overrun the country grew louder and the same harrying techniques that had been levelled against the Chinese were put to use. But in this case the very virtues of the Japanese were unashamedly cited to justify the attack. "We admire their industry and cleverness," explained Senator James D. Phelan of California, "but for that very reason, being a masterful people, they are more dangerous."[23]

As the Chinese had been condemned for their imputed vices, so the Japanese were condemned for their virtues, sobriety, industry, intelligence, and skill, for their respect for law and for their honesty. Dr. Benjamin Ide Wheeler, president emeritus of the State University of California, said "Their good taste, persistent industry, their excellent qualities and their virtues render their presence amongst us a pitiful danger."[24]

Infiltration of a neighborhood or a farm area was seen as a prelude to a beachhead for the invasion of America itself. From the San Francisco earthquake to World War II, the Japanese were targets of anti-Oriental invective and repression. The general elections of 1910 in California found all three party platforms with anti-Japanese planks. The California Alien Law of 1913 prohibited Japanese aliens from buying or leasing agricultural land for longer than three years. In 1919 the American Legion demanded a permanent denial of citizenship to Japanese nationals and an amendment to the Constitution of the United States denying citizenship to American-born children of ineligible aliens. In 1922 the Supreme Court held Japanese were not "whites" and thereby disqualified them for citizenship. The Initiative Land Law in California prohibited Japanese aliens from leasing land on any terms, buying stock in any organization owning or leasing agricultural land, and becoming guardians over minor citizens if the estate consisted of land. In 1921 the State Legislature empowered local boards to establish separate schools for children of Indian and Oriental parentage and in 1923

[23] "Why California Objects to the Japanese Invasion," *The Annals* of the American Academy of Political and Social Science, vol. XCIII, January, 1921, p. 17.

[24] Col. John P. Irish, "The Japanese Issue in California," *ibid.*, p. 75.

even share-cropping was forbidden to Japanese aliens. In 1924 Congress barred Japanese from entering the country altogether.

The various sanctions against the Japanese made their mark. Racial housing covenants and labor union proscriptions checked their progress in the cities and the Alien Land Act checked it on the farms. Inability to attain citizenship kept the Japanese from voicing effective political protest. In the West Coast cities they lived in "Little Tokyos" where they provided goods and services for other Japanese in the produce enterprises and operated service trades for each other, ran rooming houses or catered to tourists. Yet despite oppressions, the native born (Nisei) were mostly high school graduates, many of them attending college. By 1941, Japanese farmers were raising about 42 per cent of the produce crops of California.[25]

By 1940 there were 127,000 Japanese in the United States, of whom only 37 per cent were foreign-born and most of the others were of an older generation, only 8 per cent of them being under 35 years of age. Despite all the efforts to contain them, most of the Nisei were bi-cultural, observing American customs more than Japanese. There was no evidence of disloyalty to America and in fact there was positive evidence that most were loyal.[26]

Nevertheless in the spring and summer of 1942, after the Pearl Harbor attack, Americans of Japanese descent in the Pacific Coast area were rounded up and shipped to internment camps in the interior. Some 75,000 American citizens of Japanese ancestry had to leave their homes for these camps. It was the first time in American history that racial characteristics became the determinant of an individual's liberty, the first time citizens were marched out of their homes because of their ancestry.

There is much about this odd deviation from democratic tradition that must be viewed in context. The Japanese had sunk our fleet. Anti-Japanese sentiment was running high; emotions were not easily controllable, and long-standing prejudices were finding their outlets

[25] R. A. Schermerhorn, *These Our People*. Boston, D.C. Heath and Company, 1949, p. 216.
[26] Carey McWilliams, *Prejudice. Japanese Americans: Symbols of Racial Intolerance.* Boston, Little Brown and Company, 1944, p. 114; see also Carey McWilliams, *Impounded People, Japanese Americans in Relocation Centers.* Department of Interior, War Relocation Authority, Washington, Government Printing Office, 1944, p. 37.

in odium and demands for vengeance. Nor did the Fourth Estate help to keep heads cool. Scribes like Henry McLemore of the San Francisco *Examiner* screamed "Herd 'em up, pack 'em off and give 'em the inside room in the badlands . . . let us have no patience with the enemy or with anyone whose veins carry his blood. . . . Personally I hate the Japanese. And that goes for all of them."[27]

Westbrook Pegler urged that "the Japanese in California should be under armed guard to the last man and woman right now, and to hell with habeas corpus until the danger is over." Resolutions demanding evacuation were approved by responsibles as well as irresponsibles. While popular passion may be expected to rise during war, prejudice seems to have seized the sober Army leaders and the responsible federal agencies as well.

The classic statement of General J. L. DeWitt, who had charge of the corral, is illustrative: "A Jap's a Jap. . . . It makes no difference whether he is an American citizen or not. . . . I don't want any of them here. . . . They are a dangerous element. . . . There is no way to determine their loyalty."[28]

Even the usually calm and sober United States Supreme Court now ruled that "ethnic affiliations" may be a source of danger per se.[29]

There is persuasive evidence that the evacuation was induced at least in part by simple economic and political motivations rather than wartime emotions. The influence of the Western Growers Protective Association—with whom the Japanese farmers were in competition—the Grower-Shipper Vegetable Association, the Associated Farmers, and the California Farm Bureau, was being brought to bear on officials.[30]

---

[27] January 29, 1942; see also, Dorothy S. Thomas and Richard S. Nishimoto, *The Spoilage: Japanese American Evacuation and Resettlement.* Berkeley, University of California Press, 1946, pp. 1–23.

[28] Another statement by the general in the same vein is "The Japanese race is an enemy race and while many second and third generation Japanese born on United States soil, possessed of United States citizenship, have been 'Americanized,' the racial strains are undiluted." U.S. Army, Western Defense Command and Fourth Army, *Final Report, Japanese Evacuation from the West Coast, 1942.* Washington, Government Printing Office, 1943, p. 34.

[29] See Chapter XXI.

[30] Morton Grodzins, *Americans Betrayed.* Chicago, The University of Chicago Press, 1949, chap. II, "Pressure Groups."

. . . mass evacuation was not the product of wartime hysteria; it was the logical end-product, the goal, of a strategy of dominance which began forty years earlier and which was closely related to a similar strategy of American dominance in the Pacific. The resident Japanese were always the hostages of this larger strategy much as Japan proper is today the hostage of the American empire. . . .[31]

The evacuation solved the problem of Japanese competition. It destroyed the sound little truck farms along the highways and the cleaning and dyeing establishments. Total losses of all evacuated Japanese were estimated at $350–500 million. The dwellings emptied of Japanese helped ease the housing shortage in the cities. The evacuation broke the ghetto. But two things it did not do: it did not solve the Japanese minority problem; it did not relieve California of new minority problems. It created an ominous judicial precedent when the Supreme Court paid homage to racial prejudice. With peace and the return to common sense, some 60,000 Japanese also returned. The rest ventured toward kindlier Boston, New York, Philadelphia, Washington, Denver, Salt Lake City, Cleveland, Cincinnati, and other cities. The victory over Japan won, one would expect that the fears of invasion would have subsided and that the new Japanese stereotype would now be more clearly like that of the Chinese, i.e., humbled and "safe." Indeed public attitudes were somewhat friendlier. Japanese American soldiers had established a fine record during the war. Some of the civic and socially minded groups which had supported the evacuation policy were ashamed and contrite. There was pity in the air, the competition of the Japanese truck farmer was no longer a factor, and more important still the Japanese were no longer so numerous.

Yet violence greeted some who returned to their former homes. Houses were spattered with kerosene and set on fire, while night riders poured rifle shots on those who were trying to quench the flames. Threats and hatred bore the marks of organization, and police were kept busy looking in other directions.[32]

Temporary housing arrangements were provided in California by the War Relocation Authority and by the Federal Public Housing

[31] Carey McWilliams, *Brothers Under the Skin*. Boston, Little Brown, rev. ed., 1951, p. 164.

[32] Emory S. Bogardus, "The Japanese Return to the West Coast," *Sociology and Social Research,* January–February, 1947, pp. 226–233.

Authority. Many privately operated hostels were maintained by social and religious groups. But the Japanese did not fully regain their former position in the American economy, nor did many win back their homes or neighborhoods they once occupied.

After the Japanese had been herded into internment camps, California again began to feel the pinch of labor shortage, particularly with the increase of war industries. Mexicans began to trek northward in greater numbers and Negroes moved in from the South. The Negroes took over the little Tokyos.

With the coming of the new groups, public attitudes toward the Japanese continued to ease just as opposition had eased against the Chinese when the Japanese appeared. Less than ten years after Hiroshima, Tokyo's movies were exhibiting Hollywood's product and its night clubs were filled with American tourists dancing with beautifully gowned Japanese girls to the tune of American jazz. The waning of resentment was speeded by the return of American soldiers with Japanese war brides, by the cooperative attitudes of the Japanese at home, by the feelings of American tourists who now began to see the Japanese as quaint, industrious, and interesting, and above all by the diversion of resentments toward the newest migrant minorities—the Mexicans and Negroes.

V

THE STREAM FROM THE GULF

Two-way Current from the Gulf

Up to the 1920's, the immigration current ran mainly one way. Most immigrants cut their ties with Europe, sank new foundations in American farms and cities, and reared their families. Only a small portion came to work and save and return to the motherland. The trip was tough, costly, and dangerous. The Atlantic was braved only after long thought, and consultation with friends already here. Though there were resentments and demands to halt further immigration there were no cries that the immigrant must go back whence he came, except in the case of the Orientals. Once the white immigrant was here he was a shareholder, entitled to all the fruits of American opportunities.

In the 1920's a new type of immigrant entered the American scene. He came from across the Caribbean or the Rio Grande, appearing first in the West and Southwest, later in the East. He was a two-way immigrant. He came to work—then left. He felled no trees to make way for the plow, he staked no quarter sections. Nor was the fruit he picked his own, for he worked as part of a dreary crew—picking crops for subsistence pay, moving North to another farm with each crop and season, and migrating back again. Sometimes he might leave the procession, legally or illegally, to seek more permanent status. Most often he would head back to his country of origin, or linger at some crude way-station far from the stream of life. His shelter was primitive, provided by the farmer or set up by himself in a squatters' village. Or he might crowd in with others as a temporary tenant. His status, unlike that of prior immigrants, was nomadic.

He was migrant, not immigrant; free to move but not to stay. The age of mobility which had produced more transportation, goods, and men, had also produced the mobile ghetto, a new phenomenon on the American scene. The dwellers in these ghettos were both citizens and aliens and were mostly Mexicans and Negroes, but they also included Puerto Ricans, Bahamians, and a scattering of other minorities.

The development was partly the by-product of a new conflict of interests between the American economy and the American society. The American economy needed labor—the tough, laborious, monotonous toil once accomplished by the European peasant immigrant. The reward for that labor included the right to buy into the American community. The new American society, however, was no longer willing to share all its fruits with those who came. It was unwilling even to have them as neighbors. It became a closed corporation. The grower needed hands for the season and wanted them cheap, but was unwilling to support those hands until the next crop. City workers would not have them compete for their jobs, while the cities to which they drifted were unwilling to pay the social costs to maintain them between seasons. Homeowners dreaded their presence and feared invasion of their neighborhoods. Federal officials made no effort to resolve the conflict, set up a national policy, or even define the problem. The executive manager of the California Beet Growers Association expressed the West's needs bluntly:

We have gone through the whole gamut. We have used Chinamen, Japs, Hindus, Filipinos, Mexican Nationals, Mexican wetbacks, if you please, Indians, Negroes, Bahamians, prisoners of war and what-have-you. . . . We have always been willing to take any kind of labor that we could get when we needed them; domestic labor when it was available. When it wasn't we had to get what we could to get our crops harvested. . . .[1]

Having missed the big pool of cheap white labor that developed the eastern seaboard and the midwestern prairie, the West now insisted on using its own methods. The Chinese and Japanese stream had stopped. Many Negroes were being attracted to factories. The Puerto Ricans, as citizens, would have had the right to remain in the cities

[1] *Migratory Labor in American Agriculture:* Report of the President's Commission on Migratory Labor. Washington, U.S. Government Printing Office, 1951, p. 13.

and claim governmental services. A big new source of labor had to be found. It lay across the Rio Grande. Here was the great pool of docile, hungry Mexicans, willing to work at stoop-labor under a hot sun for two or three dollars a day. Here within a stone's throw were two standards of life which, if separately maintained, could answer the growers' prayer.

But while the Rio Grande is easy to cross, the border it marks is legally impenetrable. Millions of persecuted people have hung on for months in the D.P. camps of Europe, waited a decade in strange ports in the hope their quota numbers might be reached. Many come within sight of American ports, only to be turned back at the gate.

How hurdle the obstacle without changing the law? One way is to violate the law, and growers and owners of western farm factories and ranches rose to the occasion with all the talent they could muster. They grasped the powerful arm of government and turned it into a catspaw for western interests. The lobby, whose influence seems to gather power on its course from the Pacific to the Potomac, "prevents the extension of social security, minimum wages, and other forms of protections to the Mexican rural workers. The same lobby inspires highly confidential agreements with the Mexican government for the recruitment of Nationals or *braceros,* whose major strategic function is to depress wages in California and Texas. Men who are highly sympathetic to the policies of the Associated Farmers sit securely in control of the machinery of the Inter-American System, thereby heading off constructive multilateral action to tackle the problems of inter-American labor migration at its roots."[2]

"We find," the President's Commission on Migratory Labor placidly confirms, "that there have been times when pressure has been successfully exerted upon Washington to have the Immigration and Naturalization Service issue orders to field officers to go easy on deportations until crops have been harvested."[3]

When, in 1949, representatives of the Federal Employment Service asked immigration officials to cut down Mexican deportations, the latter blithely conformed. The assistant commissioner of the Immigration and Naturalization Service conceded that "pressure here is con-

[2] Ernesto Galarza, "The Mexican American: A National Concern. Program for Action," *Common Ground,* summer, 1949, pp. 27–38.

[3] *Op. cit.,* p. 75.

siderable."[4] Agents enforcing the law suddenly found complaints filed against them. An "investigation" was launched out of Washington for no other purpose than to "get the enforcing agents to 'lay off.' "[5] A spokesman for farm employers insists that the border states need special consideration in the matter of illegal migrancy "because their agricultural economy was largely developed by Mexican labor," a policy which he concedes "was partly illegal, but yet condoned by our Government officials for many years."[6]

Special consideration for the big growers is obtained through a curious joint venture between the Mexican and American governments. California and Texas are fertile in fields, Mexico in people. Since the Mexicans are needed during the crop-picking season but are unwanted when their work is done, the solution is simple. The Mexican illegals will be recruited one day and arrested soon after for violating the law. While the crops are being harvested, officials wink at the hundreds of thousands of Mexicans wading or swimming the river or crossing at some point of the 1600 mile border from Texas to the Pacific. But if the Mexicans hang on when no longer needed, their children will need schooling, hospitalization, and other social services. By corralling and exporting them at the strategic moment, the law's mandate can be complied with, the growers' needs met, the nation's moral sense remain unaroused. It is no accident that arrests and deportations decline at the season's beginning and rise at the season's end.

The New Stream from the Gulf

California alone got 63 per cent of the Mexicans in 1945, but in the peak months, January through April, the figure reached 90 per cent. The other principal beneficiary is Texas, while Arizona, New Mexico, Colorado, and Idaho also benefit. Organized farmers openly send their agents into Mexico to recruit labor. Mexicans, here illegally,

---

[4] *Ibid.,* p. 76.

[5] "The United States Immigration and Naturalization Service recognizes the need for farm workers in Idaho, and through cooperation with the State employment service, withholds its search and deportation until such times as there is not a shortage of farm workers," blandly concedes the report of the State Employment Service of Idaho, another state enjoying the fruits of Mexican stoop-labor. *Loc. cit.*

[6] *Ibid.,* p. 74.

are often legalized by immigration officials who march them across the border for a few minutes and march them right back again, clothed in legitimacy. Mexicans who wait for the legal processes of entry may wait till Doomsday. It is more practical to violate the law than to comply with it. "Our government thus has become a contributor to the growth of illegal traffic which it has responsibility to prevent," says the President's Commission.[7]

The average Wetback is a fugitive—hungry, rootless, furtive, exploited, and wretched. Having the distinctive racial features of his Indian ancestors he is easily identifiable, and can be apprehended. Or if he is here legally, he finds it hard to sink roots. His wages, while reaching as much as 40¢ an hour, may be as low as 15¢. Often he pays tribute for being smuggled across the border, only to be bilked out of his earnings by unscrupulous employers. He is a victim of rent-gouging, usury, and company-store chicane.

Ignorance, exploitation, and primitive standards marked the early pattern of capitalist development in the days of Manchesterism abroad and the domestic immigrant sweatshops of a half century ago. But in time the exploited become wiser, more educated, more vocal politically; the exploiter less selfish, his oppressions halted by an awakened public conscience. Capitalism's excesses are brought within bounds, its virtues retained, its vices curbed. But there is a marked difference, becoming more emphasized in the West and Southwest today. The upward movement toward improvement and assimilation, which was democratic capitalism's greatest contribution to society, is now markedly checked in the West and Southwest. The new migrants cannot climb up from the bottom as their predecessors did. This of course suits those at the top. As one employer of migratory labor puts it: "One big advantage in using these alien laborers is that there is no social or economic problems during slack seasons." They either go back to Mexico or they are forced back.

The employers' attitude seems to run something like this: You are needed and will be used, but you must know your place; we will let you know your place; stay there! If, as, and when you are no longer needed, get out, or at least stay out of sight until we call you again. If you go where you are not wanted we will seize you and put you in your place. And though we need your labor desperately, we

[7] *Loc. cit.*

disclaim any obligation to care for you or take you in as part of our community.

"Beyond wanting migrants to be available when needed and to be gone when not needed," comments the President's Commission, "they are expected to work under conditions no longer typical or characteristic of the American standard of life."[8] There are no job standards at all for this type of employment, no housing, sanitation, or medical facilities. At a coroner's inquest in California's San Joaquin Valley, a white migratory worker, father of a four-month-old child, testified:

> On November 4, he started vomiting but stopped and seemed better. At 9 o'clock on Sunday the 6th, he was very bad, and we started for the hospital. We took him to the Coalinga Hospital but we didn't have any money and they sent us to the General Hospital in Fresno. We are not familiar with this area and we stopped at the Wallace Sanatorium. We didn't have any money so they sent us on to the General Hospital. When we arrived they told us the baby was dead.[9]

Wetbacks, Drybacks, Americans

Not all Mexicans are Wetbacks or migrant laborers. Mexicans in the United States, in fact, represent one of its most diverse groups. The Spanish Colonials, located mostly in New Mexico, are descendants of the Spanish Conquistadors and the Mexican Indians who settled in the region in the sixteenth century and won citizenship after the Mexican War. In the 1950's these formed about half the population of New Mexico and about a twelfth of the total number of Mexicans in the country.

They have attained political strength, and in fact have elected their own legislators and governors. There is no official segregation (although an informal segregation is practiced in schools, churches, social groups, and in employment). There are no restrictive covenants to bar them from neighborhoods, and relations with the Anglos are friendly. They are a substantial group numerically, but live in scattered communities relatively isolated from the stream of American life. The literacy level is low, and most spend their lives on the same farm or in the same community. Behavior, mores, and beliefs have been uniform and unchanging through the years. While not upgraded

[8] *Ibid*, p. 16.
[9] *Ibid*, p. 155.

into the American social structure, they have established a tolerable bicultural consortium. Another group of Mexican descent immigrated slowly until about 1910 and more rapidly until about 1930. A substantial number have been born here since that time. The 1950 Census lists 2.5 million persons of Mexican descent. Most are concentrated in the West and Southwest.

Up to 1917 there had been a free movement between Mexico and the United States. After the 1917 immigration law, some 73,000 entered when we waived the restrictions to induce Mexicans to take jobs in farming, railroads, and mining. Immigration since then has been legal, quasi-legal, and illegal. In the 1920's we received a million Mexicans, but conditions got so bad in the depression years that half a million drifted back to Mexico and were repatriated. With the defense program, a new wave came. From 1942 to 1947, in fact, the government at its own cost brought in 219,500 as farm workers, and in 1954 negotiations were under way to accept many more.

Although some can be found in trade, white-collar occupations, and the professions, most workers of Mexican descent are agricultural workers, migratory laborers, or unskilled industrial workers. Job turnover is high, mobility common, and a settled agricultural or industrial worker today may be migratory tomorrow. "On the whole, the Mexican-American may be called America's most unsettled minority."[10]

Though those of lighter color may have a status in the Southwest somewhat above the Negro and native Indian, the darker ones suffer the customary exclusion practices in housing and employment. Many are disadvantaged because they have never become citizens and are loath to bring their status into challenge by demanding better conditions. Attitudes of police officials are often hostile, reflecting the attitudes of the community itself. The Los Angeles "Zoot Suit Riots" in 1943, which threatened to strain the relationship between the Mexican and American governments at a time when amity was most needed and which touched off an epidemic of riots in a number of cities, were the product of antipathy by both the public and press to Mexicans and to the absence of adequate police protection.[11]

[10] R. A. Schermerhorn, *These Our People*. Boston, D.C. Heath and Company, 1949, p. 178.

[11] Carey McWilliams, *North from Mexico*. Philadelphia, J. B. Lippincott & Co., 1948, p. 244.

Communities in the United States might have absorbed and accepted some of them—like the early northern Negroes—were it not for the inspired Wetback invasion. The sudden swarm of men willing to work for a pittance depressed wages, making it hard for other unskilled labor, particularly Mexican-Americans, to maintain whatever standards they had attained. It also sharpened the antagonism between Mexican and American labor. When earlier immigrants struck for better wages or working conditions, employers or contractors would sweep down with a "task force" of several thousand fresh Mexican labor recruits and break the resistance.

Many Mexicans and Mexican-Americans have found themselves pushed farther north by the competition, inviting social tension as they move forward. Matters became worse when the Wetbacks followed, invited by northern farmers anxious to get a turn at the cheaper labor. As long as they are needed but stay out of sight their hinterland colonies may be tolerated. If there is no longer a need for them they may be told to leave for "sanitary reasons" or because they are trespassing. Transient life makes it difficult for Mexican children to rise in the social or economic milieu. The ill, infirm, and child-bearing must all move with the demands of the season, or starve. Relief aid, unemployment insurance, and other benefits are rare. The Mexican migrant is a peon cut off from the responsibility a master might have to assume. Nominally he is free, actually he is forsaken. If he is an illegal entrant, he has no rights at all. If he is a contract laborer he has the meager protection required by the contract, and no more.

Housing of Mexicans

The housing and neighborhoods of Mexicans and Mexican-Americans vary as does their status. In San Antonio, the west side Mexican slum of 60,000 is called "the largest solid bloc of under-possessed in the United States."[12] Slum life, exploitation, segregation, and social subordination are virtually complete.

New Mexico villages are composed of one-story adobe houses grouped around the church and stores. Though the village is picturesque, the houses lack the necessary water, electricity, or screening to make them livable. The sense of community is strong, however, and the Mexican here has found a place in it. Discriminations do not

[12] John Gunther, *Inside USA*. New York, Harper & Brothers, 1947, p. 832.

compare with those in the cities, and are a far cry from those to which Mexican migrants are subjected.

There are also Mexican communities within urban metropolitan areas, such as Los Angeles, San Diego, Phoenix, Denver, and Chicago. Here migrants dwell during the winter. When menial labor is needed they often succeed in getting a city job and becoming city dwellers. But the shift from rural to urban life has not taken place as frequently as with the recent Negro migrant. When the Mexican does get into the city he may be classed as "nonwhite" and excluded like the Negro, or he may be rated as a lower-class tenant than even the Negro.[13] Owners may be reluctant to rent to him except when other tenants are unavailable. Restrictive covenants are common, and there are few homeowners among the Mexicans.[14] In one town the instructions to real estate agents were:

"Care should be taken not to get people of the African, Mexican, Chinese or other similar races in this quarter." The reason given was "protection of property values against depreciation." In another case a citizen of a small town with an adjoining Mexican colony said, "The townspeople won't let the Mexicans come any closer. Three Spanish-American families want to rent in town now but we will have to find some way of keeping them out."[15] The Los Angeles City Housing Survey of 1939 showed that Mexicans were more overcrowded than any other group.

A large group entered Chicago and the Calumet area where some set up their own ghettos while others moved into Negro, Irish, or Italian neighborhoods. Wherever they went they were met by efforts to drive them out or to restrict the areas of their residence. The reasons given were that they were "dirty," "always fighting," and "depreciated property values." Mexican in-migration was met by window-smashing, assaults, and even murders. "Mexicans will pay $30 rent for property for which the Irish will pay only $20. The Mexicans can't get in many

[13] See for example Homer Hoyt, *One Hundred Years of Land Values in Chicago*. Chicago, University of Chicago Press, 1933, p. 314.

[14] *Mexicans in California*, California Mexican Fact Finding Committee, Part IV, "Social Aspects of the Mexican Immigrant Problem." San Francisco, California State Printing Office, 1930, pp. 175–207.

[15] Paul S. Taylor, *Mexican Labor in the United States*, University of California Publications in Economics, vol. 6, no. 1, "Imperial Valley, Cal." Berkeley, University of California Press, 1929, p. 81; *ibid*, vol, 6, no. 2. "Valley of the South Platte, Colo.," p. 209.

places, so they pay more in order to get in; they can afford to because they take in boarders."[16]

The migratory worker has the worst housing. His low living standards make it unnecessary, in the farmer's opinion, to provide him with adequate shelter. He sleeps on the ground, in a cave, under a tree, or in a chicken house. He cannot bargain or protest. Water for washing, cooking, and drinking is frequently from a muddy irrigation ditch, and there are no sanitary facilities within sight.

The domestic Mexican or native Negro migrant worker has a better chance of getting some shelter from the elements, but even this is generally a ramshackle shed, tent, or cabin, or a ditch-bank camp of tents or canvas stretched across a pole with boxes, brush, or burlap across the end. This may be a squatters' camp or the land may be owned by the employer. Another type of house is the labor shack in the beet fields, built of rough lumber and covered with tar paper. It is not proof against the weather, has been frequently condemned by investigators and sometimes by an enlightened employer. In one case, a sugar company refused to contract for beets after seeing the housing provided for the field workers. "There is not much excuse for that sort of thing now after 25 years of beet-growing."[17] But, though a quarter of a century has passed since then, conditions are no better in the beet fields and, in fact, have worsened considerably.

Shacktown "communities," occupied by resident Mexicans and Negroes for the six to eight months they are not picking crops, are graphically referred to as "The Jungle" or "Ragtown." They may be a dozen or more blocks square, having populations of as many as 10,000. The raw land is rented by the month, sometimes at outrageous rental. The writer visited one of these Mexican communities in Los Angeles County outside the city limits. The huts, two or three to a lot, are homemade from stray boards, burlap, or other waste material. Cardboard or old corrugated scrap is used to block up the open spaces. Few if any were secure against the elements, none against vermin. A single room will be occupied by as many as ten people. The unpaved streets are full of mud-holes which serve doubly as play spaces for children and breeding grounds for mosquitoes. There is of

---

[16] Taylor, *op. cit.,* vol. 7, no. 2, 1932, "Chicago and the Calumet Regions," pp. 220–222.

[17] Taylor, *op. cit.,* "Valley of the South Platte, Colo.," pp. 162–163.

course no plumbing, drainage, or screening and no running water. The whole community fronted on a railroad, with no barrier to protect the roving children. Other similar communities abut city dumps, cactus patches, or ditches.

The contact between these people and the government is through the county sheriff, the most feared man in the community. He visits occasionally to see that the Mexicans are "in their place." The county will do nothing to improve the standard of housing or to provide health supervision and safety from fire or other hazards. The sites are, it seems, deliberately set outside the city limits and on unbeaten paths where they cannot be seen. If the colonies appear too conspicuous and citizens' pride is affected or their shame aroused, a movement may be started to get the Mexicans off the highway and out of sight. The attitude is, "They are breaking our citizens' hearts, so get rid of them."

These communities dot California wherever there are crops to be harvested. They have expanded two- or threefold in the last decade, but not even federal officials know how many there are. A similar condition exists throughout Texas. When Los Angeles County was offered more than $300,000 by the federal government to survey its slums, it turned the offer down. Exponents of public housing were called "communists" by a member of the County Redevelopment Authority. The county needs no federal help for slum clearance, for it can clear its slums by having the sheriff order the Mexicans out. But so long as the Mexicans are needed to pick crops, they might stay—out of sight of course.

When the writer in 1950 addressed a meeting of Mexicans and Mexican-American workmen who had occupied permanent houses within the city of Los Angeles, he was surprised to find them opposed to the public housing program. An intelligent Mexican girl complained that after they had been assured of getting better housing, their houses were torn down and they were relegated to the streets. Many were not citizens and were therefore ineligible for new housing. Others were barred because of income requirements or other technical considerations. They feared slum clearance as a new pretext for ousting them from their humble homes. The limited statistics available spotlight the generally deplorable conditions. In Imperial County, California, the infant death rate from diarrhea, enteritis, and dysentery is more than seven times as high as the statewide average. Mexican children represent the major proportion of the victims. In Hidalgo County, among 83 children between the ages of six and twelve in 55 families, 21 were found to be in need of immediate medical care, and for 27 others "medical care was considered to be indicated but less urgent."[18]

A physician told the President's Commission of the frequent cases of pellagra and "ordinary starvation" due to the diet of cornmeal and rice "and very little else." In one Texas camp 96 per cent of the children had not consumed any milk whatsoever in the last 6 months while 8 out of every 10 adults had not eaten any meat in 6 months.[19]

Thus, in the case of the migrant Mexican, and to some extent other migrants, we have a unique kind of internal colonialism. The native laborer works hard for pitiful wages, suffers the social inferiority of a native in the eyes of his master and the community, and lives under the subhuman conditions so often characteristic of native colonial life. The difference between the traditional and the new colonialism is that our colonial natives are kept with us within distance when we want them—and then driven out of the community when no longer needed. They go back to the "colony" at the season's end, often under armed guard. In this novel system, a dual standard of capitalist morality has been constructed. We have on the one hand a minimum wage, a 40-hour week, social security, and a living standard that rates among the highest in the world. On the other hand we tolerate conditions as primitive as any that existed under feudalism.

A social dichotomy has developed which is not bridgeable as time erases distinguishing customs and language. Stratification has displaced evolution for those at the bottom. The process of enlightenment and upgrading through education does not function for them, nor even for their children.

Fortunately this anomaly has not escaped exposure and public investigation. When the facts are better known, the American public may be expected to enforce corrective measures despite the counter pressures from those who benefit by the status quo.

[18] *Migratory Labor in American Agriculture, op. cit.*, p. 154.
[19] *Loc. cit.*

VI

THE PUERTO RICAN AIRLIFT

EVERY day a few hundred Puerto Ricans can be seen at the San Juan airport waiting to board airliners for New York. There are women with babies, young people, some older people, some colored, some white. Their belongings are at their sides in suitcases or crude bundles. There are gesticulations, the bustle of hurried farewells, some tears. Soon the packs are weighed, an announcement in Spanish comes over the loud speaker, and a roar of engines signals another departure from America's teeming little island in the Caribbean.

Shift the scene to the airports of New York and there are similar crowds of Puerto Rican out-migrants, the same gesticulations, the same tears, the same belongings in suitcases and bundles; the same bustle of farewells, and the roar of engines. But this time it signals the end of an adventure—the road back to America's teeming little island in the Caribbean.

The Puerto Rican journey is unique in the record of American migrations.

1. It is an air migration.

2. It is a six-and-a-half-hour trip, not the laborious two to three week sailing from Europe a half century ago, and the pull-back to the island is ever-present.

3. Like alien immigrants, the Puerto Rican comes with his native tongue, traditions, and customs, but he is an American citizen.

4. The migration, instead of moving outward to take advantage of the wider opportunities the country offers, has seemingly bogged down in a single port of entry.

Prior to 1940, emigration from Puerto Rico averaged only a few thousand persons a year. From 1942 to 1945, however, out-migration from Puerto Rico increased, effecting a net settlement of 29,000 on the mainland. Then in 1946 the number of settlers on the mainland spiralled, so that by 1953 more than 500,000 had settled here. Between 1940 and June, 1953, migrants who had left the island numbered more than 1.85 million, and those who had returned 1.4 million.[1]

How many returned to the island because they were transients in the first place or because they were disillusioned is not known, for no sample surveys have been made at the American airports to determine the reasons for departures. Doubtless, some are students or small businessmen, others visitors who come to look around and stay; still others who came to stay decided a visit was enough. A recent study, however, showed that more than half already here would like to return to the island with its mild climate and more familiar patterns, if they could support their families there.[2]

What has turned the Puerto Rican migration into the Puerto Rican problem is not its size. By comparison, no less than 2.7 million Negroes migrated between 1940 and 1947, 1.18 million moving between noncontiguous states.[3] Between 1942 and 1947 the federal government itself brought in 219,500 Mexicans. In 1950, the known Wetback traffic was ten times as great as the net Puerto Rican in-migration. In 1952 1.5 million Mexicans came in, and it is authoritatively estimated that from one to ten times as many escape periodic corralling as are caught. In fact, Puerto Rico's whole population of 2.25 million could be absorbed in America's expanding economy in a few years, as were previous migrants.

The main obstructions in the Puerto Rican problem are the inability to establish secure footholds on the continent, the sordid conditions under which the migrants live, and the seeming hopelessness of the island's position unless two bottlenecks are broken—one that

---

[1] A. J. Jaffe, "Demographic and Labor Force Characteristics of the New York City Puerto Rican Population," in A. J. Jaffe (ed.), *Puerto Rican Population in New York City*. New York, Bureau of Applied Social Research, Columbia University, January, 1954, p. 8.

[2] Sophie M. Robison, "Social and Welfare Statistics on the New York Puerto Rican Population," *Ibid*, p. 54.

[3] *Housing of the Nonwhite Population 1940 to 1950*. Washington, D.C., Housing and Home Finance Agency, July, 1952, p. 3.

blocks a permanent migration from the island, the other that confines it to a single city when it reaches the mainland.

The Rural Migration

The Puerto Rican migration to the mainland consists of two streams of labor: one rural, the other urban. Agriculture is the island's main source of employment, and in 1950, 60 per cent of the population lived in rural areas. The rural migration is largely seasonal and consists of a temporary migration of contract laborers composed of some 15,000 farm workers, of whom only a few thousand are independent farm workers. Yet only a trickle of agricultural labor ever settles here permanently.

While farm workers are in constant demand on the mainland, unemployment and underemployment in agriculture on the island are greater than in any other economic activity. There are several reasons for the mainland's failure to draw off the island's surplus farm population: One is the American policy of preferring alien labor to citizens. A citizen has rights—we cannot let an American starve or have his children roam barefoot on the main highways. An alien Mexican, however, can be corralled when no longer needed and forced back across the Rio Grande.[4]

The president of the Florida growers' group told the Secretary of Agriculture:

> The vast difference between the Bahama Islands labor and the domestic, including Puerto Ricans, is that labor transported from the Bahama Islands can be diverted and sent home if it does not work, which cannot be done in the instance of labor from domestic United States or Puerto Rico.[5]

A large Connecticut tobacco planter employed a pool of labor from the British West Indies by permission of the U.S. Employment Service, which supervises the flow of contract labor to the United States. These foreign workers were, of course, returned when the season was over. Since they were not citizens, they were more controllable in the event of disagreement over wages, work, and shelter. Puerto Ricans, moreover, as citizens could assert their rights to go where they chose.

---

[4] *Migratory Labor in American Agriculture.* Report of the President's Commission on Migratory Labor. Washington, U. S. Government Printing Office, 1951, p. 16.

[5] *Ibid,* p. 39.

They might drift to cities and seek jobs, presenting a minority problem which would cause pressure on the erstwhile employer by the city's public officials. Though protest against this discrimination by Puerto Rican officials in 1953 succeeded in winning equal hiring privileges on paper for Puerto Rican farm labor, British Colonial labor is still being largely used in the tobacco fields.

The Puerto Rican government could, of course, do more than file a formal protest with a government department. It could demand full rights for American citizens from the island. But its odd status as the nation's first and only commonwealth has given rise to some curious contradictions. A New Yorker or an Alaskan is an American first and a New Yorker or Alaskan second. A Negro is a Negro but the right to his absolute equality is continuously asserted. The Spanish heritage in the Puerto Rican, however, remains strong, as does the difference between an Islander and an American. Puerto Rico has never asked to become a state. This difference between the "Puerto Rican American citizen" and the "American American citizen" remains prominent and conditions official policy on both the island and the mainland. And it may partly explain a curious agreement between the U. S. Employment Service and the Puerto Rican government under which no Puerto Rican contract labor will be transported to any state unless the state director of employment certifies that a shortage of labor exists. Puerto Rico's Bureau of Employment and Migration acknowledges its duty to be to regulate the flow of migration so that migrants "will not dislocate their American workers who are already in the areas to which they migrate."

The Puerto Rican government asserts that this certification agreement protects the worker against unscrupulous farmers and agents. It might. But the Puerto Rican still comes last. Priorities go to aliens who do not have to wait for certification and neither, of course, do American citizens on the mainland. Thus the Puerto Rican waits his turn after other American citizens, and often after Mexicans (legal and illegal) and West Indians.

The competition from foreign labor and the limitation of permanent opportunities for its rural labor on the mainland have prevented a much-needed outflow of Puerto Ricans to farm areas throughout the country. In the sense that many citizen farm workers are sooner or later absorbed into the urban labor pool, the assimilation of Puerto

Ricans into American urban communities has been markedly checked as well. The upward social mobility which has always been available to foreign immigration and should certainly be available to these American citizens has been limited. Decrowding of the island is being accomplished not through a permanent rural emigration followed by gradual absorption into the mainland economy, but by a concentrated urban migration aimed almost exclusively at New York City. About eighty-three per cent of the mainland Puerto Ricans are in New York City, where one in every 20 persons is of Puerto Rican origin, most of them recent arrivals.

The Urban Migration

To the majority of Puerto Rican migrants, New York and the United States are synonymous. New York is where friends and relatives live, where the home language is spoken, where the air lanes end. San Juan is dotted with tantalizing signs about New York, Puerto Rican shops call themselves "New York Department Store," New York is where the cargo boats come from, a kind of dream world one is carried to on the wings of an angel. And in the planes to the new utopia, a guitar will often call up the vision of the new land-a-coming, with its magic casements opening up on electric refrigerators, flush toilets, and bathtubs.

Yet the formidable skyscrapers that greet the migrant soon fade ominously into the dark and dirty tenement district that becomes his new horizon. Here the Puerto Rican faces his first disillusionment.

New York's Puerto Rican sections in 1953 probably ranked among the worst in the world. This was not because of the age or the exteriors of the buildings but because of the number of people crowded into small spaces—and because rents are so high that little is left for other needs. An American missionary described Harlem housing conditions as worse than what he had seen in China, the primary evil being the psychological collapse caused by overcrowding. It is not an overstatement.

In March, 1950, the writer saw a six-story, 25-foot wide tenement on East 100th Street into which 170 Puerto Ricans had been herded. Rents were about $16 a month per room; the apartments had to be shared and there were twelve people living in a single three-room apartment. Every hall window was broken. Splintered stair treads sank perilously with each step. Almost every toilet was out of order. Loosened plaster hung from the hall ceilings; great heaps of garbage rotted on the floor under the stairways; a dead rat lay on a landing. Gaping holes in the toilet walls served as passageways for the rats and one tenant said she kept two dogs and a cat to prevent them from attacking her children. There were 481 officially reported cases of rat bites in 1952, and since it is estimated that only 1 in 5 cases is reported, some 2500 human beings—mostly babies—are bitten by rats every year. Most of the cases are in the Harlem slums.

In another ancient tenement in the same street there were 15 people in a four-room apartment; in another, 18 people occupied a three-room unit. On 105th Street, between Park and Lexington Avenues, 30 people lived in a building sharing a single broken toilet without a seat. Here too there were rat holes in the walls.

In East 108th Street, two stores were rented for living quarters, a condition now common throughout the city. The Puerto Rican tenants said they paid $28 monthly per store. The plate glass was broken, the windows boarded up. There were no closets, no lights, no baths. Clothes were laid on trunks or on the floor. Children slept in dark and airless rooms, separated from their parents by makeshift curtains.

On East 100th Street the writer found 25 human beings living in a dark and airless coal cellar ten feet below the street level. The cellar was divided into two vaults—one under the sidewalk, the other in the rear. The vaults had stored coal, old furniture and garbage cans, but were now rented as dwellings. Each vault had been divided by a brick wall into coal bins, and in each bin lived a family. Under the city sidewalk were the two coal bins occupied by the other two families. Iron cellar doors at sidewalk level kept out both light and air. Here these people ate, slept, washed, and reproduced. No animal could live here long, yet here were 17 children, the youngest having been born here two weeks before. Almost all the 17 children had been sick during the preceding weeks. One had been hospitalized only a few days before. One of the mothers was confined to her bed under the sidewalk while trying to feed, clothe, and care for her children. Each of the four spaces, including the coal bins, brought rent—a total of more than $50 monthly.

In Brooklyn and elsewhere, flimsy one-family firetraps shelter 10

or more families, each family herded into a single room and doing
its own cooking on a coal or oil stove. Even minimum accommodations in these districts of the city cannot be procured without key-
money of several hundred dollars and the payment of ransom rental
thereafter.

Bad as the situation is for the white Puerto Rican, it is worse for
the colored. New York City has a famous skyline, and an equally
famous color-line. Both have occasional rainbows, like the city's
interracial housing program and anti-bias laws. But, though New York
City is one of the nation's most tolerant areas, it has never been able
to put an end to discrimination nor can it open its housing to its
minorities in the suburban sections beyond its boundaries. Black is
not white even in the metropolis.

When the darker Puerto Rican lands, he suddenly confronts the
city's color-line. The hue that made no difference in San Juan, Puerto
Rico, does make a difference at San Juan Hill, New York City.
Migration transforms the darker Puerto Rican into a Negro. He feels
strange even among his own lighter countrymen who soon learn that
difference in color means difference in status. The colored migrants
have fewer opportunities and less incentive to become part of the
mainland culture. Their only chance is to look and act conspicuously
different from the American Negro.[6]

But there is housing bias against all Puerto Ricans—light or dark.
The "spick," as the Spanish-speaking slum-dweller is scornfully called,
is rated a less desirable tenant than the Negro. The Puerto Rican
influx is following the pattern of infiltration, inundation, and out-
spread characteristic of Negro expansion, but is virtually confined to
the metropolis. It is also meeting similar resistance. Most landlords
with a long-term interest in their property can never be sure how many
people will eventually live in the apartment, whether the tenant's job
is permanent, or whether the migrant will have enough left from his
earnings to pay the rent. The family does not always come at one time,
and since relatives on the island are prone to share huts, the in-
migrating folk may follow the practice, thereby dividing the costs.

There are landlords, big and little, who make a specialty of buying
slum properties for Puerto Rican occupancy because they yield 30 to

[6] C. Wright Mills, Clarence Senior, and Rose Kohn Goldsen, *The Puerto
Rican Journey*. New York, Harper & Brothers, 1950, p. 87.

100 per cent a year on investment. Some of the landlords are operators attracted by the high yields; others are former profiteering tenants who have branched out into landlordism; still others are small-time lessees seeking to recover their investment in one or two years by exacting illicit bonuses and charging all the traffic will bear. The properties bring high returns because repairs are nonexistent; because the legitimate real estate investor and mortgage-lender generally shun this type of investment despite its attractive yield; because the owners (some of them shoestring operators or lessees from the minority groups themselves) are willing to run the risks of operating properties plastered with violations, and have mastered the technique of evading rent control or dodging or appeasing an examining inspector. Strict enforcement by city officials of violations is difficult since there are no alternative accommodations when the houses are ordered vacated. Prosecution in the courts has become a tedious and often impossible task.

A grand jury investigating the death of seven Puerto Ricans herded into an illegally occupied Brooklyn tinderbox in 1952 reported:

> Shocked as we were by the death of seven persons, we were more appalled as the evidence adduced before us disclosed that the greatest city in the world is surely but not slowly being permitted to deteriorate and decay. . . . Occupancy of dark, damp and filthy cellars that defy description, and families of six, seven and more, cooking and eating and sleeping in one room lacking proper toilet facilities, are spreading the slum blight.

Puerto Rican officials in New York City have tried to minimize the situation by urging that previous immigrants had to experience similar hardships. But housing conditions for the Puerto Rican migrants are far worse than they were for the nineteenth-century immigrant. The American frontier was open until 1890 and land was available to those who could make no adjustment in the cities. Building material was virtually free. In New York City, new though substandard tenements were built in the last century to provide housing at rents the immigrants could afford.

Nor are conditions like those between 1900 and 1930. Though housing was bad then, it was hardly comparable to what the Puerto Ricans must accept today. Not only is the Islander forced into some of the slums built 60 years ago, but he is paying up to $60 monthly per room. The unbelievable overcrowding is undermining family life and precipitating social, economic, and psychological disruption, as evidenced by the large number of Spanish names in the Family Court and in Youth Term.

Nor does there seem to be a ready answer to the housing problem facing the in-migrants. Limiting the number of persons per room and strict enforcement of violations would mean more evictions. Slum clearance is already forcing thousands from homes and intensifying overcrowding. Curbing conversions into smaller units would only hold down the housing supply.

New York's combined city, state, and federal postwar housing program, designed mainly to replace slums and producing some 6500 dwelling units a year, has become meaningless against the influx of new candidates for its slums. It has added little to the over-all housing supply and even if doubled would mean little if the migration continued at the current rate.

Despite the depressing housing picture there are some brighter aspects. The in-migration has been a blessing to employers and made the city a rich source of cheap labor. Less than 8 per cent on relief in 1953 were Puerto Ricans. About 20,000, mostly women, were absorbed into the garment industry and about 16,000 men in hotels and restaurants, while tens of thousands of others found light factory work or employment in building and domestic service. They have earned the respect of employers and are considered dependable workers. They are, however, the lowest paid workers, often exploited because few of them know about the 75¢ minimum wage.

Many earlier migrants have found decent housing, made adjustments, and have been absorbed into the metropolis' social community. While conditions are not uniform, many of the earlier arrivals and some of the later ones have succeeded in breaking through to the Central Park West section, Chelsea, the Bronx, and Brooklyn. The overcrowding of some of these once fashionable areas, the inundation of the schools by Puerto Rican children, and the out-migration of older residents, however, have spread resentment. The possibility of depression adds to the danger of racial tension. "We will have a real powder-keg," admits a Puerto Rican official. Housing and concentration in a single city still pose the most serious problems.

Although four of every five settlers remain in New York City, a number of small clusters do exist in Bridgeport, Newark, Passaic,

Trenton, Camden, Philadelphia, Pittsburgh, Buffalo, Youngstown, Cleveland, Lorain, Gary, Chicago, Aurora, Joliet, Savannah, and Milwaukee. These, if they last, will draw more migrants from their present concentration. But there is no sign that this is occurring to any appreciable extent.

Impartial appraisals of the implications and aspects of the immigration are wanting. No one is prepared to face the problem, much less discuss it openly. City officials have been swayed by the political stakes. Congressmen have been beset by farm groups who prefer illegal Mexicans to citizen labor. The Puerto Rican Government fears unfavorable public reaction. Even civic-minded individuals and the press are chary of exposing themselves to accusations of bias. The consequence is the ignoring of the factors responsible for the problem and of the remedies which might help to alleviate it.

The Problem of Population

Puerto Rico's main problem is that a fecund people is being confined to a barren island. In 1950, population density was 645 persons to the square mile—at a similar density the United States would have a population of 1900 million. The average married rural woman has about 7 children during her child-bearing period, and 29 per cent of the rural women average 10 or more. This falls sharply among the urban population where about 29 per cent give birth to 1, 2, or 3 children. The rapidly declining mortality rate coupled with the rising birth rate makes Puerto Rico one of the fastest growing populations in the world.

Competition for work is keen, wages low. The median income of all money-earners 14 years and over in 1949 was $378—it was $617 in the urban and only $275 in the rural areas. About half the total population 14 years and over earned no income at all. Low incomes are reflected in poor living conditions. About 40 per cent of the population sleep in rooms with 4 or more persons, many of the houses are ramshackle and cannot withstand the island's hurricanes, most of the families have no ovens, many drink water from ditches.

Yet though the island is crowded and conditions bad, its climate is warm; children are in a land where 70 per cent of the people live in open country or little villages; social relations are intimate, and though the Negro population is 25 per cent, there is so much intermarriage that color distinctions are of no importance except among the white elite; rents are a tenth of what they are in New York, and though the slum of Puerto Rico may drive social life into the street, it is apt to be the Puerto Rican plaza rather than the cold and impersonal slum street of the metropolis.

The federally aided public housing program has helped, too. Puerto Rico's three housing authorities built more than 10,000 low-rent dwellings by 1953 and moved several thousand salvageable houses from squatter villages to new areas. But when the writer asked the director of the Housing Authority in San Juan if he thought public housing would ever solve the island's housing problem, he pointed to the birth chart and shrugged his shoulders.

Tax exemption to firms establishing factories on the island has improved work opportunities.[7] Since 1940, thanks largely to the efforts of President Luis Munoz-Marin, net income has risen from $228,000,000 to $891,000,000, lifting per capita net income from $122 to $399, and wages per employed worker from $229 to $917. Public school enrollment has gone up from 68.5 per cent to 78 per cent; unemployment fell from 122,000 to 76,000. A new land law has distributed acreage to 28,000 farm families and another 60,000 are expected to be settled in six years. Life expectancy went from 46 to 61 years, and the death rate fell from 18.9 per thousand to 9.3, all of which helped double the population and increase the pressure for migration.

Despite all these aids and efforts, the population pressure continues and demands a solution. One proposal is to give the Islanders the independence they do not want. This would cut off migration and imperil the overcrowded island and its people so severely that eventual aid would be inevitable. We cannot escape our obligation by this route, and the island's people have consistently rejected it when it was proposed.

A second proposal is education in contraception. This is difficult, partly because of Catholic opposition, partly because of the Islanders' indifference, and partly because of their stubborn insistence upon hav-

[7] The gainfully employed increased 64 per cent in the 38 years 1910–1947; 51 per cent of the increase was accomplished in the last 7 years. Per capita income doubled in the war years, but was still less than $260. Mills, et. al., op. cit., p. 18.

ing babies. Which reason counts most has never been determined, though poverty and babies seem to have gone together long before Malthus exhorted the poor to continence. Poverty will continue to bring babies to the poor, if only because the parents hope that sons will keep them from starving in their old age. When social security is lacking, production of filial reinforcements seems the only rational substitute.

Thus, one way to stem the increase in Puerto Rican babies is to raise the standard of living, educate the Puerto Ricans in all things, including contraception, and preserve them against the hazards of insecurity.

Yet statistics show that the mainland needs all the babies the Puerto Ricans can produce. It is estimated that with an out-migration of 35,000–50,000 annually, there is a fair chance that the population of the island would be stabilized in the next generation. And it can be safely ventured that 35,000–50,000 Puerto Rican migrants is only a fraction of what American industry can absorb.

The solution to the Puerto Rican problem lies not in limiting their numbers but in our willingness to treat these people as fellow citizens and help to settle them throughout the country in communities where they are desperately needed.

The period of labor shortage in the 1950's proved the most opportune for economic assimilation in the nation's history. Poor white families, millions of Negroes, and others have been absorbed into the American labor pool and into American communities. Not without protest, resistance, and even violence. But no migration of a new people is easy, and unless some way is found for making the country's opportunities available to the Islander instead of hemming him into New York and Puerto Rico, no solution will ever be in sight. There has been no substantial net movement out of the city after 1950, and since April, 1950, nearly 83 per cent of the total on the mainland had settled here. A migration limited mainly by space and the ability of the human body and spirit to endure overcrowding and hardship can never be a healthy one.

The concentration in New York City moreover threatens to construct an unfounded stereotype of the Puerto Rican worker which, if it reaches out to other cities, will curtail opportunities for wider settlement and progress. In Youngstown, Ohio, for example, opposition was aroused in 1952 against a thousand Puerto Ricans who had come to take jobs. Quoting from an unfortunate column in the New York *Daily Mirror,* one Youngstown city official argued that the Puerto Rican was unable to assimilate, that he was a criminal and diseased. "They soon become marijuana addicts, throng into cheap and crowded dives which cater to their trade, and many become violent criminals with gun and knife. Many of them are dope peddlers. The crime rate is stupendous and it is increasing and spreading."[8] Puerto Rican officials, a progressive Youngstown mayor, a courageous newspaper, and enlightened churchmen and laymen challenged the indictment and overcame the opposition.

Experiences like these are inevitable. Every migration to America has had its crusader for "Americans" and against outsiders. But if faced intelligently, opposition can be overcome.

In face of such problems the Puerto Rican government has chosen a policy of caution. It not only carefully supervises and limits farm contract labor to the precise number certified by state authorities, but it also functions as the principal employment agent and adviser for its industrial migrants already here. It fears the strictures, oppressions, and rioting against minorities in Chicago and other cities. It hesitates to encourage its citizens to go to the South because of discrimination there.

In its efforts to protect the Puerto Ricans and avoid any local protests, the Puerto Rican government's general policy has been to send Islanders from its employment offices in the United States only when, as, and if the U. S. Employment Service or an employer requests workers. This is in sharp contrast to the Negro practice of moving directly into the city where the jobs are, and competing for them openly.

Theoretically, of course, the Puerto Rican is as free as the Negro to move where he pleases. But in practice, foreign-speaking or insecure migrants head toward areas where others of their group already live. And unless other communities are opened up faster than they have been and more settlements are established, New York City and Puerto Rico will continue to be the principal areas of opportunity for the Islander and that opportunity will continue limited. The decline in migration to the mainland indicated for 1954 can neither

[8] Youngstown *Vindicator,* March 17, 1952.

be permanent nor ease the surging population pressures on the Island.

However well-intentioned may be the Commonwealth's policy of cautiously settling migrants outside New York City, it means that the Puerto Rican labor supply is being unfairly subordinated while the good jobs are pre-empted by others, including aliens. The blame for this situation must of course be shared by our own federal government, notably the U.S. Employment Service.

With foreign immigration to this country curtailed, with only 2.25 million people on the island, and with an urgent need for the semi-skilled, farm, and other labor that Puerto Rico offers, the problem here is not one of Puerto Rican labor surplus or of overpopulation or of discouraging migration to the mainland, but of evolving a constructive policy to make America's opportunities more available to citizens whose labor we desperately need.

VII

THE QUEST FOR SHELTER AND THE
COMPULSORY GHETTO

THE housing problem faced by the new crop of migrants has been troubling us ever since the time of the first American settlers. But there are marked differences between the problem then and the problem today.

The nineteenth-century immigrants, like the current crop, were insecure in their new environments and preferred to live with people of their own country, tongue, tradition, or faith. Poor when they arrived, working at small wages, able to afford only the cheapest kind of shelter, they lived in run-down housing or new dwellings of low standard built especially for them. Some of the houses were described as "unfit for beasts," as indeed they were. Good citizens were aroused as far back as 1835 when Gerret Forbes, City Inspector in New York City, reported on the unprecedented number of deaths due to over-crowding and filthy living quarters.[1] Twenty years later the Association for Improving the Condition of the Poor found that "hundreds upon hundreds of paupers pour into the hospitals stricken by disease contracted in those hotbeds of pestilence—the tenements."[2]

But the problem for the nineteenth-century immigrants was not insurmountable. Building costs were low enough for private builders to erect new buildings in the port cities. They had no running water, toilets were in the yards, and the inside rooms were windowless. Yet, though low in standard and crowded, they were new and could be built almost as fast as the prospective tenants disembarked. As social

[1] James Ford, Katherine Morrow and G. N. Thompson, *Slums and Housing*, 2 vols., Cambridge, Harvard University Press, 1936, pp. 95-96.

[2] See author's brief on behalf of the Authority in *New York City Housing Authority v. Muller*, 270 N.Y. 333.

protest matured, running water was supplied on each floor, toilet and ablutionary facilities were improved, and the buildings were made safer.

In addition to the cities there was another frontier. It was not an easy frontier but immigrants could push out and select land within fifty miles of a railroad and build from materials gathered nearby. Thus the Russians in the Dakotas put up good two-room adobe houses with their own hands, laid the board floors, and protected themselves from the elements until more permanent shelter could be built.

Dr. Alvin Johnson, the educator, whose Danish father settled in Nebraska, told the writer:

> The house I was born in and spent my first years in comfort cost my father twenty-five dollars for windows and outside door. There were four rooms, in two stories. The walls were logs, the floors were split logs hewn smooth; the roof was a stack of hay. Later my father blew in fifty dollars for a shingled roof. Of course he did all the work himself.
>
> A bachelor neighbor had a house twenty feet long and twelve feet wide, built of prairie sod, cut in foot squares and laid like brick. Its roof consisted of stout poles laid close together with sods built up to a gable structure, where after a year the sunflowers ran riot. He blew in ten dollars for two windows.[3]

The important difference between frontier houses and town dwellings was that in the case of the former a man owned the land and the house he built. Occupancy did not depend on the ability to buy land and multiple materials, the constancy of a job, or the unremitting payment of one fourth to one third of one's earnings. Though self-help housing is still being built in the underdeveloped areas of the world, and occasionally in America, we are now mainly a nation of machines and specialists. The American worker is either completely unskilled or he is trained in a single skill and no longer knows the difference between a level and a bevel. Though industrialization rationalized production in other fields and brought many items within reach of the rank and file, home building compared with other industries is still largely a handicraft operation by twelve to fifteen specialist trades. Building is done directly on the site and at costs far above the average worker's means. Specialization brought

[3] Letter of April 27, 1951.

efficiency to manufacture but housing specialization only split the building unit into hundreds of separate segments whose myriad sub-segments must be put together in some five hundred operations.

Despite a remarkable increase in income, in 1951 25 per cent of all families still had incomes under $2000 annually, more than 40 per cent had incomes under $3000. Almost 31 per cent of families of two or more persons received less than $3000. Almost no new housing was provided for these even under the federally aided FHA mortgage insurance program. Many others buy new housing only by scrimping on food, clothing, medical care, and recreation. A large percentage cannot pay for a decent house no matter how drastically they cut down on other expenditures, while many others pay for their shelter only by overcrowding or sharing dwellings with other families.

The year 1950 saw the biggest home-building boom in America's history—1.4 million new dwellings.[4] It also saw considerable improvement of old structures. Yet while there was a 42 per cent gain between 1940 and 1950 in the number of occupied nonfarm dwellings with an interior flush toilet, almost 6 million were still without one—the same in 1950 as in 1940. According to the 1950 Census, 10 million nonfarm dwelling units were either dilapidated or lacked running water. More than 1.7 million families were without separate housing facilities in 1950 and more than 2.5 million families were living "seriously overcrowded," i.e., with more than one and a half persons per room.

The consequences of slum life have been told often.[5] But the housing problem is more than the slum and the crime, disease, and social distortions which are its by-products. It has become a complex of problems which affect the whole national economy and its well-being. Since 1900, public intervention has shifted from one

[4] *Housing Statistics*. Washington, D. C., Housing and Home Finance Agency, January, 1953, p. 1.

[5] Charles Abrams and John P. Dean, "Housing and the Family," in Ruth Nanda Anshen (ed.), *The Family: Its Function and Destiny*. New York, Harper & Brothers, 1949, Chap. xv; E. R. Mowrer, *Disorganization: Personal and Social*. Philadelphia, J. B. Lippincott Company, 1942; R. E. L. Faris and H. W. Dunham, *Mental Disorders in Urban Areas*. Chicago, University of Chicago Press, 1939; Ford, Morrow, and Thompson, *op. cit.;* Jay Rumney and Sara Shuman, *The Cost of Slums in Newark*. Newark, N. J., 1946 (pamphlet).

policy to another—increasing the standards of privately built immigrant housing, improving building codes, clearing slums, subsidizing lower-income families, preserving home ownership, insuring mortgage lenders, and reducing down payments for homes. Federal intervention since 1933 has been prompted by motivations running the gamut from economic pump-priming to social improvement to defense needs, to war requirements, to postwar rehousing of war veterans, and in 1954 to economic pump-priming again.

But the race and color problem which emerged as an important factor ever since the 1920's has been all but neglected. It was now mainly the minorities who were being increasingly identified with slum life. They were suffering most from lack of shelter, overcrowding, burdensome rents, absentee landlords, discrimination and oppression, lack of new housing, despair, lack of financing, unsettlement or eviction, and the general social consequences of housing failure.

Housing conditions became worst for the three minority groups moving up to take jobs in the expanding economy. They were not only the lowest paid workers but they shared in common the effects of discrimination.

The darkest skinned Mexican faces the same exclusions and discriminations as the Negro.[6] So too, those Puerto Ricans rated black by mainland standards cannot compete with whites for shelter or find it at normal rents.

Thus, the three important groups of migrants—American Negro, Puerto Rican, and Mexican, all with a higher visibility than the Europeans—cannot conceal their identity from a home developer or their would-be neighbors. There are other complications. Not only are costs and rentals higher and financing more costly (if available at all) but the incomes of nonwhites are less than one half the incomes of whites. The median income of white families in 1950 was $4135; for nonwhites it was only $1569.[7] These figures of course

[6] If the child is not obviously a blend of Negro or Indian blood, he may be allowed to attend a white school. In Texas, Mexican-American children are segregated particularly in the lower grades, producing a three-way school system—for Negroes, whites, and Mexican-Americans.

[7] U.S. Bureau of Census, *Income of Families and Persons in the U.S.: 1950,* P 60, no. 9, March 25, 1952.

conceal the fact that migrants to farms earn so little they can spend nothing for shelter.

The general characteristics of nonwhite housing are:

1. Most houses are in older sections where signs of marked neighborhood deterioration have long been evident.

2. In 1950, more than 27 per cent of the housing was dilapidated, about five times the proportion of those of white families. The proportion of substandard housing was close to six times as high as for whites.[8]

3. Buildings lack the basic amenities of other dwellings. Outdoor privies are the only toilets for 47.8 per cent of all nonwhite homes. Nearly 42 per cent of nonwhite urban homes lacked a private flush toilet as contrasted with 10 per cent for whites.[9]

4. Repairs to the buildings are either not made by the owners or not worth making. Rotten floors, broken windows, cracked walls, water dripping from the ceilings, plumbing that serves as a promenade for rats, are common in New York, Chicago, and other cities, large and small.

5. Lending institutions have rated the areas as out of bounds for mortgage investment. They refuse funds even when offered FHA insurance.

6. Little or no investment in new building is ventured in nonwhite sections because of financing problems, prejudice, restrictions, and other causes. Public housing is the exception, but it meets only a small fraction of the need. Often it destroys as much housing as it builds.

7. Tax arrears are higher in these sections than in others. Owners are more interested in "milkability," in liquidation of their investments in a brief period out of rents, instead of being satisfied with a moderate return on a long-term investment.

8. Nonwhites receive less housing value for their housing dollar than do whites.[10]

9. Garbage collections, building inspections, street maintenance,

[8] *The Housing Situation—1950*. Washington, Housing and Home Finance Agency, February, 1951.

[9] *Ibid.*, p. 12.

[10] Corienne Robinson, "Relationship between Condition of Dwelling and Rentals by Race," *The Journal of Land and Public Utility Economics,* August, 1946, pp. 296–302; Sara Shuman, "Differential Rents for Whites and Negro Families," *ibid.*, pp. 169, 174.

and other city services are less satisfactory than in other areas. The abnormal number of rat bites in Harlem, for example, may be ascribed not only to lack of proper upkeep but to the ready supply of uncollected garbage in the streets. Southern cities and some in the North omit street paving and sidewalks in Negro sections. In hilly sections the residents try to fill gullies in the streets with broken masonry, worn-out linoleum, old tires, and other trash.

10. Building values are lower in relation to rents than in other areas. This is due to financing difficulties and the low esteem in which such ownership is regarded.

11. The proportion of occupants' incomes allocable for rent is higher in nonwhite areas, while payment of bonuses as a condition for renting is frequent.

12. Overcrowding of land and within buildings is greater. Although 5 per cent of white families were extremely overcrowded in 1950, the figure for nonwhites was 18 per cent.[11] (In Chicago Negroes lived 90,000 to the square mile, while whites in neighboring apartments were only 20,000 to the square mile.) While the proportion of overcrowding decreased for whites between 1940 and 1950, it increased by more than 11 per cent for nonwhites.

13. Schools, hospitals, and recreation facilities are inferior.[12]

14. Many of the houses were not designed originally for boarding or multiple occupancy; in some cases commercial buildings were subdivided into dormitories. In Chicago large houses are being broken up into dozens of small apartments. In New York City one-family houses are being rented to ten or more families.

Conditions such as these translate themselves into statistics on disease, mortality, and crime. The infant mortality rate, which is the most sensitive index to urban social conditions, is two and a half times higher among families with two or more persons per room than among families with one person or less per room.[13] In New York City, in the three years 1945-1947, the annual average non-white infant mortality rate was 87 per cent higher than the rate for

[11] "Non White Housing," House+Home, April, 1953, p. 44.
[12] Gunnar Myrdal, An American Dilemma. New York, Harper & Brothers, 1944, chap. 15.
[13] Robert M. Woodbury, Causal Factors in Infant Mortality. U.S. Children's Bureau, Publication No. 142. Washington, Government Printing Office, 1925, p. 129.

whites. In 1940, the Negro infant mortality rate in cities with populations over 100,000 was 62 per cent higher than the white rate. In 1946 it was 63 per cent higher.[14] In a survey in New York City, it was calculated:

> If the non-white mortality rates in neighborhoods with less than 5 per cent of Negro population had prevailed among all Negroes, 1,400 fewer Negro deaths would have occurred. If the white mortality rates in neighborhoods with less than 5 per cent Negro population had prevailed throughout the city, 2,600 fewer deaths would have occurred.[15]

The Woodbury study, cited earlier, showed an infant mortality rate of 52 per 1000 live births for families with less than one person per room, 94.9 for one to two persons, and 135.7 for two persons or more.

Merger of Slum and Ghetto

Yet, bad as slums are, the slum and ghetto long remained two separate patterns. Though often merged into a single neighborhood, the ghetto was not always a slum nor the slum always a ghetto. People of low income who could afford nothing better lived in slums. People lived in ghettos when they were unfamiliar with the country's customs or language, felt socially insecure, or preferred living with their own people.

The slum-ghetto was created when those of a single ethnic minority group lived not only in a ghetto but also in bad housing. Characteristically the residents were socially as well as economically insecure.

Thus, slum, ghetto, and slum-ghetto all evolved within the rough limits of choice, not compulsion. With economic security the slum-dweller moved out of the slum into better or more dignified surroundings. He might still choose to live with his own group in a

---

[14] National Office of Vital Statistics, "Infant Mortality by Race and by Urban and Rural Areas: United States, Each Division and State, 1946," *Vital Statistics: Special Reports*, vol. 29, no. 7, F.S.A., USPSHS, November 22, 1948; M. Gover, "Negro Mortality. II The Birth Rate and Infant and Maternal Mortality," *Public Health Reports*, vol. 61 (October, 1948), p. 1529, cited in Alfred Yankauer, Jr., "The Relationship of Fetal and Infant Mortality to Residential Segregation," *American Sociological Review*, vol. XV, no. 5, Oct, 1950, p. 644.

[15] Yankauer, *op. cit.*, p. 646.

more attractive ghetto or in a better house in the same ghetto. Or, as he prospered, he might make the break and move to a more diversified neighborhood. Here he, or at least his children, could begin the ascent toward social or cultural parity.

In slum, ghetto, and slum-ghetto of a few decades ago, ability to pay was the determining factor in the dwelling market. There were no lasting compulsions or legal restraints on social mobility. If the physical frontier was closed, the social frontier was still open. Price, not status or race, usually delineated the chosen neighborhood.

Internal migrations have always been the means for improving one's status or opportunities and for effecting a required personal or social readjustment. The underprivileged, the victims of droughts or dust storms, of economic and social misfortune have had open to them the right to move. From 25 to 30 million persons move annually and about a third of these move across county lines.[16]

With the new nonwhite in-migrations, however, an element of compulsion began to characterize the slum-ghetto. The element of choice narrowed and five kinds of compulsions now kept minorities in their place—physical, structural, social, economic, and legal.

Physical compulsion implied the use of force—bombs, arson, threats, or mobs.

Structural controls meant walls, fences, dead-end streets, closed cities.

Social controls included the snub at the grocery, refusal to accept the family in the community or club, and segregation in the schools and public facilities.

Economic compulsions represented the use of pressures by private owners to keep the minority in its place—racial covenants, refusal to make mortgage loans, and "codes of ethics" among realtors to keep the minority out.

Legalized compulsions involved the use of the powers of government to control movements of minorities—condemnation powers, pressures by officials of the FHA, removal of tenants through urban redevelopment, slum clearance, and the use of various administrative devices summarized later.

[16] E. E. Ashley, "Mobility and Migration as Factors in Housing Demand," *Housing Research.* Washington, Housing and Home Finance Agency, October, 1953.

The compulsory slum-ghetto combined the worst features of slum life and ghetto life and added to it either enforced immobility through confinement to a designated area, or enforced mobility. Enforced immobility cut off escape from the slum, restricting the residents and often their children to a section rampant with social problems. The schools were segregated. Obvious race or color identification meant discrimination in the street, playground, church, and club. It perpetuated the slum and slum-living, emphasizing the difference between "ins" and "outs," and intensifying tensions between neighboring groups, fanning antiracial prejudices all along the line and frustrating the healthy process of social fusion and rapport.

Within the compulsory slum-ghetto are now found: (1) higher income families who could pay for good housing offered by private enterprise outside the slum-ghetto but who are barred from it by their race or color; (2) families in the middle-income group who could afford cheaper housing but are also excluded from the outside market; (3) families in the lowest-income group who cannot afford standard private dwellings but are kept from moving to other slums outside the ghetto.

The chief characteristics of slum life are high rents in proportion to income and the quality of the facilities offered; structural deterioration; absence of minimum facilities; and overcrowding. The population in the area continues to grow. In-migration of minority members from other parts of the country swells the population further. But the available space does not swell. In fact, the more the population grows the greater is the resistance by those in the surrounding areas. Sometimes there is a break-through to adjacent streets or areas, but often the minority continues to stew in the boiling slum-pot. The dweller is barred from purchasing peripheral land on which to build a new house because suburban owners fear a beachhead by the ghetto-dweller will be followed by a new ghetto settlement. If those who control the community want an expanded ghetto to be limited, moved, or eliminated, powers are now ample to do any of those things.

Enforced Mobility

Even worse than enforced immobility is enforced mobility. Compulsory confinement to a section, however congested, at least provides a roof and allows a man to keep his job and friends intact.

Enforced mobility, however, shakes the family from home, friends, and environment, often forcing the breadwinner to give up his job as well. It does not permit permanent settlement or the building of a community where the processes of economic and social improvement might develop.

Enforced mobility penalizes Mexicans, Negroes, and other unsettled minorities who are no longer allowed to lay roots in a given community but are forced to rove from place to place. They perform their jobs in farm and field and move on. Their mobility is often accelerated by local police, acting under local laws or no laws at all. These people are feared as a charge on the local budget or a drain on the community chest. Although itinerancy and nomadism may still be tolerated, vagrancy has lately become a particular form of iniquity. If poverty has not yet been officially made a crime, lacking "visible means of support"—as vagrancy is defined—is. Local police and local judges have had no difficulty arresting and holding those who, though American citizens, linger on in cities when they are not wanted.

The newest form of forced mobility affects even settled minority citizens. Tens of thousands of slum-dwellers are being dislodged through slum clearance, urban redevelopment, and public works operations. While many of these programs are undertaken in good faith, others are deliberately designed to oust "undesirable" settlers who had obtained a foothold. Various other administrative devices are now available to unscrupulous officials. It is no coincidence that the public's bulldozers are often aimed against shacks on central tracts that have long been coveted by private developers. Compulsory mobility is a new phenomenon in the slum-ghetto. It is intended to blast the grim effort of an unwanted group to subsist on the fringe of society.

Inside the city is the slum, abutting the city the suburb. Outside both is the mobile ghetto of makeshifts, put together to shelter the rover from the elements. The occupants of city slum and peripheral makeshifts are now both subject to displacement. The most important aspect of social mobility—the right to live in any community one chooses—now depends on being permitted to sink roots until a job can be found. But the never-ending housing famine makes this difficult for the minorities in the urban slum, and for those on the city's outskirts virtually impossible. Inside the city, the slum-dweller rests uneasily as he wonders when the descent of public power will turn him into a transient searching for the lost frontier. Outside the city, the seasonal worker is not even hopeful of ever finding it.

VIII

INVASION AND COUNTERATTACK

THE movement of southern Negroes to the cities provided the first major test since the Oriental influx of how the challenge to American neighborhoods would be met. From 1920, when the European immigration trailed off, to 1930, which signaled the end of the boom years, 615,000 Negroes left the South. Georgia, South Carolina, and Mississippi lost the bulk. They headed mainly east, concentrating in the big cities. Others moved to the Middle West, notably Chicago and St. Louis. Once the trek had started there was no substantial letup, even during the depression years. Chicago alone received no less than 43,000 between 1920 and 1930.[1]

The Negro at first headed toward already established Negro areas. He had less difficulty doing this in cities which were already punctuated with Negro districts. But soon expansion into new sections became inevitable and once-stabilized white belts began to feel the pressure as the Negro spread outward from his bulging ghetto. Sometimes he moved into all-white slums, sometimes into more costly neighborhoods. He was able to do this by doubling up and sharing the cost, because of the rise of a small professional class able to pay for better housing, because of the tendency of unionization to establish equal pay, or because of the presence of more than one breadwinner in the family.

The whites met the problem in a number of ways:

Some elected to stay put. This occurred where the Negro migration was small and no major challenge felt.

[1] R. A. Schermerhorn, *These Our People*. Boston, D. C. Heath and Company, 1949, p. 134. From 1930 to 1940, the Negro population of the Southeast and Southwest dropped from 6,395,000 to 6,289,000, while urban Negro population jumped from 2,966,000 to 3,616,000, (p. 120).

Some elected to escape the whole business by moving to new territory. The suburb was the city's sub-frontier and wider rings of new land were within time distance, thanks to the automobile and fast commuters' trains. The exodus made some of the vacated space available to the Negro.

The reaction of others, however, was to stay and fight it out with legal devices. The introduction of zoning made it possible to ban Negroes by the simple addition of a new prohibition of occupancy by black human beings. When racial zoning was struck down by the courts and the racial covenant succeeded it, application of the covenant proved more difficult in the older neighborhoods. The opposition then often resorted to the third means—force, one of the oldest devices for keeping minorities in their place and one of the most effective.

In the South, where intimidation had been the established procedure to protect the social structure, there was no absence of leaders to organize the required resistance to unauthorized Negro movements. As long as the necessary subordination patterns remained undisturbed, however, southerners took no action. The Negroes in turn were not disposed to move where they were not wanted. But sometimes the Negro's necessity overcame his caution, and the white man's temper ran ahead of his senses. The records of the period show the results.

In 1929, shots were fired into a Negro house in Memphis, and the house burned down.[2] A riot in Phillips County, Arkansas, resulted in the killing of 25 to 50 persons in 1919. There was also a riot in East St. Louis, Illinois, during World War I which took the lives of 39 Negroes and 8 whites. In Houston, in 1917, 17 whites were killed, 13 Negroes hanged, 41 imprisoned for life.[3] There were bombings or riots in Louisville, Kansas City, and Baltimore.

Violence had been less common in the North which had once espoused the Negro's cause and even welcomed him. Nevertheless, in 1924, Negroes were forced to give up their homes in Garfield Heights, Ohio, because "they had no right to buy such a nice place."[4]

[2] *The Negro Yearbook* (Monroe W. Work, ed.). Tuskegee, Alabama, Negro Yearbook Publishing Co., 1931.

[3] Gunnar Myrdal, *An American Dilemma*. New York, Harper & Brothers, 1944, p. 567.

[4] *The Crisis*, vol. 29, no. 1, November, 1924, p. 20.

In 1931, after a cross-burning in Pittsburgh, organized threats were made to withdraw financial support from the Y.M.C.A. and the Community Chest if these organizations did not force two Negro doctors and a Y.M.C.A. secretary to move from their recently bought homes. Thereafter, a mob of 3000 whites attacked a new home built by a Negro post office employee.[5]

There were explosions in westward areas, too. A Negro's house was torn down in Denver in 1926.[6] In fact there were 26 riots in American cities in 1919 alone, the most notorious of which was a Chicago outburst which took the lives of 15 whites and 23 Negroes, besides injuring more than 500 persons. This outbreak had been preceded by a concerted campaign marked by organized meetings, circulars, and antiracial propaganda led by a property owners' organization which was said to have been responsible for the bombing of 58 Negro homes in a period of less than four years.[7]

Despite the violence, however, the Negro established his foothold in the cities. By 1940 there were 4,000,000 Negroes in the North, and it was only a prelude to a greater march in the years to follow. Housing, however, remained the big problem. In Chicago, where there were now 240,000 Negroes, a seven-room flat on East 56th Street, which thirty years before had been rented to middle-class whites at $27.50 a month, had been broken up into four one- and two-room apartments occupied by three to seven persons each. A single bathroom served the seven families. The Black Belt now stretched southward from the central business section for seven and a half miles. Eighty per cent of the city's property was said to be covered by restrictive covenants, and property owners' associations were actively organizing opposition against Negroes. Population density was 70,000 to the square mile, compared to 34,000 for whites.

In Cleveland, Negroes in 1940 were 9.6 per cent of the population; Columbus 11.7, Dallas 17.1, Detroit 9.2, Gary 18.3, Houston 22.4, Indianapolis, 13.2, Los Angeles 4.2, New York 6.1, Philadelphia 13, Youngstown 8.7.

The early war boom years 1940-1942 saw no great movement of

[5] *Negro Housing,* President's Conference on Home Building and Home Ownership, vol. VI. Washington, 1932, pp. 46–47.

[6] *Ibid.*

[7] *The Negro in Chicago.* The Chicago Commission on Race Relations. Chicago, University of Chicago Press, 1922, p. 122.

Negroes but when the bars to Negro employment were relaxed they migrated to the war centers in droves. Some 750,000 Negroes moved across state lines into new industrial centers. The Detroit area alone gained 80,000. A larger group moved to the West Coast cities, and between 1940 and 1944, Los Angeles, Portland, Vancouver, Seattle, San Diego, and the San Francisco area acquired 121,000, a gain of 113 per cent. The Los Angeles metropolitan area gained 59,000. Simultaneously, a northward move saw 80,000 going to Chicago alone.

As the labor shortage sharpened, an inflow of Mexicans began across the Rio Grande. The number of Mexicans recruited for agricultural work leaped to 120,000 in 1946. Later they came faster. The Puerto Rican migration was stepped up simultaneously. More Islanders were seen in the New York subways and the streets of Harlem, Brooklyn, and the Bronx.

Racial tensions accompanied the migrations: the usual rumors of "rape" or the general feeling that the servile Negro servant was now becoming insolent. There were stories of impending attacks by Negroes in mass—"We've got to kill them before they kill us." There were also some fiery crosses burned as far north as Newark, New Jersey. In Missouri a group of 200 farmers in an all-white community seized some Negro tenants on a farm, forced them into trucks, and drove them out. The superintendent of the high school was forced to flee the building when 100 senior students threatened him because his father was the first landowner to bring Negroes into the community. A series of anti-Negro demonstrations in southeastern Missouri communities followed. When enforcement officers were threatened for protecting the employees, the FBI stepped in to investigate.[8] The most serious incidents during the war were in Detroit, where rioting erupted in 1942 and 1943. On the whole, however, racial tensions during the migrations were held in check by the patriotic fervor of the war period and its emergent considerations. The enemy's emphasis on race purity and its extermination of "impure" races sublimated confused emotions at home. Some Negro-white neighborhoods exhibited heroic cooperation and boasted a

[8] The New York *Times,* January 15, 1944; New York *Herald Tribune,* January 16 and 18, 1944; New York *World Telegram,* January 17, 1944.

patriotic tolerance. The rumors of race riots, though plentiful, never grew to serious proportions.[9]

Toward the end of hostilities and the relaxation of war controls, the tensions blew into the open. The first serious disturbances in the South followed the rise of the Columbians, whose aim was to prevent Negroes from moving into homes formerly occupied by whites. Donning uniforms with special insignia and openly advocating dictatorship, the Columbians proposed to solve the Negro problem by deporting every Negro. A race riot in Columbia, Tennessee, in February, 1946, culminated in the shooting of four officers and two white civilians and the maiming of dozens of Negroes. It was the climax of a series of assaults upon Negroes in the streets and even in their homes. Others were falsely charged by white ruffians with stealing. In Monroe, Georgia, two Negroes and their wives were assassinated.

A report on November 4, 1946, to The New York *Times* on the Columbians in Atlanta read: "Throughout the South are heard predictions that the housing problem may succeed the overcrowded buses of the wartime period as the greatest potential for inter-racial quarrels and, perhaps, violence."

The rumors were not unfounded. A wave of violence swept through the country from the South to the North, from East to West. A Negro's home was burned in Redwood City, a suburb of San Francisco, in December, 1946. In Chicago, in the same month, a hundred policemen swinging nightsticks, battled a mob that had hurled rocks at a truck moving a Negro veteran's belongings into a housing project. The crowd stoned police cars as well and only when the police charged into the crowd did the barrage stop.[10]

Birmingham "Created by the Lord"

The wave hit Birmingham, Alabama, where Negroes comprised 43 per cent of the population. A series of zoning laws had been enacted and re-enacted despite invalidation by the courts. A Negro's home which had been the object of three court suits involving the

[9] James A. Dombrowski, "The Southern Conference for Human Welfare," *Common Ground,* summer, 1946, pp. 14–25; also, Florence Murray, "The Negro and Civil Liberties During World War II," *Social Forces,* vol. 24, no. 2, December, 1945, p. 212.

[10] The New York *Times,* December 10, 1946.

ordinances was blasted by dynamite. Thereafter, tensions rose and on March 26, 1949, three more Negro homes were dynamited.[11] Two months later the City Commission voted a "Buffer Zone" between white and Negro sections on the west side of town, consisting of a 50-foot strip running six blocks north from a housing project to a highway. The zone was for "commercial construction only."[12] At a federal court hearing on the law, the mayor testified, "There would be bloodshed and tragedy. . . . There are some things that go beyond the written law . . . things created by the people and the Lord."[13]

Threats continued to be made to Negro residents. The K.K.K. was active. There were assaults and attempts to lure Negro leaders into traps where they could be manhandled. One night seven Birmingham police officers and detectives swooped down without warrant on a Negro home. They said they had heard that white people were living there with the Negro family.[14] On August 13, 1949, two midnight blasts rocked Negro houses zoned for whites only. The explosions were heard over most of Birmingham. When they occurred, several Negroes, on guard in anticipation of the attack, fired at a speeding automobile from which the bombs had been thrown. The shots missed. The police commissioner charged the Negroes as "partly to blame for the incident for not informing police."[15]

In April, 1950, a blast ripped through the home of a Negro minister in Birmingham. It was the second dynamiting of the house in less than a year. It was followed in nine days by another blast at the home of a Negro dentist, causing $11,000 damage.[16] In December, 1950, the home of a Negro woman who had led a court fight against the city zoning law was dynamited. The heavy explosion was set off shortly before midnight and was heard for several miles. The bomb apparently was placed or thrown on a screened porch. The contractor who had completed the house only a month before estimated damage tentatively at about $8000. It was the fifth bombing of a Negro house since the spring of 1949. Three were blasted then and another the April before.[17]

[11] Washington *Times Herald*, March 26, 1949.
[12] The New York *Times,* June 1, 1949.
[13] New York *Post,* December 14, 1949.
[14] New York *Post,* June 10, 1949.
[15] New York *Herald Tribune,* August 14, 1949.
[16] Atlanta *Constitution,* April 24, 1950.
[17] Atlanta *Journal,* December 22, 1950.

In May, 1951, the two homes which had been the targets of the dynamiters for three years were finally burned to the ground.[18]

Elsewhere

Nor were the Birmingham outbreaks an isolated affair. Chicago had a wave of riots after World War II, plus hundreds of minor incidents. Bombings were occurring simultaneously in other areas and in 1950–1951 there were bombings in Nashville, Wake Forest (N.C.), Miami, Dallas, Rome (Georgia), and Crossville, Phenix City, and Cottonwood, Alabama.

In Chattanooga, in May, 1950, a Negro home in a previously white section was bombed for the second time, almost killing two children. In Nashville, after cross-burnings, a bomb was hurled from a passing automobile which shook houses in a six-block radius. In March, 1951, several sticks of dynamite were exploded in the backyard of a house recently sold to Negroes, touching off a whole wave of dynamitings in the area. In seventeen months preceding August 11, 1951, Negro homes were the target of 13 dynamitings in Dallas.

Considerable violence occurred elsewhere that the press never reported. These sample news items will give a running idea of what was happening from 1949 through 1952:

GEORGIA ACTS TO ENFORCE HOUSING SEGREGATION
Georgia is moving to halt sales of white neighborhood homes to Negroes, a practice that has brought sporadic violence to the South. . . . Saturday night, dynamite ripped a home in a white section of Atlanta. Negroes had just purchased the house.—New York *World-Telegram,* March 9, 1949.

NEGRO'S LICENSE REVOKED IN SALE OF "WHITE" HOMES
Georgia today took away the license of a Negro real estate dealer who sold homes in a white neighborhood to Negroes.—The New York *Times,* March 24, 1949.

WASHINGTON MEMO
. . . A Negro family moved into a home in a "white neighborhood" over the weekend; within a few hours the house had been stoned, a trash fire was discovered in the backyard and a "citizen's meeting" protesting the advent of the Negroes had been held. Reports of Klan activity in the area are current.—New York *Post,* April 6, 1949.

[18] New York *Post,* May 7, 1951.

BIG CROSS BURNED

Nashville, Tenn.—A fifteen-foot cross was burned last night near the site of a proposed Negro housing unit in a section of town predominantly occupied by white persons.—New York *Sun,* April 7, 1949.

NEGRO DOCTOR'S WIFE BLAMES PREJUDICE IN BOMBING OF HOUSE

Warren, O.—A homemade dynamite bomb which heavily damaged a Negro doctor's incompleted $50,000 home was set off in spite motivated by race prejudice, the doctor's wife told police today.—Chicago *Tribune,* April 8, 1949.

BRONX HOME STONED IN NIGHT AFTER TALK OF SALE TO NEGRO

New York *Post,* June 17, 1949.

NEGRO HOUSING HALTED; HOMES AT NASHVILLE BLAST SCENE NOW SLATED FOR WHITES

Plans have been abandoned for a Negro housing project in an area here that has been the scene of a cross burning and an explosion.—The New York *Times,* January 7, 1950.

BLASTS DAMAGE CAROLINA HOMES

Richmond (Va.) *Times-Dispatch,* April 7, 1952.

POLICE ALERTED AS WHITES THREATEN NEGRO NEIGHBORS

. . . A group of spokesmen suggested . . . "If you leave this neighborhood you will live longer and be happier."—Houston *Chronicle,* June 17, 1952.

RACIAL ECHO IN BLASTING OF HOUSE

An explosion here early Sunday morning blasted the front of an empty house about to be occupied by a Negro family. Police said the house is in a predominantly white neighborhood.—Atlanta *Constitution,* June 18, 1951.

NEGRO HOME BUILT NEAR WHITE AREA IN DALLAS BOMBED

The bombing was the twelfth in the area in recent months.—St. Louis *Post-Dispatch,* July 12, 1951.

THREATENED NEGRO GUARDED ON COAST

Since Gary moved in the neighbors have been protesting his presence. Last night a stone crashed through the kitchen window and at 4:30 A.M. today another rock was hurled against the house. A reinforced guard of sheriff's deputies was thrown around Gary's home.—The New York *Times* dispatch from Richmond, California, March 18, 1952.

Los Angeles (UP)—Two home-made bombs were exploded yesterday outside the home of William Bailey, a Negro science teacher, and a residence, across the street, occupied by white persons. No one was injured but both buildings were damaged extensively.—The New York *Times,* March 17, 1952.

CHICAGO MOB FIRES HOUSE ON "NEGRO" RUMOR
Chicago (UP)—A mob of about 4,000 persons attempted to burn a two-family house last night after they heard rumors that Negroes planned to move into the building.—New York *Post,* July 2, 1952.

An article in the *New South* for June–July, 1952, published by the Southern Regional Council at Atlanta, sums up the violence in the South for an 18-month period as follows:

Since January 1, 1951 more than 40 bombings have been perpetrated in the South by terrorists and vandals, and many more have been attempted . . . most of these depredations have grown out of racial and religious tensions. . . . Not a single case of bombing growing out of racial and religious tensions has resulted in conviction of the perpetrators.[19]

A group of homeowners originally from Georgia and Arkansas spearheaded a mob scene in Contra Costa County in the San Francisco Bay area. Despite urgent appeals law enforcement was represented only by two policemen in a parked car who made no effort to disperse the crowd. A riot was avoided by the firm intervention of the California Attorney-General.[20] There were a series of bombings of Negro homes in Houston, in August, 1953.[21] A Negro was shot at in Madison, Wisconsin, and on September 30, his home vandalized.

Organized opposition in a Cleveland neighborhood brought tension and vandalism for almost two weeks. The sale of a home to a Negro was protested by organized meetings of hundreds of owners. Intervention by the mayor, the Community Relations Committee, churches, and civic officials brought the situation under control.[22] In 1953 there was arson, violence or bomb-throwing in Kansas City, Atlanta, Chicago and East St. Louis, Cleveland, Indianapolis, Long Island, and Los Angeles County.[23]

Bombings continued in 1954. In Sacramento, California, dynamite

[19] "Blighted Housing and Bomb Violence," pp. 1-2.
[20] Letter from Edward Howden, Executive Director, Council for Civic Unity of San Francisco, August 8, 1952.
[21] Houston *Post,* August 31, 1953.
[22] *Memorandum on Housing Situation, Lee-Harvard Area.* Confidential report, The Community Relations Committee, Cleveland, Ohio, July 23, 1953.
[23] *Civil Rights in the United States 1953. A Balance Sheet of Group Relations,* New York, American Jewish Congress and the National Association for the Advancement of Colored People, 1954.

blew a hole in the cement porch of a Negro couple while they were sleeping. Chicago continued seething. The Supreme Court decision barring school segregation unleashed new antagonisms in Southern communities. Three successive explosions rocked Norfolk County, Virginia, between August 24 and September 11, causing extensive damage.

On June 27, in Louisville, Kentucky, where 17 per cent of the population is Negro, a bomb shattered the wall of a house belonging to Andrew E. Wade IV. The house had been bought for the Wades through a Mr. and Mrs. Carl Braden, a white couple who were their friends. The explosion had been preceded by crossburning, rock-throwing, and gunfire. The prosecutor started an investigation. Instead of finding the hoodlums responsible for the outrages, he raided the Braden home and the homes of their friends. Literature characterized as "Communistic" was seized. With a passion for irrelevancy, a grand jury then indicted the Bradens and three of their friends for advocating sedition. Another friend of the Wades was indicted for causing the explosion. The jury's finding was simple. The conflict over homes in Louisville was not between whites and blacks but between whites, blacks, and Reds. It was all found to be a Communist plot. "It is very significant," said the jury knowingly, "that the case seems to follow the pattern used by the Communist party in this country to create trouble between the respective races . . . and then causing incidents such as this."[24] In December, Braden was convicted, the jury recommending a 15-year jail term.

Yet in the face of violence, slurs, and threats, the Negro continued pushing his way into the cities. He was there to stay. Racial covenants and mob action made things harder, but they could not force him back to the cotton and tobacco fields. He was establishing his new base. He was completing the migration he had put off while European immigrants had poured in. It was one of the momentous efforts of a subordinate race to rise to its place in the American sun. If it was met by resistance, prosecutions, terror, and violence, and left traumatic marks on the body politic, they were the price for the gains that were being achieved.

[24] The New York *Times,* October 10, 1954.

IX

THE OPEN AND CLOSED CITY— DETROIT AND DEARBORN

DETROIT was reared in a series of booms and explosions. The booms were land-booms in which lots were bought for ten dollars down in prairieland subdivisions and sold overnight at bonanza profits. The explosions were the sound of ingenious new engines contrived by men in little sheds and attics, engines that changed the pace and face of cities everywhere and brought the many worlds nearer to one.

But there were other kinds of booms and explosions in Detroit which rent those worlds further apart than the fastest planes could link them. They were the sounds of dynamite and shotguns leveled at Negroes trying to move into their homes. They were the sounds of fanatics, the verbal blasts of mischievous little men like Father Charles Coughlin, Gerald L. K. Smith, and William D. Pelley, who preached race hatred and religious intolerance.

In most American cities their tirades would get nowhere. But there were folk in Detroit peculiarly vulnerable to their explosions—southern whites, isolated hill-folk, insecure migrants, uneducated Negroes, and men who could not think for themselves. Much of the population was new, their roots still unfirmed, their jobs tentative. Competition for jobs was always keen, competition for housing even keener. Detroit grew faster than her building industry. From a mere 205,000 in 1890 the city spiraled to a million in 1920, 1.6 million in 1940, 1.8 million in 1950. Because she grew so fast, Detroit seemed always a city of strangers.

Detroit's streets, laid out beautifully after the fire of 1805 which leveled every house but one, were lined with good, well-planned houses. But soon the city outgrew its plans. There was no longer any room in the central areas, so Detroit spread. Land speculation was so rampant and uncontrolled after the turn of the century that the abortive subdivisions could have housed millions if fully developed. Then, thanks to the automobile boom which gave both employment and access to the new land, some of the water was pumped out of the subdivisions. When the FHA system came along, the water poured out even faster.

The FHA system was a catalyst to a new set of up-and-coming building entrepreneurs drawn from miscellaneous fields toward an inviting new game. FHA enabled the more enterprising shoestringers to clean up millions. In a hundred years, the slogan "Forty acres and a mule" changed to "Front money and a contact." To fit the workers' purses, FHA cut standards to a substandard minimum. Today Detroit's landscape is littered with thousands of "economy houses" which will be full-fledged slums in the not distant future. By filling the surrounding suburbs, however, FHA helped the automobile companies house their workers without company outlay. FHA did more. It espoused racial exclusion and when Negroes moved into an area adjoining a proposed FHA project, it approved walling them off. The wall in Detroit is now referred to as "The Wailing Wall."

By the time of World War I, Negroes were 10 per cent of Detroit's population, and by the close of World War II, 16 per cent. Many were from the South; so were a goodly number of white workers. There were also mountaineers, Poles, Irish, and people of every race, class, and denomination drawn to Detroit's factories by the magnet of high wages. Thanks to an enlightened labor leadership, they worked side by side without too much trouble, and even joined the same unions. But when they left the factories for their homes there was trouble. Workers had been told that Negroes make bad neighbors and destroy real estate values. Kept from buying homes in most of the outlying areas, the Negroes crowded into the city slums and expanded into other sections wherever they could establish beachheads. The movement took on all the aspects of a cold war, each side waiting for the other to fire the first charge.

The first charge was fired in 1925. Dr. Ossian Sweet, a successful

Negro doctor, had bought a house in a white section. The Negro population had risen from 5741 in 1910 to almost 82,000, and tensions were mounting with the influx. But the whites had done nothing more serious than make threats and break a few windows. Another Negro doctor, whose house had been stoned, had picked up his belongings and moved a few years earlier. Sweet was not so accommodating. His white neighbors formed a mob and attacked his house. Sweet was said to have fired and killed an innocent bystander, wounding another. Clarence Darrow and Arthur Garfield Hays defended Sweet and the men who stood at his side. The case got worldwide notice. The argument used was that a man's home is his castle, even though the man is a Negro and the home not a castle. Sweet was freed. Liberals thought a Negro's right to live where he chose was established for good and that mob rule in Detroit was ended.

They were wrong. Little explosions continued. In the midst of World War II came a big explosion at a housing project built in a mixed neighborhood by the Federal Works Agency for Negro occupancy. It was named "Sojourner Truth Houses," after the famous Abolitionist. The government officials vacillated between making the project white and making it Negro. Realtors and homeowners filed thousands of written protests. A local Congressman threw his weight around the Washington housing offices, and another from Alabama who had headed an investigating committee vowed the project would never go to Negroes. Two fiery crosses were burned at the site. The state FHA director, true to form, wrote that "the project occupied by Negroes could be expected to have an adverse influence on mortgage payments in the neighborhood." When, after rocking back and forth under pressure and fear, the government finally decided on Negro occupancy, the top blew off in Detroit.

The Negro families eligible for occupancy in the new project had given up their old quarters. At 7 A.M. on Saturday, February 28, 1942, twelve Negro families started to move their belongings into their new homes. The trucks got to within two blocks of the project when a mob of several hundred whites met them with clubs, stones, and sticks. The mob was well organized. Instructions were relayed by a commandant from a sound truck. Under an elaborate plan of action, automobiles manned by lieutenants were to be driven through the area calling out all residents as soon as the Negroes arrived at the project. In 20 minutes a mob of 500 could be corralled.[1]

In anticipation of trouble, 200 police were brought to the scene. A riot squad should be trained to suppress trouble, not to rationalize the prejudices of their fellow citizens with their own. But the police were unsympathetic with the Negroes, some inoculated with the same anti-Negro poison which had affected the mob.

As the first three Negro families approached on trucks, the mob leaders warned them not to get any closer. The police inspector told housing officials on hand that his men could not adequately protect the tenants. Housing Director Charles Edgecombe decided to hold up any further moving until more adequate protection could be provided. The Negro tenants protested that they had given up their homes and had nowhere to go. Meanwhile, some 100 Negroes from nearby Conant Gardens had assembled. The two antagonistic groups faced each other. Soon a few rocks came at the Negro families. The whites moved on the Negroes. The Negroes stood their ground.

The police made no effort to push the whites back, but struck at the Negroes with clubs. Only 3 of the 104 arrested were whites, while 33 of the 38 persons hospitalized were Negroes. Most were victims not of the rioters' rocks but of policemen's clubs and fists.

Throughout the day there were skirmishes between police and Negroes, between rioters and Negroes. By the following day the mob had grown to about 1000 whites. A group of 30, mostly women, picketed the project office, carrying two American flags. John B. Blandford, then head of the National Housing Agency, exhorted, "We are at war. This is a war housing project." Government officials pointed to the incalculable loss of prestige on the international front. But outbursts of violence continued. The militia was finally called to protect the Negroes in the project, and they moved in.

Tensions did not subside. The riot was the prelude to another the next year which caused 35 deaths, 500 injuries, and millions of dollars in property damage—aside from the loss of millions of man-hours in war production plants.[2] The ineptitude of police organization and

[1] Travel report by Robert R. Taylor, February 29, 1942, and interoffice memoranda of various members of the Federal Works Agency (mimeographed).

[2] Robert C. Weaver, *The Negro Ghetto*. New York, Harcourt, Brace & Company, 1948, p. 94.

the absence of a race relations policy stood out as responsible factors.

The records of the Sojourner Truth riot disclose the nature of the fears, biases, and emotions which had affected the white residents. Protests filed against the project read:

Concession by cheap politicians to Negro votes.

Negroes will rape white girls.

Negroes should be rehoused on farms.

Contiguous property will lose its value.

Our property was bought on the understanding there would be restrictions against colored or yellow races.

Two races cannot be combined in any community; "white and black won't mix."

If Negro families are forced in, it will lead to discord.

Negroes are filthy and drive white people away.

"We have the right to choose our own neighbors."

Negro housing project will bring too many Negroes to Detroit.

Negro occupancy is the result of "colored and yellow communistic propaganda working on the Mayor."

"How would you like a filthy Negro neighbor?"

Mayor is playing politics ("He is as low as a white prostitute who marries a black man").

Negroes are zoned off together in other cities, why not in Detroit?

Blacks coming in means a "run-down" community.

United States Government does not put Negro soldiers in with whites; each have their own camps. Why not their own neighborhoods?

FHA will guarantee no further home loans in Negro neighborhoods.

I want to fight for U.S.A. and not for Africa.

It's not wise to encourage intermingling and intermarriage of the races.

Nazis drove Polish out of their homes; we are no better off here.

Negroes have not earned the right to live with whites.

"This land is restricted to white occupancy and by God we intend to keep it so."

Whites pay taxes; Negroes get housing and relief.

Polish communities are integrated in their churches and schools which are restricted to Polish people.

These statements disclose the presence of the familiar stereotypes associated with the Negro, i.e., Negroes are filthy, shiftless, and socially dangerous; their presence means loss of values of white homes, inferior and run-down neighborhoods, a withdrawal by the whites from the community, and an inundation by the Negroes.

Coupled with these fears and stereotypes are sporadic rationalizations, loose and attenuated charges, justifications all apparently born of hearsay and gossip but sufficiently influential to activate uncontrolled emotion and violence.

After the riots, measures were taken to prevent their recurrence. The most important was the establishment in 1944 of an official "Mayor's Interracial Committee," composed of eminent citizens and directed by George Schermer, an expert in racial problems. Schermer set out to awaken civic groups to responsibility for the city's racial problem. These things were done: The police were reorganized, educated, and oriented to riot control. Police officers were given instruction at the University of Michigan and Fisk University. Four uniformed Negro sergeants, a detective, and 100 Negro policemen were appointed in a force of 4200. They were required to work closely with Schermer and his assistants. "Hot" areas were carefully watched for disturbing symptoms. The committee developed techniques for "tension control," including reviews of public policies, mass education, neighborhood speakers, and pamphlets, posters, and films for school and public meetings. Schermer himself lived in one of the tension areas so he could keep close watch at the roots.

After several years' work, Schermer was able to say that a riot could no longer occur in Detroit and no matter where a Negro moved, the police could maintain order. Indeed, with modern equipment and organization, no mob should ever develop the potential to take over.

Despite these gains, underlying factors still made Detroit a troublesome area on the American horizon. Its housing shortage was worse than ever before. The Negro population more than doubled in the decade since 1940, most of the newcomers being jammed into the old ghetto—though a small number moved into the periphery and into temporary public war housing. Bigotry and opposition to Negro expansion have established deep roots in the sump of Detroit's politics. Rabble-rousers achieved an important political status and there were often discernible in the *vox populi* the strident notes of demagogy.

In the 1949 "nonpartisan" election campaign public housing became a leading issue. Detroit had received a federal earmarking of money for some 10,000 low-rent dwellings to house its low-income workers. The candidate for mayor was George Edwards, who had CIO's support and favored public housing. He was attacked as a friend of Negroes and communists. Albert Cobo, the successful candidate, came out as the guardian of the small homeowner, the taxpayer, and the "best people." A backbone of Cobo's support was the self-styled "neighborhood improvement association," which is associated with Detroit's history of violence. Its main purpose is to resist every intrusion of minority population into white neighborhoods. Some of these organizations have been linked to the remnants of the Gerald L. K. Smith groups, Father Coughlin, and southern white lunatic-fringe groups.

After the war, the associations spread all over the city and became one of its most important political factors. Their rise was championed by a string of suburban newspapers which kept fever high against reds, Negroes, and "socialist" (public or cooperative) housing.

The newspapers thrived on the advertising support of local businessmen, developers, and even churches. The publisher's gimmick for recruiting readers was editorialized news items provoking fear and hatred. It has demonstrated that prejudice can produce profits and fantasy can be marketed as fact. For example, public housing in the newspapers' view means intrusion of "colored citizens" into white neighborhoods. Readers should therefore rise to the defense of their homes and oppose the intruder.

Though the CIO and the United Auto Workers have worked to educate their members in race tolerance, the rank and file is by no means free of prejudice. A Detroit Council for Better Housing was formed to bring together leaders from the CIO, AFL, and church and community groups, but it was only a valiant minnow in a rising sea of prejudice.

The city councilmen fear the neighborhood associations which send noisy delegations to council meetings and threaten freely whenever they are displeased by the council's actions. The councilmen make decisions on an *ad hoc* basis. When a Negro developer tried to build housing, they simply condemned his land for a public park. That was years ago. There is still no park nor was the site ever suited for one.

Employment in Detroit remains volatile. To mountaineers recruited from the Carolina backwoods, unemployment or a strike may simply mean a bus home to hill country till they are needed again. But to homeowners, it might spell foreclosure. The equity in the home to these folk is their life's savings, all that stands between them and destitution. When the associations let it be known that one Negro settler will ruin not only the values of the white's houses but also the chastity of every pure young daughter, the frightened homeowners naturally take alarm. The socials in many a church in Detroit are kept in lively ferment by the discussions of the black menace to America's most sacred institutions, property and womanly virtue. A number of churches have refused their meeting halls to social organizations which have a different point of view.

No sooner was Cobo elected than he made an unprecedented appearance as mayor-elect before the city council to voice his opposition to public housing projects "in outlying areas where single homes are located." This meant abandonment of all vacant-land projects and the demolition of slum areas in which some 9500 Negro families lived. Cobo insisted that a number of these areas be developed by private enterprise, which meant that few of the dispossessed Negro families would stand a chance of ever getting back into the new housing. As for public housing, he said, "the council should allay the fears of homeowners in outlying areas that public housing projects will be built nearby." This supported the position of the suburban press and the neighborhood associations.

Of course if the city tore down only the Negro areas, the displaced Negro families would have no place to go in the meantime. In 1950 the writer addressed the city council at the request of citizens' groups and urged it not to dispossess the Negroes from the slum sites and to adopt a mixed housing policy to end the battle over sites. The councilman frankly replied that Cobo's election had been on the issue of segregation and no public housing in outlying areas, and this was a political commitment.

In recent years Negro buying power has improved and more Negroes have moved into the older white sections of Detroit. A somewhat more liberalized FHA policy has helped to ease credit for some Negro homes and race bias is no longer being fanned by FHA officials. The Supreme Court's decision on restrictive covenants has opened some new sections, and small clusters of Negroes have escaped from the ghetto.

With the increase of Negro population, the political power of Negroes is getting more respect. Detroit's housing authority (not without trepidation) finally admitted Negroes into one of its segregated housing projects located in a mixed area. Under the low income limits set by the federal government, however, there has been a scarcity of eligible white applicants and an excess of Negro applicants. Another temporary project for whites located in a Negro area has been opened to mixed occupancy. All other projects, however, remained lily-white in 1954.

The churches have become more cooperative as some ministers and church leaders have striven to bring about interracial accord and allay the panic of white residents of their parishes. In 1952 the Right Reverend Richard Emrich, Protestant Episcopal Bishop of Michigan, addressed a letter to every clergyman in the diocese saying: "The Church is not the church of any one race, class, or nation. It is God's family. Every Parish and Mission is in its location the representative of the universal Church, and all peoples of every kindred, nation, and tongue, are welcome in its fold."[3]

But the Detroit area still seethes. The neighborhood improvement associations have now federated to strengthen their political power. The city government often finds it easier to heed than to buck them. In 1950 they exerted strong pressure to oust Schermer and curb the work of his committee. In 1952, Schermer resigned to head Philadelphia's Commission on Human Relations. After his resignation a new fifteen-man commission on human relations was set up by Mayor Cobo, eight appointed by Cobo, the other seven representing city departments. The mayor has the power to appoint and remove the executive director. Civic organizations fear for the commission's future, Detroit politics being what they are.

Dearborn

The worst aspect of the Detroit situation today is found outside the city limits. It is a new and ominous phenomenon. Detroit, as the country's fifth biggest city, contains the mixed elements and varied interests which prevent democratic cities from sinking irretrievably into the quicksands of race prejudice. The situation is different in

---

[3] Quoted in article by Walter White, "How Detroit Fights Race Hatred," *Saturday Evening Post,* July 18, 1953, p. 95.

nearby Dearborn, a city of 94,994 (1950) and the site of the Ford Motor Company.

Dearborn is composed of thousands of little homes similar to suburban Detroit's. In fact, but for the legalized boundary, Dearborn would be just a borough of Detroit.

Dearborn elected Orville L. Hubbard, who campaigned for the mayoralty on the racial issue. Hubbard's big boast was that he had kept Negroes out of Dearborn. In 1948, the John Hancock Life Insurance Company decided to build a private rental housing project on land owned by the Ford Motor Company. The company had no intention of housing any Negroes. But Negroes were the problem in Detroit, and though there were almost no Negroes in Dearborn, the city was close enough to Detroit to give the issue political appeal. Hubbard found something to be against—Negroes. He also needed to show that it was he who was saving the day for Dearborn's white citizenry. The life insurance company provided him with the opportunity. He organized meetings and attacked the project as the opening wedge for a Negro inundation of Dearborn. Handbills and stickers were circulated and a "conspiracy" was laid to the Ford Motor Company and the insurance company, as unlikely a pair of racial conspirators as can be imagined.

One of the circulars read:

> KEEP NEGROES OUT OF DEARBORN
> X   VOTE *NO* on (Advisory Vote)
> (The John Hancock Rental Housing Project)

> PROTECT YOUR HOME AND MINE!
> X   VOTE *NO* on (Advisory Vote)

Another circular, printed on official stationery and bearing the city seal, read:

> WAKE UP, DEARBORN!
> WAKE UP!
> OPEN   YOUR   EYES   W I D E!
> JOHN HANCOCK GIVES HOUSING DOUBLE-TALK

With none of the 15,000 Ford Rouge Negro workers living in Dearborn, don't be "lulled into a false sense of security" that John Hancock—with 8,500,000 policyholders of every race, color and creed—can build in Dearborn a multimillion dollar terrace-type rental housing project from its huge insurance funds, including incomes from Negroes, and exclude Negro families from living in the Hancock row-housing project in Dearborn, "if" you allow it to be built here. *Keep Dearborn a home-owners city by voting NO on the (ADVISORY VOTE) which by "stooping, squatting and squinting" you will find at the bottom of the right column on your voting machine.*

The project was defeated and the citizens of Dearborn were happy. Orville L. Hubbard was reelected for his achievement in saving the city from the mythical corps of black invaders.

The Closed City

The exclusion practices of Dearborn are practiced in Grosse Point, Bloomfield Hills, and Birmingham, which also adjoin Detroit. They are being repeated in other parts of the country. They are significant because the American symbol has always been the open road, not the walled city. Most Americans move on an average of once every five years—to recast opportunities, establish firmer roots, find a better environment for their children, or enjoy a milder climate in the evening of life.

The right to buy or rent land underlay America's early abolition of feudal tenures and restraints on alienation. It exhibited itself in the break-up of colonial latifundia and in the various state declarations against land monopoly and primogeniture. Federal law guarantees the right to buy, own, rent, and lease land.

When industrialization produced walled company towns from which union organizers were kept out by company guards and in which employees were confined, libertarians were outraged.[4] Repressions of free speech and free assembly in the company towns were successfully challenged. Later, company towns like the Gulf Oil Company's Chickasaw, Alabama, were restrained by the courts from keeping out religious groups.[5] Efforts to zone areas "for whites only" were also struck down. All these were viewed as inconsonant with the American ideal.

But more recently it has become possible for whole races to be banned from a city. It is done officially, as in Dearborn, or by subtler forms of exclusion. With FHA and other federal housing aids, it has now become possible to build a whole city and to tenant it

---

[4] Arthur Garfield Hays, *Let Freedom Ring.* New York, Boni & Liveright, 1928.

[5] *Marsh v. Alabama*, 326 U.S. 501.

with a group of a single race or color. After developers build communities which are then incorporated, their own police are hired, their own laws enacted, and the "wrong kind of people" kept out. Cicero and Berwyn, Ill.,[6] and the Levittowns (New York and Pennsylvania) are other examples of communities with populations of 50,000 or more, but no Negroes. Fairless Hills, near Levittown, Pennsylvania, financed by the U.S. Steel Corporation, is another community with an all-white population. Most of the Negro workers in the new steel plant near Levittown and Fairless Hills have had to crowd into the nearby cities (Trenton, Camden, Philadelphia).

The closed city is still in its beginnings in America. It may make no further progress, particularly if the public is alerted to the dangers. There are also many safety factors in the work of racial relations agencies and citizen groups. But the pattern that leads to the closed city exists at a number of points, and unless it is broken it is apt to spread.

A clue to what more closed cities could mean may be gleaned from what happened in Cicero, Illinois, in July, 1951.

[6] The Census of 1950 lists less than 100 Negroes in Berwyn and Cicero, but these are either household workers, building superintendents, or others; there are no Negro neighborhoods or Negro "pockets" in any of the cities mentioned.

X

COOK COUNTY, ILLINOIS

O N THURSDAY, July 12, 1951, Governor Adlai Stevenson declared martial law in Cicero, a city adjoining Chicago, after police and sheriff's forces declared themselves unable to cope with a mob of 4000 which had assembled to keep Harvey E. Clark, Jr., a Negro war veteran, from moving his family into a $60 apartment. The rioting had started the previous Tuesday and raged without interruption up to early Friday morning. Law and order collapsed as the mob ran free and the police looked on. Flares, bricks, and burning torches were thrown into the $100,000 apartment house; radiators and walls were ripped out; furniture was thrown from the windows, and trees were torn up by the roots to be burned as the mob cheered. Policemen joked with the mobsters as though it were a prank. The mayor and the chief of police were "out of town." When the militia tried to push back the mob at bayonet point, four militiamen were felled and only the superb discipline of the others as they saw their men go down kept the riot from turning into massacre.

The implications of the riot were too ugly for many people to face. The riot was variously held to be a nasty incident that does not happen too often, a wicked occurrence in a wicked city that is the haunt of Al Capone's former mob, an eruption provoked by "alien" Czechs and Poles who have not yet learned the American way of life, a teen-agers' lark that got out of control, and a rumpus started by communists. It was not at all surprising that a Cook County grand jury even added the interpretation it was all a "Negro plot."

Yet behind the Cicero affair lies one of the most disturbing violations of civil rights in American history. Its most ominous aspect is the growing use of legal processes to flout civil rights. The Cicero riot was only a recent phase of this development.

The Cicero rioting started when a Mrs. DeRose, who owned the apartment house, got into a controversy with her tenants and was ordered to refund a portion of the rent. Shortly after, out of spite, profit, or both, she rented an apartment to Clark, a graduate of Fisk University. Movement of Negroes into white areas is nothing new in Chicago. But it was new in Cicero which, like Dearborn and many similar communities, had successfuly resisted Negro settlement.

When it was learned that a Negro was moving into the apartment house, a high Cicero official arrived to warn Mrs. DeRose there would be "trouble" if Clark moved in. The city, he said, could not be responsible for keeping order. Two policemen then came to tell Mrs. DeRose she could not "get away with it." At 2:30 P.M. on June 8 a moving van containing $2000 worth of Clark's furniture drove up to the house and was halted by the police. The rental agent was ushered out with a drawn revolver at his back. A jeering crowd had gathered and Clark was then told to get out or he would be arrested "for protective custody." A detective warned him, "I'll bust your damned head if you don't move."

"At about 6 P.M.," reads Clark's affidavit, "the chief of police of Cicero rushed out of the alley nearby followed by twenty men and grabbed my arm." The chief told him to " 'get out of here fast. There will be no moving into this building.' . . . He hit me about eight times while he was pushing me ahead of him toward my car which was parked across the street. I was trying to walk but he was trying to make me move faster. When we reached my car, I opened the door and the chief shoved me inside and said 'Get out of Cicero and don't come back in town or you'll get a bullet through you.' "

When suit was brought against the Cicero police through the National Association for the Advancement of Colored People, United States District Judge John P. Barnes, on June 26, enjoined the city from "shooting, beating or otherwise harassing Clark"—one of the most unusual injunctions in legal annals. "You are going to exercise the same diligence in seeing that these people move in as you did in trying to keep them out," said the judge.

When Clark moved in, word was passed along that there would

be "fun" at the apartment house. Crowds gathered, tensions rose, and a rock smashed the window of Clark's apartment.

On Wednesday, July 11, some of the white families in the apartment house, warned of impending trouble, stored their furniture and moved out. By dusk a crowd of 4000 cut the ropes put up by the police. Only 60 policemen were assigned to the scene. The uniformed policemen in front of the building stepped out of the way when the crowd moved forward; the plainclothesmen simply mixed with the crowd as fires were set inside the building. Women carried stones from a nearby rockpile to bombard the windows while policemen stood by.

A few state police and twenty deputy sheriffs under County Sheriff John E. Babb, who arrived Wednesday evening, were at the scene, but little was done to disperse the mob. When the sheriff's deputies asked Cicero firemen to turn hoses on the crowd, the firemen refused to do so without orders from their lieutenant, who was unavailable. After $20,000 in damage had been done to the building, Babb requested the Governor to send in the state militia. The troops arrived and finally pushed back the mob at bayonet point. Four of the militiamen were felled in the process.

The Cicero riot received more than usual notice in Chicago, although for two days the news had been played down. In fact, most Chicagoans saw the riot on television before they read it in their newspapers. But when the Governor called out the National Guard, the news broke all over the country, forcing the grand jury to investigate.

On January 18, 1952, the grand jury brought in its findings. Instead of indicting the hoodlums responsible for the vandalism which denied Clark the right to live where he chose, it indicted the NAACP attorney who was defending his right. It also indicted the owner, her lawyer, and her rental agent, charging them all with conspiracy to injure property by causing "depreciation in the market selling price." The right of a Negro to buy or rent a home, which is guaranteed by the federal Civil Rights Law of 1866, was thus declared to be null and void in Illinois.

Ultimately, after protest by civic groups, the indictments were dropped and the United States Attorney General ordered an investigation. Indictments were then obtained against the town president, the fire chief, the police chief, the town attorney, and three policemen. The charges were dismissed against the town president and fire chief. Later the police chief and two policemen were fined a total of $2500.

The federal prosecution was hailed as a courageous step forward. It could more accurately be called rare, since incursions upon civil rights in housing have not often stirred action by federal officials.

Also forgotten was the fact that the Cicero riot was only the most recent of a series in Cook County. The other riots were either not publicized, or were reported like local fires. From July, 1949, to July, 1952, there were four such riots in Chicago, and there have been nine altogether from 1945 to 1954. In addition, from 1949 to the day of the Cicero outbreak there were more than a hundred lesser incidents in the Chicago area: bombings, fires, or organized assaults against Negro families, one of these by a hit-and-run incendiary who started a fire that cost ten lives. Another incident was the bombing of the home of Dr. Percy Julian, the eminent Negro scientist.

A major outburst, unmentioned by the newspapers, took place only a few days before the Cicero climax. It began toward evening on Sunday, July 1, when Leon Yonik, publisher of a local Lithuanian newspaper, gave shelter to three Negro delegates to the "American Peace Crusade," a leftist organization then meeting in Chicago. A crowd gathered, the Negroes were spirited out the back door by policemen, a co-editor of the newspaper was slugged, and rock-throwing began. The windows in Yonik's house and the plateglass in his newspaper shop were shattered. The cops stood around the house three or four feet apart, ducking the missiles as the crowd cheered. Only a sergeant was in command. Next morning a false fire alarm was sounded and the mob rushed in with the hook and ladder. One of the men leaving the house, which was being "protected" by the police, was assaulted in their full view. He went to the police station to sign a complaint and was jailed. When arrested rioters came up for trial, policemen failed to appear as witnesses.

The Chicago Council Against Racial and Religious Discrimination called the police action "a poor job of mob diagnosis, mob dispersal, force deployment."

In November, 1949, Aaron Bindman, a union organizer, invited some Negro labor representatives to his new home on Peoria Street. Quickly the rumor spread that Negroes had bought or rented the building. A crowd formed, but as usual only a small police detail was assigned. The first rock was thrown by a twelve-year-old boy and a general barrage followed. There were no policemen on the side of the street from which the stones were being thrown; as each stone sailed through the air, the crowd of about two hundred cheered. The next night the crowd gathered again and moved toward the house, crying, "Let's get them out," "Burn the house," "Communists," "Get the sheenies." Children cried, "Lynch 'em!" Other catcalls were aimed at the University of Chicago.

The small crowd could easily have been dispersed, but police sympathies were again with the mob. Soon gangs of young men organized, and the pattern was set for a more general outbreak. A few days later the crowds had increased to about two thousand. Gangs roamed the streets, beating up Jews. Two University of Chicago students were set upon by the mob, beaten, and their car overturned. The men who came to the police station to bail out mob victims (arrested for fighting back) were soundly pummeled in front of the station, while another student vainly begged the officers inside to help them. Another man, on whom the mob found a B'nai B'rith card, was mauled. Outsiders who visited the area were attacked because they were strangers. One policeman told a Chicago *Daily News* reporter that he thought it was all right to beat up certain people "because they were Communists." "How do you know they were Communists?" the reporter asked. "Because they were Jews," answered the policeman.[1]

Finally, Mayor Martin H. Kennelly ordered his police to be more diligent in dispersing the crowds. After five days of rioting 200 policemen were sent into the area, some 70 persons were arrested, order was restored. Thirteen persons were reported injured and many others took their bruises quietly home. Pressed by social agencies and warned that Jewish veterans might organize for reprisals, Mayor Kennelly said a new crowd-dispersal policy would be adopted.

A riot in August, 1947, at a veterans housing project known as

[1] For further details see the reports of the Chicago Commission on Human Relations which are full records of the outbreaks and the incidents that preceded them.

Fernwood Park Homes required 1500 policemen to quell it. A roaring crowd threw rocks, smashed cars, stoned Negroes in automobiles, started grass fires along the walks. As usual, only minor reports of the outbreak were carried in the newspapers. More than 100 persons were arrested in one evening, about half of them youngsters.

The immediate cause of the flare-ups differs in each case, but the underlying cause is always the same: Negroes try to move out of their overcrowded slum areas and are met with violence, or the presence of an occasional Negro is interpreted as signalizing an influx. Groups are permitted to gather around the target; they draw larger groups, including the subnormal, the prejudiced, the emotionally immature, and youth seeking "fun." These are encouraged to take the lead. Rumors begin to fly, emotion rises, order breaks down, and normally law-abiding citizens become part of the mob action. Frustrated by not being able to get at the target, the mob looks for a scapegoat— Negroes, Jews, communists, strangers, intellectuals. In five of the recent outbreaks, police showed no willingness to protect the Negroes in their rights, and in some their forces were even deployed to let the victims take their beatings. The potential for similar miniature race wars exists in other parts of urban America.

Causes of the Tensions

The underlying factors responsible for the continuing wave of explosions in Cook County are:
1. The in-migration of Negroes and other minorities to take jobs.
2. A shortage of housing.
3. Their inevitable movement into white areas to compete for existing housing.
4. Failure of the citizenry to insist upon a solution of the problem and bring pressure upon their public officials.
5. Creating fears of loss of property values and fears of Negroes as neighbors.
6. The fanning of tensions by troublemaking groups.
7. The hostility or apathy of public officials and police.

Conversion of Chicago from a prairie to one of the world's great industrial centers was made possible by labor that kept pouring in.

Much of this labor was foreign-born or Negro. Between 1900 and 1920, however, while the number of foreign-born in Chicago increased by one third, the Negro population trebled (Table II). When foreign immigration was curtailed, the Negro kept coming. He not only increased in numbers but in his ratio to the total population:

TABLE II.   NUMBER AND PERCENTAGE OF NEGRO TO TOTAL POPULATION IN COOK COUNTY

| Year | Total | Negro | |
		Number	Per Cent
1900	1,838,735	31,838	1.9
1910	2,405,233	46,627	1.9
1920	3,053,017	115,238	3.8
1930	3,982,123	246,992	6.1
1940	4,063,342	249,157	6.1
1950	5,508,792	521,007	11.1

Violence accompanied the movement. A race riot in 1908 was among the first of its kind in the North; it cost six lives and left hundreds of Negroes homeless.[2] A riot in East St. Louis led to a Congressional investigation. A series of bombings held Chicago in its grip for seven days in the summer of 1919.[3] Yet Negroes continued to pour in and so long as housing was available these flare-ups were not too frequent. Negroes, in fact, were accepted as were any other in-migrating groups. They got their housing and, though it was costly and substandard, they were not as badly housed, up to World War I, as the Italians. But soon building costs rose; so did rents, and vacancies disappeared. There was rising resistance to giving the Negro any good used housing either in the city or the suburbs. The Negro began to pierce further into the all-white sections of the city.

In 1940, 73 per cent of the colored residents lived in three census areas which were almost solidly Negro. By 1950 close to 15,000 Negro families had purchased or occupied dwellings beyond previously

[2] "The Massacre of East St. Louis," *The Crisis*, September, 1917, pp. 219–238; *The Negro in Chicago*, The Chicago Commission on Race Relations, Chicago, University of Chicago Press, 1922, pp. 1–78.
[3] *The Negro in Chicago*, pp. 123–133.

established Negro residences. The movement occurred principally at the edges of the older areas.[4]

Since there was never enough housing for the newcomers, rents rocketed. Houses were cut up to provide little more than standing room. Decaying mansions were converted into kitchenette apartments, pseudo-hotels, and rooming houses. Slums ripe for demolition teemed with new occupants. "Despite local building codes and regulations 'anything goes' in the Negro-occupied areas in terms of dwelling standards."[5]

The Chicago Housing Authority in June, 1949, listed 272,000 substandard homes in the city. It said, "Rental housing is virtually not available." The Negroes, as the group most hard-hit, might have made good customers for private developments, but FHA, principal sponsor of housing after the 1930's, discouraged building for Negroes. It advocated racial covenants in Cook County as elsewhere. Building and loan associations refused to make loans for new Negro housing. The few Negro home-builders who tried to build on vacant land outside the established Negro zones found their houses burned to the ground. Fire insurance companies refused to write insurance, which made it impossible to obtain financing from any source. After a chain of riots followed by protests against FHA's exclusion policy, FHA in 1950 called together builders and mortgage-lenders to find out whether some Negro housing could be built. The associations and white builders blamed the helpless Negro builders and nothing happened.

To resist Negro expansion, neighborhood civic associations sprang up throughout the city. Racial restrictive covenants appeared everywhere and owners were importuned to sign up in an effort "to resist the invader." Where a white owner sold to a Negro, some associations followed him to his new section and publicized his betrayal. As restrictions were broken, anti-Negro violence followed. Much of it was not even reported. Violence was repeated against the same property on as many as nine occasions while police guarded it.

[4] Memorandum of August 3, 1950, from George B. Nesbitt, Field Representative, to C. L. Farris, Field Operations Branch, Division of Slum Clearance and Urban Redevelopment, Housing and Home Finance Agency, in re: Chicago, Illinois Field Trip—July 24 through 29, 1950, p. 9 (mimeographed).
[5] *Ibid.*

Attitudes of Local Officials

One of the keys to race peace in a city is held by the mayor and governing officials. A riot does not start because 4000 people organize all at once into a mob. There are those who instigate the violence, encourage incidents, and fan the fury. The original crowd grows to mob size only when police allow it. Irresponsible elements in a neighborhood are emboldened into overt action when they sense active or passive support from the political or official machines. Before the Negro tenants moved into the Fernwood housing project, for example, anti-Negro delegations from the Fernwood community called upon Mayor Kennelly to persuade him to abolish the Chicago Housing Authority's nonsegregation policy in some of its public housing projects. The Authority's courageous but beleaguered executive director Elizabeth Wood had asked for Kennelly's support, and Thomas H. Wright, director of the Chicago Commission on Human Relations, had asked the mayor to warn the delegation that anyone who used violence on move-in day would be arrested. Kennelly wavered and tried to appease the delegation, which left the session pleased and full of smiles, some even convinced that Kennelly was for them. A week before move-in day, the captain of police told one of Wright's assistants that he expected to have only 2 policemen at the project when the Negroes arrived. It was not long before the mayor discovered that 1500 policemen were required to disperse the mob.

Kennelly had another chance to take leadership in 1949 when the Carey ordinance came up for a vote. This sought to ban racial discrimination in the selection of tenants for any urban redevelopment project to which the city gave aid in the form of land acquisition or cash subsidies. The proposed ordinance was vigorously opposed by the neighborhood civic associations, the hate groups and, oddly enough, by some respectable citizens' groups and the Chicago press. Supporting the ordinance were citizens' organizations, public housing officials, and others who had become sensitive to the growing race frictions and their dangers.

The ordinance met its first test when it came up for debate before a committee of councilmen. The balconies were crowded with frightened people who had been told that the new law would speed

Negro invasion of their areas. Also present were large groups of city employees whom some city officials had corralled for the occasion. They joined in booing those who spoke for the ordinance.

Though the cards appeared stacked against the measure, the council committee after a heated debate voted its adoption. But Kennelly interceded to demand the ordinance's defeat. The mayor had his way. Anti-Negro groups then interpreted the defeat as a "victory of the Whites against the Negroes." Its most serious aspect was that it undermined if not destroyed the moral base essential for resolving the race issue in housing.

An intelligent public housing program might have helped house some of the Negroes and demonstrated that nondiscriminatory housing was feasible. But in August, 1950, the Chicago City Council approved a housing program to build 21,000 dwellings. Only half of these could ever be erected, only about 2100 units were to be on vacant land, and only 1200 of these would be built. Instead of easing the pressure for minority housing, 10,500 families would be displaced, 9000 of them Negroes. About 70 per cent of those Negroes would be ineligible for the new public housing. There also appeared to be an unwritten agreement not to put Negro tenants in certain of the projects.[6]

Next, Chicago's urban redevelopment program also promised to displace additional Negro families in the name of slum clearance. Eviction of Negroes and their inevitable entry into more white areas was bound to make tensions worse than ever.

It would, of course, be inaccurate to lay all blame on Mayor Kennelly and public officials. A pattern of uninterrupted tension and disorder like Chicago's is the result of a number of factors, not the least of which is the attitude of the city's influential groups:

1. Business and Industrial Groups

These profited from the influx of cheap labor but shunned all responsibility for housing their workers. Many were the mainstay of chambers of commerce and other organizations which stood behind the anti-public housing lobby on the local and national fronts.

[6] Chicago *Defender*, May 2, 1953.

2. *The Savings and Loan Associations*

The central office of these powerful organizations is in Chicago. Their political strength, as shown by the lobby investigation, is immense.[7] They are the most formidable opponents of the public housing program and while they make loans for Negro housing, insist on keeping the Negro within established areas.

3. *Real Estate Interests*

Chicago is the home base of the National Association of Real Estate Boards and its allied organizations. This organization originated the "Code of Ethics" binding its members to oppose occupancy by minorities. It organized the National Home and Property Owners Foundation in Chicago which operated with other neighborhood civic associations to keep Negroes in their place. It also opposes public housing and has done nothing to help Negroes increase their living space. Many leading realtors favor segregation.

4. *Building Operators*

Despite the vast minority market, they have done little to provide housing for minorities. They have built huge developments closed to Negroes and helped accentuate the pressure for housing within the city.

5. *Civic-Minded Citizens*

In a situation as volatile as Chicago's, there is need for concerted leadership by civic-minded citizens. But some of Chicago's prominent citizens are also prominent in strange places. John Gunther calls Chicago "the chief breeding area and headquarters of Fascism in the United States."[8] It is the birthplace of "American Action, Inc.," a secret organization with a dubious membership and an avowed determination to purge 187 Congressmen whose liberalism it does not like. Gunther insists American Action cannot be lightly dismissed: "They have a considerable substance. . . . The folk who think that it was Roosevelt personally who sank the American fleet at Pearl Har-

[7] *United States Savings and Loan League.* A Report of the House Select Committee on Lobbying Activities, House of Representatives, Eighty-first Congress, Second Session, Created Pursuant to H. Res. 298, October 31, 1950.

[8] *Inside U.S.A.* New York, Harper & Brothers, 1947, pp. 382–383.

bor, the least sophisticated tycoons and really rabid anti-New Dealers, the would-be totalitarians and secret and not-so-secret sympathizers with Coughlin, Gerald L. K. Smith, *et al.*, applaud its aims."[9] The president of the organization, he says, was a former national commander of the American Legion, Edward A. Hayes; its treasurer W. Homer Hartz, former president of the Illinois Manufacturers Association; and among its contributors was General Robert E. Wood of Sears, Roebuck, who claimed that the movement had "the blessing of the topmost Republican and Democratic leaders." Ernest T. Weir, of Weirton Steel Company, Lammot Du Pont, chairman of the board of E. I. Du Pont de Nemours, are also mentioned as supporters, and "one member of its Executive Committee is Robert Harriss, a New York business man with a Coughlinite past. . . ."[10]

But even some of the so-called best citizens have rationalized their opposition to Negro movements and thereby lent passive support to bigotry. The respectable Chicago Citizens' Association, composed of some of the city's most influential citizens, should either have supported the Carey Ordinance or at least stayed out of the picture. Instead, the association helped defeat the ordinance. The support supplied by prominent bankers and businessmen to organizations like the Southtown Planning Association, one of the leaders in the fight for more and tighter racial covenants, is another demonstration of how to bring on the mischief-makers.

6. The Press

An educated public opinion at the start could have halted the tide of prejudice and violence. But the Chicago newspapers have curious attitudes about the Negro and how to handle the problem. They are mildly friendly, with the exception of the *Tribune,* which has vacillated. Yet three major papers openly opposed the Carey ordinance, including the liberal *Sun-Times.* One complication is that some of the more enlightened citizens have asked the papers to screen racial news unfavorable to the Negro and play down riot stories. Some felt it was bad for Chicago's reputation. Others seriously believed that sensational reporting by some of the papers might spread whatever violence occurred, give dangerous publicity to certain hate groups, or rouse the

[9] *Ibid.*
[10] *Ibid.*

Negroes to reprisal. Today it is also argued that making a fuss about such incidents plays into the hands of Russian propaganda, which indeed it does. But the result of the self-censorship of the press is that far more coverage is being given to these outbursts in the European and Asiatic press than in our own. They remain secret only to some Americans.[11] Another result is that the papers, perplexed by the whole business and unequipped to handle the race problem on the spot, have surrendered to the irresponsibles the leadership they should have assumed and maintained.

Meanwhile a vested political interest is built up in race prejudice. Anti-Negro and anti-Semitic rabble-rousers flock in to supply an ideology, and unscrupulous politicians attempt to ride into power by appealing to race hatred. While the more prominent newspapers are silent from a misguided feeling of responsibility, another section of the press has fanned anti-racial feeling with complete freedom. The *South End Reporter* and the *Southtown Economist* have been notorious examples. The openly hostile editorials of the *Calumet Index,* the inflammatory "Letters to the Editor" signed by odd pseudonyms, and the anti-racial undertones that accelerate fears, hates, and fever, are other examples.

The Cook County outbreaks were no isolated incidents chargeable to local conditions or to some single criminal segment of the population. They are only one of the most recent symptoms of a major disease in the American scene. The police that stood by as Negroes were beaten and their homes burned were echoing the sentiments of those they thought were the "good people." The Cook County jury that accused the landlady, her lawyer, her agent, and the NAACP lawyer was not corrupt but only converting those sentiments into a formal indictment. Nor were the rioters all vandals or gangsters. They often had the sanction of their elders, of the community, of the police, and of parts of the press. The Cicero police who tried to prevent the Negro family from moving in undoubtedly believed they were acting in the interests of their community. When the mayor and the chief of police "couldn't be found," it was because they knew that if they stopped the riot they would lose any chances of reelection. The sheriff

---

[11] Three weeks after the Cicero riot, Governor Thomas E. Dewey of New York was forced to apologize for Cicero to a Singapore audience that had read the story on the front pages of their newspapers.

of Cook County felt politically embarrassed when he tried to enforce the law. The anti-Negro councilmen in Chicago were only speaking the view of their constituencies in inveighing against Negroes, while Chicago's mayor in opposing civil rights laws and non-discriminatory public housing felt he could thereby gain more votes than he would lose.

Chicago and Cicero are cities where opposition to housing for Negroes may pay off politically. It is one of the outstanding examples of two cities where too many people have lost their ethical sense on the race issue. It will take a long and laborious effort to restore it. Nor will it ever succeed until its press and enlightened citizenry, its responsible businessmen and its public officials, all shift from their attitudes of indifference and give the cause leadership.

Epilogue

On July 1, 1952, on the eve of the Republican national convention in Chicago, a small clique of experts and politicians were going over the last drafts of the Republican national platform. It did not matter who was nominated—the platform was to be one any candidate could accept. Over the objection of Negro leaders, the platform omitted all reference to public housing or the housing of minorities; it advocated more slum clearance as part of their aids to "small business." And the whole matter of civil rights was glossed over with the customary generalizations about "equality," and so forth.

On the same evening and only a half-mile from convention headquarters, a mob of 4000 was trying to burn a two-family house because it had heard rumors Negroes were planning to move in. The mob stoned the building, breaking every window. It started burning the house, and after the fire was extinguished, it tore off the wooden porch with crowbars and sledgehammers. When a squad of 200 policemen came to quell it, the mob tore the antennas from the police cars. The jeers and roar of the mob were loud enough to reach the platform committee, but either it did not hear it or did not want to.

After the platform committee had filed its generalizations and repaired for the political campaign, another type of campaign continued germinating in Chicago. The monthly reports of Chicago's Commission on Human Relations in 1952 and 1953 began to read like field bulletins in a war. There was one incident after another of arson, attempted arson, property damage, vandalism, tension, threats, anonymous warnings, assaults, crowd gatherings, stone-throwings, hurling of firebrands, anti-Semitic incidents, rumors, murder by "nigger-hunters," intimidation of workmen building Negro housing, and so on. There is the little group of teen-agers or hoodlums and the crowd of several hundred threatening to grow to mob proportions. Then the police invoke "Plan 2" or some other tactic, disperse the crowd, and all is quiet until the next incident, an incident which may or may not burgeon into a riot, depending on the police.

On July 30, 1953, Donald Howard, a Negro mail carrier and World War II veteran, moved into Trumbull Park Homes with his wife and two small children. Trumbull Park Homes is a 462-unit public housing development in a neighborhood of one- and two-family homes occupied by Slavic, German, and more recently Mexican workers from nearby steel and machine plants. They were first- and second-generation immigrants often working side by side with Negroes at the plants. It was always a peaceful area of law-abiding people no different from hundreds of other areas around the country.

Then a rumor started its rounds about the tenants being Negroes. Small groups of teen-agers gathered around the project. A small detail of plainclothesmen was assigned to the job. When a brick was thrown through the window, a small uniformed police detail was posted at the Howard apartment. Every night there were demonstrations, the Howards' windows were smashed, and burning sulphur hurled through them. The hoodlum elements were feeling their way with the police but too often the men just stood by, sometimes laughing or cursing. One shouted, "Those who moved the niggers out here should be hanged."

A few days later the sporadic disturbances became more organized. By now the rumors were that 30 Negroes would be moved into the project. On August 9, a crowd of 500 gathered and 35 police squadcars were rushed to the scene. But by nightfall the crowd had grown into an unruly mob of 1000. They stoned windows; bands of hoodlums darted through the crowds throwing lighted torches, while the Howard family sat huddled in their apartment. The hoodlums then stoned Negroes in passing buses and automobiles. As the mob grew to 2000 violence mounted, 750 policemen were assigned to patrol the area, and barricades were set up a half mile around the project. By this time the police became energetic and after a number of arrests and the issuance of a report by the Chicago Housing Authority that it was investigating into the Howards' eligibility for the project, temporary order was restored.

The Housing Authority which had been under attack for its segregation policy in four of its projects now agreed to move three other Negro families into the project, ordered all segregation eliminated, condemned the mob violence, and ordered the eviction of tenants who had participated. But violence was resumed with demonstrations, brick-throwing, and arson. On August 28, four fires broke out, a local tavern catering to Negroes and whites was almost completely gutted, and two policemen injured in scuffles with mobs.

Five months after the first disturbance, demonstrations were still on with bands ranging from 150 to 200 milling around making trouble. There were now a hundred arrests.

The Trumbull Park riots were part of the pattern that has made Chicago a seething caldron since 1945. There was the passiveness of leading citizens. There was the police action that became efficient only after the large crowds had formed, but lent sympathy to the anti-Negro element when vigilance was indispensable. There were the neighborhood improvement associations and the local South Side press playing their part as in former riots. There was also the *Daily Calumet*[12] with its daily harangues:

> . . . The Negro can turn his neighborhood into a slum overnight.
> . . . These areas have been terrorized by sex offenders and thieves. If we don't wake up soon we'll be steam-rollered. Where next to flee— Australia, or perhaps New Zealand? . . . The people on the East Side better wake up, before it is too late. . . . Most of them [Negroes] live like savages. . . . Why don't they stay where they belong? . . . A white man will always be a white man and a colored man will always be colored. Thus by a divine law higher than that of any court or housing authority, the whites and colored are separated. . . . Protesting the move-in of Negroes the three past commanders of the American Legion Post sent a telegram to Senator McCarthy "to investigate the Americanism of the officers of the Chicago Housing Authority." . . . We firmly believe that the whole setup has communistic backing.

There were also the local aldermen now crying the "community has the right to choose its own neighbors"; the Howards were "profes-

[12] October–November, 1953.

sional agitators." Another alderman attacked the housing authority as being "shot through with radicals in control and pinkos."

The White Circle League was on hand too, with the *Daily Calumet* quoting its founder, Joseph Beauharnais, on "the negro cancer"— ". . . thank God that there are a few white men who will risk all to fight for the preservation of the white race." Speaking before the South Deering Improvement Association, Beauharnais asked for "a march on the city hall with banners and rolling pins, to show Mayor Kennelly that we mean business."[13]

As tension seethed months after the move, a petition with 17,000 signatures asked that the police guard be withdrawn. As many as 1200 policemen had been doing round-the-clock duty at the project. Arrests were few despite the violence. When the police were accused of looking the other way they said the local magistrate would not convict anyway.

Meanwhile, peaceful citizens unwilling to participate in the violence found their property afire. Many others cooperated with the troublemakers out of fear. There were 165 fire alarms in the neighborhood from July 30, 1953, to April 10, 1954, 86 of them false. There were 41 fires in sheds, garages, and barns, 8 in the Trumbull Park project and 13 of "undetermined origin," 9 of them ascribed to arson or attempted arson.[14]

In May, 1954, after living behind barricaded windows for nine months, the Howards at the urging of the police moved out. "We were too nervous to eat or sleep," Howard said. The other Negro families held on. How long only time will tell.[15]

[13] *Op cit.,* November 2, 1953. See also Chap. XIV, p. 189.
[14] Chicago *Daily News,* April 10, 1954, p. 1.
[15] Shortly thereafter, Elizabeth Wood, the Chicago Housing Authority's able but beleaguered executive secretary, who had held out for a Negro's right to equality in public housing, was fired.

XI

MIAMI: A Case Study in Dynamite and Crackpots

BETWEEN June and December, 1951, a mysterious wave of dynamitings swept the Miami area like a freak tornado. Negro homes were blown up, synagogues blasted, a Catholic church attacked, and the population seized with a hysteria unparalleled in Florida's history. After twenty actual or attempted dynamitings the wave of violence moved northward, taking the lives of the state director of the National Association for the Advancement of Colored People, and his wife. It thereafter kept moving further north, devastating homes and terrorizing whites and Negroes in the whole southeastern area. More than fifteen additional incidents were recorded.

How the wave started, why it veered toward religious desecration and murder, and who all the guilty are may never be fully known. Despite a swarm of FBI men, months of investigating, a few perjury indictments, and a score of attractive rewards, the mystery remains unsolved. Yet when all the pieces of evidence are set into their grim jigsaw, the Miami episode suggests that it may never be entirely solved by the professional detective. Much of what happened in Miami may lie within the sphere of social pathology. The ugliest aspects of the story are the uncontrollable nature of the violence, the attacks upon houses of worship, and the rise of the crackpot as an important factor in the race issue.

The event which touched off the Florida dynamitings was the bombing of a housing project known as Carver Village in Edison Center, Miami. The underlying reason for the tensions before and after the violence was the effort of Negro families to find decent places in which to live.

Negro in-migration to Miami followed in the wake of the city's phenomenal rise from a town of 5000 in 1910 to a city of 250,000 in 1950. Between 1940 and 1950, Miami's white population more than doubled, while the Negro population rose by less than 10 per cent. The Negroes supplied the unskilled labor, the hotel workers, food handlers, and household servants. In the drive of the whites for housing the Negroes were steadily pushed out into areas eight to twenty miles from their workplaces. Only about 40,000 Negroes remained in Miami proper.

These Negroes were herded into a few dense slums that had no running water or inside toilets and were so termite-ridden that a gaping hole could be made by pressing a finger against a wall. Broken windows were replaced by makeshift boards, roofs leaked, and open holes in floors accommodated the rats. These older cabins brought upwards of $10 a week, while newer ones of three tiny rooms and kitchen brought $18.50 a week or more. Four to six of these cabins were jammed onto a single lot. Because of the prohibitive rents, doubling up with other families and taking in lodgers were common practices. While 11 persons to the acre is the normal density in Miami, Negroes were being crowded in at the rate of 200.

The high rents paid by the Negro would seemingly make him a good customer in this real-estate-minded area, except for the difficulty of obtaining land for Negro projects. Though 15,000 Negro families would be almost lost in the vast acreage subdivided during the abortive Florida boom, a Negro family is about as welcome in a Miami neighborhood as a Miami Beach Jew would be in a swank Fort Lauderdale club.

Miami is the center of a tropical resort belt which includes Miami Beach, Coral Gables, Hialeah and Fort Lauderdale. It is not a southern city by character or tradition. Unlike New Orleans and other southern cities in which Negroes and whites have lived along the same streets ever since Emancipation, Miami's patterns are new. The population consists of northerners and westerners as well as migrants from nearby southern communities. The northern and western migrants, persuaded by builders and realtors in their old communities that Negroes hurt property values, have imported these fears and carried neighborhood segregation into a region where segregation existed in everything but neighborhoods. Simultaneously, the many white migrants from Georgia and Alabama imposed the customary southern pattern of segregation on schools, churches, and transportation. The northerners accepted the southern brand of discrimination and the southerners reciprocally obliged by endorsing neighborhood segregation. The result was an odd merger of the old southern discriminations without the redeeming feature of interracial proximity and the new northern discriminations, uncompensated by northern legislative protections of civil and political rights.

The concentration of Jews in Miami Beach and their pressure for more space against the adjoining resort belt has generated local opposition to Jews as a group, making them a more convenient object of anti-Semitic expression. Miami has accepted the stereotype of the "city Jew": successful, fur-coated, arrogant, self-satisfied, and pushy.

Simultaneously, the Negroes' desperate search for housing has exposed them to the charge that they want to go where they do not belong, that they are challenging white supremacy. The Jew has gone too far, the Negro is trying to. The Miami area is a fertile field for professional bigots to whom the fanning of hatreds is stock-in-trade. Jew and Negro are brought into closer focus, and hate, frustration, and prejudice find a broader and even an interchangeable target.

The Miami area has had a long history of association with the Ku Klux Klan. The prime mover of the hate clique recently has been Grand Dragon Bill Hendrix. The Klan lost all its old primacy when the federal government bore down on its leaders. But it never was crushed completely, and in 1951 it still had considerable strength in Tallahassee, Tampa, Orlando, and in the Groveland area made famous by the case of Samuel Sheppard and Walter Lee Irvin, two Negro boys who had been convicted of raping a white woman. The case inspired the Klan to stampede through the Negro area, burning homes and terrorizing the community. After a reversal of the conviction, Sheppard was shot to death by Sheriff McCall, who had been escorting the prisoners handcuffed to their re-trial. The sheriff said they had tried to escape. Irvin, who survived McCall's bullets, said Sheppard was shot down in cold blood.

At the time of the Miami dynamite epidemic, Hendrix had announced his candidacy for Governor and was trying to pick up strength by inveighing against the Miami Jews. He proclaimed that if elected he would send "every bulldozer in the state road department down to Miami Beach to rip out all the sea walls and give the beaches back to the Gentiles." Hendrix's chief strength was not in the number of his followers, who were said to be less than 1000, but in his occasional effectiveness as a catalytic agent for the hates and obsessions of warped minds.

A few housing projects for Negroes have been built on the distant periphery of Miami. But the prohibitive prices, the distance from work, the high daily bus fares, the crowded backseat transportation, and the need for automobiles ultimately discouraged or bankrupted many of the home-buyers.

There was some hope for the Negro in public housing, but since no one wanted him to live nearby, the housing authority had trouble getting a site. The problem was finally met by selecting the Edison Center area in northwest Miami. The city then surrounded the new Negro housing project with a solid six-foot stone wall to separate the Negro area from that of the white. The walled-in area for Negroes is called "Liberty City."

All remained quiet until two Miami builders named Wiseheart and Bouvier decided to build a 400-unit FHA private project for whites on the white side of the wall, and a Negro project on the black side to be called Carver Village. Since the Negro project was inside the wall no one objected. But the white dwellings remained half empty, so the owners, sensing the larger profit in Negro rentals, decided to rent some of these units to the home-hungry Negroes.

The white residents retained William J. Pruitt, a Miami lawyer, to find ways of pushing the Negroes back inside the wall.

When the Negroes refused, the residents placed a three-quarter page advertisement in the Miami *Daily News* (owned by the interests of James M. Cox, 1920 Democratic presidential candidate), announcing an "Indignation Meeting" under the auspices of the Edison Center Board of Trade and the Edison Center Civic Association. Citizens of Miami were invited to join a "Mammoth Motorcade" which would parade around Carver Village and demonstrate "white supremacy."

The meeting was opened by a white minister who, after solemnly invoking God's aid, denounced Wiseheart and Bouvier as traitors to their race. Pruitt then declaimed that there was a "Divine Plan" which made one man black and one white. The people of the South, he cried, intended to "retain white supremacy until our dying days. . . ." A representative of the Miami *Daily News* passed out sample copies of the paper and took subscriptions, while the paper was praised from the floor for its support. (The vice-president of the paper explained to this writer later that he had hoped by accepting the ad to bring out the more "rational leaders." The Miami *Herald* turned down the ad.)

After the meeting, cars circled Carver Village, honking horns and flashing searchlights into Negroes' windows. A subscription man from the Miami *Daily News,* who had stopped his car in Edison Center, shot and wounded a Negro. He said the man was approaching him in a "threatening manner." The windshield of another Negro's car was shattered. But there were no other incidents.

In the weeks that followed, tensions mounted. They were kindled to fever point when the owners set up a new corporation with Negro directors to run Carver Village. Soon Ku Klux Klan literature began to appear throughout the area inveighing against Jews and Negroes. (Neither Bouvier nor Wiseheart was a Jew, though the rumor spread that both were.) But it appeared fairly clear that the Klan was merely trying to capitalize on the situation. The prime movers in the opposition at this time were not the Klansmen but the perturbed residents of Edison Center.

By the end of August everyone in Miami except the police knew there was to be trouble at Carver Village. The area buzzed with it. The faces of men revealed it. The newspapers warned of "the explosive situation" and of the "violence" that was coming. The Negroes were cautioned to get out as soon as possible. *Miami Life,* a sensational sheet run by one Ervin Clein and operating on the style of the anti-Negro newspapers in Detroit and Chicago, headlined "Race Riots May Be Caused By Greed." (Clein was a friend of Governor Fuller Warren and had been appointed shortly before to an important state commission.) In a mixed brew of prophecy and suggestion, Clein warned that if the Negroes were allowed to stay, "We will all be sitting on a keg of dynamite. . . . Miami may look for anything." He suggested zoning the project out, raising its taxes, and "endangering the mortgage investment of the insurance or other companies holding the FHA paper. . . . Oh! something must be done—and should. Or else look for trouble as the people in the Northwest section are seething and fearful."

Instead of policing the project to protect the Negroes' rights, Miami found a simpler solution. The five Miami city commissioners in mid-September ordered the new $2 million Carver Village project condemned for public use. They did not know the precise use but listed several possible uses: a park, public housing, county fairgrounds, rental to school teachers, playgrounds, a swimming pool, a stockade for city prisoners. When asked how brand new apartment houses could be used for a park or swimming pool, City Commissioner Bandel had a ready answer: "Knock 'em down." The public purpose finally arrived at was for office facilities, "in connection with the building and construction of its sewage disposal system and for other municipal purposes." The two million dollars it would cost to acquire Carver Village was $1,300,000 more than Miami then had in its treasury.

The decision to condemn solved nothing and only heightened the tensions. It riled some taxpayers who saw themselves burdened with a big expense, while Edison Center residents interpreted the move as meaning that the city officials were on their side—which indeed they were.

On September 22, at 2:11 A.M., and while police were supposed to be guarding against expected violence, three cases containing 300 pounds of dynamite were moved up to Carver Village. The houses were unoccupied except for one tenant then on vacation. The fuses were lit by a professional hand. Hundreds of windows were shattered and ten apartments were destroyed or damaged. The concussion was felt fifty blocks away. "It's a miracle no one was killed," said a Miami detective. "It was a well-planned job meant to be a warning rather than to kill."

Blasting Negroes out of places they should not be in is not new in the South. This device had been used only a short time before in Birmingham, Chattanooga, and elsewhere. Dynamite spreads terror, does its damage efficiently, and is more controllable than fire. The blasting aroused no serious public reaction. The feeling in fact was that Wiseheart and Bouvier deserved it, that now maybe the city would not need to condemn the property and spend taxpayers' money to keep Negroes inside the wall. Police Chief Headley said his investigation "pointed strongly to the conclusion" that communists were involved, and a "police source" whispered for publication that communists were even paying the Negro tenants to stay in the project. After the dynamiting, police went around the project handing out a host of summonses to Negroes for parking their cars in front of their own property.

Simultaneously, two Negroes in a truck, who had stopped off for a beer while delivering some dynamite to a construction job, were hauled into jail, held incommunicado, charged with being "hired for the job," grilled, threatened, submitted to lie-detector tests, and even after every detail of their story had been checked satisfactorily, detained behind bars.

Miami Life cited the indictment of Mrs. DeRose and the NAACP lawyer for conspiracy to "reduce real estate values" in Cicero, Illinois,[1] and urged the grand jury to "condemn and indict them in whatever manner that is within the power of the Grand Jury to do so." Every Negro tenant still remaining in Carver Village, it urged, should be subpoenaed before the grand jury. The president of the Dade County Property Owners' Association echoed this sentiment.

Up to September, 1951, Carver Village had been a dispute between Negroes and whites. The Jews were in no way involved except for the rumor that Wiseheart and Bouvier were Jews. About a week later, however, a mysterious flurry of anti-Semitic incidents began to sweep through Miami:

On October 1 (Rosh Hashana), the president of Tifereth Israel Northwide Jewish Center in Miami got an anonymous telephone call that the Center would be blown up. A hurried visit disclosed a sign three feet long with a swastika and K.K.K. emblem. It reviled Jews and "dirty Negroes."

On October 9 (eve of Yom Kippur) two sticks of dynamite were found at Temple Israel. A fuse had been lit but failed. A red cross and "K.K.K." were painted on the Temple's door.

On October 15 (first day of Succoth) two sticks of dynamite were found at the Miami Hebrew School and Congregation. The lighted fuse had failed to reach the dynamite.

A few weeks later, Jewish gravestones in Woodlawn Cemetery were defaced with bullets.

Some unexploded dynamite was also found in a high school and in the Dade County Court House.

All these incidents seemed amateurish, as distinguished from the expert job at Carver Village, but since they caused no major damage, they created no major stir. No one was arrested.

[1] See Chapter X.

In November, Chelsie J. Senerchia, the new mayor, and his city commission took office. Senerchia supported public housing and had made it a main issue in his campaign. Soon after election, Mrs. Senerchia got two telephone calls to the effect that "if we didn't get the Negroes out of Carver Village within a month they would bomb it to pieces." On November 30, just after the warning to Mrs. Senerchia and 69 days after the first dynamiting, a second blast shook Carver Village. Like the first, it was timed for ten minutes after 2:00 A.M. Twenty-two sticks of dynamite were again excellently placed, professionally discharged, and $22,000 in damage caused. Concrete rubble flew fifty yards. The police were not on hand. Police Chief Headley explained to the press: "It's obviously an attempt to create racial discord. It closely follows the known pattern of Moscow-directed propaganda, the idea being to foment violence and thereby gain U.S. dateline stories for use in their own newspapers."

After the second blast, City Commissioner H. Leslie Quigg announced a simple solution. He called upon Headley to warn the Negroes to move out of Carver Village. David Hawthorne, spokesman for the county real estate group, concurred. "Someone ought to do something about the situation," he cried. "I'm afraid there's going to be bloodshed." Obviously the thing to do was give in to the dynamiters so there would be no more trouble.

By this time, however, emotion was running high in the Negro quarter. Some Negroes had left Carver Village, fearing for their children's lives. But most decided to stick it out. They charged that the police could have prevented the blasts if they had wanted to; that they knew who the culprits were; and that in fact there was a police car in the project at the time of the first blast. They accused the police of harrying them with threats and summonses. Some of the Negroes applied for gun licenses. The police proceeded to disarm them, license or no license. When policemen tried to arrest two Negroes in Edison Center for carrying guns, a riot almost followed and Negroes forced the police to release the prisoners. Dade County Sheriff James B. Henderson thereupon asked Governor Fuller Warren to call out the National Guard because "these were inflammatory conditions here, with Negroes carrying guns. We don't want a repetition here of race riots such as they have had elsewhere." The implication was that it was the Negroes who were the real menace and the militia was needed to "take care of them."

On Sunday morning, December 2, the day after Commissioner Quigg's statement that Headley should have the tenants moved out by force, Carver Village was dynamited for the third time. There was no damage this time, and the blast would have aroused no more protest than the other two. But that same day there were two other amateurish blasts which finally shook the community out of its lethargy.

One took place in the southwest section of Miami, the other at the Miami Hebrew School and Congregation. Forty-four of the school's stained-glass memorial windows were shattered. The blasting of the synagogue now put the violence on the front pages of the nation's press. The Miami *Herald,* the only newspaper in the area to criticize the inaction of the police, wrote: "Common ordinary prudence dictated that the police department maintain a round-the-clock patrol of Carver Village. The terrorists knew the inadequacy of the Miami Police Department."

Jewish as well as non-Jewish elements were now aroused to more positive action. A group of citizens led by Councilman Burnett Roth of Miami Beach, which had organized a Coordinating Committee Against the Bombings, demanded protection of all synagogues. The Anti-Defamation League and its director, Gil Balkin, assumed a leading role. A committee of rabbis marched on police headquarters to register their protest.

After a heated session with law-enforcement officers representing the Miami-Coral Gables area, Coral Gables Safety Director W. G. Kimbrough told the Jewish delegation that starting midnight Sunday in Coral Gables "each place will have a 24-hour guard, regardless of cost."

Less than a week later, Kimbrough got a call from a man who said politely he had tried to reach him three times. "We're going to blow the synagogue up," the voice said. Kimbrough got out of bed, rushed to the police station, and ordered a policeman to Rabbi Morris Skop's Coral Gables Jewish Center. Kimbrough's man watched until exactly 7:00 A.M and left. No sooner had he gone than an automobile drove by and a stick of dynamite with a lighted fuse was hurled at the Center. The loaded stick hit a tree before it landed, dislodging the cap.

On December 23 there was another call to Kimbrough's home. "To show we aren't prejudiced against the Jews, we plan to celebrate Christmas by bombing a Catholic church. You have nothing to worry about. We wish you a merry Christmas." Police searched the Catholic church in Coral Gables and found nothing. On Sunday morning a stick of dynamite was hurled at the door of St. Peter's and Paul's Church in Miami. The fuse had smoldered and gone out.

The bombing of the church strengthened the campaign of the Jews just as the bombing of the synagogue had strengthened the Negroes. Police Chief Headley dismissed the incident with a statement that it was an "amateur job." But the public was becoming aroused. The Miami *Herald* aptly summed up the now general feeling: "Miami is afraid, disgraced and ashamed."

But the violence could seemingly no longer be stemmed, not even by a now alerted police force. After another advance warning to Kimbrough there was another blast at the Hialeah Springs Community Center. This was the fifteenth case in the epidemic.

Miami was by now developing an acute case of dynamite jitters. School boards of all denominations were demanding guards for their children. Attendance at Sunday schools had dropped by 50 per cent. Police switchboards were kept busy answering calls inspired by firecrackers or backfiring. A bridegroom caused a near panic in Hialeah when he celebrated his wedding by shooting off an aerial bomb. A driver lit a match in his car only to be rushed at by police with a machine gun, who thought he was about to light a fuse. Anonymous calls by pranksters and crackpots added to the confusion. A Protestant minister publicly offered his whole congregation to guard synagogues, while the Jewish War Veterans voted to throw a cordon around all synagogues in the Miami area. The sheriff offered to deputize the veterans and floodlights were thrown upon the synagogues while the veterans waited for the dynamiters to appear.

By this time, too, the press (including the finally-aroused Miami *Daily News*) was hot with columns and editorials denouncing the violence. No less than thirteen offers of bounty were posted, ranging from $5000 by the cities of Miami and Miami Beach to $50 offered by the Miami Beach Optimists. Simultaneously, a host of FBI men descended upon Miami with instructions to "turn the dogs loose." With this, violence in Miami ceased.

But if the chain of explosions was now checked in Miami, the spark seemed to have got through to the North. Florida Negroes, it had been said, were getting out of hand. The Carver Village Negroes were only one example. Some whites blamed the Negroes for the nationwide publicity on the bombings, not the kind of news that attracts tourists. The sentiment aroused for Sheppard and Irvin, who had been sentenced to death and ordered re-tried, was another example of Negro orneriness. NAACP activities by northern meddlers was resented widely.

On Christmas night, the sixteenth incident in the chain of violence occurred in Mims, Florida. A dynamite charge exploded under the house of Harry T. Moore, state director of the NAACP, killing him instantly. His wife died of wounds a few days later. Moore had criticized Sheriff McCall for shooting down Sheppard and Irvin. The murder was deplored in Florida for a short time, then forgotten. In fact, a few weeks after the Moore murder, Grand Dragon Hendrix himself was invited to address the annual conference of the politically potent Florida sheriffs at Daytona Beach (an event which of itself should sober those who feel that his was a lone whoop in the wilderness). The Grand Dragon told the sheriffs he deplored "the furor which had arisen over the Groveland case (Sheppard and Irvin), and the Harry T. Moore murder." He said Moore "wasn't just a Negro, he was a Communist and a troublemaker in this state. The whole commotion over the Groveland case and Moore's murder was inspired by the Communists." Sheriff McCall was in the audience. He was warmly applauded and offered the chairmanship of the sheriffs' association.

The invitation to candidate Hendrix was reported by the Florida press as straight news, and neither the public nor the press seemed shocked by it. None of the sheriffs protested Hendrix's statements— in fact they let it be known that too many of them had been troubled with problems of "radicals" and did not want any "liberal" for governor.

The epidemic of violence continued, touching one city after another in rapid succession. Two days after Moore's death an attempt was made to dynamite a railroad engine at Rome, Georgia.

Two days after that, two men set a dynamite charge near a Negro social club.

The same day, in Crossville, Alabama, a cross was burned and dynamite exploded to scare off an antiliquor campaigner about to reveal violations of the liquor laws.

On January 3, 1952, a bomb was exploded in the middle of a street in Atlanta.

On January 9, 24 sticks of dynamite were exploded under the home of Hugh Bentley of Phenix City, Alabama. Bentley, an antivice crusader and an officer of the Russell County Betterment Association, had launched a vice clean-up campaign. One of his children was hurled 30 feet by the explosion.

A few days later an explosion in Cottonwood, Alabama, wrecked the home of a convict's wife who was said to have figured in an investigation into parole activities. Her children were injured and her three-room house virtually demolished. The culprit was arrested and later confessed he got the idea from reading about the bombing of Bentley's home in Phenix City.

Next, in Pikesville, Kentucky, the automobile of a United Mine Workers organizer was destroyed. The home of a Negro physician in Cairo, Illinois, was dynamited on January 29. A grudge blast near Norfolk, Virginia, wrecked the Sycamore Inn, leased to a bootlegger, while a fire bomb was thrown into a synagogue window as far north as Philadelphia. The rapid succession of blasts now began to be featured in the nation's press as something shockingly unusual.

As the violence moved northward, panic and hysteria moved with it. Florida continued in a state of jitters. Telephone calls to police continued to jam switchboards. The Rev. G. E. Hodges of Jacksonville called the local press and announced he had received a call threatening to dynamite his church "in the same way as happened in Mims, Florida," unless Hodges stopped his "strong preaching." The minister laid the threat to "Miami communists" and shouted: "I've had right smart things to say about them in my preaching for the past several months." Addressing 2000 listeners who had gathered in response to the publicity, he dared the communists to speak up from the audience. "They don't have the guts to do nothing," he said after a dramatic pause. Twenty armed men then guarded his church waiting for the communists to show up. The Florida press gave the clergy-man's challenge front page treatment.

A deranged lady threatened to leap from a Florida hotel balcony because the communists were after her. An audience watching a basketball game in Coral Gables coliseum was evacuated after an anonymous call warning that the place was wired for bombing. More offers of rewards continued pouring in and FBI men combed race-tracks, beaches, and movie houses for dynamiters.

But as the season got under way on the Florida coast, the swarm of tourists, undaunted in their desire for fun or rest, superimposed itself upon the troubled atmosphere. The violence had been stopped in Miami just in advance of the season, and it looked as though business would not suffer too badly. The new tourist invasion submerged the fears, veered the interests, and changed the conversation. Airplanes carrying undulating streamers across the skies promised tasty dishes in the restaurants and the best of Broadway's comics in the night clubs. Rabbis, ministers, and civic leaders, still inveighing against the dynamiters, found their audiences getting sparse and bewildered. The boom of dynamite receded as the boom of business rose to its seasonal crescendo.

In this chronology one must grope for clues and inferences. The Carver Village episode resembled in some respects the outbreaks in Cicero, Chicago, and Detroit, in that all grew out of the effort to keep Negroes from filtering into white sections. There was the same use of the "civic associations" to consolidate resistance and stimulate fears that the Negroes would soon swarm in like locusts and ruin the neighborhoods; the same lack of cooperation by the police, the same fanning of tensions by sections of the press.

But while there has been a fringe in Chicago led by Beauharnais and his White Circle League stirring up trouble against scapegoat targets such as "Jews," "radicals," and "intellectuals," his efforts never could be credited with being the big wheel. The situation is different in Florida and the South where terrorism has had a long history in cross-burnings, floggings, tarrings and featherings, whippings, and occasional lynchings. The principal motivation for these outbursts has been the effort to maintain "white supremacy" and keep Negroes "in their place." The issue, like most issues, has been fought by rational and irrational people and along both rational and irrational lines. It has been accompanied by political pressuring, lawful action, and lawlessness. When violence has been used, the participants have included not only those who think they are fulfilling substantial justice by holding the Negroes down but also adolescents in search of fun, misguided adults who fear loss of realty values, pseudo-patriots lured by the cry of "communism," and the easily gullible drawn by excitement from the masses into the mobs.

The chain of violence in Miami bears the imprint of the fanatic and the mentally disabled. These are the folk to whom the line between right and wrong is blurred. Their frailties and degrees of tolerance vary but their hates or obsessions either remain impacted or, when activated, exhaust themselves in harmless episodes. Danger arises when their hates and obsessions acquire moral justification, and they begin to identify their own distorted values with those of the community. Unable to focus on rational means of achieving their aims, they seek retributive justice through the easiest means at their disposal. These people are grist for the mills of men like Hendrix.

The Carver Village dynamitings (at least the first two) were motivated, as in Chicago and Detroit, by the effort to keep the Negroes from moving where they were not wanted. When business and civic associations, portions of the press and church, police, and public officials created an atmosphere in which a Negro's right to live where he chose became a wrong—a wrong for which neither police nor officials could find a legal remedy—it seemed to Edison Center residents that it was justifiable to use force to frighten the Negroes out of the section. Reprehensible as the dynamitings were, they were professionally handled and designed to evict rather than to kill. The dynamiters probably felt they were merely carrying out the will of the neighborhood and were not violating community mores or offending police officials. No doubt they resented the amateur irresponsibles who were horning in on the show and causing the forces of law and public opinion to bear down upon violence of all sorts, including the professionals' own brand of "constructive" violence.

Once the Carver Village dynamitings were under way, and the community had acquiesced in the promiscuous use of dynamite as a weapon of terror, the involvement of the weaker layer of the community was inevitable. The community then got more than it had bargained for, but that was the cost of the alliance.

As in riots, the target could not be prevented from broadening to embrace other objects of local hatred—Jews, Catholics, radicals, reformers, squealers, union organizers, and anyone who could be conveniently fitted into the category of "enemy." The amateurish throwing of dynamite, the bizarre signs threatening Jews, the anonymous warnings, all follow the prescribed pattern of irresponsibles seeking a butt for their obsessions, a target for their hates, an outlet for their frustrations. The recent addition of the "communist" to the catalogue of targets is natural. The label serves as a contemporary image of the Jew, and may include the militant Negro, labor leader, libertarian, dissenter, radical, the unsubmissive, the different, and the generally disliked.

Grand Dragon Hendrix and his type become dangerous when their actions are given the authority of popular sanction and official acquiescence. A Hendrix can then expand his circle to include the credulous and the weak-minded in search of leadership. He not only inspires them to bizarre activities but gives implied sanction for what might otherwise be reprehensible. The socially immoral action becomes a right, a public benefit, a duty.

The sanction of mischief by the press, the police, or public officials can thus set off a whole chain of irrational actions by those on the margin of normal society. In that sense, when violence or crime ensues, they are responsible for the result.

While there has been considerable study of the actions of crowds and mobs,[2] there is less known of the equally suggestible and contagious quality of individual irrational action. Yet in some respects, though the acting individuals may not be present in groups, a number of the same symptoms seem to occur. Here, too, the heterogeneous may be "swamped by the homogeneous, and the unconscious qualities obtain the upper hand . . . by various processes an individual may be brought into such a condition that, having entirely lost his conscious personality, he obeys all the suggestions of the operator who has deprived him of it, and commits acts in utter contradiction with his

[2] One of the classics is Gustave LeBon, *The Crowd: A Study of the Popular Mind*. London, Ernest Benn, Ltd., ed. 17, 1930.

character and habits."[3] The irrational person and the marginal mind may transform suggested ideas into acts. The suggestion of the leader which may be strong enough to move him to action in a crowd may not suffice to move him when acting apart from the crowd. The approval or even apparent acquiescence of officials, the sanction of the more respected, the inflammatory writings of the press, are all forces which can reach the irrational person and fire him to individual action.

The role that modern mass communications may play in touching off the abnormal is further illustrated by the frequent reaction to publicity about prominent persons. Most of those publicized receive some crank mail. The anonymous writers are generally harmless and fear punishment. But among them are also the dangerous. Those in whom the line between right and wrong is shadowy can be induced to commit violence when the respected agencies of the community authorize or inspire it. The Negro and the Jew, traditional objects of abnormal fears, biases and obsessions, are easy victims.[4]

[3] *Ibid.*, pp. 32, 34.

[4] On a purely speculative basis this writer suggests that the murder of Arnold Shuster, a young Jew who spotted Willie Sutton, the nationally famous bank robber, may illustrate this point. Sutton had been given a big play in the nation's press, and had become a hero to many mentalities. After Shuster turned in Sutton, he received anonymous threats and calls, but the New York City police failed to guard him. He was shot to death by still-unidentified killers.

Another New York City crime might also be cited. A Jewish lawyer was featured in the press as having fallen heir to a $200,000 legacy from a client, an elderly gentile woman. In a will contest he was charged by the natural heirs with winning the legacy by unduly influencing his client. He was followed to his door by two men, and shot. When a jury acquitted one of the men accused of the attack, the judge called the jurors "naïve" for believing the defendant's alibi.

In both cases the victims were Jews whose acts might be considered "typically Jewish." Both were the subjects of wide publicity and the acts of neither were popular, i.e., "squealing" in one case, and "pirating a fortune from a gentile lady," in the other. In both cases the police could find no motive.

If the same sequence of violence as was generated in the Miami area can be started elsewhere by a newspaper reaction, it may yet prove possible to commit murder by publicity. Indeed, in a recent feud between two newspaper men, one of them, a well-known columnist, charged that the other, a Jew, was a "commie," and gave his home address. The result was a series of threats, anonymous telephone calls, and other forms of molestations by the feeble-minded.

It is significant that just as the tide of violence in Miami had risen with public attitudes of support, it began to subside with the rise of moral indignation and the reassertion of the community's insistence upon law enforcement. To restrain outbreaks of lawless action in areas of stress, therefore, it is essential to understand not only the nature of the actor but the nature of the community itself; the officials who set the measure of right and wrong and the respected agencies of public opinion, particularly the press.

XII

HOUSING AND THE SUBURBAN MILIEU

THE TENSION, fear, and bias afflicting American communities stem from a number of causes, one of the most important of which is the housing problem. This problem is more than the slum, the housing shortage, or the high cost of plumbing.

The housing problem is not enough housing and not the right kind; bad housing or no housing at all; houses too large or too small; the damp wall or vermin; the endless trek to and from work, school, or grocery; the four flights of stairs, or the desperate need to get one's mother-in-law a separate flat; the unbearable rent, or the exodus of an industry that leaves you jobless; the strange-looking neighbors or the hostile ones; inability to pay the tax bill or the case-hardened mortgagee; uncertainty of tenancy or the hazards of ownership; the company landlord who thinks you're a troublemaker, or your tenant downstairs to whom all landlords are anathema; absence of children your daughter's age, or the bad climate for your asthma; the quest for privacy, or the child that died on the highway; the tensions, weariness, monotony, boredom; the smoke, soot, smog; the traffic; crime and delinquency; the longing for trees, room, play space, or change of scene; the noise, smell, heat, or darkness.

Housing, in fact, is one of America's biggest headaches and one of the underlying reasons behind many of its discontents.

The word "home," one of the symbols of the problem, embodies the deepest sentiments of American folklore. Home is the seat of one's leisure hours, security, memories, where the family is raised, where hopes are built, where treasured possessions are kept and good friends are fed. It is the place one lives and dies in. Or, as Robert

137

Frost says, home is the place where when you get there, they've got to take you in.

Unable to solve their problems completely, the majority of bread-winners try to merge dream with reality by buying their homes. Others hope to buy a house some day.

The decision to own is one of life's major decisions. It represents not only a desire to achieve housing peace but also an emotional experience, a vision that is always realty but not always reality. It bespeaks freedom and security; it is tied up with pride, confidence, and the search for popularity or position. It connotes fun and gaiety, privacy without loneliness. It nourishes ambition and grants relief from the pressure of daily routines. It is the mysterious gadget that promises to resolve life's frustrations and conciliate one's desires.

In its permanence the owner sees the stabilization of his own values; in the firmness of its foundation he follows his own roots into the community; in the warmth of its fireplace he grasps the deeper attachments and inner comforts for which he has long aspired; in its completeness he sees the completeness of his own wants and needs; in its ownership he sees release from the fears and uncertainties of life. The two-bedroom house on 800 square feet of land amid hundreds of other two-bedroom houses on 800 square feet of land has become the post-frontier symbol of what we call "the American way of life," the "vine and fig tree" of the Bible and Thomas Jefferson, transposed to the industrial scene.

For those who can afford the risk, buying a house is wise. The feeling of security, false as it often is, can be as important as security itself. But for many individuals, the investment is a hazardous com-mitment entailing the delivery of one's savings and the pledge of his name to a debt two to four times his annual wage. It means pay-ment of 20 to 40 per cent of his weekly earnings. Failure to pay a single installment may bring foreclosure, eviction, and despair.

Home ownership has thus become a complex of brick and fantasy, security and hazard, fact and fiction, functional fulfillment and in-adequacy. Thanks to government propaganda, magazines, and realtors, it has also become a dream-world of magic casements opening up on well-stocked larders, of mythical hearths and carpet-slippers under unmortgaged roofs, a sure cure for malaise and a lasting anchorage from church-aisle to the grave. Model home displays are launched by personalities ranging from chorus girls to cabinet members. No president of recent years has failed to lend his name to the cause, while newspapers, magazines, and brochures continue to play up the great American dream with a skill that makes even the wariest capitulate.

In many ways, the house has not changed much since Neolithic man discovered the flint axe and adze.[1] The porch has often been omitted for the sake of economy, there is still the same pitched roof, the same 700–800 square feet of space, and the same warm, glowing fireplace. But there are two important factors that have recently come upon the scene. The first is the change in the nature of tenure. This has come about since the rise of the modern mortgage system. One no longer buys a house today but an equity in one; not a fee simple but a fee conditional, not "to have and to hold" forever but so long as one can afford the mortgage payments; not a heritage for one's children but a conditional right to possession.

A second factor is social deterioration—and the aspect of social deterioration most frightening of all is the threatened infiltration into the neighborhood of the wrong kind of neighbors. This fear is real, is reflected in the estimates of the homeowner, his friends, the real estate appraisers and lenders who mortgage the house, the government which insures the mortgage. The factor of social deterioration functions with unremitting pressure whether the house is costly or cheap, well preserved or shabby, mortgage-bound or mortgage-free. It is no longer the type of house but the type of neighborhood which reflects social standing. This is now true in America's little towns as in its Middletowns and Bigtowns. Fine looking homes in Chicago may be still as fine looking but are considered blighted when Negroes or other minorities live in the neighborhood. The once aristocratic old east-end section of Muncie ("Middletown"), Indiana, has yielded to the new, more fashionable subdivision on the other side of town "to which the ambitious matrons of the city are removing their families."[2]

In city after city, status depends on whether one lives on Swank Street or Blight Alley, and in suburb after suburb it depends on the

---

[1] Charles Abrams, *The Future of Housing*. New York, Harper & Brothers, 1946, p. 20 and photograph opposite p. 22.

[2] Robert S. and Helen M. Lynd, *Middletown in Transition*. New York, Harcourt, Brace and Company, 1937, p. 82.

status the suburb denotes. On Long Island, a man's status is plain when he lives in a public housing project or in Garden City. In Beverly Hills, California, certain street addresses tell whether the scenario writer earns $250 or $2500 a week. "One can no longer count on being known for what one is, but must declare visibly and substantially the symbols of one's class belonging. . . . The neighborhood left behind by this kind of competition for status may still remain desirable, but only to the families whose psychological standard of living and aspiring is lower."[3]

Status has become more emphasized than ever since the rise of the suburb where social deterioration now affects value even more than physical deterioration does. Though Americans have always striven for vertical mobility, the emphasis had been on income or capital and the social limelight it generated. They made every effort to protect that status. But with the rise of income and the leveling of some social and economic groups, a different pressure set in for new marks of prestige and status. The neighborhood one lived in became a main index and new protections had to be devised to resist any assault upon it. The suburb and the quest for status are shaping the American personality of the future as the frontier once shaped the American personality of the past.

The Suburb and the Suburban Personality

In the twenty-five years preceding the end of World War II, no less than 75 per cent of new developments for owner-occupancy were built in peripheral sections.[4] While the big cities (excluding their suburban communities) were getting less than a third of the population growth between 1940 and 1950 and all other areas (rural regions, small cities, and villages far from metropolitan areas) got barely a fifth, suburbs jumped in population 35.5 per cent. In ten years, well over nine million additional residents moved into fringe communities. Nearly half the recent national population rise was in the city outskirts.

The big cities managed to hold their proportionate share of the

[3] John P. Dean, *Home Ownership—Is it Sound?*. New York, Harper & Brothers, 1945, p. 144, citing Federal Housing Administration *Underwriting Manual*, Revised 1938, Sec. 1379(2).

[4] U. S. Department of Commerce, Bureau of the Census, *Sixteenth Census Reports*, Vol. IV, *Housing*, Part 1. Washington, 1943.

total population—about 33 per cent—and a large portion of their population increase was being supplied by minorities. Baltimore suburbs claimed 73 per cent more residents in ten years while the city itself grew only by 10.5 per cent. Fringe communities around Galveston, Ogden, Oklahoma City, Washington, Sacramento, San Diego, the San Francisco-Oakland area, and the Norfolk-Portsmouth area all had gains of more than 100 per cent. Houston and Dallas increased by well over 50 per cent.

These suburbs were the answer to a number of thorny problems and disaffections flowing out of industrialization and the rise of big cities. The nineteenth-century city had been built up to suit the endowments of the horse. How far he could draw a tram marked the distance of neighborhoods from workplaces, and how far and fast a pair of horses could pull a fire engine determined the boundaries of the neighborhood. It was the era of equine city planning, equine streets, equine architecture, equine industrialization. It was equine even in its effect upon personality, for it slowed the human pace to that of the horse. In a world rapidly yielding to the smoke of bituminous coal and the noise and stench of crowded life, the horse remained the surviving link to the pastoral environment from which man had emerged only a few generations before.

The city had many interests, but it was big, cold, impersonal—and humbling. It was also discordant, ear-splitting, dangerous, ill-adapted to man's leisure, unsatisfying to his yearnings for greenery, quiet, calm. With the fast train and automobile, new sections opened up five or ten miles from the city's center, but still within reach of the factories and shopping centers. The automobile which made the suburb possible simultaneously made the city less bearable. It added to the fumes, made travel within the city difficult, and produced new dangers for children.[5]

The suburb in an expanding world met the struggle for space, privacy, and the nostalgia for country life. Land was cheaper here, too; a family could get a house on two lots with trees, a garden, and play space for children. Here was the place to find a home and the bundle of rights, dreams, satisfactions, and illusions that come wrapped with the deed.

---

[5] More than 6000 children are injured annually on New York City streets, according to the National Safety Council.

Additional city growth pushed the suburbs farther and farther away, isolating them from the city. Although the man kept some contacts with the city during working hours, the wife saw it less and less, particularly as movies, radio, television, and chainstore shopping made the suburb more self-contained. Reduction of the size of the house also dispossessed the father- or mother-in-law who had been the traditional contact with the previous era and with the city. When the television set was moved in, the house got even smaller. But all this contributed to further confinement within the home and further withdrawal from the city.

Houses in the suburbs were bought largely by "little people"— skilled and semiskilled workers, clerks, small merchants, young professionals, people comprising America's great middle class. Their contact with the city, its culture and civilization was now *en passant*. At 5:30 every evening they would be disgorged from factories and offices, herded into commuters' trains and buses, and dispatched to waiting wives who would lead them to their television sets. Here, as in the local cinemas, they would meet the mythical characters properly glorified or depraved to fit the elementary responses at the extremes of human emotion. For them the city was the crucible, the suburb the cooling dish. Some had come straight from the cities with the conscious or subconscious wish to escape from neighborhoods where they once had brief contacts with Negroes, Jews, and Italians in shops and schools. Others had heard so many remarks about the city's undesirables—the "dirty Negro," the "money-grubbing Jews," the "knife-carrying Italian"—that they were occasionally surprised to encounter "good" Jews, "nice" Negroes, or "gentle" Italians. Lacking regular communication with these strange characters, these suburban dwellers had little opportunity for education through personal experience.

The Jew had long served as the symbol of city life anyway. He was the city capitalist, and the city communist, shrewd and sharp, rootless, feared, and envied. "The symbolic projection of hatred of the city onto the Jews allows the prejudiced person to destroy the city and to escape the city, and at the same time to keep it and live in it."[6]

[6] Arnold Rose, "Anti-Semitism's Root in City-Hatred," *Race Prejudice and Discrimination*. (Arnold Rose, ed.). New York, Alfred A. Knopf, Inc., 1948, p. 507.

The alien immigrant also became involved with the city and its evils, while the once rural Negro, now concentrated and moving en masse, changed overnight into an urban stereotype: bold, uninhibited, brutish, pushy, and dangerous. As he became more visibly numerous, the dangers of his presence increased as well, and so did the suburbanites' fear of the city and its life.

The suburbanite, in contrast, became the prototype of what is known as "American." Suburban residents were considered "homogeneous" not only by home builders, banks, and the government, but by each other. The quarry of salesmen, they soon became the quarry of the speculative builder, of the rumor-monger and the hate-hawker.

Owning one's home was a badge of social prestige. The 10 per cent down payment delivered a higher social status along with a house. The rough rule is that a man can afford to buy a home costing twice his annual income; the suburbanites generally pledged themselves for a little more. Although the owners were in debt, the houses looked free and independent. The chaste little villas were paid for with $1000 down payments and a 25-year mortgage of $8000 to $10,000, which with other carrying charges and maintenance regularly sapped a quarter or more of the buyers' incomes. This group represented the great market for mortgaged refrigerators, mortgaged vacuum cleaners, mortgaged washing machines, and mortgaged cars. But the little white door, the quaint blue shutters, the brass knocker, the blue half-tiled bathroom, and the unfinished attic had an honorific elegance of their own. These were all good people who sought privacy and a roof over their heads. They composed the readership of the home magazines and the Sunday supplements—suburbs were never good library communities, for the "public library is a little too democratic for them."[7]

Withdrawal from the city altered the suburbanite's outlook, his friends, attitudes, and interests. In the city, relationships may have been more distant, but he had been able to choose his friends on the basis of a common interest—in business, music, art, theater, or sports. He could also withdraw from friends he didn't want to see and enjoy greater privacy in the things he wanted to do. If he made an enemy, it was not devastating. He would be a New Deal Democrat with impunity.

[7] Harlan Paul Douglass, *The Suburban Trend*. New York, The Century Company, 1925, p. 202.

But in the suburb he felt the proximity of people as he felt the proximity of weather. He found himself drawn into circles he might have shunned as a city man. He saw more of the bridge tables, heard more talk about radio and TV, the material virtues of icebox cake and the refrigerator it was made in, or the immaterial virtues of someone else's son or daughter. Gossip, a minor factor in city life, became the daily bread of conversation. Many housewives relaxed at the telephone as soon as the breakfast dishes were washed. This pattern was bearable and even pleasant for many. The city had too much talent to tax one's mind. It was above them and beyond them. Here they could find people of a more common stamp. If they were not alike in their interests when they arrived, they soon got that way.

One of the common threads that bound the suburbanites together was not culture or tradition, or civic pride or national welfare. It was neighborhood dignity. The magazines told them so repeatedly and so did the realtors, the neighborhood associations, and even the government housing officials. Suburban groups had a sanctuary to protect. They knew that blight of any kind has an eroding quality that engulfs whole neighborhoods and might affect their investments. Neighborhood dignity became synonymous with neighborhood homogeneity, while neighborhood homogeneity gave rise to a concerted effort to keep out the "wrong people" and the "foreign element."

In the pre-automobile century some groups lived in voluntary ghettos, but there were also mixed formations which represented a variety of cultures, languages, colors, interests, tastes, and idiosyncrasies. The tendency over the long run was to blend interests and to subordinate biases. In contrast, the suburban community strove for a pattern of one-type occupancy, to be established with private and governmental encouragement. It was to be preserved against inharmonious intrusions by compact and even by law.

Among the first to play up class in the suburb were the railroads. In 1905, the Central Railroad of New Jersey published a monthly magazine to entice the city-dweller toward the periphery. One issue read:

One of the most encouraging features of suburban growth is the high class of population that the suburb draws to itself. It seems to sift out the most desirable element in the city population, leaving the superficial and the tawdry to continue its cooped up life.

The truth is that there is nothing about the suburbs that could possibly appeal to the unsubstantial element of city dwellers. To such, suburban life appears tame and uninviting. But for the man who wants to put as many leagues as possible between his home and the Tenderloin, to keep his wife and children apart from the contaminating sights and influences of a metropolis, to rear a family altar which shall be worthy of the sacred name of home, there can be no question but that the *suburb is the place.*[8]

In the next issue:

Suburban society—I use the word in its real sense—is not only more available, but contains few of the undesirable elements of city environment.[9]

And a still later issue carried an article entitled "The Movement of the 'Smart Set' Towards the Suburbs."

A spate of new magazines found the suburban personality rich bait for their lines. In an age in which mass production demands mass advertising to reach a mass market, mass circulation became imperative. Mass circulation is gained not by rising above the level of the masses, but by reaching down to it—not by challenging its biases but by catering to and even stimulating them.

For fifty cents Americans could now buy one of a series of magazines filled with colorgravures of prize homes (building costs omitted) which only a fraction of them could afford. But if they could not buy they could dream. And economy menus were simultaneously supplied to console the dreamer. The "middle class" was told to be homogeneous, not mix with the rich or poor, and to use "restrictions" to keep the "wrong people" out.

The suburbs attract real people because their appeal is wide. They offer permanence. . . . The city seems to have a place for the children of the very rich and the very poor, but none for those between . . . choose your suburb carefully. Real estate experts will give you advice on all sorts of material matters—restrictions, taxes, assessments, and all that kind of thing. Use your own power of observation on some other points that may tell you whether or not this is your town. . . . You will fit more easily into a town where there are not too great extremes of wealth. . . . Pick a town

[8] *The Suburbanite*, A Monthly Magazine for Those Who Are and Those Who Ought to be Interested in Suburban Homes. Published by Passenger Department, Central Railroad of New Jersey, vol. III, no. 1, April, 1905, p. 16.

[9] G. G. Given, "Getting Acquainted in the Suburbs," *ibid*, May, 1905, p. 8.

where most of the "nicest" children go to public school. Aside from the expense, it means a more homogenous place.[10]

Home ownership was repeatedly referred to as the American ideal (suggesting of course that renting is low class). It was intimated that Washington's ragged troops had bled and died for this cause:

> The American house of today is also a house which clearly expresses the fundamental American aspirations and ideals about the dignity of every man, which are still pretty much the same as they were in 1776.[11]

In a later issue, *House Beautiful* began a campaign against foreign architects of the Bauhaus school, punctuating the attack with hints of the sinister and possibly communistic nature of foreign art.[12]

"Exclusiveness" and restrictions were coupled in another magazine with patriotism and "The Golden Rule":

> "Nowhere is this doctrine [The Golden Rule] better illustrated than in the ten-year-old community of River Oaks in Houston, Texas. Handsome homes, blending well with each other, and all equally well cared for, they face the future free from possible blight. Neighborhood restrictions protect them from the fate of once-fine neighborhoods now become "the wrong side of the tracks."[13]

In the February, 1937, issue of *Good Housekeeping,* a "shield of honor" was given to ten "exclusive suburban communities." The importance of class, the difference between "right or wrong groups," and the qualification of "social standing" were carefully emphasized. The article asked: "Does the property have restrictions? What are they? Proper restrictions are a great asset." Another article refers to the importance of "a restricted residential environment."[14] The next month *Good Housekeeping* emphasized the importance of "protection of type of residences . . . maintenance and enforcement of the restrictions."[15] And another article illustrated houses in "Roland

[10] Elizabeth Orford, "There's No Substitute for the Suburbs," *The American Home,* vol. XX, no. 5, Oct., 1938, pp. 4, 67.

[11] Jean Murray Bangs, "How American Is Your Way of Living," *House Beautiful,* vol. 92, no. 9, September, 1950, pp. 81, 161.

[12] Elizabeth Gordon, "The Threat to the Next America," *ibid.,* April, 1953, p. 126.

[13] "Personality in a Community," *Good Housekeeping,* vol. 106, no. 3, March, 1938, p. 48 (unsigned).

[14] Helen Koues, "Good Building Materials," *ibid.,* vol. 104, no. 2, March, 1937, pp. 50–51.

[15] Helen Koues, "Beauty in Community Planning," *ibid.,* April, 1937, pp. 51, 235.

Park a beautiful restricted suburb of Baltimore."[16] One had only to see these communities to sense what the restrictions meant—the "wrong kind of people."

Realtors and realty boards followed the line. A professor at New York University quotes President Hoover's welcome to the President's Conference on Building and Home Ownership:

> Those immortal ballads "Home Sweet Home," "My Old Kentucky Home," and "The Little Gray Home in the West," were not written about tenements or apartments. They are the expressions of racial longing which find outlet in the living poetry and songs of our people. . . . That our people should live in their own homes is a sentiment deep in the heart of our race and of American life. . . .[17]

Professor North continues:

> And this is the atmosphere that the broker and salesman must absorb. It is the air he must breathe. He is not selling bricks and mortar or shingles and siding, but "Home." He is not a salesman taking orders, but a missionary, a pioneer with a vision . . . leading on to new fields and frontiers.[18]

He was right, for it was as missionaries that the real estate men went into the field. The individual buyer, said the realtor, was too shy to take action when his neighbor sold his house to the wrong person. It was up to the builder to act.[19]

The National Association of Home Builders urged forming "homes associations" with "enforcement functions, developing prestige for the builder." The homeowner was assured of "enhancing and protecting his investment, enforcing protective covenants, promoting community activities, insuring stable and attractive neighborhoods."[20]

Developers put ads in newspapers and in magazines puffing up exclusiveness and exclusion:

YOU'LL FIND CONTENTMENT IN A HOME OF INDIVIDUALITY
AT CHEELCROFT
In the Heart of the Ridgewood-Saddle River Section. . . . The atmosphere of Cheelcroft is one of harmony and impeccable good taste. The people

[16] Helen Koues, "Enduring Value of Good Architecture," *ibid.*, vol. 104, no. 5, May, 1937, p. 51.

[17] Nelson L. North, *Real Estate Selling and Leasing.* New York, Prentice-Hall, Inc., 1938, p. 139.

[18] *Ibid.*

[19] "Homes Associations for the Small Operator—Their Value in Building Sound Neighborhoods," *Land Planning Service.* National Association of Home Builders, Bulletin no. 3, November, 1947.

[20] *Ibid.*

who live there are of the type that you, yourself, would select for neighbors.[21]

The Seven Bridges Realty Corp. of Chappaqua, N. Y., advertised: "A carefully restricted community [for] families of the right type."[22]

Ironically, it is the suburban house itself which has invited social deterioration. It is small and rigidly planned, allowing for neither expansion nor contraction to fit changing needs. The two bedrooms are provided on the supposition that the American family will have no more than two children, of the same sex and everlastingly compatible. Most houses are flimsily built and no matter how much is spent on upkeep, shabbiness becomes apparent. The stock plans used by developers thwart any expression of individuality in taste, leveling all buyers to the same pitch and standard. As costs rose in recent years, the builders cut standards still further. The owners' maintenance costs went up still higher, generally beyond their ability to pay. This accelerates deterioration of the neighborhood and makes it an early candidate for a lower economic group. The buyers are often so homogeneous in age composition that all of them grow old together. They are so alike in income and social levels that the neighborhood becomes a dull place. It soon becomes obsolete socially as well as physically.

Parlor conversation has dwindled with the pre-emption of the parlor by television. But one of the livest subjects at the supermarket, over the telephone, and on commuters' trains is the alien interloper and the Negro intruder who are waiting for the first opportunity to engulf the neighborhood with their kind. The fear is not without foundation. Owners, ever-suspicious that their neighbor might be the first to sell out, often take no chances and themselves become the first to sell. Among the buyers may be home-hungry minorities willing to pay a premium price. Once a few minority members move in, others in the neighborhood yield to the call of lucre and the press of fear.

The most effective promoter of class exclusion as we shall see was the federal government itself. For more than a decade and a half the United States had a concerted, rationalized, publicized, government-supported program under which a great section of the new generation was set apart, sterilized against infection by alien culture, taught to live with and respect only its own kind, trained to oppose intrusion

---

[21] *The American Home*, vol. XII, no. 5, October, 1934, p. 263–o.
[22] *Ibid.*, June, 1934, vol. XII, no. 1, p. 3–h.

by those who were different. A man should never live with those in a "higher or lower income scale than his own. It is the part of wisdom to buy in a neighborhood where people are of his own racial or national type," wrote a government housing economist.[23]

"Homogeneity" became a crucial determinant of value and government field agents were instructed to inquire whether the neighborhood was homogeneous in population.[24]

The antipathetic or nonhomogeneous type of neighborhood was not a good risk, while even the children were not to mix with others of "an incompatible racial element," or go to the same school.

The worker who may have had no prejudice against a Negro co-worker was now taught to be prejudiced against him as a neighbor. Housing was being built up as a wedge to split class from class. The American neighborhood was turned into a breeding ground of bias, fear, and discrimination.

Millions of homes in thousands of neighborhoods were now all patterned upon the placement into isolated areas of people of a common stamp. It led to a division of these neighborhoods into those of the elite and the unwanted. It created sensitive communities that in the long run were economically and socially unworkable. It subordinated intelligence to race, religion, income, color, or social status. It enjoined the children of one section from mixing with those of another. It created thousands of homogeneous islands which were homogeneous only in their fears and were more foreign to the American tradition than the outsiders they sought to exclude. Finally, it won a place in the national political scene by developing a large bloc of voters who saw their interest threatened by the espousal of democratic precepts of equality of opportunity and of equal right to shelter.

[23] See A. M. Weimer and J. J. Rowland, *When You Buy or Build a Home.* New York, Ronald Press, 1937, p. 17.
[24] I ¶2321, Social Item B 3(a). *Rental Housing Manual,* Washington, Federal Housing Administration, 1940.

XIII

THE REALTY CODE

THE prejudice which has spread through American neighborhoods has been nourished by the organized real estate enterprise, an enterprise and an organization which have changed so markedly since the New Deal that their old form is no longer recognizable.

Up to the 1930's the real estate business consisted of small-time operators, builders, real estate brokers, managers, and appraisers operating on a local basis. Operations were financed through mortgage lenders with large capitalizations drawn from the savings of the rank and file. These lenders were usually savings banks, savings and loan associations, or insurance companies operating under state laws. The savings banks and associations were limited by law to intrastate business, while the insurance companies operated on an interstate basis. Fearing government regulation, the insurance companies fought intervention with all the political power they could muster.

Ignoring the general trend toward concentration in every industry from steel to the orange drink, real estate remained one of the country's last localized enterprises. It was a personalized business which resisted standardization and subordination to large-scale operation. Racial difficulties consequently remained local problems, too, to be tackled and resolved by the local builder, the local lender, or the local landlord.

Collective action developed with the appearance of racial restrictive covenants, racial zoning, and with the concerted action of mortgage-lenders. But these instruments continued to originate at the local level, varying with the racial pattern of each area, with the extent of racial infiltration, and with the intensity of local reactions.

Before the New Deal, moreover, the federal role was largely supervisory. If the personalized oppression against a racial minority became official, the courts would enjoin it as a violation of the Fourteenth Amendment. Both entrepreneurial and government patterns thus tended to delimit anti-racial practices and hold them within local bounds. Anti-racial agitation was checked by the prevailing spirit of the public policy and no ready liaison could be effected between federal officialdom and bigotry.

The New Deal altered the real estate operation, and with it the racial housing problem. There was no central theme to influence the New Deal program and many of the efforts were merely "experiments" or "demonstrations." But it soon became evident that one of the main directions of federal aid was toward real estate. It took form in aid to homeowners burdened with debt; to mortgage-lenders with soured mortgages that threatened depositors' and shareholders' savings; and to home-builders, contractors, and building workers needed to resume homebuilding, one of the great economic pump-primers. Soon some 30 federal agencies emerged, all with an interest of one kind or another in landed operations—homes, farms, buildings, or realty credit.

In a few years the federal stake in real estate operations passed the $10 billion mark. Three billion dollars of loans were rescued from institutional portfolios. Building and loan associations received federal loans and their depositors were guaranteed against loss. The FHA system enabled builders to engage in real estate subdivisions without investment, while lenders were insured against any loss on their mortgage loans, though not required to reduce interest rates.

It was a welcome intervention indeed, from the point of view of the entrepreneurs and lenders. One effect of this federal expansion was the encouragement of larger operations by local builders while land subdividers might acquire larger tracts than ever before and sell them to a dozen or more builders under a single plan of subdivision. Homebuyers too could now acquire houses with only a 10 per cent down payment.

Another effect was the organization of a lobby designed to preserve and improve the dividends of federal expansion. Not all lobbies are bad, and in a society increasingly dominated by government, many are inevitable and necessary. But the Washington real estate lobby and its allies were as unique as the policies they proffered. The lobby grew to such strength and influence that President Truman characterized it as the most dangerous in Washington.

The real estate lobby was described by Herbert U. Nelson, executive vice president of the National Association of Real Estate Boards, as "18 working organizations interested in building, construction materials, and real estate. We have a common end and a common interest, and it works fine. Included is the United States Chamber of Commerce."[1]

By 1950, NAREB was composed of 1100 member boards and 43,539 "realtors" who contributed dues of more than $420,000 annually. There was also a Washington lobbying committee with a separate budget. Other parts of the organization were an "Appraisal Institute," a "Management Institute," and a "Brokers Institute." Working closely with NAREB was the National Association of Home Builders with a membership of 16,350 dedicated to the perpetuation of the new dividends and blessings of federal intervention. A third wing was the United States Savings and Loan League directed by a skillful lobbyist, Morton Bodfish, who kept his influence in the foreground and his name in the background. Other wings of the lobby included the National Association of Lumber Dealers and the Producers' Council, representing the powerful materials interests.

While these organizations are nominally separate entities, they exert joint pressure on Congress and the federal housing agencies. Public officials consult the lobbyists on forthcoming regulations, and accept their fees for speeches. Payment of a $10,000 fee for a pamphlet on prefabrication, bearing the name of Senator Joseph McCarthy,[2] was held by the Attorney General to violate no law. The newspapers print column after column of the lobby's propaganda. The lumber-dealer lobby alone boasted that in a single year it wangled 149,000 free lines of print (about 700 columns) and $900,000 of free advertising.[3] In one month newspaper stories of the NAREB totaled 2500, an average of 83 a day. The realtors have 250 newspaper contact committees which flood their local papers with letters to the editor and

---

[1] *Housing Lobby,* Part 2 of Hearings before the House Select Committee on Lobbying Activities, House of Representatives, Eighty-first Congress, Second Session, Pursuant to H. Res. 298, April 19–28, May 3, 5, 17, 1950, p. 48.

[2] *Ibid.,* pp. 55, 135.

[3] *Ibid.,* pp. 486, 493.

arrange for favorable editorial comment—or supply canned editorials which are used widely.[4] At least once a month the big wire services—AP, UP, INS—put the lobby's releases to real estate editors on the wires as if they were authoritative market comment.[5] The releases are rarely impartial judgments on trends, but consist of self-serving announcements, optimistic puffing, or propaganda directed for or against legislation.

Radio and television are not neglected. Fulton Lewis, Jr., is known for his faithful reflection of the lobby's views, and many other commentators lend support.

The United States Savings and Loan League campaigns against social issues such as public housing. Campaign funds sometimes come out of savings deposits. The main influence of the savings and loan associations lies with the important committees of Congress. Bodfish keeps a sharp eye on committee appointments to assure a sympathetic membership.[6]

Main attention by all the lobby components is centered on contacts with federal agencies. The lobby groups will suggest the appointment of a friendly administrator or try to destroy one who offends them. The most important work, of course, is carried on by the lobby behind the closed doors of the administrator—the preparation of legislation which grants subsidies or lightens obligations. Bills have been drawn by the lobby jointly with the federal agency. Here the lobby has wielded strategic power because it can do things the agency may not —such as pressing individual congressmen for higher budgets, large appropriations, and expansion of the agency's powers. The lobby is the unofficial right arm that can manipulate conveniently in coves and recesses forbidden to official agencies.

In return, the agency has worded its rules and manuals so as not to displease its benefactors. In fact, the ethics of the lobby, its credenda, and even its social values will often be engrafted on the policies of the federal agency. The occasions are rare when there has been no complete rapport. One reason for this, according to Nelson, is that

[4] *Ibid.*, p. 737.

[5] *Ibid.*, pp. 484–486.

[6] See, for example, the interesting correspondence and memoranda between the League and friendly senators that run through *United States Savings and Loan League,* the 750-page report of the House Select Committee on Lobbying Activities (House of Representatives, Eighty-first Congress, Second Session, Created Pursuant to H. Res. 298, October 31, 1950).

"we put several hundred of our people, whom we found and persuaded to go into government service, into positions where they could give their services."[7] But a more basic reason is implicit in the nature of the joint government-private venture in which the private, more dynamic partner is apt to impose his lower standards upon the presumably higher-principled public agency.

The attitude of Nelson toward government aid is simple: "I do not oppose government intervention in housing. I only believe that the powers of government should be used to assist private enterprise." His opinion of democracy is short and simple too: "Democracy stinks."[8]

A main objective of the lobby is to expand the benefits for its members, and this has been done effectively indeed. Its whipping boy has been the little public housing program which it attacks in the press and in Congress on every occasion. In 1953 Congress bowed to the lobby and voted to immolate the low-rent program. As part of its strategy during the fight in 1949 the lobby, tongue in cheek, proffered the Cain-Bricker amendment which would have prohibited any segregation in public housing, thereby alienating southern support and threatening the bill when it seemed most likely to pass.

The lobby's growing influence might be of less concern to minorities except for the anti-racial policy that has permeated the philosophy of many of its members. The anti-racial slant became apparent in the 1920's, and was accepted without resistance or fanfare. Then, like Topsy, it just grew. Unlike Topsy, however, it was anti-Negro, anti-alien, and anti-anybody-who-was-different.

In 1922, when the NAREB was still a small trade organization of local real estate brokers, Nelson helped launch a series of textbooks on real estate. "When I came into the picture in 1922," he said, "there were two textbooks available on real estate practice." He then made arrangements with Professor Richard T. Ely, land economist at the University of Wisconsin, and the Macmillan Company for the publication of twelve textbooks.[9] The liaison with Ely gave prestige to the real estate group, which was then of small-fry caliber. Ely was one

---

[7] *Housing Lobby, op. cit.,* p. 12.

[8] For Nelson's views on the desirability of a republic, see *ibid.,* pp. 25, 30.

[9] *Housing Lobby, op. cit.,* p. 57. Although Nelson said the arrangement was for eight, there appears to have been twelve.

of the most liberal and able economists of the era and his own interest in urban land economics and real estate brought many good students into the fields.[10] There is nothing in his own writings to suggest a belief in racial segregation; rather they point to a developed sense of the true democratic spirit. The probabilities are that Ely, who was advanced in age and busy with his own writings, paid little attention to all the texts which he co-sponsored.

The first books dealt with a variety of subjects—real estate advertising, land economics, roadside development, real estate law, public land policy history, land planning, and other technical subjects. Some, indeed, were original contributions to the new and little-known field of urban land economics. But the books dealing with current real estate practices introduced the racial question in no uncertain terms. Among the first to be sponsored by Nelson was *Principles of Real Estate Practice* by Ernest McKinley Fisher, then assistant executive secretary of NAREB.[11] Fisher emphasized the character of the community as the most important aspect determining value ". . . sometimes a relatively poor location may be so improved and restricted as to greatly enhance its natural value. It is a matter of common observation that the purchase of property by certain racial types is very likely to diminish the value of other property in the section. In general, people of similar social standing live near together."[12] Dr. Fisher, now professor of urban land economics at Columbia University, like Ely is a man without racial bias, has made constructive contributions in the field and, like some others in the profession, was merely stating what he thought was fact.

The religious element in real estate values was introduced by another author:

Residential values are affected by racial and religious factors. . . . A home utility seeks location near people . . . but always near persons of the same social standing, same races, near to churches, schools, and all phases of social life and with access to places of business and shopping. . . . And so the habits, the character, the race, the movements, and the very moods of people are the ultimate factors of real estate value. . . . The real factors are buying mood, hours, purchasing power, motives at the moment, di-

[10] Among his students, for example, were Coleman Woodbury and George S. Wehrwein who have made important contributions.
[11] New York, The Macmillan Company, 1923.
[12] *Ibid.*, p. 116.

rections of movement, race, occupations, religion and standards of living. . . .[13]

In another work, part of a series called the "Standard Course," the author, then general counsel to NAREB and listing himself as "Sometime Lecturer" at a string of universities, argued for the legality of racial restrictive covenants in a manner reminiscent of Anatole France's definition of equality:

> The individual citizen, whether he be black or white, may refuse to sell or lease property to any particular individual or class of individuals. The power of the whites to exclude the blacks from purchasing their property implies the power of the blacks to exercise the same prerogative over property which they may own. There is, therefore, no discrimination within the civil rights clause of the Constitution.[14]

These expressions coincided with the official position of NAREB which took them out of the realm of theory and implanted them into ethics. Until 1950, the official code of ethics of the Association carried the following canon:

> A realtor should never be instrumental in introducing into a neighborhood a character of property or occupancy, members of any race or nationality, or any individual whose presence will clearly be detrimental to property values in the neighborhood.[15]

Violations of the rule exposed a board to expulsion. Supplementing its official code, the association issued a brochure in 1943 entitled "Fundamentals of Real Estate Practice." This bulked the Negro seeking an education with strange company:

> The prospective buyer might be a bootlegger who would cause considerable annoyance to his neighbors, a madame who had a number of Call Girls on her string, a gangster, who wants a screen for his activities by living in a better neighborhood, a colored man of means who was giving his children a college education and thought they were entitled to live among whites. . . . No matter what the motive or character of the would-be purchaser, if the deal would instigate a form of blight, then certainly the well-meaning broker must work against its consummation.[16]

[13] Frederick Morrison Babcock, *The Appraisal of Real Estate.* New York, The Macmillan Company, 1924, pp. 70–71.

[14] Nathan William MacChesney, *The Principles of Real Estate Law.* New York, The Macmillan Co., 1927 (vol. X in the Standard Course), p. 586.

[15] *Ibid.*

[16] Quoted in *Equality of Opportunity in Housing.* New York, National Community Relations Advisory Council, June, 1952, p. 15.

In 1950 the association modified its "Code of Ethics" so that it now reads:

A realtor should never be instrumental in introducing into a neighborhood a character of property or occupancy of any race or nationality, . . . which will clearly be detrimental to property values in that neighborhood.

Whether this was altered on the advice of counsel after the association had been indicted (for fixing commission rates) is not clear. There is reason to believe that the original canon violated the federal Civil Rights Act and might have subjected NAREB to legal action by a federal administration which then appeared unfriendly. In any event, there is little evidence that the realtors' official view has altered. To reinforce discrimination, in fact, many local "codes of ethics" continue to prohibit any member from introducing "detrimental" minorities into neighborhoods; violation would bring local expulsion. Expulsion would mean loss of livelihood since the title "realtor" is the association's copyrighted property, and mortgage companies, banks, insurance companies, other "realtors," and larger property-owners generally deal only with "realtors."

Since his modest initial venture into real estate literature, Nelson now reports that some 800 books on the subject have sprouted.[17] For what proportion of this rich fruit NAREB deserves credit cannot be known. It is clear, however, that many of the texts were written by NAREB brokers and by appraisers who learned the gospel from members of NAREB's American Institute of Real Estate Appraisers.

Recently, NAREB announced that there were 165 universities and colleges offering courses in real estate, 40 providing a major in the subject. Out of the NAREB group have come many of the texts used in these courses, and out of its annual realty "institutes" have graduated thousands of brokers steeped in the teachings of the profession. Out of these groups have come the teachers who have passed on the racist gospel to thousands of students. A search failed to reveal a single book in the field that disputes the racial line, though a few recent articles have ventured strong criticism.[18]

[17] *Housing Lobby, op. cit.,* p. 12.

[18] Belden Morgan, "Values in Transition Areas," *The Review of the Society of Residential Appraisers,* vol. 18, no. 3, March, 1952; Luigi M. Laurenti, "Effects of Nonwhite Purchases on Market Prices of Residences," *The Appraisal Journal,* July, 1952, are among the most recent and effective examples.

The local realty groups have encouraged communities to accept their ideas of what people should be like, what colors or races are socially desirable, with whom people should live, and what their social standards should be. These ideas have been mostly anti-Negro, frequently anti-alien, sometimes anti-Semitic. The rule of value is often hinged to the "100% American community" or the "ideal neighborhood" made up of the "ideal" or "right" people only.

This racist theory of value is not only taught in many schools and colleges and incorporated into texts published by responsible publishers, but is widely circulated in real estate magazines, newspapers, and home magazines. It is made the subject of state examinations in which an applicant who might take a democratic position on the racial issue would be marked wrong.

Worse still, the theory became part of the unwritten official policy in government appraisals. Here it helped deprive minorities of government-aided housing. It set up thousands of FHA neighborhoods inhabited by "homogeneous" groups who had been sold both the racist line and their houses on the representation that their neighborhoods would be forever secure against pollution if they would only cooperate.

The real estate fraternity believes in a "Gresham's Law of Neighborhoods." The theory is that just as bad dollars drive out good ones, so do bad people of the wrong complexion or status drive out good people and depress neighborhood values.[19] From this it appears proper to encourage exclusion practices, thus assuring the safety of the home investment and making community life desirable.

The earliest studies on the influence of minorities on real estate value appeared at about the time Negro migrations to the North increased. The alien immigrant was still prominent in those days, and he shared the cavil with the Negro.

Of two texts published in 1923,[20] one argued that the Negro is the threat; the other emphasized the "foreigner." McMichael (whose works are still authoritative to real estate men) and Bingham say:

[19] The new Gresham theory is adopted by Henry E. Hoagland in *Real Estate Principles*. New York, McGraw-Hill Book Co., Inc., 1940, p. 148.

[20] Stanley L. McMichael and R. F. Bingham, *City Growth and Values*. Cleveland, The Stanley McMichael Publishing Organization, 1923 (quotations from pp. 181, 182); John Spilker, *Real Estate Business as a Profession*, Cincinnati, Stewart Kidd, 1923 (quotations from pp. 123, 128).

There is a natural inclination of the colored people to live together in their own communities. With the increase in colored people coming to many Northern cities they have overrun their old districts and swept into adjoining ones or passed to other sections and formed new ones. This naturally has had a decidedly detrimental effect on land values for few white people, however inclined to be sympathetic with the problem of the colored race, care to live near them. Property values have been sadly depreciated by having a single colored family settle down on a street occupied exclusively by white residents. . . .

A simple proposal for dealing with the problem is then made:

Segregation of the Negro population seems to be the reasonable solution of the problem, no matter how unpleasant or objectionable the thought may be to colored residents. Southern cities have a habit of taking care of the problem which is well known and seems to be entirely effective. Northern cities, more sympathetic towards the negro, have been so backward . . . in coping with the problem that serious race wars have resulted. . . . Frankly, rigid segregation seems to be the only manner in which the difficulty can be effectively controlled.

Then follows an epic of constitutional ethics:

The colored people certainly have a right to life, liberty and the pursuit of happiness but they must recognize the economic disturbance which their presence in a white neighborhood causes and forego their desire to split off from the established district where the rest of their race lives.

The text by Spilker applied the theory to foreigners:

A marked change in the social character of the people coming into the section to live is clearly seen, sinking lower and lower until foreigners of the lowest and most undesirable type, begin to infest the section, living in overcrowded quarters and under unsanitary conditions.

Then, comparing a city to the human anatomy and including patriotism, purity, and idealism as part of the gruel that keeps neighborhoods healthy, the author says:

Its life-blood will depend on the character of its citizens, pure and warm if its citizens are 100% American, in education, patriotism, and lofty ideals; anemic and even diseased if polluted with a large percentage of unassimilated aliens who neither understand nor are in sympathy with American ideals and standards.

In 1927, George A. Schneider, lecturer on real estate at the University of Southern California, wrote a text which referred to both race and nationality as factors which affected values.[21] "The mere threat," he wrote, "of an undesirable encroachment must many times be recognized by a reduced unit value for the house."

In 1932, foreigners from both Europe and Asia were grouped with Negroes in a text by Charles T. Male, of Union College at Schenectady, New York.[22] "Rigid segregation" was again stressed as a remedy. Dismissing all arguments against segregation with a shrug, the author advocated temporary segregation for the "undesirable elements of Southern Europe and Asia."

Sociologists have a fine theory about quickly assimilating the white races by preventing them from segregating in our cities, but from the economic standpoint it seems highly desirable for them to be more or less segregated in sections by themselves for at least one generation. And the solution of the negro problem seems to depend upon rigid segregation. Southern cities have by hard experience evolved a method of handling the situation which may appear objectionable but which seems to be effective.

With the appearance of a study[23] by Homer Hoyt, a sincere and respectable economist, an effort was made to view the problem with a semblance of scientific approach:

The significance of these racial and national movements upon Chicago land values lies in the fact that certain racial and national groups, because of their lower economic status and their lower standards of living, pay less rent themselves and cause a greater physical deterioration of property than groups higher in the social and economic scale. Because of the instability of the tenants, high collection losses, and the aversion of persons higher in the social order to living near these classes, the rents received are capitalized at higher rates, so that they yield lower capital values than property yielding the same net income in the most desirable areas. Land values in areas occupied by such classes are therefore inevitably low. Part of the attitude reflected in lower land values is due entirely to racial prejudice, which may have no reasonable basis. Nevertheless, if the entrance of a colored family into a white neighborhood causes a general exodus of the white people, such dislikes are reflected in property values. Except in the case of negroes and Mexicans, however, these racial and

[21] *California Real Estate Principles and Practices.* New York, Prentice-Hall, Inc., 1927, p. 315.

[22] *Real Estate Fundamentals.* New York, D. Van Nostrand Company, 1932, pp. 210–211.

[23] *One Hundred Years of Land Values in Chicago.* Chicago, University of Chicago Press, 1933, p. 314.

national barriers disappear when the individuals . . . rise in the economic scale or conform to the American standard of living.

Hoyt's statement that Negroes and Mexicans are the exceptions is of course a speculation. But without any investigation, Hoyt then swallowed a local realtor's evaluation of how land values are affected by 13 races and nationalities. From most favorable to least favorable, the list was:

1. English, Germans, Scotch, Irish, Scandinavians;
2. North Italians;
3. Bohemians or Czechs;
4. Poles;
5. Lithuanians;
6. Greeks;
7. Russian Jews ("lower class");
8. South Italians;
9. Negroes;
10. Mexicans.

This hierarchy became commonly accepted in textbooks and schools, and by teachers.

Hoyt conceded that in many cases the undesirable racial factor is so merged with other unattractive features, such as proximity to factories, etc., that the separate effect of race cannot be disentangled. These qualifications were ignored by the real estate profession which quoted Hoyt to justify bias. Hoyt made a later study[24] at the request of Ernest M. Fisher, who had become FHA's director of research and statistics. Hoyt now amplified his theory to show that in the structure and growth of American cities there was a general tendency for the formation of fairly homogeneous residential sectors and a similar tendency for upper-class sectors to deteriorate when "inharmonious" groups penetrated them. He reiterated, too, that racial elements were one of the factors responsible for blight.

This theory had already received unofficial sanction within FHA. Hoyt's untested assumptions underscored FHA's emphasis on insuring loans only in "good" sectors and for neglecting aid in the declining areas where minorities lived. The theory has been challenged by Professor Lloyd Rodwin, of Massachusetts Institute of Technology,[25]

[24] *Structure and Growth of Residential Neighborhoods in American Cities.* Washington, U.S. Government Printing Office, 1939.
[25] "The Theory of Residential Growth and Structure," *The Appraisal Journal,* July, 1950.

who demonstrated that Hoyt's conclusions were based on questionable assumptions and an *ad hoc* theory of class structure. It assumed that locations were selected for class attractiveness while ignoring all other considerations including the functional adequacy of established environments which might be attractive despite the presence of other groups. More recent studies have also given concrete evidence to contradict Hoyt's thesis.[26] But the real estate profession still accepts the old racial theories as dogma. Hoyt was not responsible for them. All he did was to accept their assumptions uncritically and lend them respectability.

By 1935 the racist doctrine had become so deeply rooted that the FHA had no trouble imposing it without modification upon the egalitarian ethic of American democracy.

If any doubt had survived about the effect of certain people on land value, the official FHA *Underwriting Manual* now laid it to rest. Since almost every recent rental project and most individually owned homes have been built under FHA supervision and received their racial rating in accordance with its manual, the real estate group may be credited with shaping the racial and social patterns of American neighborhoods in the last generation. The FHA rules, according to McMichael,[27] were in fact formulated by Frederick Morrison Babcock, who was one of Nelson's earliest authors.[28]

The FHA underwriting manuals not only adopted the phraseology of "inharmonious races and classes," but advocated racial restrictions, physical barriers, racial covenants, and racial zoning as methods of excluding certain racial and national groups. Pigpens and unwelcome races were classed as equally objectionable.[29]

What began as private prejudice was thus converted into public policy, approved by public agencies, enforced by the full panoply of public power and backed by public credit. More complete excerpts from the government manuals are given later.

[26] Laurenti, *op. cit.*

[27] McMichael and Bingham, *op. cit.*

[28] His most notable work in addition to *The Appraisal of Real Estate* (*op. cit.*), is his *Valuation of Real Estate*. New York, McGraw-Hill Book Co., Inc., 1932.

[29] *Underwriting Manual*. Washington, Federal Housing Administration, November 1, 1936, Part II "Risk Rating Restrictions," §2, 284(3). The Home Loan Bank Board followed the policy as well.

After the FHA manual had embraced prejudice, text-writers re-echoed the racist doctrine. In 1937, Arthur M. Weimer, former FHA economist, and John J. Rowland advocated inquiring into the same "inharmonious racial or national groups" referred to by FHA, recommended "deed restrictions against inharmonious races," and the setting up of "clubs" which allow sale of property only to members.[30] The authors, however, contributed a new suggestion: the poorer classes were advised to stay put for their own best interests: "The prospective home buyer should not locate in an area inhabited by people who are on a considerably *higher or lower* income scale than his own. . . . It is the part of wisdom to buy in a neighborhood where people are of his own racial or national type."

The idea that it was good for the American to stay in his place attained popularity in the years to follow. It was widely taught and as widely accepted. The word "homogeneous" began to appear more often in both unofficial and official publications.[31] "It is usually best to buy a home in a neighborhood where the other residents have about the same income and social standing as your own," wrote Roland K. Abercrombie.[32] He advocated restriction against non-Caucasians. Weimer and Hoyt repeated that "the migration into a neighborhood of families with certain readily distinguishable national, racial or religious characteristics frequently stimulates the out-migration of previous residents in the area."[33] Presence of "inharmonious racial, national, or income groups in an adjoining area represents a threat to property values," said the authors.

The religious element as a factor of value was also mentioned in that year by *The Real Estate Handbook*. Advocating "protective covenants," the authors, employees of the National Association of

[30] *When you Buy or Build a Home.* New York, Ronald Press, 1937, pp. 14, 15.

[31] See "Neighborhood Rating" (suggestions drawn up by Division of Research and Statistics of the Federal Home Loan Bank Board) *Review of the Society of Residential Appraisers*, vol. 6, no. 8, August, 1940; Ayers J. DuBois, "Valuation of Residential Properties in Small Towns, *ibid.,* vol. 5, no. 10, October, 1939; Hoagland, *op. cit.,* pp. 147–150; George L. Schmutz, *The Appraisal Process.* Los Angeles, published privately by the author, 1941.

[32] *How to Buy or Build Your Home Wisely.* New York, The Macmillan Co., 1941, pp. 14, 18.

[33] *Principles of Urban Real Estate.* New York, The Ronald Press, rev. ed., 1948, p. 127.

Home Builders and NAREB, wrote: "A neighborhood of homogeneous dwellings, parks, schools, churches, stores, and other structures properly designed and built should retain its character during the life of its component units. Adverse influences and unregulated uses should be excluded. . . .[34]

The Intellectual Hierarchy

The appraisal group is the intellectual wing of the NAREB. In 1950, the American Institute of Real Estate Appraisers had some 1300 members. "The Army and Navy asked us to give them our most skilled brokers and appraisers and technicians," said Herbert U. Nelson, and he did.[35] The appraisers value property for many other federal agencies. They set the official criteria for value, advise federal administrators on rules to be promulgated in building, financing, and disposing of homes. They are the social and intellectual guides in matters of real estate in which official and unofficial agencies are involved.[36]

More recent thoughts include those of Arthur A. May, former dean of the American Institute of Real Estate Appraisers, teacher at Yale University, Tulane University, and the Detroit Institute of Technology, and also director of the federal government's Liquidation Service of the General Services Administration. Commenting on American neighborhoods, he wrote:

What we should have in mind is the homogeneity of the people who live within the area, their sameness of income and their sameness of social habits . . . when . . . the infiltration of the antipathetic racial groups begins to gnaw at the edges, it will not be long until direct access will be had to the very core of the neighborhood itself.[37]

In a textbook, May repeats that warning. He then discourses on the social structure of neighborhoods:

The historical background of the inhabitants of the neighborhood is important to the valuation study. It is necessary to know where they come

[34] Lawrence G. Holmes and Carrie Maude Jones, eds., New York, Prentice-Hall, Inc., 1948.

[35] *Housing Lobby, op. cit.,* p. 12.

[36] Some 46 per cent of brokers were engaged in real estate appraisal in July, 1949.

[37] "Appraising the Home," *The Appraisal Journal,* January, 1951, pp. 22–23.

from, their habits of living and their cultural attainments. The nation is a polyglot mixture of many races, creeds and nationalities. The preponderance of any particular nationalistic or racial group in the neighborhood will evidence family traits and social customs indigenous to that particular group.[38]

Whether the average appraiser is qualified to judge another's habits, backgrounds, and cultural attainments does not seem to worry May. "The encroachment of the antipathetic racial or nationalistic group brings with it, first the threat and ultimately the effect of decreased values." May then applies his rule not only to the foreign-born but to their children as well:

From this we may generalize that, in the city that houses a large percentage of people of foreign birth, *or their children,* or that contains a substantial minority percentage of people of races other than white, residential real estate values in the older districts bordering those at present inhabited by the minority peoples will exist in a state of threatened status quo.[39] [Italics supplied.]

May has recently extended his theory of homogeneity to religion as well as race. Writing of the advice he gave a customer who wanted to buy a lot for $2500, he says:

I told him . . . he had to satisfy himself that these people were of about his same economic level, that culturally they were approximately his equal, that they were of his same race and preferably his same religion in order to assure him that the interests and living habits of himself and his neighbors would lie parallel.[40]

The effects of minority infiltration on value has seemingly been one of the main interests of the appraisal profession. Its Education and Research Committee, in an official glossary, defines a blighted area as "A declining area which is seriously affected by destructive economic forces, such as encroaching inharmonious property usages, infiltration of lower social and economic classes of inhabitants. . . ." It then defines a slum not by physical dilapidation alone but in terms of people—"the lowest social and economic class of the population."

In 1941, George L. Schmutz, another dean of American real estate appraisers, rated "deviation from the typical" as a depressor of values:

[38] Arthur A. May, *The Valuation of Residential Real Estate.* New York, Prentice-Hall, Inc., 1942, p. 99.

[39] *Ibid.,* p. 75.

[40] "Appraising the Home," *op. cit.,* p. 19.

. . . the most significant observation of residential neighborhoods is an exemplification of the aphorism that "birds of a feather flock together." By this is meant that there is a tendency toward the neighborhood grouping of people of the same race, nationality, income and social position.[41]

The *Journal of the American Institute of Real Estate Appraisers,* which since 1933 has been the institute's official publication, and the *Residential Appraisers Review,* published by the Society of Residential Appraisers, are replete with similar doctrines. This writer found no less than fifteen articles written between 1933 and 1945 dealing with the subject, and fourteen which followed the NAREB view on race and value.[42] The writers included FHA zone managers, presidents of real estate boards, officials of HOLC, and college instructors. These articles generally parrot the theories and often the same dogma on the need for racial and social homogeneity if value is to be maintained. In at least one case, factors affecting value include not only race and color but religion, wealth, occupations, and reputation.[43] In another, the author, an assistant editor of the Institute's *Appraisal Journal,* asserts, "Property owners should reserve and have the right to restrict

[41] *The Appraisal Process, op. cit.,* p. 50. No one seems to have challenged his observation by showing that blackbirds and white do get along together, though both dread white weasels.

[42] In the *Journal of the American Institute of Real Estate Appraisers:* Philip W. Kniskern, "Some Value Factors in Residential Property," October, 1933, pp. 6–10; Harry S. Cutmore, "The Appraisal of Single Family Dwellings," *ibid.*; Charles B. Shattuck, "What Price the American Home," *ibid.*; August B. Schulte, "Residential District Permutations," July, 1936; Robert H. Armstrong, "Neighborhood Analysis," Frederick M. Babcock, Maurice R. Massey, Jr., and Walter L. Greene, "Techniques of Residental Location Rating," April, 1938.

In *The Appraisal Journal:* Boyd T. Barnard, "The Appraisal of Old Homes," January, 1940; John E. McGovern, "Appraisal of Large-Scale Suburban Apartment Projects," April, 1940; Elsie S. Parker, "Two Sides of the Color Line," January and July, 1943; Talmage D. Auble, "Residential Appraising in the Postwar Period," January, 1944; K. Lee Hyder, "Over-Accenting the Slum Problem," April, 1945.

In *Residential Appraisers' Review:* Edward V. Walsh, "The Obsolescence Factor," November, 1935; H. O. Walter, "Appraising Residential Property—From Application to Loan Disbursement," December, 1935.

In *The Review of the Society of Residential Appraisers:* Louis M. Pratt, "Racial Restrictions and Their Effect on Valuation," April, 1939; Ayers J. DuBois, "Valuation of Residential Properties in Small Towns," October, 1939; "Neighborhood Rating" (suggestions drawn up by Division of Research and Statistics of Federal Home Loan Bank Board), August, 1940; Leslie H. Bamburg, "Values Guarded by Owners' Alliance," June, 1944.

[43] Kniskern, *op. cit.,* p. 8.

the area in which they live. If this is to be a free country, we should be able to choose in the larger sense our neighbors, our schools, our parks, our churches."[44]

This "freedom of choice" has become the subject of a California crusade to amend the state constitution and ultimately the federal constitution to bring the government into line.[45] Freedom would presumably not apply to the white who chooses to sell to a Negro or to the Negro who chooses to buy. According to Miss Parker, "Are we to restrict, segregate and bar the Negro? This is a matter which each city must decide for itself."[46] According to this, therefore, if a city decides to "restrict, segregate and bar the Negro," it should be within its right.

Infiltration of incompatible races has always been a red flag to the appraiser, but one appraiser admitted: "During the war former racial barriers have broken down to some extent," and "The white and the colored can work side by side in certain industries." But, he continues, "the mixing of races in family life cannot be countenanced."[47] Why the gains in one area cannot be carried on to another, the author does not say.

For maximum desirability, writes still another appraiser, people in a neighborhood must "be more or less alike in their manner of living, their education and their financial status, and not antagonistic or incompatible in their racial characteristics or nationalities." Restrictions, he says, are not "a matter of intolerance but an attempt to 'make everybody happy' in their home surroundings."[48]

Another writer describes the sequences in a neighborhood "invasion": (1) The native-born whites of the best class shift to the next best location, (2) a "slightly inferior class," first of native-born whites, takes over the old residences, (3) next come "successively lower classes of native-born whites," (4) the foreigner then enters, (5) the foreigner is followed by the Negro or other colored races, (6) finally the Negro is pushed out by business.[49]

[44] Parker, *op. cit.,* p. 248.
[45] Stanley L. McMichael, *Real Estate Subdivisions.* New York, Prentice-Hall, Inc., 1949, pp. 204ff.
[46] *Ibid.,* p. 236.
[47] Auble, *op. cit.,* p. 48.
[48] Pratt, *op. cit.,* p. 13.
[49] Schulte, *op. cit.,* p. 283.

Another says: "To the layman, people are mostly just people and he gives little or no thought to the slight difference in the quality of the various classes of people." But the appraiser, he says, must not consider people as people. He "must constantly be on the lookout for differences in the classes of people . . . should even so much as one family of questionable racial characteristics or customs move into the neighborhood, the market value of such single family homes will react almost at once to this adverse influence."[50]

Possibly the values of such laymen may be nearer right than the valuations of some appraisers. In the last few years *The Appraisal Journal,* under the editorship of Robert H. Armstrong, has published a few articles taking the contrary view.[51] It is a hopeful sign and a credit to the editor, but there is still no evidence that appraisers are ready to see that the resistance to minorities which may affect values in some areas may not affect values in others. Nor have they sensed that opening up living space to the small proportion of minorities who need it might ease the shortage for them and remove the very threat to value they assert is uniform and inevitable.

[50] Shattuck, *op. cit.,* pp. 38–39.
[51] Charles Abrams, "The New 'Gresham's Law of Neighborhoods'—Fact or Fiction," *The Appraisal Journal,* July, 1951; Rodwin, *op. cit.,* Laurenti, *op. cit.*

XIV

HOMEBUILDING AND IMPROVEMENT ASSOCIATIONS

THE biases of realtors and appraisers should have nothing to do with the home-builders—theoretically. Homebuilding is operated for profit and turnover. A builder builds, sells, and moves on. As with bananas or washing machines, color of coin not complexion should count. But the logic of bias is not always the logic of the market—except when bias is part of the stock-in-trade.

Prior to the advent of federal aid to private housing, the home-building entrepreneur averaged no more than four to six houses a year. In contrast to the mass production and scientific techniques that broke costs in other industries, the builder continued with eighteenth-century tools and methods to fumble along in a twentieth-century environment. Though building a house was an operation of major financial proportions, which should have attracted the big industries looking for mass markets, the average builder marketed no securities, developed no research staff, employed no permanent labor force, and often had his office in his hat. He commanded no sizable personal credit and depended on mortgages for his financing from the time the land was purchased until the finished product was sold.

The rise of FHA and the Home Loan Bank System changed matters. It produced more big-timers like the Levitts and Bohannons and enlarged the operations of most other builders. But in 1950, a substantial majority of the membership of the National Association of Home Builders still built less than 50 houses a year. Those who built a thousand or several thousand were still the few.[1]

[1] Frank W. Cortright, in *Housing Lobby,* Part 2 of Hearings before the House Select Committee on Lobbying Activities, House of Representatives, Eighty-first Congress, Second Session, Pursuant to H. Res. 298, April 19-28, May 3, 5, 7, 1950, p. 234.

Though federal intervention failed to make the industry large-scale, it did highlight for the builders the attractive qualities of federal subventions and insurance. Bigger and better profits could come only with bigger and better organization. This meant closer contact with the National Association of Real Estate Boards. The National Association of Home Builders became a wing of the real estate lobby, but after 1942 it broke off into a separate organization with a new arrangement under which its president became a director of NAREB and each organization appointed a director to the other's board.[2] Though the bodies were now different, the voice remained the same. The bigger builders dominated the organization and maintained an active liaison with the national lobby and with the federal agencies, supporting the latter's legislation and exacting liberal concessions in return. The smaller ones went along passively on the theory that what was good for the goose was good for the gosling.

A by-product of the association with the realtors was a greater cohesion of thinking. In November, 1947, NAHB issued a bulletin prepared by the Urban Land Institute, the realtor-financed research organization which shared offices with NAREB, advocating "homes associations for the smaller operator,"[3] and urged the advantages of "protective covenants." The individual home-buyer, the bulletin complained, too often hesitates to protest an "infraction" by a neighbor. To get real action the developer himself should take the initiative and do what the home-buyer does not. The homes association should be set up with five to seven dummies appointed by the builder, said the bulletin.

The first function of the organization is listed as "enforcement of private covenants and restrictions." Large developers, said the bulletin, can control their neighborhoods but small builders who have greater difficulty could, by pooling efforts with other small builders, achieve wider and more effective restrictions. Where efforts cannot be pooled, "it may be possible to adopt covenants which are similar to those already in force in adjacent developments and to form associations which may affiliate or merge with a neighboring organization." Of course, says the bulletin, keeping the wrong people out should not

[2] *Ibid.*, p. 229.
[3] *Land Planning Service,* National Association of Home Builders, Bulletin No. 3, November. 1947.

be the only purpose of the organization. To make it attractive, it can include recreation for the younger generation, dances, theatricals, picnicking, and "nature study." The nature study did not include that portion of anthropology which teaches that all people belong to the same genus and species, that most of their physical traits are external, that there is no pure race nor any superior or inferior races.

Some home-builders had been practicing race restrictions for years. The others now found the response of their customers encouraging too. Buyers liked the idea of being accepted into an "exclusive" neighborhood. To be discriminating, they were told, you must be discriminatory. The dream of the warm fireside, of the security and pride of ownership would be enlarged to include a whole community of neighbors, friendly, similar, socially acceptable, interesting, and white.

Unlike the tiled bathroom, venetian blinds, and television outlets, the promise of racial exclusiveness cost the builder nothing. Builders began to advertise the "absolutely restricted" neighborhood (no Negroes, Jews, or other minorities), and "reasonably restricted" neighborhoods (Jews, etc., but no Negroes). They soon learned too that the more types they excluded, the more exclusive their neighborhoods would be. They vied with each other in their quest for more groups they might exclude. After selling exclusion of Negroes in the North and Orientals in the West, they began to bar Mexicans, Jews, Armenians, Syrians, Puerto Ricans, American Indians, non-Caucasians, and a host of other "objectionables" who challenged the great American vision of peace, comfort, and security.

A special handbook, edited jointly by the administrative assistant to the National Association of Home Builders and the information director of NAREB, was prepared. The manual advised the home-builder to use "protective covenants" to protect the individual home-buyer against "the thoughtlessness or selfishness of his neighbors. A neighborhood of homogeneous dwellings, parks, schools, churches, stores and other structures" was advocated. Ideas which "may be enlarged upon in institutional advertising of a community" included the "types of neighbors."[4]

Until 1948 the principal medium for keeping the new neighbor-

[4] Lawrence G. Holmes and Carrie Maude Jones, eds., *The Real Estate Handbook*. New York, Prentice-Hall, Inc., 1948, pp. 218, 331.

hoods pure was the restrictive covenant. All the builder had to do was covenant the land with restrictions banning various types of people and he or his buyers could invoke the aid of the courts to enforce it against a violator.

The larger builders had a signal opportunity to set up democratic neighborhoods. There were in fact a number of defense projects built under the Lanham Act in Ohio and Connecticut where nonwhites lived near whites without trouble. But the larger builders did not set the example. The Levitts of Long Island simply wrote a standard provision into their deeds and leases forbidding Negro occupancy. After the Supreme Court barred enforcement of restrictive covenants, the policy against Negro occupancy was continued—though no longer in writing. The Levitts carried the same policy to Levittown, Pennsylvania, where a new community of 70,000 was being built. A similar policy was adopted in nearby Fairless Hills, financed by the U.S. Steel Company, and by other large developments from one coast to the other.

Nor was the Negro the only victim. In Baltimore and Cleveland suburbs, Jews were barred, and a visible pattern of higher-class Jewish ghettos began to appear in the new fashionable areas. In Baltimore there were even a few Jews among those who discriminated against Jews, lending justification to the practices of the non-Jewish discriminators. It required continuous pressure from the Jewish community to make them change their policies.

Blaming the Builders

In the 17 years since 1935, less than 1 per cent of new dwelling construction was for the nonwhite families who comprise 10 per cent of the population. In the war and postwar periods there were many Negroes who could pay for the product. According to Albert M. Cole, administrator of the Housing and Home Finance Agency, there is "a very substantial waiting market for Negro housing ranging from $40 to $90 in rents and from $6500 to $15,000 for sales housing, with a fair number of minority families able to enter the luxury housing market."[5] In 1950, 5.4 per cent of the total Negro population were earning $5000 or more a year.

[5] "What is the Federal Government's Role in Housing?" address to the Economic Club of Detroit, February 8, 1954.

Nor was the Negro a bad risk, a fact accepted by home-builders who had treated fairly with the Negro buyer. Few buyers wanted ownership more than the Negro. The State FHA Director of Georgia has said, "My experience during the past 15 years has convinced me that the Negro is a good credit risk on home finance so long as he receives a fair deal in value for his money."

The problem may be explained partly by what has been described as "the self-fulfilling prophecy," i.e., "If men define situations as real they are real in their consequences."[6] If, justifiedly or not, Negroes are thought to be bad risks, dirty, undependable, and poor customers, appraisals will be low, mortgage money hard to get, interest rates exorbitant, sites undesirable, profits and costs extravagant. The Negro will be forced to pay prices he cannot afford and become the bad risk he would not be were he treated like the white buyer. This has been happening in a great many cases.

The Negro has been forced to pay too much for his houses; land is so far from the source of employment that he spends more for automobile and bus transportation than he can afford; he pays duress prices for his land; sites often lack the benefit of schools, streets, and city services; land often entails inordinate outlays for improvements and utilities; cities penalize him with a high assessment when he has moved out of his place; he pays usurious premiums for building loan money, if he can get it at all, and excessive interest on his permanent loan; oppressive zoning ordinances or other kinds of official opposition prevent him from completing the house or carrying it; FHA officials set appraisals so low that the Negro cannot put up the extra cash required.

Doubtless the anti-Negro propaganda has had much to do with discouraging Negro operations. A building operator does not relish fighting local bias—the builder who puts a Negro development near a white one is viewed as a heel (see the case of Bouvier and Wisehart in Miami cited in Chapter XI). There has been, moreover, enough demand by white families without engaging in specialties. Besides, local public officials and, until recently, the FHA, frowned on builders who ventured into housing for Negroes.

[6] Robert K. Merton, "A Social Psychological Factor," in Arnold Rose, *Race Prejudice and Discrimination*. New York, Alfred A. Knopf, Inc., 1948, p. 510, originally published as "The Self-Fulfilling Prophecy," *The Antioch Review*, Summer, 1948.

The problem therefore calls for a series of demonstrations spurred by the federal government which can break down the folklore, ease the pressures, and create a normal investing environment and a sound home-buying policy. It also calls for an analysis of a number of other specific problems, the more important of which are:

1. Absence of Mortgage Money

Ever since the spiraling of home costs, the rise of the mortgage system,[7] and of the equity system of home buying, the building flow has become dependent on mortgage money. The average man who earned $4000 a year could not put up $10,000 for a house, nor could the builder finance him. The latter depended on permanent and short-term mortgage money, chiefly from life insurance companies, banks, and savings and loan associations.

These mortgage-lenders were conditioned by the same attitudes on the racial issue as were the realtors and home-builders. Their mortgage officers read the same texts, swallowed the same myths. Their appraisers were generally allied with NAREB or its affiliate, the American Institute of Real Estate Appraisers. And though there were men among the group who could do their own thinking, there was rarely any inclination to question the premises on which the hallowed practice rested.

The attitude of Frederick H. Ecker, chairman of the board of Metropolitan Life Insurance Company, to the effect that "Negroes and whites don't mix,"[8] was fairly typical. New York City savings banks agreed among themselves to ban loans in Negro areas, and the Department of Justice, on August 6, 1946, filed a complaint in the Southern District of New York against the Mortgage Conference of New York and 38 of the city's leading bank and trust companies,[9] charging them with agreeing "to use their control of credit to cause the exclusion of certain minority racial and national groups from certain areas." The government alleged that the defendants "prepared, published, kept current and distributed maps of each section

[7] Charles Abrams, *The Future of Housing*. New York, Harper & Brothers, 1946, Chap. 8.

[8] Frederick H. Ecker, Record on Appeal, *Dorsey v. Stuyvesant Town Corporation*, 299 N. Y. 512, 339 U. S. 981.

[9] *United States of America v. The Mortgage Conference of New York, et al.* File No. Civil 37-247.

of New York City showing blocks on which Negroes and Spanish-speaking persons resided; refrained from making mortgage loans on properties in such blocks; and induced owners of real estate in certain sections of New York City to refuse to permit Negroes and Spanish-speaking persons to move into such sections."

The effect of this conspiracy, according to the complaint, was that "Negroes and Spanish-speaking persons have been restricted to residence in certain sections of New York City; have been compelled to pay higher rents than those charged for comparable dwellings in other sections of the city; and owners of properties occupied by Negroes and Spanish-speaking persons have been denied the mortgage financing required to maintain real estate in habitable condition and to operate it successfully at reasonable rental levels."

The defendants did not contest the suit, agreeing to the entry of a civil decree on June 16, 1948.

Despite the injunction it does not appear that interest in New York City's Negro areas has revived. Mortgage loans are now made predominantly by individuals, with bonuses ranging up to 25 per cent of the mortgage principal.[10] It is of course only fair to say that institutions in New York City were not the only offenders, nor the most blameworthy. A few of their number have in fact recently made loans on interracial projects. Moreover, the prosecuting arm of the government was charging the banks with doing exactly what the administrative arm, through FHA and the Home Loan Bank System, was then sanctioning and encouraging.

Savings and loan associations are linked directly with the national real estate lobby by working arrangement, and their leaders share the prejudices of the realtors, appraisers, text-writers, and the real estate professors. In fact, many who wrote or taught the racist doctrine were officials of the United States Savings and Loan League, or its local associations. Their thinking was accepted by some of the very federal officials in the Home Loan Bank Board whose duty it was to regulate the associations.[11]

The local associations are the watchdogs of neighborhood purity

[10] *Halley Investigation,* New York, August 26, 1952; see also, "Is Harlem Realty Being Abandoned by New York Savings Institutions?" *Real Estate Forum,* New York, September, 1952, p. 6.

[11] See Chapter XIII.

in the cities. If there were any attempt to build for minorities where they are not wanted, they would rate the areas out of bounds for future loans. Some loans, however, are made for housing of Negroes in established Negro sections at higher interest rates and though the total of loan funds made available is small, the savings and loan associations are still one of the main sources of mortgage money for segregated housing.

When the federal government, after one of the Chicago riots, called a conference of builders and savings and loan associations to see whether more housing for Negroes could be built in the Cook County area, one of the top building loan lenders said this was the responsibility of Negro lenders.

Negro savings and loan associations make some loans for Negro housing but the total assets of 21 Negro-operated lending companies in 1947 were only $8,864,342.[12] The organizations find that raising adequate capital is all but impossible. Their loans are viewed as undesirable by non-Negro institutions; hence the Negro companies have difficulty in hypothecating or rediscounting their mortgages. Even when the federal government has offered to insure the mortgage loans unconditionally, most lenders have persisted in their refusal to accept the mortgages at par value. Finally, since loans are rated below par in the general market, the companies are not so attractive to savers as are the white companies.

2. Demands for Exorbitant Profits

The fact that mortgages cannot be had through regular channels even when insured by FHA has had a depressing effect on the minority housing market. Mortgages taken back by sellers have been sold at fantastic discounts, though bearing government insurance, and some lending institutions have even rated these mortgages as undesirable at any price. This has contributed to the discouragement of building entrepreneurs.

Trading in older minority property is often marked by low values and fantastic profits. At hearings before City Council President Rudolph Halley in New York in 1953, professional operators in Harlem said they bought property serving Negroes and Puerto

[12] *The Negro Handbook 1949,* Florence Murray, ed. New York, The Macmillan Company, 1949, p. 204.

Ricans for about $6500 a parcel and resold it for $13,000 with $3000 cash, taking back two mortgages for the balance. The first mortgage would sell at a discount of 30 to 40 per cent, the second for whatever the market would bring. The new buyer would then lease the property to a special operator (often a member of a minority group or a petty investor), who would put up $1000 and expect to earn about $1000 a year on his investment. Profits ran from 50 to 100 per cent on investments, depending on the condition of the property and the risks involved. The chief risk is prosecution, not loss of investment.

Many of these properties are subject to violations. They are bought or leased by those skilled in avoiding compliance with the law. Public ire, not always tempered by a willingness to explore underlying causes, asserts itself in demands for prosecution of the landlords whenever lives are lost in fire-trap tenements. Magistrates and prosecutors get more than their quota of newspaper space by inveighing against the owners and exacting dramatic penalties. Newspapers tend to reduce the problem to one of identifying a culprit in each crime, rather than exploring the case and the causes. Thus, when a fire burns some tenants to death, the public conscience is assuaged by sending the owner to jail. Forgotten are the thousands of other victims who are similarly threatened. The ultimate effect is a demand by landlords for ever-growing returns to compensate for ever-growing risks. These risks, however, do not exist on new property sold to responsible members of minority groups and large mortgage discounts are unwarranted, particularly when the mortgages are FHA-insured.

3. Land Acquisition Problems

Even where there are builders willing to build and mortgage-lenders willing to lend, the obstacle of getting land remains. The area occupied by all cities and villages of the country covers only 10 million acres out of a 1903 million total. There is enough room in the United States to house its entire population at a density of twelve families to the acre within a portion of a single state, or within view of the Pacific Ocean. Much good land is available in and near most cities.

The difficulty is not land shortage as such but land shortage for minority housing. The only available land for minorities is usually so far from utilities, transportation, shopping, and other facilities that it is undesirable. A builder who has put up hundreds of houses in Long Island with the financing of the Bowery Savings Bank and FHA insurance listed three reasons for the dearth of Negro housing: Land, Land, and Land. Building housing for whites encounters no trouble with neighbors, landowners, or zoning authorities. But the moment the community hears that a Negro community is intended, the land is either not for sale or becomes impossible to build on because of threatened sanctions. *House + Home* lists the trade secrets for those venturing into homebuilding: "Before you commence be sure your site will not involve you in a civic hassle. Go quietly to the planning commission."[13] The planning commission is not apt to be friendly unless the site is in an established Negro area or is totally unwanted for whites. A single protest, warranted or not, is enough to ban the site.

Obtaining land for Negro housing is both an art and a science. An ingenious southern Negro builder told the writer how he worked out the process of "ripening" land for Negro use. He would buy a farm, send Negroes over to take care of the barns, fields, and livestock. After a few years, the community "would kinda get used to seeing the black folk around those parts, and finally they'd give the nod." The condition was that the builder would separate the project from the surrounding area and keep it "contained" by a "greenbelt." While southern paternalism could effect such compromises, possibilities in the North would be dimmer, for every advance by minorities is viewed with fear and suspicion.

4. Inability to Obtain Fire Insurance

Before erecting his building, the builder usually requires a temporary building loan. Fire insurance is essential to protect the lender during construction. Upon completion of the building, the mortgagee then requires fire insurance for its replacement value. When the Negro builds in an "approved area," he usually gets insurance. When he ventures where he is not wanted, his house may be burned before it is even enclosed. In Chicago, a Negro savings and loan association is willing to advance money to builders for Negro housing, but has found it impossible to obtain insurance coverage when the houses

---

[13] "Non White Housing," *House+Home,* April, 1953, p. 44.

are in hostile sections. With arson and vandalism rampant, some insurance companies have learned not to venture, for they have been burned too often.

5. Imposition of Sanctions

Those willing to venture often face trouble. In Ayreshire Village, Houston, Texas, builders were instructed not to sell homes to Jews. One builder and a real estate agent, in 1949, unwittingly sold a home to a Jewish family. The builder was thereafter denied the opportunity of building any more homes in the village, while the real estate agent was refused property listings in the area.[14] Similar restrictions were applied to at least nine separate subdivisions in the Houston district. The restrictions against Jews force the building of all-Jewish sections, which in turn spurs opposition to any Jew moving into a section of non-Jews.

6. The Club

Special efforts were made in 1953 to encourage lenders to lend and builders to build and a few mortgage-lenders are ready to take a few loans. Civic organizations have tried to clear the air and, in a few cases, have succeeded. But the amount of Negro housing remains negligible.

Builders continue to exhibit an interest in refining exclusion practices, for they have found it a paying device. One of the most popular forms is the "neighborhood club." Prospects not acceptable in the club are not eligible as home-buyers. A majority can therefore keep a minority out. The device is being used against Jews in some cases as well as Negroes, Mexicans, and Puerto Ricans in most.

From the attorney for the California Real Estate Association has come the following suggestion now widely approved by writers on subdivisions:

A homes association could be formed, the members of which are the owners of building sites within the residential tract, and prohibiting the occupancy except to those persons or families, who hold an occupancy permit issued by the homes association. The issuance of the permit is dis-

[14] *Gentlemen's Agreements Situation in Houston,* Memo from Southwestern Jewish Community Relations Council, Houston, Texas, September 14, 1951. Through the intervention of civic organizations, some progress has been made in the Houston situation.

cretionary and without reference to race or color but based entirely upon personal qualifications as a good neighbor, or in other words, cultural status. This is an extension of the idea that any club may regulate admission to its membership. Many a country club restricts occupancy of home sites on its grounds to its members. Religious colonies have long been established upon the same basis. This arrangement would likewise operate against undesirable Caucasians as prospective buyers.[15]

This idea has spread. Exclusion is even openly advertised in the more enlightened newspapers, viz, the New York *Herald Tribune,* September 20, 1953: "Smoke Rise for Ideal Community Living . . . Club Plan Protection." On June 26, 1953, the *U. S. News & World Report,* edited by David Lawrence, featured an article headed "New Ways to Pick a Neighbor."

> There still may be ways to control who lives next door. One way is to form a co-op. Another is to start a club or association, . . . the club imposes any qualifications it chooses for membership. . . . A "veto power" over resale of property in real estate developments is being tried by a number of builders. The development company imposes restrictions on the first purchasers. This is believed to be thoroughly legal. Any owner may designate a buyer. Then, as a condition of sale, the company requires the buyer not to resell his home unless the next purchaser is approved. This method allows the company to control the character of residents in the neighborhood.
> A variation of this plan is to require buyers to give the development company the first opportunity to buy back the property if the purchaser wants to sell. This method is known as "first refusal" and is often used in new subdivisions. By exercising its option to buy, the company can forestall sales to persons to whom it objects. This device also is used by neighborhood associations and clubs.[16]

In June, 1954, the National Association of Home Builders seemed at last to recognize the existence of a housing problem for minorities and urged its members to explore the possibilities of building segregated housing. The social and political pressures are growing and something must be done soon, said its president. "The advocates of integration, however, will continue to put pressure on governmental policy and private selling practices in the general housing market."

[15] See, for example, Stanley L. McMichael, *Real Estate Subdivisions.* New York, Prentice-Hall, Inc., 1949, p. 207.

[16] P. 30. When the American Jewish Committee communicated with the editor about the implications of the article, a later article appeared citing authorities repudiating the argument that minority infiltrations inevitably depress values, (" 'Restricted' Area: Does it Pay?" *ibid,* October 23, 1953.)

Mortgage lenders were challenged to make loans. An information kit was distributed to builders.[17]

Though the proposal threatened to stratify neighborhoods by race, it represented a departure from the previous practice of building almost no housing at all for minorities. Whether the exhortations will have any effect in producing housing for minorities, whether they are only surface efforts to satisfy the increasing pressures on FHA, or whether they represent a new attempt to effect segregation in the schools by segregating Negroes in neighborhoods, all remains to be seen.

NEIGHBORHOOD IMPROVEMENT ASSOCIATION

One of the remarkable phenomena of the American political and social scheme is the vast network of clubs and organizations. These exist for many purposes—political, professional, social, and economic. There is hardly a cause in American life, from a universal language to the preservation of barber shop quartets, that sooner or later does not spawn an organization to sponsor it. The action organizations or public interest groups serve a constructive purpose by providing the individual protestant with the collective strength to press a cause and the personal anonymity that protects him against reprisal.

One of the more recent organizations is the neighborhood improvement association, also known as the "improvement club," "taxpayers association," "civic association," "taxpayers' league," "chamber of commerce," "property-owners' association," "homeowners' association," "homeowners' foundation," etc. They have long existed to improve physical patterns, oppose tax increases, press for parks or schools, keep the streets clean, or zone the area against industrial intrusions and nuisances.

The migration of minorities prompted many of these organizations to mobilize against possible intruders or to oust minorities who have already settled. Meetings are now called by them to arouse owners to the "perils of invasion," urge them not to sell or rent to minorities, exert moral pressures and sanctions against owners who have done

---

[17] *Housing for Minority Groups.* Suggested Activity for Local Associations of Home Builders. "Package Program" and Agenda for Local Meeting. Prepared by Mortgage Finance Dept., National Association of Home Builders under supervision of Minority Group Housing Committee, Wallace Johnson, Chairman.

so, and often engage in intimidation and violence. They are also an important factor in the discouragement of builders from venturing into minority housing.

Most owners organize out of a genuine fear that entry of minorities will hurt values and speed deterioration. But the associations are also sponsored by promoters of jobs paid for by panicky home-owners or troublemakers who earn a living from race hate. Small owners are thrown into fits of trepidation and join a common front to preserve home and fireside against an "invader." A patriotic glow and a crusading fervor mark these efforts. The organizations have grown by leaps and bounds.

The waves of violence against Negroes in Chicago during and after the war years coincided with the activity of these associations and the circulation of their inflammatory propaganda.[17a] The Kenwood and Hyde Park Property Owners Association became prominent in 1918 to "make Hyde Park white." It described itself as "a red blood organization who say openly, we won't be driven out. We make no secret of our methods, they are effective and legal. . . . Every owner has the right to defend his property to the utmost of his ability with every means at his disposal. . . . Any property owner who sells property anywhere in our district to undesirables is an enemy to the white owner and should be discovered and punished."[18]

Some 58 bombs exploded in white houses rented or sold to Negroes were attributed to the activities of this association.[19] Detroit's rioting was also inspired by a neighborhood association dedicated to keeping the Negro out of white neighborhoods.

The Associations and the Restrictive Covenant

The associations received a big fillip through the rise of the racial restrictive covenant. The fact that state courts had sanctioned the

---

[17a] Robert C. Weaver, *The Negro Ghetto*. New York, Harcourt, Brace & Company, 1948, p. 39; St. Clair Drake and Horace R. Cayton, *Black Metropolis*. New York, Harcourt, Brace and Company, 1945, p. 73; *The Negro in Chicago*, The Chicago Commission on Race Relations. Chicago, University of Chicago Press, 1922, pp. 117-31; Zorita Mikva, *The Neighborhood Improvement Association: A Counter Force to the Expansion of Chicago's Negro Population:* A Dissertation submitted to the Faculty of the Division of Social Science in Candidacy for the Degree of Master of Arts, Department of Sociology, Chicago, June, 1951 (in manuscript).

[18] *The Negro in Chicago, op. cit.*, pp. 118–123.

[19] *Ibid.*, pp. 122-24.

covenant, and that even the government itself was approving and encouraging its use, legitimatized their project and even gave it moral purpose. In the West, organizations specialized in spreading the covenants against Negroes, Chinese, and Japanese for a set fee.

Associations acted to threaten or cajole owners into observing their covenants, brought suit against them for violations, threatened Negroes with damage suits when they moved in despite the covenants, and organized intimidation campaigns when other methods failed. As two consultants said in their report to the government:

> There is no such thing as a neighborhood which does not need an improvement association. Such organizations in addition to their effect on the neighborhood would have great value as educators in citizenship and democracy, and would give people a proper vehicle for approaching the city government on matters relating to their home territory. . . . There can be initiated a drive for restrictive covenants.[20]

The Community Builders' Handbook of the Urban Land Institute, research organization of the realty groups, cites J. C. Nichols, a developer with a long success in employing the association device and restrictive covenants in home development: "We now have 19 such associations, all functioning in an excellent manner under one common staff, and every lot is sold subject to a land assessment for such associations."[21]

World War II did not stem their growth, and despite the patriotic atmosphere, there was some incitement to violence. In 1945, a San Francisco association set out to attack Negro infiltration and kept fanning hate throughout the war period. In 1945, one of the organizations in Los Angeles appeared before the Mayor's Interracial Committee and threatened violence and bloodshed if Negroes were admitted into one of the war housing projects.[22] Associations also played their part in the Sojourner Truth riot in Detroit in 1942.

Research on the associations is sparse. One study[23] of the associa-

---

[20] *Appendices to the Preliminary Report on Conservation of Middle-Aged Neighborhoods and Properties,* National Housing Agency, Office of the Administrator, Urban Redevelopment Division, Report U.D. 3, October 16, 1944, a confidential report cited in "The 'Neighborhood Unit' Is an Instrument of Segregation," by Reginald R. Isaacs, Part II, *Journal of Housing,* August, 1948, p. 216.

[21] *The Community Builders' Handbook,* Urban Land Institute, 1947.

[22] Weaver, *op. cit.,* p. 252; San Francisco *Chronicle,* July 24, 1945.

[23] Mikva, *op. cit.*

tions in Chicago suggests that their strength is derived not from the number of members. Eighty of the groups claim memberships of less than 300, nine claim between 300 and 600, and another eight claim membership between 600 and 2000. These claims are apt to be wishful. The South Manor Improvement Association reported a membership of 200, but when the president warned in a published notice of meeting that the association would disband if attendance were not better, only 50 persons showed up.[24] Yet it would be an error to measure organizational importance by membership alone. A realistic test is the organization's effectiveness in mustering political support on a given issue at a particular time.

A number of the Chicago associations operate through block captains who solicit membership from each family. Local aldermen are importuned for their help, in return for which they are given political support. While many still function to keep their neighborhoods free from smoke, noise, factories, and other unwholesome intrusions, the main purpose of most is to keep minorities in their place.

In Washington, D. C., the Federation of Civic Associations promoted restrictive covenants, sought to block public housing, and tried to bar aid from the Community Chest to organizations supporting expansion of housing for Negroes.

In Baltimore, an association functions to organize owners not to sell their properties to Negroes and to post their houses with signs reading "Not For Sale." Los Angeles in 1953 had about 13 associations organized to keep Negroes and other minorities out of white neighborhoods. They are usually dominated by a few persons, mainly real estate men. Dues are collected from families in each tract.[25] The Los Angeles associations meet in school buildings, a restraining locale. Speakers confine themselves to exhorting owners not to sell to minorities, but stronger methods may be used between meetings.

In one case, a woman who had shown a house to a Filipino was threatened with a $10,000 damage suit. In another case, the owner was warned her house would be burned.

Much of the money collected by Los Angeles associations has

[24] *Ibid.*
[25] Letter from T. Dale Gardner, Executive Secretary, Committee on Human Relations. County of Los Angeles, May 27, 1953.

been used for court cases, but as cases dragged on or were lost, "it became frustrating to the more neurotic white residents of the community. It was under these circumstances that vandalism occurred. The police often attributed these acts to youths who were motivated by their parents. To my knowledge, no person has ever been arrested or convicted for committing such vandalism."[26]

Miami's Carver Village incidents were sparked by a neighborhood association. In Houston, a Riverside Home Owners Protective Association organized "to keep Negroes from purchasing properties in the residential area." The organization followed purchase of a $35,000 home by a Negro. The usual threatening telephone calls were accompanied by the sending of fake ambulance and police alarms. According to the Houston *Chronicle,* a group of "several hundred white neighbors gathered in front of the house and a spokesman suggested 'If you leave this neighborhood you will live longer and be happier. . . .' "[27]

In the Rolling Wood subdivision in the San Francisco Bay area, a neighborhood association representing about 100 of some 700 homeowners tried to buy off a Negro who had bought a home in the area. When the offer was refused, the president of the association publicized his personal opposition to his Negro neighbor and the next day a crowd formed, hurling stones. A major riot was averted by the intervention of state officials.[28]

The Neighborhood Association and the Neighborhood Press

The local community newspaper often plays an important part in the growth of the associations. The latter are stoutly supported by the newspapers which announce association meetings, publicize their activities, report neighborhood news from the point of view of the associations, and favor them in editorials. The larger urban newspapers generally avoid the racial question, partly because it is viewed as a hot potato, partly because they do not know how to handle race news, and partly because their wide circulation includes both white and black, liberal and bigot. The suburban paper, often distributed free, is less troubled by these conflicts.

[26] *Ibid.*
[27] June 17, 1952.
[28] Letter from Edward Howden, Executive Director, Council for Civic Unity of San Francisco, August 8, 1952.

An increasing portion of the suburban and neighborhood press seems to have discovered that racial bias and circulation can go hand in hand and that anti-Negro sentiment pays off. Before one of the major riots in Chicago, the Southtown Planning Association was active not only in spreading the racial restrictive covenant but in exerting pressure against property owners to resist Negro infiltration. The *Southtown Economist,* whose publisher is a leader of one of the federated associations, supported the association's point of view in "keeping the Englewood Community homogeneous." During the aldermanic campaign immediately preceding the riot, candidates openly advocated "keeping the community white." Anti-Negro cartoons were displayed and loudspeakers broadcast anti-Negro propaganda. Neighborhood social institutions, including even some religious institutions, openly cooperated in the campaign against the Negro.[29]

Another example of cooperation between the local press and the associations is the Calumet Civic Council's fight against Negroes in the Fernwood public housing project in Chicago in 1947. The Council represented twelve individual civic associations that aroused opposition to Negro occupancy. The *Calumet Index,* in an editorial on June 9, 1947, headed "Protect Your Homes," said:

Negro interests in the state have again seen fit to try to force themselves on the white population by having bills introduced in the state legislature which would wipe out all property restrictions. Unless these bills are defeated, every white neighborhood in the city and state will find itself defenseless against the wanton destruction of property values by a Negro minority intent upon forcing itself upon white neighborhoods.

The paper also published scores of letters, the writers often using pseudonyms, typical of which was the following signed "A Chicago Policeman":

. . . I'm in a position to know the Negro intimately being a policeman and handling so many of them during 18 years on the force. They've pushed the whites around plenty these last five or six years and because we ignore them they have you bluffed and get bolder as the years roll by.

If we have to have a showdown with them to protect our homes and families, I'm in favor of it. God knows I wouldn't want one alongside of me. . . . You can't argue a point with a Negro because he's going to

[29] Report of the Commission on Human Relations, City of Chicago, December 10, 1949, p. 16 (mimeographed).

have his way whether he's right or wrong and he'll back himself up with a knife or other deadly weapon. . . . I hope the whites some day soon will organize and stop this menace to our way of living and the sooner they do it the better. I'm not prejudiced . . . but. . . . They want the bright lights and a bottle—not a quiet life.[30]

From another letter, dated June 16, 1947:

. . . Sister, if you had heard your daughter or your little granddaughter scream as I heard a little girl scream recently, who was receiving a treatment of your "brotherhood of all men" from a Negro. . . .
(Signed) A HOMEOWNER, A VOTER

A few months after these and similar letters, the Fernwood riots broke out. Blame for the bloodshed was then placed on the mayor for allowing the few Negro veterans to move into the public housing project. One letter exhorted:

Citizens, is this the America our forefathers fought to establish? Let us rise to the challenge.

A MOTHER

The Fernwood riot, instead of inspiring contrition, was urged as justification for removing the Negro families from the project. The Calumet Civic Council wrote the mayor that inclusion of the Negroes was a "shameful disgrace."

Federation of the Associations

The Supreme Court's decision outlawing enforcement of the racial covenants in 1948 at first gave the associations a sharp setback. It crippled the device which gave them personal contact with the individual homeowner whose signature was sought to the covenant. But it did not eliminate them. Opposition to public housing became the new rallying call. The claim was broadcast that public housing would increase the homeowner's taxes, locate cheap-looking housing near his home, and invite "undesirables."

More organizations were formed in Chicago, including the Fortieth Ward Civic and Improvement Association, National Home and Property Owners Association, Southwest Neighborhood Council, Taxpayers' Action Committee, and Tenth Ward Citizens Association. By 1950 there were some 200 local improvement associations in

[30] The *Calumet Index,* June, 1947, letter dated June 9, 1947.

Chicago, many of them linked in a city-wide federation.[31] Other programs on their agenda called for enactment of subtly worded zoning ordinances which would ban Negroes, and for the cooperation of the police and public officials to help keep "intruders" out.[32]

Federation has facilitated the merger of activities and the directing of influence where it can be most effective. The homeowner was generally content to remain aloof to organizations except on neighborhood problems immediately affecting him. Now he is being urged to exert pressure upon his Congressman to protect his home and fireside. The local improvement associations, an established force in city and state affairs, are now operating on the national level through their federated associations. The main attack has been aimed at public housing, which is held up as a threat to white supremacy in American neighborhoods.

In Chicago, the interracial housing policy of the housing authority and the placement of temporary war housing projects throughout the city have been the associations' favorite targets and new associations were organized in the two years following 1949, with the public housing issue their chief focus. Public housing is viewed as a threat to the homogeneity of white communities.

The Southtown Planning Association in Chicago, which sponsored a pamphlet entitled "Choose Your Neighbor," was supported not only by small property-owners but by businessmen, led by the publisher of the *Southtown Economist,* and included among its other officers a prominent businessman, a realtor, and a banker who was the president of the Chicago City Bank and Trust Company, the president of the Mutual Bank, and a past president of the American Bankers Association. Its budget for signing up restrictive covenants was $30,000.[33]

In Los Angeles, fear of Negro infiltration was played upon by real estate groups to defeat public housing in a local election. The federations are better financed than the individual associations, hold meetings with member groups, and call mass meetings when mobilization is

[31] A list of 153 neighborhood improvement associations has been compiled from notices in community newspapers alone. Mikva, *op. cit.*

[32] For a list of these devices, see Chapter XVI.

[33] Mikva, *op. cit.*

needed. Prominent real estate men are among the leaders of the federated associations. Despite the distinct anti-racial purpose, these organizations attract some of the presumably most respectable citizens.

Neighborhood Associations, Boards, and Bigots

On the periphery of some neighborhood associations operate the openly fanatical organizations. The monthly report of the executive director of the Chicago Commission on Human Relations for September, 1950, states:

> Factors have come into the most recent disturbances which add significant danger to them. Extremists on the left and right are agitating in these already upset communities. The White Circle League, an openly anti-Negro organization, is operating on a white supremacy program in these areas where Negroes are purchasing homes. This organization is so vicious that its leader, Joseph Beauharnais, has been convicted and fined in Municipal Court for vilifying the Negro people. . . . The activity of this group has intensified the anti-racial hatreds, and attacks have been made upon property owned by Negroes, or where Negroes are prospective buyers the property has been vandalized. Whenever these anti-racial demonstrations occur, they serve as an open invitation to communist groups and their sympathizers to use the event for agitational purposes.

Los Angeles was the birthplace of the Small Property Owners of America and America Plus, Inc. The former has dedicated itself among other things to the defeat of public housing. It is said to be linked through its president to a Klan-type secret organization called the "Royal Order of American Defenders for White, Gentile, Protestant, American Citizens."[34]

America Plus, Inc., is campaigning for the right of the American neighborhood "to protect its own property values and to fix its own standards of culture, congeniality and happiness through its association voluntarily created to achieve these ends." A "Freedom of Choice" amendment is proposed to the state constitution as a model for similar movements throughout the nation. It would give owners of restaurants, landlords, barber shops, skating rinks, etc., the same right to discriminate. "Private property owners living in the same neighborhood shall have the right to contract with each other concerning the occupancy of private housing accommodations in such

[34] *California Eagle,* May 21, 1953.

area, and that they may form local associations for that purpose."[35]

In an editorial on December 6, 1951, the San Franciso *Chronicle* summed up America Plus, Inc., as well as it counterparts in other areas of the country:

WHAT'S THIS "AMERICA PLUS"?

The "freedom of choice" label is, of course, window dressing. What the measure seeks to sell to the people of California is the freedom to discriminate.

There is nothing new about this pitch—it has been the stock-in-trade of such men as Huey Long, Father Coughlin, William Dudley Pelley, and a list of kindred demagogues as long as your arm. But it is always dangerous, for it always turns to the unthinking a plausible face, and proceeds to strum upon their own prejudices. . . .

The Communists, to suit their purposes, are trying to destroy it [America] by dividing class against class, rich against poor, worker against manager. The extremists at the other end, in their turn and for their own obscure ends, are trying to destroy it by setting race against race, creed against creed, as in this so-called "Freedom of Choice" amendment.

It would be a mistake to assume that either of them could not succeed. . . . This country, comprising the most complicated patchwork of racial origins and religious faiths of any Nation in history, draws its great strength from this heterogeneity, but its vulnerability springs from the same fact. If ever the process of racial and religious fission gets off to a fair start here, it can sweep us to destruction. That's why an obligation of vigilance rests upon every American. That's why outfits like the one calling itself "America Plus" need to be exposed and rejected promptly and decisively, before they can get started with their divisive work.

[35] *Fact Sheet #2,* California Committee for Human Rights, January 22, 1952.

XV

DISCRIMINATION IN HOTELS AND RESORTS

A N OLD rule of the common law is that an innkeeper may not arbitrarily refuse a traveler shelter. If the wayfarer is behaved and willing to pay, he may not be relegated to the manger when there is room at the inn. The rule was originally less a product of Christian ethics than British convenience. It was extended to include the hostelries that replaced inns in the burgeoning cities, became part of the common law in America,[1] and was implemented by penal statutes in a number of states. After the Civil War it was enacted into federal law but voided by the Supreme Court as an invasion of states' rights.[2]

Despite statutes and custom, discrimination in hotels and resorts of all grades is common. Negroes are discriminated against in most hotels and resorts. Jews are apt to be barred from many resorts. Discrimination against Chinese, Indians, Japanese, Mexicans, and other minorities is frequent, varying with the place.

Exclusion from hotels may curtail a man's chances to make a living. No matter how competent, a Negro may find it impossible to hold a job that requires extensive travel. If his job is important enough to involve attendance at conventions and business conferences, he may be kept out of meeting rooms, banquet halls, and restaurants. These practices block the path to a leveling of economic and social differences.

[1] Refusing a guest without cause gives rise to an action for damages, and the Civil Rights Laws affording specific remedies and penalties have not abrogated the common law rule. But damages, in the absence of specific statutory penalties, are generally hard to prove.

[2] *Civil Rights Cases,* 109 U.S. 3.

The ordinary worker suffers, too. The Negro who moves to a strange city in search of a job must first find a bed. Inability to get temporary shelter may force him to give up, whereas the white mechanic will be accepted at almost any hotel he chooses. Minorities cannot enjoy freedom of opportunity so long as hotels admit them only as porters and dishwashers.

The written rule of hotel practice is to refuse rooms to "undesirables." The unwritten rule includes as undesirables people of the wrong race or color. Refusing a guest is an art. It is simple to say "There is no room." But a Negro may have a written confirmation of his reservation or he may decide to sit in the lobby and wait for a check-out. The standard practice on paper is:

Front Service Division—When undesirable persons attempt to register, they must not be just refused accommodations, but offered only the highest-priced rooms. If they agree to purchase the room at that rate, they must be given a room that sells regularly at that rate.[3]

Offering an undesirable the best suite may not make social sense but it seems to make business sense. The Negro who is offered the de luxe suite at $30 a day is not apt to stay long.

To spare embarrassment to dignitaries from Haiti, Liberia, India, and other nations that do not conform to the American standard of whiteness, the State Department has often provided rooms in Blair House or Lee House in Washington.[4] In Boston, a young Haitian lawyer visiting the United States under State Department auspices was evicted from a hotel and forced to pay triple the rates charged whites in a second-rate rooming house.[5] These incidents are common but they break into print only through the clumsiness of a desk clerk followed up by the orneriness of the visitor. President-elect Eisenhower was surprised to hear about them from a Negro delegation in December, 1952. Six months later Winston Churchill told the House of Commons he would not change the site of the Bermuda Conference because there was "insufficient evidence" of discrimination against

[3] *Standard Practice Manuals for Hotel Operation.* National Hotel Management Co., Inc. New York, Harper & Brothers, 1935.

[4] *Segregation in Washington.* A Report of the National Committee on Segregation in the Nation's Capital. Chicago, November, 1948.

[5] *PM,* January 17, 1944.

Jews by the Mid-Ocean Club where the conference was to be held.[6] Their unawareness was a sign of isolation from the realities of discrimination, not unusual among persons who have never been snubbed by a room clerk.

Denying hotel accommodations to people of unwanted color or faith is another product of the exclusiveness which has pushed its way into the American scene. The dowager from Atlanta visiting her daughter and new son-in-law in a big northern city would be humiliated to find a Negro in the elevator, unless he were running it. The hotel therefore tries to accommodate its patron's prejudices along with her person, no matter how much humiliation is suffered by the excluded minority.

New York City, whose polyglot population has been fusing together for centuries, is one of the nation's most liberal cities. But when the Jehovah's Witnesses held their 1953 convention in New York City, a number of hotels declined to provide rooms because the sect has a sizable proportion of Negroes and is nondiscriminatory.

The policy of hotels in the Times Square district has become more liberal since the war, but the liberalism is far from uniform. One manager, a veteran of almost twenty-five years in the business, summarized the situation:

"First-class hotels are choosy toward everybody, regardless of race, color or previous conditions of servitude. They will, however, let in a famous Negro, such as Lena Horne." Third-class hotels will admit a few Negroes, especially if the manager is worried about the loss from empty rooms. One of these hotels reported three regular Negro tenants: a well-known actor, a night club singer, and a minister. The manager remarked that they were among his best patrons. "They are quiet and they pay their bills on time," he said. "I have never been cheated by a Negro."

The most discriminatory hotels, this manager declared, are the

[6] The evidence submitted was an acceptance of a reservation from a Vincent O'Connor and a simultaneous rejection of a reservation by a Jacob Goldberg. Discrimination was also charged by The Travel Agents Committee to Combat Discrimination in the Travel Industry. The committee reported that the club "has a policy of religious discrimination. It will not accept Jewish guests." The club explained that its policy is to accept guests who "will be congenial to the members and will themselves be happy during their stay." (Anti-Defamation League release, June 12, 1953, published in New York *Herald Tribune,* June 24, 1953.)

second-class hotels that rank beneath the status of the Waldorf and the Pierre. Despite their precautions, they are occasionally caught when a registration has been confirmed and the registrant turns out to be a Negro. He may then be given a room for a single night or offered a costly room. The second-class places rarely accept a Negro who appears without a reservation.

One liberal-minded hotel-keeper east of Times Square, catering to an intellectual and literary clientele, once decided to take all comers on the theory that his regular guests were opposed to discrimination or would not care. This was a pioneering move at the time. The new policy soon became generally known and the hotel got increased applications from Negroes. Fearing the effects of a disproportionate balance, the hotel went back to the old policy of limited Negro registration. The fear may well have been groundless and certainly would have been if other hotels also had an open policy. Another Times Square hotel now actually encourages Negro registration. Room clerks in other hotels regularly send Negro applicants to it.

Ordinary arithmetic shows that there is little reason today for hotel managers to worry about an inundation if they admit Negroes on the same basis as other applicants. Negroes form only a small percentage of the population, and proportionately fewer Negroes than whites can afford the normal rates of good hotels. If only a single hotel in a large city would accept a Negro applicant, then there might be risk of many more Negroes choosing the one hostelry that would accommodate them. But, despite the persistence of discriminatory practices, Negro applicants in northern cities may choose among as many as a dozen respectable hotels—particularly if they take the trouble to write or wire for reservations in advance.

The improvement in recent years has been perceptible. Test suits have prompted hotel owners to show more respect for law suits and anti-bias laws. Labor unions have helped to break down discriminatory policies. "The elevator operators are Negroes and they would squawk if we discriminated," one manager frankly explained.

A. H. Feller, late counsel to the United Nations, told the writer that the problem of accommodations for colored personnel and delegates had worried the Secretariat. After conversations with the Waldorf, it was agreed that UN guests and dignitaries would be accepted without frowning at their complexions. In return, the UN promised to favor the Waldorf with its recommendations.

Negroes fare better when they are delegates to conventions of predominantly white organizations. The hotels reckon that the presence of a few Negroes is not so damaging as the loss of several hundred reservations. The recent practice of many public-interest organizations in turning down convention cities where hotels discriminate has had a salutary effect.

A no-discrimination commitment must be arranged well in advance. The National Municipal League scheduled its annual conference in Nashville several years ago and discovered when its members arrived that Negroes could not have rooms. Since then the League has held meetings in San Antonio, Texas, and Richmond, Virginia, without any hotel troubles.

The National Association of Intergroup Relations Officials held its 1953 meeting in Washington. A number of its members are Negroes. Four first-class hotels were willing to house the conference and give Negroes both rooms and free use of hotel facilities. The organization chose the Hotel Willard as conference headquarters.

The improvement, however, has been far from uniform. In St. Louis, Walter Gordon, eminent California penal authority, his wife, and other delegates to the convention of the Congress of Correction were denied accommodations by the Statler Hotel because they were Negroes. The Statler manager explained that segregation was the rule at all St. Louis hotels and that the hotel had offered to obtain accommodations for the three Negroes at hotels "catering to members of that race."[7]

New Orleans has made some concessions to South Americans of dubious hue in order to compete as a port city with Miami. An American Negro professor returning from a trip to South America and stopping off at New Orleans told the writer that when he entered the airport bus for the ride to the city he was advised to sit with the whites—because the driver had overheard him talking in Spanish.

Discriminatory policies are even more common in semi-transient and resort operations than in ordinary hotels. These policies have prevailed for a long time. This writer was shown a letter dated May 8, 1897, from the proprietor of the Pocono Mountain House, Mount

[7] St. Louis *Post-Dispatch,* October 9, 1950.

Pocono, Pennsylvania, to a Maryland bride-elect who had inquired about reservations for the honeymoon. The letter read:

DEAR MADAM:

Replying to your esteemed favor of the 6th inst., would say we can accommodate you with one good double room to be occupied by two persons from $10 to $12.50 per week each person during June. You may also be pleased to learn that we do not cater to the patronage of Hebrews. Trusting we may hear from you further, we remain

Very respectfully yours,
E. E. HOOKER

Fifty-seven years later, the Anti-Defamation League charged the Poconos' High Point Inn with having mailed to various residents of Pennsylvania cards stating that the hotel caters "to a young Gentile clientele between 20 to 35 years of age."[8]

The groups proscribed today and the rigidity of the restrictions vary. The resort belt from the Adirondacks to Bermuda and Nassau will turn a cold shoulder to Jews in some places and to Negroes and Orientals in most. The devices for keeping out the unwanted may be a sign reading "No Jews allowed," "Christians only"; or the desk clerk may politely refuse the visitor accommodation. Most often the tip-off will be given through advertisements reading "Protestant church nearby," "Restricted clientele," "Discriminating clientele," "Our clientele is 100% Christian," "Admission through club membership only." The *Hotel Red Book* a passenger picks up on any train is punctuated with these tips and neither the railroads nor the hotel associations have voiced protest.

In other cases letters to applying guests will make clear the hotel's preferences in advance. A resort owner in Falmouth, Massachusetts, for example, wrote: "Our clientele is gentile and consists mostly of young people." Similar practices are pursued in Ulster and Warren Counties, New York.[9] A Wisconsin study in 1947–1948 listed more than 100 hotels and resorts in that state which advertised such discriminatory policies either in brochures or letters. The information conveyed was either by the blunt "Gentiles only" or the more protracted "Although we hold no prejudices, for the good of all

[8] *Jewish Chronicle*, Columbus, Ohio, November 13, 1953.
[9] New York *Daily News*, December 1, 1952.

concerned we must adhere as closely as possible to a restricted clientele policy. . . ."[10]

Enactment in 1951 of a Wisconsin law barring the use of discriminatory advertising and the activities of a state commission on human rights may have helped but not eliminated discriminatory practices. A survey made just prior to the law showed 39 out of 79 resorts had a restrictive policy; 14 had a questionable policy; 8 failed to answer; and only 18 indicated no discrimination.[11]

Though one member of the commission says progress has been "reasonably good" since the law, civic groups say discrimination is not decreasing. A survey by an American Veterans Committee post showed that five out of six resorts in an area still discriminate on the basis of religion. At the legislative hearings the position of the resort owners was put as follows by J. W. Johnson, president of the National Resort Association and the Selected Resort Association: "We do not intend to lose our right to choose our friends, associates and companions."[12] Other resort owners said they only follow the prejudices of their guests and that they would lose the patronage of the prejudiced if they changed their policy.

In May, 1952, Lyle Olson, a resort owner in Somo Lake, Wisconsin, who refused to discriminate, charged that he was visited by a belligerent group of Tomahawk citizens and threatened. "Minority groups ruined the country," he was told. His liquor license, he charged, was revoked on a technicality and his credit with liquor suppliers cut off. At a meeting of resort owners, the president of the Tomahawk Chamber of Commerce was reported as saying: "The Governor's office is 100% behind us (in opposition to accepting Jewish and Negro guests). They all believe as we do but they're playing politics

[10] Milwaukee *Journal,* November 21, 1948.

[11] Some 6500 resort and hotel operators were thereafter sent letters explaining the new law and one member of the commission reported that almost all discriminatory signs and advertising had disappeared. Another member said: "If a resort owner wants to accept the bounties of tax money by having a paved road built past his property, his business advertised nationally and his lake stocked with fish, then he must be willing to recognize not only the law of the land but the basic American principle that all men are created equal." (Statement of Bruno Bitker, *National Jewish Post,* Indianapolis, Ind., May 16, 1952.)

[12] *Op. cit.*

and have to keep under the table." Governor Walter Kohler, Jr., called the charge "ridiculous."

The chances of a guest with a Jewish name being accepted by a resort chosen from advertisements in the New York *Herald Tribune* are 27 per cent, 48 per cent in The New York *Times*. Persons with non-Jewish names have an 88–91 per cent chance.[13]

A survey by the Anti-Defamation League revealed 675 hotels in 21 states where prejudice is a matter of public record.[14] A survey in 1953 of 809 Florida resort hotels and real estate agencies[15] showed that Jewish applicants were acceptable in only 28 per cent. Non-Jews applying for accommodations in the same hotels showed an acceptance rate of 62 per cent. One hotel wrote that it followed a restrictive policy with regard to "pets, children under 12 years of age and the Hebrew Religion." Another said, "We have most denominations of churches with the exception of Jewish Synagogues"; a prominent realtor assured his clients that "we do not sell property to Miami Beach elements or their cousins from Brooklyn." The survey showed that almost every resort center on Florida's east and west coast has establishments which bar Jews. Fort Lauderdale and Delray Beach are notorious for their discriminatory policies. In Fort Lauderdale, 56 per cent of hotels indicated discrimination against Jews in replies to requests for reservations, while another 4 per cent used discriminatory suggestions, such as "near churches." A spot check showed that 73 per cent displayed discriminatory signs such as "Restricted Clientele" and "Selected Clientele."

Delray Beach openly boasts that it is "the only city in the East Coast fully restricted to Gentiles." Half the replies received in answer to a request by a Jewish applicant contained categorical discriminatory statements while the rest used subtler phraseology.

There is no discrimination against Jews in northern and central Florida, and in St. Petersburg, where discrimination formerly existed,

[13] Ruth G. Weintraub, *How Secure These Rights?* Garden City, N. Y., Doubleday & Company, Inc., 1949, p. 30.

[14] Benjamin Epstein and Arnold Foster, *The Troublemakers.* Garden City, N. Y., Doubleday & Company, Inc., 1952.

[15] *A Survey of Resort Discrimination in the State of Florida.* Prepared by the National Discriminations Department and the Florida Regional Office of the Anti-Defamation League of B'nai B'rith, May 15, 1953 (mimeographed).

90 per cent of resorts no longer discriminate due to a vigorous anti-discrimination campaign.

Another Anti-Defamation League survey[16] showed that 40 per cent of resorts in Maine follow a discriminatory policy. A bill to outlaw discrimination was defeated after opposition by hotel owners. When a similar bill was introduced in New Hampshire, *The Concord Monitor* opposed the measure editorially: "Why run the risk of losing a lot of recreation dollars furnished by vacationers who refuse to sleep under the same roof with Jews? It is a matter of business, nothing else, with the proprietors." Counsel for the Maine Hotelmen's Association opposed the measure and came to the hearings armed with photostats of the *Monitor* editorial. Despite support by other newspapers, the bill was defeated.

The exclusiveness which has become part of the stock-in-trade of the resort hotels costs nothing and may enhance prestige. By advertising that it bars Jews, a hotel emphasizes the care with which it selects its clientele; the guest is honored by being accepted and feels a perceptible improvement in his social position.

This policy of discrimination may be more elastic than it is in permanent neighborhoods. It may be relaxed in some places if business is bad or the seasonal peak has passed. When Alvin Smith is given a mail reservation and appears as an identifiable Jew, a high room rate is quoted, an undesirable room offered, or a limited reservation accepted, but most Jews avoid places where they might be embarrassed. Though hotels and resorts in some states fear law suits by rejected guests, discriminatory practices persist. Sometimes even the prominent suffer embarrassment, as when the late George Gershwin was turned down by an Adirondack resort because he was a Jew.

One of the principal media for effecting segregation is the travel and tourist agency. The agencies have instructions from resorts throughout the world and they parcel out accommodations to conform to the biases of each hotel. A memorandum to travel agencies by the Jug End Barn, Inc., in the Berkshires, for example, read: "We rely on you to 'screen' any prospective guests and to send us only those who will fit in with our high type Gentile following."[17]

When a customer applies to any major travel service office for

---

[16] New England office, 1953.
[17] *Jewish Weekly Times,* Boston, February 9, 1950.

accommodations, the clerk will size up the applicant, then refer to a code on an index card which tells him what kind of people are accepted at a particular place. He will then suggest the hotel where the customer should go. Some agents have stopped recommending hotels which cater to Jewish customers, believing they are doing their gentile clients a favor. All too often the guest finds himself diverted from an area he might have liked or shunted off to an inferior hotel.

The technique used by travel agencies in culling applicants for exclusive resorts is illustrated by this letter from the Male Travel Bureau, 274 Madison Avenue, New York, to a traveler with a suspicious name who had asked in October, 1953, for reservations at a Nassau hotel:

Thank you for your letter of October 26 and your deposit of $50 to cover reservations at Balmoral Club, Nassau.

The text matter in the Balmoral folder is not a routine matter. The hotel is operated on a club basis and all of its members must provide proper references before arrival. While it is true that the acceptance of your deposit will permit you to register, the hotel places the onus on this agency to provide the type of client they will accept.

Before sending your deposit to the hotel, would you kindly send the writer the name of your golf club and its address. Should you not be a member of a golf club, the name of a church group would do. Any good reference will help. Please do not think we are stickey (sic) about this as it is for the protection of all.

Thank you very much for your patronage.

Very truly yours,
ELMER W. GRIMES

A few weeks later another person telephoned the same agency and asked for a reservation at the same hotel ($48 a day for two persons, including breakfast, dinner, and bath). "Will there be any problem about references?" the caller asked. "Not with a name like Crosby," was the reply.

Not all travel agents sympathize with the policy of exclusion. The American Society of Travel Agents has officially condemned it, and a Travel Agents Committee to Combat Discrimination in the Travel Industry has pledged itself to defeat it. But discrimination is so widespread that many agents say they might have to go out of business if they refused to accept the practice. The American Automobile

Association has removed discriminatory phraseology from its directory of hotels and resorts.

Travel agents in the Southwest say 90 per cent of the first-class resorts in Arizona discriminate, 50 per cent in Palm Springs, and 90 per cent in Laguna Beach, California. Cook's has indicated that some 50 per cent of the resorts in Vermont, New Hampshire, and Maine are restricted.[18] Hotel owners say that if they opened their doors to Jews their gentile guests would leave and the resort would soon become all-Jewish. Both fears are dubious, to say the least.

In the first place, gentiles who really like a vacation spot, who may have been coming to the same hotel for years, are not going to flee because Judge and Mrs. Bernard Botein, Groucho Marx, or Bernard Baruch are seen in the dining room. A hotel manager with too little savoir faire to exploit top-grade Jewish guests as an asset would be less than competent. To suggest that a large number of educated and knowledgeable citizens would not tolerate the presence of Jews in a resort hotel is a reflection upon the good sense and decency of gentiles.

Prejudice will ultimately dwindle to insignificance in America because most people cannot be made to believe what their own experiences controvert. The great need is to provide opportunities for experiences which will demonstrate that prejudice has no foundation in truth. The Ashfords and the Prentisses, exposed to Jewish guests at their summer hotel for the first time, should find nothing more objectionable in them than in the Baylors and McBridges and other members of the old crowd. Nor should they feel challenged by the presence of a Jew in a resort any more than by his presence on an ocean liner.

The fear that resorts would soon become all-Jewish if they admitted any Jews is wrong on two counts. It could not happen unless all gentiles pulled out, an extremely remote possibility. And even if the gentiles did stay away, there simply are not enough Jews in the United States to swamp the resorts, just as it would be impossible to pack the hotels with Episcopalians or Unitarians who could pay the tariffs. Jews represent about 3 per cent of the population. Only a small minority can afford to vacation at resorts—assuming that they all wanted to, which they don't.

[18] Weintraub, *op. cit.*, p. 26.

The proprietors of discriminatory hotels in the United States should weigh the examples of England and France. Hotels in those countries do not discriminate and they have no Jewish problem. The problem here is a man-made mirage which would vanish if the hotel-keepers approached it honestly.

Apologists for discrimination cite the almost solidly Jewish hotels of Miami Beach, the Catskills, and Lakewood, New Jersey, as examples of what would happen if hotels and resorts in other places opened their doors to Jews. The existence of these Jewish vacation centers, established partly because of the closed-door policy, in fact supplies another argument against the fear that Jewish guests would inundate the gentile resorts. There are literally hundreds of resort areas in the United States, most of which are cold to Jews. Yet the volume of Jewish demand for resort space has been so small that only a few areas have been occupied by Jews who could not go elsewhere. Miami Beach and the other Jewish vacation centers will stay in business, serving clients from past years and thus decreasing the potential number of Jewish applicants when the gentile hotels finally open their doors.

There may indeed be an initial chill when persons accustomed to hearing about the various stereotypes have their first meeting on the beach or veranda. But rapprochement is always around the corner, and strange circumstances often make it possible to turn the corner. The rise of common causes, interests, and civic aims is one of the most effective levelers.

In Ocean Beach on Fire Island, New York, a Jewish infiltration of summer residents aroused opposition in the 1940's, but a common threat also appeared in the form of a colony of homosexuals. Though not classified as minorities, homosexuals often suffer similar disabilities and oppressions. Many of the Fire Island group were competent designers, decorators, and artists seeking the same security which minorities feel when they herd with their own kind. Most of the residents objected to the "blemish." Non-Jews and Jews found a common aim and ultimately a satisfactory rapprochement was achieved between them—though not with the homosexuals. A new scapegoat had supplied the essential diversion and the new common interest.

In Fire Island, a number of communities still exclude Jews and other minorities, using the club device. One new community has coined the term "Swejon" ("No Jews" in reverse) to signal its policy. Another, known as Point O'Woods, has a gate at its entrance attended by a uniformed guard who sees to it that none but the few hundred pure-blooded residents enter. The pure-bloods, however, are not barred from the adjoining communities and their services, amenities, and enjoyments, which they partake of freely. These communities with free-entry for the elite and a no-trespass sign for the less desirable are becoming a familiar example of snobbery in the resort belts.

The club device has made headway in recent years as a means of excluding minorities. In theory no one is permitted into the resort club unless he has been formally introduced and approved by the members. In fact, however, introduction is no more than a recommendation by another guest or by a tourist agent and approval is not by the membership but by the resort operator. In Eleuthera, Nassau, British West Indies, a resort owned jointly by the British Government and the president of the Aluminum Corporation of America, proposed a restriction which would prevent occupancy by "undesirables." How desirables and undesirables were to be distinguished did not appear, but the project illustrates the ethical conflict when public and private agencies join hands.

The resorts' exclusion policies have taken a toll greater than the frustrations and indignities experienced by minorities. One by-product is the encouragement of residential segregation. Resort centers have become growingly popular as permanent settlements, and developers have tended to extend the discriminatory patterns of the resorts into the new neighborhoods. "When I first came to Laguna Beach," wrote the publisher of *South Coast News*,[19] "I soon discovered that the town harbored a considerable sum of racial prejudices, including anti-Semitism. There exists an unwritten law against selling property to Jews. In the case of one of the most prominent subdivisions, it is a written law."

When the policies of resort hotels are finally relaxed, a more democratic distribution of their guests will take place. There will of course still be those preferring to spend their vacations with their own kind. The Miamis and anti-Miamis will continue to flourish without challenge by one to the other. But there are also many people who find

[19] June 17, 1947.

homogeneity a bore, whether the guests are Jews only, Catholics only, or Quakers only. Those who are class-enthralled at home are by no means unanimous in their desire to make their vacation diet more of the same. Heterogeneity, not homogeneity, is what makes cities like New York City and Paris not only tolerable but fascinating.

XVI

SEGREGATION AND GOVERNMENT

UNTIL THE 1930's, most decisions in American economic life were made by businessmen. Government was in the nature of an impartial overseer, interfering with private enterprise only when the public conscience was shocked into action by a substantial violation of the rules. The occasions when the federal government became involved with the racial question were rare: an official might have to rule on how to classify a Negro in the Civil Service, or how legally to provide a Jacksonville post office with separate toilets for Negroes and whites. The local official was guided by the "states rights" and "separate but equal" doctrines, and racial issues at the local level were resolved primarily through civil rights legislation.

Two distinct levels of ethics governed social conduct. The private entrepreneur functioned under the ethic of "caveat emptor," and "I am not my brother's keeper."[1] The government's ethic was higher. It was the ethic of the arbiter, the guardian against immoral conduct, the defender of the weak against the strong. Its function was rooted

---

[1] That is not to say there are no morals in business. But primarily they are the morals of honesty as a policy more than as a virtue. To take an extreme example: a man may beat his wife at home yet be scrupulous in maintaining his A-1 credit rating. So, too, the competitive requirements of business and profit do not often leave room for giving the competitor an advantage or giving the worker a higher wage than he asks for, or telling the consumer the bad as well as the good things about his product. It must speak for itself in an economy of competitive goods. When a businessman exhibits Christian virtue it may be as a vestryman, philanthropist, or as a plain human being but not as a businessman, and society cannot criticize him for it, anymore than it would censure the lawyer defending the murderer. The average mortal in our complex society is required to operate under several variations of morality which society recognizes as proper and reconcilable, and which in their own way make for a functioning economy.

in the thinking of Harrington, Locke, and the French philosophers, and was thought to be that of a counterpoise between diverse interests. Its inspiration was derived from a vague blend of Christian conscience, natural rights, bills of rights, and Anglo-Saxon equity. The higher ethic stood over the lower one, divided by differences in duty, aim, responsibility, and function, and interceding when the lower ethic moved beyond tolerable bounds. Despite pressures and occasional deviations, the ethical concepts of both government and enterprise improved.

In human relations, we witnessed such advances as the Fourteenth Amendment, the Civil Rights Acts, and other gains. Passions and prejudices rose from time to time but, unsanctioned by government, they exhausted themselves in minor incidents. Though far from perfect, this private enterprise economy regulated by state and federal governments promised to emerge into one of the most favorable patterns of fair play ever known to proletarian man.

Under the higher moral standards embodied in government constitutions and legislation, hotels, restaurants, theaters, ice cream parlors, public conveyances,[2] barber shops, and public places were often forbidden by state law from discriminating. A federal law banned discrimination in the sale or lease of real estate. Employers were forbidden to discriminate in carrying out public contracts and occasionally in private employment. Recently unions were bound to the constitutional ethic when beneficiaries of public aid or power.[3]

In the operation of the private enterprise system there were of course discriminations and prejudices, but they were the exceptions. The guiding principle of the system has been profit, not caste. When competition and the free market ceased to function, it became the duty of the government to intercede and break up the blocs. The free market system, checked by constitutions, courts, and civil rights legislation, thus fostered a favorable formula for social and economic opportunity.

The increasing complexities of industrialization challenged the

[2] *State Anti-Discrimination and Anti-Bias Laws.* New York, American Jewish Congress, 1948. A federal law forbidding discrimination in public places was held unconstitutional in the *Civil Rights Cases,* 109 U.S. 3 (1883).

[3] 14 Stat. 27 (1866), 8 U.S.C.A. 42 (1942); *Steele v. Louisville & Nashville R. R. Co.,* 323 U.S. 192 (1944); *State Anti-Discrimination and Anti-Bias Laws, op. cit.*

formula in a number of places. The piratical practices of some businessmen needed checking. Speculation required regulation. A higher standard was needed for the tenements and human incinerators packed with immigrants. A new social conscience asserted that the entrepreneur had duties as well as rights. Both the contraction of rights and the enlargement of duties found their expression in expansion of the police and tax powers of the government.

These regulations, while aiming to restrict private enterprise, nevertheless ratified the private enterprise system. Essentially they aimed to limit not destroy, to guide not supplant. Their underlying principle was reasonableness, which meant they would not undermine the profit or property systems, discourage incentive, or replace the entrepreneur. Government operations in areas where private enterprise was not doing an adequate job, or government subsidization of the poor, was until the 1930's unthinkable.[4]

As long as state and federal power was limited, the possibility of public abuses was also limited. Whether people subsisted, starved, or prospered was determined largely by competition. When, however, the public power was expanded, the minority stood to benefit but also took the risk that the very reforms aimed to help it—health laws, zoning, public improvements, park programs, slum clearance, urban redevelopment, licensing, mortgage insurance, and even civil rights legislation—might nevertheless be abused far beyond the intentions of their sponsors.

Power not only corrupts but is itself corruptible. While the physical scientists were learning how to unleash *physical power* and simultaneously harness it in the public interest, a parallel trend was in process to harness *public power* in the private interest.

One of the by-products of this newly released public power was its corruption into instruments of oppression against minorities. The premonitory signs of this process had appeared with the advent of the Chinese on the West Coast. As the potentialities of the licensing and regulatory powers were realized, a city ordinance imposed a license fee of $15 per quarter on laundries not using a vehicle. Another required vegetable peddlers to pay $2 if they drove a wagon and $10 if they were peddlers on foot. Both laws were aimed at the

---

[4] *In the Opinion of the Justices,* 211 Mass. 624; *Salisbury Land and Improvement Co. v. Commonwealth,* 215 Mass. 371.

Chinese, who rarely had wagons. Another device was the "queue ordinance" providing that every person convicted of any criminal offense should have his hair cut to within an inch of his head—a lasting affront and disgrace to a Chinese.[5]

In 1850 a foreign miner's license tax law compelled payment of a $20 fee every month for the mining privilege.[6] This had originally been directed against Spanish-Americans, French, and other foreigners, but was ultimately aimed and applied specifically against the Chinese. When California officials discovered that many counties could not exist without the revenue, they modified the tax so that it yielded an income of more than $5 million between 1850 and 1870. No less than 95 per cent of it was paid by the Chinese.[7] A head tax of $2.50 upon all Chinese 18 years of age or over was also imposed. Tax collectors were authorized to seize and sell the property of Chinese delinquents. In 1852, California required masters of vessels to put up a bond of $500 per capita as indemnity against medical costs and other aid to alien passengers. The income from this tax was to be apportioned among principal state hospitals, from which the Chinese were excluded.[8] The law was declared unconstitutional.

A major test of these laws came with the enactment of a San Francisco ordinance in the 1880's barring any person from maintaining a laundry without the consent of the Board of Supervisors except in buildings of brick and stone. Since the Chinese lived and worked in frame buildings, they would have been forced out of business. On the surface, however, it all seemed a reasonable exercise of the health power. Fortunately, the Supreme Court looked behind the apparently innocent wording to discover the real intent of the statute and declared it unconstitutional.[9]

In 1909, a bill was introduced in California giving school trustees the "power to remove children of filthy or vicious habits or children

[5] Roy L. Garis, *Immigration Restriction*. New York, The Macmillan Co., 1927, p. 287.

[6] Mary Roberts Coolidge, *Chinese Immigration*. New York, Henry Holt and Co., 1909, p. 29.

[7] Elmer Clarence Sandmeyer, "The Anti-Chinese Movement in California." Urbana, University of Illinois Press, *Illinois Studies in the Social Sciences*, vol. 24, no. 3, p. 43.

[8] Coolidge, *op. cit.*, p. 70.

[9] *Yick Wo v. Hopkins*, 118 U.S. 356.

suffering from contagious or infectious diseases, and also to establish separate schools for Indian children or for children of Mongolian or Japanese or Chinese descent." This and a series of similar bills became a *cause célèbre* when President Theodore Roosevelt interceded to ask that these bills be killed in the interests of our relations with Japan.[10]

Racial Zoning

The mushroom growth of cities precipitated a demand for the regulation of city development and land use. In its modern sense, zoning had been adopted by German municipalities to keep undesirable uses from encroaching upon residential neighborhoods, and it gained more widespread popularity in the United States. But in its application to racial segregation, zoning already had a longer history. It was long used in Europe as a device to exclude Jews or to confine them to ghettos—a device which in Africa has now been broadened to confine blacks and Indians to prescribed areas.

When the modern derivative of zoning was introduced into cities, in the interests of better planning, it was not long before private interests and municipal officials saw it as a practical instrument for restricting the movements of American minorities. Though a Baltimore ordinance of 1910 is generally referred to as the first racial zoning law in America, it was the Chinese in California who became the first victims when a local law required all Chinese to move from one area occupied by them to another. This was struck down by a federal court as an arbitrary classification of property in violation of due process and equal protection.[11]

In the main, American racial ordinances were designed to exclude Negroes, especially in the South.[12] The usual zoning ordinance made it unlawful for both Negroes and Caucasians to occupy houses on any street in which the larger number of houses was occupied by members

[10] Gilbert Thomas Stephenson, *Race Distinctions in American Law*. New York, D. Appleton and Company, 1910, p. 162.

[11] *In re Lee Sing*, 43 F. 359 (1890).

[12] *Hopkins v. City of Richmond*, 117 Va. 692, 86 S.E. 139 (1915); overruled in *Irvine v. City of Clifton Forge*, 97 S.E. 310 (1918); *Hardin v. City of Atlanta*, 147 Ga. 248, 93 S.E. 401 (1917); overruled in *Glover v. City of Atlanta*, 96 S.E. 562 (1918); *Harris v. City of Louisville*, 165 Ky. 559, 177 S. W. 472; overruled in *Buchanan v. Warley*, 245 U.S. 60, 38 S.Ct. 16 (1917).

of the opposite race. These ordinances were upheld by state courts on the theory that equal protection was afforded, since the ordinances applied to both whites and Negroes. The United States Supreme Court in 1917 declared racial zoning ordinances unconstitutional.[13] The court held:

> Property is more than the mere thing which a person owns. It is elementary that it includes the right to acquire, use, and dispose of it. . . . The Fourteenth Amendment was designed to assure to the colored race the enjoyment of all the civil rights that under the law are enjoyed by white persons and to give to that race the protection of the general government in that enjoyment whenever it should be denied by the states.[14]

While the court's decisions have put an end to racial zoning legislation legally, they have not ended the use of the zoning weapon against minorities. In Pennsylvania, a zoning ordinance was employed to harry a housing cooperative.[15] In Los Angeles, zoning devices were used to keep out cooperatives that might take in Negroes. In Bannockburn, Maryland, zoning sought to bar construction of a cooperative which, it was feared, might sell to minorities.

Communities no longer resort to the clumsy device of racial zoning laws, thereby exposing themselves to judicial attack. The methods are more subtle, motives less discernible, and exclusions more effective. Thus, an ordinance might be written to permit no more than one building to an acre or otherwise make any housing development impractical. Those who build for whites can get a modification *pro forma*. But the moment an unwelcome group appears, the officials stand firm on the written ordinance. In other cases, stricter zoning ordinances are enacted just when a minority is about to start building. Or an ordinance may compel an expenditure of a larger amount of money on each house, or require that the house be of an excessive square footage. As long as the officials do not openly give the reason for their action, recourse to the courts is often futile.

[13] *Buchanan v. Warley, op. cit.*

[14] Other efforts were made to salvage zoning as a discriminatory device (*Harmon v. Tyler,* 273 U.S. 668, 1927; *City of Richmond v. Deans,* 281 U.S. 704, 1934). One involved an ordinance prohibiting any person from living in a city block where the majority of residences were occupied by those with whom such person was forbidden to enter into marriage under state law. But the court struck it down.

[15] *American Veterans Housing Co-operative, Inc. v. Reginald M. Budd,* 69 Pa. D. & C. 449 (1949).

In Miami, land which public officials thought would be used for Negro residences was summarily zoned for industrial uses only. The same technique was used outside of Philadelphia.

In Birmingham, Alabama, in May, 1949, the city actually created a buffer zone for white and Negro homes after several houses bought by Negroes had been dynamited. The zone consisted of a 50-foot strip running six blocks north from a Negro housing project to a highway. The strip was zoned for "commercial construction only."[16] In the same year, in Lockport Township, St. Joseph County, Michigan, Negro families bought land on which to build houses, only to be confronted with a new ordinance preventing them from building on parcels of less than 20 acres.[17] Home-owners' and builders' organizations were openly pressing in Chicago "to get some good zoning laws so we can have the kind of people living next to us that we want."[18]

Long after the decisions outlawing zoning, "the medium of appropriate and well-drawn ordinances" was still being recommended as a method for barring "inharmonious groups."[19]

Public Works and Parks

Another device for checking minority movements is condemnation for public improvements. A Negro builder owning a site for subdivision might first meet technical objections to his plans and then find difficulty in getting his sewers or utility lines approved. If these devices fail to discourage him, the municipal authorities may discover that the land must be condemned for a public park. This device was employed in Detroit though the site was neither suitable for a park nor ever used for one.

In other cases, sites abutting Negro developments have been acquired for railroad stations, incinerator dumps, urban redevelopment, public housing projects, roads, and similar improvements. These

[16] The New York *Times,* June 1, 1949.

[17] New York *Daily Compass,* August 4, 1949.

[18] David Nelson, chairman of the Westown chapter of the National Home and Property Owners Foundation, an organization associated with the National Association of Real Estate Boards, at a meeting, July 10, 1950, cited in Zorita Mikva, *The Neighborhood Improvement Association: A Counter Force to the Expansion of Chicago's Negro Population,* University of Chicago, 1951 (in manuscript), p. 87.

[19] *Underwriting Manual.* Washington, Federal Housing Administration, 1938, §933.

improvements sometimes tend to cut off the minority area from the rest of the city and stem the expansion of its living space. Where minority groups have already settled on the land they may be summarily evicted. They are frequently forced to pay their own moving expenses. The owner is usually barred from raising any objection to the condemnation except that the use is not public in nature or that adequate compensation is not being paid.

The citizens' sensibilities may be assuaged by the belief that the minority owner has been paid in full. Actually, the owner is fortunate if he gets two thirds of his actual damage. For besides his outlays for attorneys' and appraisers' fees, moving costs, and income taxes, he must find another house, and all too often he discovers that as a member of a minority he must pay more than market price. The neighborhood demolition, moreover, shortens the supply of dwellings available to his group and often makes purchase of a house in that community impossible. Frequently, condemnation of his house leaves no alternative but to abandon the community, his job, and his friends.

In Los Angeles, Mexican-Americans were dispossessed under the condemnation power to make room for public works. In Miami, the city council ordered a brand-new $2 million housing project, into which Negroes had moved, condemned for public use. In Detroit and Chicago, Negro owners were told to move in the name of urban redevelopment. In Washington, a Negro area was torn down to make room for a new Senate office building. In Baltimore, 1000 Negroes are scheduled to be evicted to make room for a state office building. All too often the choice of a particular site occupied by minorities is more than a coincidence. When the improvements also happen to clear slums, they receive public acclaim as well as official approval. No compensation is paid to evicted tenants and little thought is given to their plight.

City Planning

A term which starts sympathetic palpitations among civic groups and other well-intentioned citizens is "city planning." Pioneers in the movement hoped to educate both the public and its officials in the advantages of urban order and in the beauty of tree-rimmed cities with built-in schools, shops, and work places that functioned as independent units free of the crowding and stresses that characterize the modern metropolis. Each area was to be self-contained. The rural was to be carried into the urban. Everything was to be provided within the neighborhood confines, from the bucolic to the alcoholic, from the church one is baptized in to the funeral parlor he is embalmed in.

The plan had great attraction and merit in a world of chaotic metropolises that made living hard. A new type of physical environment would help take people out of the megalopolises and make a new life for the children. It would even improve the general morals of their fathers and mothers, for the guiding spirits of city planning argued that more decent environment would produce more decent human beings.

Sparked by these pioneers, city planning progressed into a discipline in England and America, and contributed much sound thinking on the improvement of neighborhoods and the building of better cities. The working city planners proved eager to talk about the physical aspects of civic design, but were mute when asked about the people who were to live in the projects. The proper distribution of people, certainly a basic part of city planning, remained outside their public calculations.

Like all other reforms, a number of city planning devices were soon betrayed by the same processes of perversion that zoning had experienced. The cul-de-sac became the device for keeping the dark-skinned neighbors on the outside of the new development; the dead-end street became a method for keeping out the dead-end kids; the greenbelt became the medium for separating the black belt from the white belt; the "neighborhood unit" concept followed the same course; the boulevard was no longer the terraced walk where the shuffling poor could observe the strutting rich, but emerged as a new barricade against minority invaders. Even walls were built ostensibly for beauty and amenity, actually for exclusion and discrimination.

New authority and new powers are being conferred on city planning officials, giving them jurisdiction over zoning, public works, urban redevelopment, neighborhood improvements, and even city budgets. But most planning officials continue to interest themselves in the physical pattern of their idealized neighborhoods rather than face up to the minority problem as one of the most vital aspects of planning. They are reluctant to assume those tougher responsibilities that go with assumption of public power. They have not only ignored the racial problem in their calculations but the problem of mixed social and economic groups generally. Their vision is too often restricted to new neighborhoods developed as all-white, all-one-class, all-exclusive enclaves. Thus another great reform may go the way of others, to be perverted into another device for exclusion and oppression.

Administrative Devices

Administrative chicane is difficult to detect and contest. With the expansion of government there have been numerous administrative agencies set up with wide areas of discretion. These include city departments of various kinds, planning commissions, zoning commissions, urban redevelopment and housing authorities, boards of standards and appeals, and licensing commissions. They are not prone to make a record of their discriminatory policies or give the minority the evidence on which their oppressions can be tested.

Filing of building violations is one method for keeping minorities in tow. The owner may be told his house is insanitary or unsafe, or a list of violations may be filed against his building, compliance with which would cost a ransom. Contesting an inspector's determination of what is safe or unsafe, sanitary or insanitary, complied with or not, is often impossible.

Raising the assessed valuation is another device. A substantial tax increase may destroy all or a large part of the equity value. Since value of a building is no more than an opinion of a local assessor, the action is difficult to attack, and recourse to the courts is cumbrous. Even if the victim should win in the courts, he finds the cost of the fight a heavy burden. Outside Atlantic City, a wealthy Negro woman purchased a hotel which she had intended to rent to Negroes. She soon learned that a prohibitive tax assessment would be registered if she were to carry out her plan. She then offered her property to whites.

Another device is the practice of disapproving plans or specifications. The refusal by a municipal authority is on technical grounds. It is often impossible to discover the real motive or to get at the facts on which to raise the issue in the courts.

A stratagem combining legislative and administrative power was an ordinance adopted by the Board of Commissioners in Montgomery

County, Pennsylvania.[20] Its purpose was to check a subdivision undertaken by a cooperative which might admit a few Negroes. The ordinance provided that no building permit could be issued for the construction of a building in a subdivision until the plan for the subdivision had first been approved and a bond filed insuring completion of the streets and other public improvements. The cooperative was informed by the township that the bond would be in the amount of $165,000. Then the commissioners amended the zoning ordinance by providing for building regulations which made it impossible for the cooperative to build the type of houses it had planned and to secure the bond guaranteeing the street improvements. After spending some $21,000 on plans and salaries and being hampered and delayed at every turn, the cooperators had to abandon the project.

Another method for discouraging an intruding minority group is to thwart or delay the dedication of streets and the laying of sewer and water lines or to refuse arbitrarily to interpret a building requirement. If the courageous venturers persist, there is always a legal way of chastising them, such as failing to supply city services or putting the city dump in the area.

Abuse of the licensing power is another device. In March, 1949, for example, a Georgia Negro real estate dealer's license was revoked on the charge that he falsely assured a Negro purchaser that she could move into a home without opposition. According to The New York *Times*[21] the license commission took up the case "after open instructions from Governor Herman Talmadge to revoke the licenses of dealers who sell white property to Negroes."

Police Action and Inaction

The police force is potentially the most dangerous instrumentality for checking minority movements. Since police commissioners are locally appointed and policemen are local residents, they are prone to abide by majority opinion. Police action can break up a mob or encourage it to run riot. An officer can guard or look the other way. He can seek out the culprit or lose sight of him.

The area of police discretion is vast and the number of obsolete

[20] *American Veterans Housing Co-operative, Inc. v. Reginald M. Budd, op. cit.*; see also Morton M. Hunt, "The Battle of Abingdon Township," *Commentary*, March. 1950. p. 234.

[21] March 24, 1949.

laws vaster still. In almost every state there is a roster of laws that can be enforced against some and not against others. Disorderly conduct, vagrancy, and trespass laws are general enough in their language to be enforceable as desired. A Negro's glance at a local doxy's calves might be viewed as offensive and disorderly, where a white lecher's touch might be pardoned as the understandable outlet of a Lothario. What is copulation by a white man may be rape by a Negro.

Traffic laws can be enforced strictly or liberally to suit the policeman's discretion. Arrests for exceeding the speed limit can rarely be challenged. In the Carver Village incident in Miami, the Negro residents who were given parking tickets for leaving their cars in front of their homes could do nothing about it. In the South, where considerable progress has been made, Negroes may still be indicted for technical crimes, and even where they win acquittal, have had to spend days in jail, put up bail, and pay the costs of trials and appeals to establish their innocence. Motives behind arrests or the filing of indictments cannot be questioned. Twelve home-owning white talesmen sitting in a locality aroused by a Negro intrusion can hardly be expected to judge the intruder as a jury of the accused's peers.[22]

In some cases, a Negro who tries to establish himself in a white area may expect anything from insults to open assault to a race riot. In most cases the Negro home-builder is frustrated before violence occurs. He may find it impossible to finance his building; contractors may refuse to build for him; building materials may be hard to get; FHA may be cool to his effort; and land may be difficult to buy. The contractor or lender who wants to help may find himself the object of reproach or reprisal. But the big obstacle to building in alien territory is arson. The burning of a Negro veteran's home in one southern city recently got nationwide publicity when a newspaper undertook a campaign to raise enough money for a new house. This is exemplary, but not usual.

Arson is not the only menace; police indiligence is another. In one case a Chicago house owner threatened by a mob for challenging the color line was followed by police to his job, ostensibly to protect him against assault. But the police looked the other way when their

---

[22] See, for example, the action of the jury in Cook County, Ill., Chapter X and of the jury in Louisville, Ky., in Chapter VIII.

protégé received an occasional whacking from a hit-and-run assailant. In most of the Cook County riots from 1945 to July, 1954, police action could have checked the rock-throwing and rioting had the police been disposed to act in time. By arriving at the scene in sufficient force, they can disperse troublemakers before they gain headway and start throwing rocks and flares. By arresting offenders they can restore faith in law enforcement and discourage future outbreaks. The alternative to effective police work is continuance of the organized terrorism that is common in some parts of the nation.

Restrictive Covenants

Another instance of official abuse is the racial restrictive covenant —a modern derivative of the covenant that sought to exclude glue, soap, and gunpowder factories, livery stables, forge shops, bone and charnel houses, brothels, and other intrusions upon neighborhood dignity. Before zoning, real property could be protected against unwholesome uses only by compact among vigilant owners. But when Chinese swarmed into the West Coast cities toward the close of the last century, the covenant was modified and invoked for the first time to bar human beings. In 1892, a federal court ruled against the covenant, calling it a restraint on the free alienation of property and a violation of the most-favored-nation clause of our treaty with China.[23] Referring to the Fourteenth Amendment, the court said:

> It would be a narrow construction of the constitutional amendment in question and of the decisions based upon it, and a very restricted application of the broad principles upon which both the amendment and the decisions proceed, to hold that, while state and municipal legislatures are forbidden to discriminate against the Chinese in their legislation, a citizen of the state may lawfully do so by contract, which the courts may enforce.

Little more was heard of the covenant until the accelerated Negro migration to the North in the next century. When racial zoning failed in the courts, the covenant was reinvoked. It soon became as routine in the conveyancer's glossary as the words "To have and to hold." Subdividers exalted it as a guarantee of a lastingly exclusive neighborhood. Once signed, there seemed to be no way of expunging it from the chain of title, which made it more mischievous than even segre-

[23] *Grandolfo v. Hartman,* 49 F. 181.

gation laws—which at least were responsive to the pressures of public opinion and subject to repeal.[24]

So common had the use of covenants become that all the vacant land in some cities was virtually proscribed against Negroes. Estimates ranged up to 80 per cent in Chicago and Los Angeles.[25] But if these figures were exaggerated when estimated, it would only have been a short time before they were justified, for the covenants were spreading with whirlwind speed. In the New York City suburbs, where the restrictive covenant had not even been heard of by the average real estate operator, a sudden spurt embraced large portions of outlying land. Among the larger developments of 75 lots or more, five sixths were already racially restricted. In a sample survey of 315 developments, no less than 56 per cent of all homes were forbidden to Negroes.[26]

Excluding only Chinese at first and later Negroes, developers soon found it profitable to bar other groups as well, including Mexicans, Armenians, Chinese, Japanese, Jews, Persians, Syrians, Filipinos, American Indians, and other "non-Caucasians." It became fashionable, in fact, to exclude as many groups as possible to emphasize the exclusiveness of the development. More reputable as well as less reputable groups joined in covenanting their property. One of the most widely publicized campaigns was undertaken by the University of Southern California and the Automobile Club of Southern California, which sought to sign up property owners on a wholesale basis. All the Greek letter societies but one joined the crusade.[27]

Soon, not only workers but legislators and public officials of minority races found themselves unable to buy or rent homes. A former governor of Alaska had decided to purchase a house in Washington, D.C., but found himself barred by a covenant against Jews. Such covenants are still common in the nation's capital. Jewish

[24] Charles Abrams, "A Challenge to the American Bar," address before the Bar Association of the City of New York, February 19, 1947; see also, Abrams "Homes for Aryans Only," *Commentary,* May, 1947.

[25] Gunnar Myrdal, *An American Dilemma.* New York, Harper & Brothers, 1944, p. 624; Robert C. Weaver, *The Negro Ghetto.* New York, Harcourt, Brace & Company, 1948, p. 214.

[26] John P. Dean, "No Other than Caucasian—a Study of Race Covenants," *Journal of Land and Public Utility Economics,* November, 1947, p. 428.

[27] Beatrice Griffith, *American Me.* Boston, Houghton Mifflin Company, 1948, p. 141.

groups and other minorities saw that the racial covenant was not solely a major threat to Negroes but to their own groups as well. A common front was formed to contest its validity.

But the covenant's mischief had already achieved a moral justification by gaining judicial sanction. It soon became unethical for builders and homeowners not to ban minorities. From 1918 onward the highest courts of Alabama, California, Colorado, Georgia, Kansas, Kentucky, Louisiana, Maryland, Michigan, Missouri, North Carolina, Oklahoma, Texas, West Virginia, and Wisconsin, the Court of Appeals for the District of Columbia, three lower New York courts, the Ohio Court of Appeals, the Illinois Appellate Court, and a New Jersey court, all held racial covenants legal and enforceable. The 1892 ruling in the *Gandolfo* case, involving the Chinese in California, had apparently been ignored.

In 1929 the issue came before the United States Supreme Court on appeal from a decision in the District of Columbia holding valid a covenant that barred Negroes.[28] Instead of deciding the point squarely, the Court parried the issue but supplied enough dictum to indicate its approval. On the one hand it rejected the argument that the restrictive covenant violated the Fifth, Thirteenth, and Fourteenth Amendments to the Constitution, and held that whether the covenant was against public policy did not involve a constitutional question and therefore did not have to be adjudicated. It also evaded the argument that a court, as an arm of government, should not be used to enforce segregation by covenant. But gratuitously (and unfortunately) it added that such an argument was also "lacking in substance," giving comfort to the proponents of the race covenant and speeding its spread. Courts everywhere now became the vehicles for enforcing racial oppressions. Owners were held in contempt for violating the covenants or made answerable in damages.

Between the time the case was heard and the ultimate review of the issue by the Supreme Court, the pattern of black ghettos and white subdivisions became cemented in America. Up to 1910, Negroes had been scattered in various parts of cities without major tensions. Had the building boom of the 1920's included suburban developments for Negroes, some Negroes might have established suburban footholds and the concentration in urban slum-ghettos might have been

[28] *Corrigan v. Buckley,* 271 U.S. 323.

eased. Instead, Negroes remained in the central parts of cities which swelled into larger concentrations with the later migrations.

The failure of the Supreme Court to strike down the covenant in the 1920's helped establish the current pattern of urban segregation and suburban exclusion which is accelerating racial tensions in American communities. Considering that more than seven million houses were built in the 1920's during the Negro migration, only a small fraction of them for Negroes, the restrictive covenant may leave its influence upon American racial patterns and biases for generations ahead.

In 1948 the Supreme Court finally agreed to review two lower court decisions involving enforcement of covenants.[29] The first two cases arose in Missouri and Michigan; the second two in the District of Columbia. A significant aspect of the case was the intervention by the Attorney General in support of the minority position. His brief cited President Truman's address at the Lincoln Memorial in June, 1947: "We must make the Federal Government a friendly vigilant defender of the rights and equalities of all Americans. . . . Our National Government must show the way."[30]

Without the government's intervention it is doubtful that the Supreme Court would have accepted review. Intervention was prompted by a freshened national sensitiveness to racial oppressions in Germany and by the responsibilities assumed by the nation under the United Nations Charter and the Report of the President's Committee on Civil Rights.[31]

Suddenly the restrictive covenant, sanctioned for decades by private owners and official agencies, burst into a great national issue. Arguments of counsel received front-page attention in the press and widespread comment on editorial pages. Several embassy representatives listened to the arguments and busily made notes. Supporting briefs were filed by a host of organizations including the Protestant Council of the City of New York, the American Association for the United Nations, the Congregational Christian Churches

[29] *Shelley v. Kraemer, McGhee v. Sipes,* 334 U.S. 1; *Hurd v. Hodge, Urciolo v. Hodge,* 334 U.S. 24.
[30] Tom C. Clark and Philip B. Perlman, *Prejudice and Property.* Washington, Public Affairs Press, 1948, p. 22.
[31] *To Secure These Rights.* Washington, U.S. Government Printing Office, 1947.

of the United States, the American Jewish Congress, the American Jewish Committee, B'nai B'rith, the American Federation of Labor, Grand Lodge of Elks, and others. The National Association of Real Estate Boards and other real estate groups supported the covenants. It was a heartening demonstration of how a deeply rooted practice can be uprooted by enlightened public and official leadership.

Four months later the Supreme Court ruled the racial covenant was not unlawful between the parties, but its enforcement by the courts was illegal. What could not be done by legislative and administrative branches to contravene the Fourteenth Amendment could not be done by the judicial arm of the government, said the Court.

These restrictive agreements standing alone cannot be regarded as a violation of any rights guaranteed to a petitioner by the Fourteenth Amendment. So long as the purposes of those agreements are effectuated by voluntary adherence to their terms, it would appear clear that there has been no action by the state and the provisions of the amendments have not been violated.

The Court ignored the argument that the covenant violated the United Nations Charter, but added that the Fourteenth Amendment aimed to assure "that all persons, whether colored or white, shall stand equal before the laws of the state, and, in regard to the colored race, for whose protection the Amendment was primarily designed, that no discrimination be made against them by law because of their color." In enjoining enforcement in the District of Columbia case, it cited the Civil Rights cases of 1868, and held that, even in the absence of a civil rights statute, "We cannot presume that the public policy of the United States manifests a lesser concern for the protection of such basic rights against discriminatory action of federal courts than against such action taken by the courts of the States."

The decisions did not directly ban suits for damages against a signer of the covenants, and if such suits were tenable the door would still have been wide open to use the covenants. In both Missouri and Oklahoma, in fact, suits for damages were thereafter upheld,[32] though courts in Michigan and the District of Columbia dismissed them.[33]

[32] *Weiss v. Leaon* 359 Mo. 1054, 225 S.W. 2d 127; *Correll v. Earley,* 205 Okla. 366, 237 P. 2d 1017.

[33] *Phillips v. Naff,* 332 Mich. 389, 52 N.W. 2d 158; *Roberts v. Curtis,* 93 F. Supp. 604 (Dist. Col.).

On June 15, 1953, the Supreme Court held that award of damages by courts for violating a covenant was "state action" and violated the Fourteenth Amendment. "The result of that sanction by the states would be to encourage the use of restrictive covenants. To that extent, the state would act to put its sanction behind the covenants." The Court upheld the right of the white owner, who was being sued for selling to a Negro, to raise the issue that the rights of Negroes were being violated in the process. It went further in its condemnation of the covenant than in its earlier decisions: ". . . respondent is the only effective adversary of the unworthy covenant in its last stand. [In the previous decisions the covenant had not been condemned as "unworthy" but had been looked upon as legal and valid between the parties.] She will be permitted to protect herself and, by so doing, close the gap to the use of this covenant, so universally condemned by the courts." (The covenant had not been "universally condemned" by the courts but had been almost universally approved until the Supreme Court rendered its decisions holding the covenant unenforceable though not invalid.)

Yet if the majority went further in its condemnation of the covenant than it had previously, the Chief Justice, who bitterly dissented from the majority, went further the other way. With a passion uncommon in judicial rhetoric, Justice Vinson not only condemned the Court for having agreed to hear the case at all, but stepped out of his way to defend the use of the covenant. ". . . Each had the right to control the use of his property against that event and to exact a promise from his or her neighbor that he or she would act accordingly." Then, gratuitously, he ventured into economics and ethics by observing that the covenant "raised the value of respondent's properties. By this suit, the plaintiffs sought only to have respondent disgorge that which was gained at the expense of depreciation in her neighbors' property." As in the earlier decisions, Justices Reed and Jackson did not participate.

Effect of Covenant Decisions

It is difficult to assess fully the effects of the decisions in the years to come, but a few results may be noted.

By forbidding courts to enforce the covenants and keeping an owner from being haled into court for contempt for selling to a minority the

Court extracted the judicial teeth which gave the covenants their bite. The decisions also removed an important rallying point around which hate groups had been corralling and inciting owners. On the practical side the decisions released to Negroes some property which had been denied to them.[34] These were not large tracts, nor were many in the suburban areas. But the Court rulings helped to break down resistance among owners of land bordering on minority-inhabited areas and speeded expansion into the adjoining sections and into some new sections. Much of this property would probably have fallen into minority hands anyway. The decisions also removed the cloud from the titles of properties already owned or occupied by Negroes who had bought or rented despite the covenants.

Another by-product of the decisions was a temporary improvement in the moral climate. Contrary to the dire predictions of some realtors, the Court's rulings did not touch off civil war or even a major skirmish. On the contrary, they were accepted as reasonable and demonstrated some readiness to dovetail our domestic morals with our international commitments. Public approval of the decisions may have given courage to the Court to take another step forward in the cases involving segregation in transportation and education.[35] Since, as the Court itself has said, issues of "ripeness" enter into its determinations to hear cases, the climate of opinion which the covenant decisions helped ripen can in retrospect be considered a significant gain.

Whether the decisions were to have any practical effect in improving the housing conditions of minorities depended mainly on how the government itself would interpret them. It was to FHA that developers looked for the mortgage insurance which made their financing possible. A simple FHA directive not to insure properties subject to covenants could have done more to make land available to minorities than the favorable Court decision.

At first FHA was not moved by the decisions. The agency ruled that they applied to court enforcement only and not to its own administrative enforcement—a specious form of reasoning since the whole

[34] B. T. McGraw and George B. Nesbitt, "Aftermath of Shelley versus Kraemer on Residential Restrictions by Race," *Land Economics,* vol. XXIX, no. 3, August, 1953, pp. 280–287.

[35] *Henderson v. United States,* 339 U.S. 816; *Sweatt v. Painter,* 339 U.S. 629.

point of the decisions was that *no* agency, judicial, legislative, *or* administrative, could lend its aid to the covenant.

Under continued pressure from civil rights groups and the Attorney General, FHA finally ruled that it no longer would insure mortgages on properties having covenants placed on them after February, 1950. It would continue to insure where covenants existed before that date.

The building and realty groups soon recovered from the Supreme Court's blow by capitalizing on the part of the decision which held restrictions valid between parties. The fact that the covenants were not enforceable in law did not deter them. Various devices not requiring judicial enforcement were still available to freeze out minorities. Among these methods are:

1. The "Van Sweringen covenant." Long used in Cleveland, it prevents sale of property without consent of the original owner of the undeveloped tract.

2. Joint consent for building. This requires consent of 5 adjoining owners before land will be sold for building. This device was being used in 1953 on the Van Sweringen tract to keep out Jews.

3. Joint consent for sale. Ten adjoining owners must agree to a sale or forfeit $500 in damages.

4. Club membership. No one may buy into a neighborhood unless acceptable to the board of the community club.

5. The leasehold system. The occupant leases the land for 99 years and may not sell the building without consent of the community's overseers. Before qualifying as a purchaser the lessee must live in the area for a year. Point O' Woods on Fire Island, New York, is an example.

6. The cooperative or "nonprofit" device. The house or apartment is leased from a cooperative corporation which has an all-powerful directorate dedicated to limiting occupancy to Caucasians, Christians, etc.

7. The broker's agreement. Real estate brokers agree among themselves or through associations not to rent or sell property to certain groups or races. In many communities these limitations are incorporated into codes of ethics.

8. Agreement by mortgagees. Lenders agree not to make mortgage loans where a racial infiltration threatens. Some mortgagees will not lend even where the government will insure the mortgage.

9. The reversion clause. The deed provides that sale to prescribed minorities makes title revert to a prior grantor. The buyer would acquire an unmarketable title.

10. The escrow agreement. A deed is deposited in escrow with a third party to assure against violation of a covenant. The escrow-holder, not the courts, would then be called upon to decide whether the covenant is violated.

11. The neighborhood improvement association. A group of owners, often manipulated by realtors, exercises sanctions to keep minorities out.

12. The option agreement. An option to repurchase the property is retained by the original owner of the tract.[36]

13. "Aesopian covenants." These deal with income limitations, occupant density, or "health."[37]

This is only a partial list. If one or a few of the devices are successfully attacked in the courts there will be enough left to effect exclusion. Valid or not, they are effective as delaying tactics. Discriminatory devices, old and new, are inevitable so long as the real estate men tout them as necessary for a "good neighborhood."

The Los Angeles Real Estate Board's plea for a constitutional amendment to validate the covenant and its outline of eight ways to avoid the restrictive covenant within the law have been presented by Stanley L. McMichael in a recent book for realtors.[38] He concludes by saying:

Obviously, this subject warrants the attention of subdividers and realtors generally. Whatever program is undertaken will probably be under the

[36] In Chicago an option was held by the Woodlawn Conservation Corporation, running in favor of the corporation and other white owners in the block at an increase in price of 2 per cent up to $500 above the price offered to the buyer. The option could be exercised within 30 days after a conditional contract was signed by the owner. In that way the option-holder could prevent the sale to anyone it deemed undesirable. But the agreement could not be promoted because Negroes had already moved into the area and the owners did not want to hazard their sale opportunities.

[37] George L. Schmutz, prominent appraiser, writes: "Recent surveys indicate that future deeds will carry agreements running 20 years covering health, safety and occupant density which will constitutionally exclude non-Caucasians from many areas because of their low incomes." *Review of the Society of Residential Appraisers,* June, 1948, p. 15.

[38] *Real Estate Subdivisions.* New York, Prentice-Hall, Inc., 1949, pp. 204–209.

auspices of the National Association of Real Estate Boards, comprising about 1,000 realty boards in cities all over the country, and with a membership approaching 50,000.

If all of these devices fail, there remain the officialized oppressions. These increased after the covenant decisions. Some local FHA directors, yielding to pressure from realtors, would not approve sites threatened with minority infiltration. Zoning laws, ostensibly legal on their face, moved up as community devices for checking infiltration; administrative chicane increased markedly. By 1954 a minority family was still not free to settle in a suburb where it was unwelcome. The devices to keep it out were still ample and the community bias was still strong.

XVII

DISCRIMINATION AND THE FEDERAL GOVERNMENT

The New Deal

The federal recovery program that began in 1933 sought primarily to correct economic imbalance not social inequalities. The emphasis on housing and land was no accident, for the groups chiefly affected by the economic collapse were homeowners, farmers, farm tenants, slum-dwellers, mortgage-lenders, and cities dependent upon tax revenues. No real pump-priming could be done without restoring these groups to a functioning role in the economy. Even the efforts to revive construction, to encourage lenders to finance homes and repairs and to improve houses and farms all seemed intended to strengthen the weakest points in the landed economy.

By the time intervention in urban and rural realty was added to its intervention in other economic areas, the federal government had emerged as the most important single influence in the economic pattern. It was not only the policeman but the inspirer of private activities and the maker of economic policy. It made loans to business and regulated business; it built housing for the underprivileged and insured mortgage loans on almost all the rental housing and on much of the smaller housing being built; it granted huge subsidies to selected industries and gave relief to the unemployed; it built and ran dams and other tremendous enterprises; it regulated labor and directed or controlled corporations which operated railroads, waterways, defense industries, and other enterprise. Its policies influenced full production and employment, or full collapse and unemployment; they affected interest rates, rising and falling prices, profits and losses, investments and liquidation.

This huge expansion of activities could not fail to stir perplexing racial and moral issues. As long as there was a separation between the public and the private function, there was also a separation between the public and private ethics. The government's ethics remained that of the Bill of Rights, not the marketplace; it set the good example; it was the arbiter, the guardian of justice and fair play. The higher public morality could better exert its influence upon the private sphere—through the courts in their molding of public policy, through the legislatures in the enactment of state laws; through the federal Constitution to prevent oppressive state action.

But what could be expected in the formerly private fields now aided or entered by the public itself? What could be expected when entrepreneurs with their lower standards and their overruling drive for profit operated conjunctively with government? Which standard should government follow: the standard of the color-blind, moral government intended by the Constitution, or the devil-take-the-hindmost standard of the private entrepreneur? The racial issue was the sensitive area in which the new ethical issue would be posed and tested.

Three courses were open:

1. The positive moral approach. Government could peremptorily refuse loans and subsidies wherever discrimination or segregation was practiced. It could assert that the true duty of democratic government is to educate the people in the principles of democracy (belief that public education would promote democratic equality was responsible for the very birth of public education in eighteenth-century France and America).

2. The parrying approach. The government could equivocate, postpone decisions, hide behind some device like local autonomy or states' rights, or leave it all up to the courts or the private entrepreneurs in charge of the operations.

3. The discriminatory approach. The government could discriminate openly and overtly.

Curiously, the choice was never the moral approach. The evasive, parrying approach was generally followed. In one case the policy was open and overt discrimination, and in another the discriminatory policy was not only open and overt but it sought to encourage discrimination and segregation by private enterprise as well.

In the case of federal contracts made with state and local agencies or federal loans to them, no racial restrictions whatever were imposed and the local agencies could discriminate or not as they chose. The reason given was respect for local autonomy.

The public housing projects built by the federal government before 1937, the federal public works program, and most of the federal war housing projects followed neighborhood patterns, which usually meant segregation. No real effort was made to create new mixed patterns even when the environment was favorable. But there was no effort to impose segregation, either.

In houses owned by the Home Owners Loan Corporation, the color line was followed.

In the Federal Housing Administration, representing the largest part of the federal housing program, discrimination and segregation were not only practiced but were openly exhorted. This practice continued for more than a decade without challenge or modification.

The Federal Housing Administration

The Federal Housing Administration, created under the National Housing Act of 1934, was launched in an effort to encourage home-building and mortgage-lending during the depression. Lending institutions which make loans to builders and homeowners are now unconditionally insured by the government, while builders who obtain these insured mortgages are able to borrow far more than their costs on the strength of the federal guarantee. The homeowner or borrower pays a small premium to the government for insurance given not to him but to the mortgagee.

A government offering such bounty to builders and lenders could have required compliance with a nondiscrimination policy. Or the agency could at least have pursued a course of evasion, or hidden behind the screen of local autonomy. Instead, FHA adopted a racial policy that could well have been culled from the Nuremberg laws. From its inception FHA set itself up as the protector of the all-white neighborhood. It sent its agents into the field to keep Negroes and other minorities from buying homes in white neighborhoods. It exerted pressure against builders who dared to build for minorities, and against lenders willing to lend on mortgages. This official agency not only kept Negroes in their place but pointed at Chinese, Mexicans, American Indians, and other minorities as well. It not only insisted on social and racial "homogeneity" in all of its projects as the price of insurance but became the vanguard of white supremacy and racial purity—in the North as well as the South. Racism was bluntly written into FHA's official manual: "If a neighborhood is to retain stability, it is necessary that properties shall continue to be occupied by the same social and racial classes.[1]

One of FHA's responsibilities was recorded as the "prevention of infiltration." The agency warned against "adverse influences" which included "unharmonious racial groups." It even exhorted the use of a model covenant, providing that "no persons of any race other than ———— [race to be inserted] shall use or occupy any building or any lot, except that this covenant shall not prevent occupancy by domestic servants of a different race domiciled with an owner or tenant."

The 1935 manual listed the important influences which the government considered "adverse." Among the most important was "infiltration of inharmonious racial or nationality groups" (§310). "Rapid transition to use by a lower class of inhabitants, is to be considered positive instability" (§307). The appeal of a residential neighborhood results from "the kind and social status of the inhabitants" (§315).

FHA then described methods to enforce "homogeneity" and exclusion of the "undesirable." It said:

. . . when fullest advantage has been taken of available means to protect the area against adverse influence and to insure that it will develop into a homogeneous residential district, possessing strong appeal to the class of persons expected to desire accommodations in it, a high neighborhood rating will be warranted (§330).

The 1936 manual perfected and expanded the racial and social doctrine of 1935. The "valuator must determine whether or not the coming generation will regard locations in such neighborhoods as desirable." It warned that "the mixed neighborhood" in competition with the "homogeneous" neighborhood will suffer, and that "the

[1] *Underwriting Manual*. Washington, Federal Housing Administration, 1938, §937.

chances are that within a comparatively short period of time a lower grade of social occupancy will exist" (§210d).

FHA included "racial occupancy" among the adverse influences (§228), and affirmed that "usually the protection against adverse influences afforded by these means includes prevention of lower class occupancy, and inharmonious racial groups" (§229).

The Valuator should investigate areas surrounding the location to determine whether or not incompatible racial and social groups are present, to the end that an intelligent prediction may be made regarding the possibility or probability of the location being invaded by such groups. . . . A change in social or racial occupancy generally leads to instability and a reduction in values. The protection offered against adverse changes should be found adequate before a high rating is given to the future (1936, §233; 1938, §937).

Of prime consideration to the Valuator is the presence or lack of homogeneity regarding . . . classes of people living in the neighborhood (1936, §252).

It was not the accommodations or conveniences in an area that always mattered but "the social class of occupants, or prestige created by associations." It is the future view of the "younger generation" that must be considered (§253); "presence of incompatible racial elements results in a lowering of the rating, often to the point of rejection" (§255). To FHA the evils of the parents must be visited upon the children, and in a classic defense of the children of the elite against the poor, FHA says "The social class of the parents of children at the school will in many instances have a vital bearing" on whether the neighborhood is "stable." The neighborhood will be less desirable if there is "a lower level of society or an incompatible racial element. . . . In such an instance it might well be that for the payment of a fee children of this area could attend another school with pupils of their same social class."[2]

FHA advocated not only deed restrictions but zoning to bar the wrong kind of people, and it classed the nuisances to be guarded against—"stables, pig pens," etc. In the same category was occupancy by the wrong kind of race. (1936, §284 (3)f).

"Appeal" is measured by the "social class" (1936, §249) and barriers are advocated to keep out the "lower class occupancy, and inharmonious racial groups" who might "invade" good sections.

[2] 1936, §266; 1938, §951.

Hills, ravines, a college campus, a high-speed traffic artery that might discourage the wrong kind of parents and their children from crossing over, and similar "artificial barriers" are held desirable (1936, §229; 1938, §935). High ratings are given for restrictive covenants "since these provide the surest protection against undesirable encroachment and inharmonious use." The restrictions should be imposed on all land in the immediate environment (1938, §980(1)).

Success and acceptance in the business world was no reason for letting a minority person enter the neighborhood, FHA said. The "type of people with whom the borrower associates socially, rather than those with whom he is associated in business activities" is the important thing, and it then concluded: "The highest rating could hardly be ascribed in cases where the borrower's chosen associates are other than substantial, law-abiding, sober-acting, sane-thinking people of acceptable ethical standards" (1938, §1014). The presumption, of course, is evident that all candidates eligible for an FHA subdivision would automatically qualify for the heavenly kingdom as well.

The revised 1940 manual made few changes. FHA was still asking, "Is the neighborhood homogeneous in population?" Nonhomogeneity was described as a "mixture of groups which tend to be socially antipathetic," including "inharmonious social groups" and races (1940, §207, 217). The wrong kind of people meant obsolescence. Important among adverse influences were infiltration of "smoke, odors, fog" and "inharmonious racial or nationality groups."

These were no slips of the pen nor the irresponsible utterances of a senseless clerk. They were part and parcel of FHA policy from its inception to 1948. After continued protests by the National Association for the Advancement of Colored People and other groups, FHA revised its underwriting manual. But it was not yet ready to yield on the issue. The changes simply made the language vague enough to take the heat off while still affirming the anti-racial policy. FHA continued to deny housing insurance to Negroes except in Negro neighborhoods and commitments in such areas were rare. It continued to insure properties subject to racial covenants and often insisted on the use of covenants.

Section 110 of the revised (1940) manual required the underwriter to estimate "the probability of any change in occupancy which would tend to change desirability for residential purposes." The underwriter was then told to evaluate the degree of compatibility of the inhabitants of the neighborhood since "the pressure of incompatible groups in a neighborhood tends to lessen or destroy owner-occupancy appeal" (§1215 (4)(d)).

Even as late as November, 1948, months after modification of its written policy and after the Supreme Court had held racial covenants unenforceable, FHA was still the stronghold of officialized intolerance. Assistant Commissioner W. J. Lockwood, commenting on the York Center Community Cooperative, a proposed interracial housing project in Illinois, defined revised FHA policy:

> If it is therefore apparent, with respect to the particular neighborhood or property under analysis, that infiltration will be unacceptable to the local real estate market and desirability of properties will be reduced in the market's mind, then this Administration has no alternative but to so recognize the conditions in its valuation of specific properties within that sphere of influence.[3]

The commissioner's statement of policy on housing projects restricted against Negroes is plain:

> I find nothing in such [restrictive covenant] decisions to indicate that in the absence of statutory authority the government, or any agency thereof, is authorized to withdraw its normal protection and benefits from persons who have executed but do not seek judicial enforcement of such covenants.[4]

On November 19, 1948, Lockwood said FHA "has never had a housing project of mixed occupancy," and ventured "the unofficial and informal statement that we believe that such projects would probably in a short period of time become all Negro. . . ." Referring to racial infiltration, Lockwood said FHA must have due regard "for the influence of such conditions not only upon a certain parcel of realty but also considers the reflection of those conditions upon properties owned by other citizens."[5]

In answer to a letter from Senator Robert F. Wagner protesting

[3] Excerpt from Memorandum by Thurgood Marshall, special counsel, National Association for the Advancement of Colored People, to President Harry S. Truman, February 1, 1949.

[4] Letter of Commissioner Franklin D. Richards to Thurgood Marshall, November 1, 1948.

[5] Letter to James Cassels, executive secretary, National Co-operative Mutual Housing Association, Chicago, Illinois.

FHA's policy, Commissioner Richards said that racial, religious, and national characteristics "are given the same consideration as all other characteristics. . . . If the study on any of these points indicates probable adverse effects . . . significantly increasing the risk, FHA is not warranted in accepting the risk."[6]

When protests continued, FHA finally modified its manual to exclude references to inharmonious racial groups. The 1949 edition omitted references to mortgages in areas threatened by minority infiltrations. On December 2, 1949, FHA agreed not to insure mortgages on properties subject to racial restrictive covenants filed after February 15, 1950. The fight to bring FHA within the Constitution was beginning to show results.

But the damage had been done. It was more serious than most realize. It was the first time in our national history that a federal agency had openly exhorted segregation. Before FHA, a homebuyer's prejudices were personalized, his decisions were of his own making. Although private covenants were being enforced by the judicial arm, they were unsanctioned by public policy at the executive and administrative levels and the courts too would strike down the attempt of a village, community, or city to officialize bias. Even segregation in the southern states had its condition of presumed equality and federal morality remained above any such qualification.

FHA's declarations had gathered together all the humbug of half-informed pseudo-experts—realtor-sociologists, appraiser-psychologists, behaviorist-lobbyists—and codified them into official dogma. It made the forbidden fruit of bias the required fare of the market.

FHA's espousal of the racial restrictive covenant helped spread it throughout the country. The private builder who had never thought of using it was obliged to adopt it as a condition for obtaining FHA insurance. Many far-seeing lawyers had viewed the insertion of racial covenants in deeds as an unnecessary nuisance of record that might restrain the free sale of property and enable captious owners to hold up their neighbors. They foresaw confusion fifty years later in the determination of who in the long complex web of intermarriage and succession might be called Caucasian, Negro, Chinese, Japanese, or Mexican. What fraction of man's blood makes him Negro or white?

[6] See Charles Abrams, "Anti-Negro Covenant is FHA's Own Idea in New York," New York *Post,* October 15, 1947.

And when is a Jew not a Jew? When is he a "good" Jew to whom property may be sold, and when is he a refugee kind or the long-nosed, bearded variety of the anti-Semitic caricature?[7]

FHA succeeded in modifying legal practice so that the common form of deed included the racial covenant. Builders everywhere became the conduits of bigotry. Houses new and old had long belonged to many who had never known race fear: war veterans who had fought side by side with Negroes, Italians, Jews, Catholics, Mexican-Americans, and Puerto Ricans; workers who stood at machines with them and joined the same unions. They now learned from a government agency that it was right to fear people of this sort and to keep them out of neighborhoods.

The covenant became common even in nongovernmental enterprises, for an owner never knew when he might want a government-insured mortgage on his property. Builders of non-FHA operations put in covenants so as not to be at a "disadvantage." Soon the covenant was found everywhere.

Builders, seeing the covenant as an inexpensive sales tool, began to sell "homogeneity" and freedom from "adverse influences," "inharmonious social groups," and "incompatible racial elements" for all these phrases were worth. The FHA insignia at a project entrance held out hope that one's neighbors would be "law-abiding, sober-acting, sane-thinking people of acceptable ethical standards."

---

[7] There are many realtors and suburbanites who still dread Jews, and on boring weekends at their country clubs find it comforting to elevate themselves by tearing the Jew down. All too often, a Jew is an image contrived in one's mind and signifying one's own fears and insecurities. The defamers haven't the slightest idea as to what a Jew is. During a visit to Israel in August, 1950, this writer saw Ethiopian Jews who are jet black; Iraqis who are like Turkish warriors; Chinese Jews; native Italian Jews who were once gentiles; Yemenites who are polygamous, squat on floors, and smoke big water pipes with their women; and a native tall blond Nordic type who would grace a Hollywood set. The "Sabra" or native Israeli is often blond and completely perplexing in his robustness and handsomeness. Though a Jewish nation, Israel is now one of the most heterogeneous in the world. A Jew, as one expert says, might well be anyone who calls himself a Jew or whom others call a Jew. (Melville J. Herskovitz, *The Jews* [Louis Finkelstein, ed.]. Jewish Publication Society of America, 1949, vol. iv, p. 1151.) This is perhaps an oversimplification, but it does emphasize that the stereotype Jew and the Jew in reality are miles apart. After a single generation in America, the Jew is far different from his immigrant father and is in fact becoming barely distinguishable from anyone else.

FHA's official policy simultaneously received unofficial support from thousands of realtors bound to the anti-racial code of ethics of the National Association of Real Estate Boards and its thousands of allied builders. The dissemination of racial and religious bias to homeowners, coupled with the propagation of race fears and anxieties, created a neighborhood climate often bordering on hysteria. Owners would put up their property for sale in panic at the first glimpse of a Negro in the neighborhood.

If FHA policy did not sanction violence, it inspired it. At the time of the Sojourner Truth riots in Detroit,[8] for example, FHA dogma about values declining with the entry of Negroes was generally believed. Some frightened whites declared that if Negroes moved in, FHA would guarantee no further loans in the neighborhood.

It is difficult to determine why prejudice functions, why mobs of homeowners and their teen-age children stone, bomb, or burn buildings. One thing is certain. The publication of anti-racial doctrine by a federal agency established official justification for prejudice and gave the semblance of right to lawlessness.

The evil that FHA did was of a peculiarly enduring character. Thousands of racially segregated neighborhoods were built, millions of people re-assorted on the basis of race, color, or class, the differences built in, in neighborhoods from coast to coast.

FHA simultaneously undermined the old pattern of heterogeneous neighborhoods in communities from coast to coast where people of mixed races and mixed religions had been living nearby or in the same block without a qualm or a quibble. Given time, the common sense of the American people might, as before, have insured steady expansion of this democratic way of life. But the natural trend was reversed by FHA's championship of an unnatural homogeneity. People everywhere became sensitized to differences in race, religion, and color. A newcomer who did not look, talk, and act exactly like themselves was to be viewed with the same mistrust shown by natives who encounter a wanderer from another tribe.

Finally, FHA policy succeeded in depriving minorities of the housing they desperately needed. FHA developments would not have them. Land sold to Negroes or Mexican-Americans meant, under FHA's policy, that adjoining land would be classed as undesirable.

[8] Chapter IX.

During the period of its anti-racial policy, FHA failed to encourage builders to put up housing for minorities. Instead of giving these hard-pressed citizens the priority they desperately needed, FHA gave priority to the restrictive covenant which banned them from housing. It went further than embracing "separate but equal" doctrine for whites and blacks for its policy was separate for whites and nothing for blacks.

The result was accentuation of housing shortages for the people who needed housing most, concentration of minorities into older deteriorated sections, pressure upon newer areas by minorities seeking space, chaotic competition for dwellings between majority and minority, and deepening of tensions between classes—one of the most sensitive aspects of American neighborhoods today.

The Home Loan Bank System

The Home Loan Bank System followed the FHA practice. When homes in white areas were acquired by the Home Owners Loan Corporation, no Negro could buy one. When loans were made, the policy was to respect segregation and encourage it.

The "neighborhood rating" procedure adopted by HOLC, which described a "desirable neighborhood," advised "breaking down the city or community into a number of homogeneous neighborhoods or areas." One of the factors was the "homogeneity" of the population, "economic stability and effect of infiltration of inharmonious families. . . . The price level of the properties is not a factor in judging desirability." Among the areas of the first grade were "generally restricted areas," while the third grade included those with "expiring restrictions or lack of them" and the "shifting or an infiltration of families with lower living standards." The fourth or worst grade area were those with an "undesirable population." In rating population the inspector was required to list "foreign families" and "Negro."[9]

"It is also suggested," HOLC said significantly, "that the procedure might profitably be adopted by other lending institutions or groups of institutions wishing to analyze the area in which they operate."[10]

An assistant district appraiser for HOLC in Chicago collected 3000 pieces of residential property suffering from some form of obsoles-

[9] "Neighborhood Rating," (Suggestions drawn up by Division of Research and Statistics of Federal Home and Loan Bank Board), *Review of the Society of Residential Appraisers,* August 1940.

[10] *Ibid.*

cence, and wrote an article based on them. The article was replete with references to "racial influence" and "deed restrictions." It cited the danger of being "surrounded on three sides by Negroes" and of value depreciation when Negroes move in.[11]

A former member of the Federal Home Loan Bank Board and professor of business finance at Ohio State University recommended restrictive covenants and homogeneity, putting his thesis as follows:

When two or more incompatible groups occupy any given neighborhood, the tendency is for the group having least regard for the maintenance of real estate standards to drive out the other groups—a sort of real estate Gresham's Law. The infiltration of additional representatives of the dominant group operates to put a blight on the neighborhood as effective as the appearance of undesirable uses of land.[12]

Neighborhood Conservation

Similar views ran through the thinking of almost every agency concerned with housing.

A "confidential" report for the government was issued "For Internal Use Only" by the National Housing Agency (over-all federal housing agency and predecessor of the Housing and Home Finance Agency). The report was directed at the urban redevelopment program then being prepared, and the consultants sought to write into the program the same anti-racial policy followed by FHA and the Home Loan Bank Board. The report made to the Urban Redevelopment Division by the two government consultants[13] deplored the movement of "the clannish, gregarious foreign born groups, of religious groups, of social groups (like rooming-house dwellers) and most important of all, of the great contained and semi-contained groups of Negroes and Jews."

The report continues, "We were told to say in our college economics, 'Bad money drives out good.' It is unfortunately true that, with but few exceptions, a displacement of neighborhood population by a new group results in an immediate lowering of the neighborhood

[11] Edward V. Walsh, "The Obsolescence Factor," *Residential Appraisers Review,* vol. 1, no. 8, November, 1935, p. 6.

[12] Henry E. Hoagland, *Real Estate Principles.* New York, McGraw-Hill Book Company, Inc., 1940, p. 148.

[13] *Appendices to the Preliminary Report on Conservation of Middle-Aged Neighborhoods and Properties.* Washington, National Housing Agency, October, 1944.

level." The authors then classified groups by number, from most desirable to least desirable, and argued that No. 5 people drive out No. 4 people. The lowest number was assigned to Negroes, the next lowest to Jews. To control the bad numbers, it was recommended that neighborhoods be set up by index numbers and various pressures exerted against infiltrating groups with the wrong digits.

A second recommendation was that neighborhoods be "contained" by creating "artificial boundaries" such as dead-end streets and parks against "inharmonious groups of any kind." The third recommendation was "a drive for restrictive covenants."

The principal effect is psychological rather than legal. They have, however, represented a rallying point around which neighborhood residents could gather to fight encroachment and have, therefore, been extremely successful as delaying actions where they have been used.

The report never became official but in a foreword the then urban redevelopment director called this anti-racial document a "first approach."

That this type of thinking still guides federal policy may be sensed from the writings of some federal officials. Thus, according to an article by the director of the appraisal division of the Liquidation Service of the General Services Administration,[14] "homogeneity" is still indispensable, "people of foreign birth" as well as their children and all nonwhites threaten a neighborhood's status quo, and a neighborhood should be homogeneous not only in social position but in race and religion.

Reasons for Discrimination by Public Agencies

One reason public agencies veer toward discrimination is the enlistment of "experts" from private fields where bias is taken for granted. Unfamiliar with the ethical responsibility of government, these men insinuate their own biases upon the public agency. Political economists, sociologists, and social psychologists are viewed as impractical theorists and are seldom consulted in realty operations.

Discrimination was also advanced by the desire of FHA and Home Loan Bank administrators to create business volume for their agencies. Since FHA must get enough housing insurance business to

[14] Arthur A. May, "Appraising the Home," *The Appraisal Journal*, January, 1951, pp. 19–25.

make its actuarial formulas work, it hesitated to condition its aid to builders upon nondiscrimination. The same is true of other joint ventures, such as the Home Loan Bank System, the Veterans Administration, and urban redevelopment. Public administrators are not primarily concerned with assuring equality in the marketplace or launching dubious experiments in interracial harmony. Their main interest, like that of private operators, is financial success. If in the process prejudice becomes part of public policy, it is only the price of profit.

Another reason for the degradation of democratic values is that the public agencies become dependent upon their private beneficiaries for lobby support in Congress. This is no secret in Washington. The government agencies best accommodated by Congress are those backed by strong private lobbies. Agency officials give a sympathetic ear to the pressures and prejudices of beneficiaries who also function as benefactors.

The South is of course a major factor. A national agency is apt to formulate rules that will be acceptable throughout the nation, thereby gaining maximum support in Congress. Thus a localized discriminatory custom tends to become the common denominator in racial policy. A federal regulation banning discrimination would be bitterly fought. Although there is frequently less segregation in the South's private neighborhood patterns than in the North, the southern bloc in Congress remains adamant against any proposal for mixing blacks and whites.

The final influence over the ethics of federal officials is their own environment. Though conditions have improved in recent years, Washington still is a southern city by latitude and attitude. Instead of setting the great example of equality, it chose to set the great example of segregation. It was in such an environment that a congressman debated the Constitution. If he wanted the right committee assignment and the cooperation of other congressmen for his program he found it unprofitable to be a troublemaker by challenging prevailing customs. Many northern congressmen in fact had to follow a double standard of life. In their home towns they could mix socially with minority people, but in Washington they knew it might be uncivil to practice civil rights.

So with government employees. Many who helped formulate policies were born and brought up in a segregated environment and knew no other. Others lived in the suburbs where no Negroes were permitted and where racial covenants are still common. Some lent a sympathetic ear to the Federation of Citizens Associations which has fought for segregation and has seen housing as the main vehicle for effecting it. Associations with a group advocating racial equality raised the suspicion of radicalism. A few days after the Supreme Court's restrictive covenant decision, four Negro children, members of a group of fifty who had won honors in a school safety-control contest and were scheduled to meet President Truman, were denied accommodations in Washington hotels. It was a reminder of the contrast between public pronouncements on civil rights and actual practice.

In such an environment a lobby that fights against equality for minorities has easier sailing than an antidiscrimination group. The administrators and their assistants, research men, clerks, and stenographers are all homeowners or tenants sensitive to racial movements. They are "homogeneous" and therefore fearful of "incompatible racial elements."

During the presidential campaign of 1952 it appeared that both candidates for the vice presidency lived in houses subject to racial restrictive covenants. The Democratic nominee, John Sparkman, an Alabaman, had bought a house subject to one, a common occurrence in Washington. The Republican candidate, Richard M. Nixon of California, went much further. He and his wife co-executed an agreement that the house they bought would never be sold or rented to "any person or persons of negro blood or extraction or to any person of the Semitic Race, blood or origin, which racial description shall be deemed to include Armenians, Jews, Hebrews, Persians and Syrians. . . ." At the time of its execution, the Supreme Court had not yet ruled on whether such a covenant was enforceable by suit for damages. Either because both candidates had been involved or because the public has grown to take these things for granted, the issue was not raised during the campaign.

The Court's ruling that Washington's restaurants cannot discriminate against a Negro patron and the school decisions have given courage to those pressing for a complete break in the Capital's segregation pattern. There are recent developments which may help to speed it. In the northeast and northwest sections, Negro-owned buildings are occupied by both whites and Negroes in the middle income group. The long-established dispersal of Negroes in the central areas has helped allay fears and their further dispersal in the last fifteen years has met with only occasional violence. Churches have cooperated and the press has condemned vandalism. Thousands of new homes have been offered to Negroes including some in rental and cooperative projects carrying government mortgage insurance. All these developments, coupled with the fact that Negro incomes are higher here than elsewhere, give hope that the nation's capital may yet set the good example.

FHA's policy has also been altered under pressure of civic groups. On February 18, 1949, FHA issued a directive to its field offices that "mortgage insurance shall not be precluded (1) because of a different type of occupancy, regardless of whether or not it is violation of a restrictive covenant, (2) nor shall such insurance be precluded on the ground that the introduction of a different occupancy type may affect the values of other properties in the area."[15] The Veterans Administration, the Home Loan Bank program, and the urban redevelopment program have modified their policies similarly.

"Homogeneity or heterogeneity of neighborhoods as to race, creed, color or nationality, is not a consideration in establishing eligibility," FHA has declared. Thenceforth, "determinations which adversely affect the eligibility for mortgage insurance" shall be supported by "observable conditions" rather than "discriminatory attitudes or prejudice." FHA has recently issued mortgage insurance for a few "open ocupancy" projects in New York, Philadelphia, Washington, and Chicago, and there have been some encouraging statements by Albert M. Cole, Administrator of the Housing and Home Finance Agency, and by FHA officials on the need for more minority housing.[16]

[15] Memorandum to Directors and Chief Underwriters of all Field Offices on the subject of *Eligibility of Properties for Mortgage Insurance* (mimeographed).

[16] The New York *Times,* May 22, 1954. A speech by Cole on October 29, 1954, not only promised a vigorous effort to make more such housing available but also called on the Mayor of Chicago to end the Trumbull Park rioting which he termed "a threat to the civic life of our country." (Dedication ceremony for Harkness Hall, Hampton Institute, Hampton, Va.; Letter of October 28, 1954 to Honorable Martin H. Kennelly.)

But we are still far from the goal. As of 1952, only about 50,000 out of almost three million dwellings insured by FHA were available to nonwhites. Of the nine million new homes built between 1935 and 1950, less than 1 per cent were open to them. There has been no appreciable gain in such housing since.

"In the short space of two decades, a weapon has been shaped that is almost as much an instrument of our national policy as the taxing power."[17]

Though FHA's mortgage insurance today covers almost one third of all new housing, running in some years closer to half, the question of FHA's duty under the Constitution remains one of the great enigmas of the new private-public co-partnership.

[17] Shirley Adelson Siegel, *The Legal Relationship of FHA to Housing Aided under Its Various Programs.* New York, unpublished monograph for the National Committee against Discrimination in Housing, 1953.

XVIII

SLUM CLEARANCE AND URBAN REDEVELOPMENT

URBAN REDEVELOPMENT is an outgrowth of the slum clearance movement. It enlisted federal interest toward the end of World War II as a device to prime the country out of the anticipated postwar slump, help remove the blight defacing American cities, and provide central sites for good private housing, public housing, commercial buildings, and other improvements.

Until 1950, urban redevelopment had been undertaken sporadically under a few state laws with the aid of local tax exemption. The most notable example was Stuyvesant Town in New York City. In 1949 Congress passed a comprehensive housing bill. Title I provided for an urban redevelopment program under which land cost in slum or blighted areas would be written down to a price attractive for redevelopment. The write-down subsidy would be paid two thirds by the federal government and one third by the municipality. Although public housing authorities could benefit from the write-down, the program was designed primarily to aid private developers. To take advantage of the local and federal grants, many states created urban redevelopment agencies or gave local housing authorities power to acquire land and replan it.

No sooner had the federal law been enacted than two facts became plain: (1) there were no houses available for the slum-dwellers to be displaced from the sites; (2) these slum-dwellers were largely minorities to whom housing in new areas was banned. Instead of administering the program to emphasize acquisition of vacant land or insisting on projects which would favor rehousing of the minorities, some officials and realty groups saw the program as an opportunity to get rid of the undesirables. Some of the displaced families could have been sheltered by the public housing program, but in 1953 and 1954 Congress jettisoned the public housing appropriations.

Urban redevelopment was thus deflected from its original social reform course and pointed toward ousting minorities. The implications, however, were far more serious than the perversion of racial covenants or zoning ordinances. Racial covenants were private arrangements; urban redevelopment was publicly subsidized and backed by official power. Racial zoning ordinances and covenants sought mainly to bar minorities from new housing. Urban redevelopment evicted them from housing they already had. Zoning ordinances were often written to require "equal" zoning restrictions for minority and majority; in urban redevelopment the land on which minorities lived and the homes they owned could be taken from them by forced sale in the name of slum clearance without so much as a solatium for their discomfort.

After acquiring the land the urban redevelopment authority was authorized to turn it over to the private developer who would have freedom to pick the new occupants. The legal justification was established in the Stuyvesant Town litigation.[1]

The federal enabling statute provided that accommodations had to be available for the displaced families. In practice, if the tenants were forced out or scared out, bought off or crowded in with others, the condition was considered "complied with." Overcrowding, the worst aspect of slum life, has been intensified by urban redevelopment and the conditions of minorities were made still more unbearable.

Eve of an Exodus

In July, 1952, this writer received from the Housing and Home Finance Agency a summary of urban redevelopment projects approved as of June 23, 1952. It showed the following:

1. There were 70 urban redevelopment projects initially approved, all of which would displace families. The total number of families to be displaced was 45,450.

2. Not a single project was an open-land project as authorized by the statute and only five were "predominantly open."

[1] *Dorsey v. Stuyvesant Town Corporation,* 299 N. Y. 512, 339 U.S. 981.

3. Of the 45,450 families to be displaced, all but 13,650 were listed as "non-white." If Mexican-Americans, Puerto Ricans, and other Spanish-speaking people were added, the figures would be much greater.

4. Only 1778 families were to be provided with low-rent public housing units (1000 of these were in Norfolk, which has always been held out as a model project).

The perversion of the program was accomplished by

1. Corrupting the definition of the word "slum."
2. Distorting the enabling legislation.
3. Sanctioning the procedure by judicial decision.

Slum Clearance—A Concept Re-examined

The word "slum" has meant different things in different eras. The nineteenth-century definition placed emphasis on the people who lived in slums. Living in a slum was thought to be the fault of the inhabitants. The country's frontiers were open and those who chose to rot in the cities' wretchedness had nobody to blame but themselves. The protest against the slum was by the quick against the socially dead; by the hardworking and sober against the indolent and drunkard. There seemed no reason for poverty or squalor in those days except one's own laziness.

Thus it seems understandable that the *Encyclopedia of Social Reform,* published in 1897, which listed drunkenness as among the prime reasons for poverty, would define a slum as a name loosely given to "dirty back streets or alleys occupied by the poor and wretched and often by criminals or semi-criminals."[2] Slums were caused, said a court in the same year, "to a very considerable extent, if not entirely, by the filthy habits of the people who inhabit them."[3] Under such definitions, the way to get rid of slums was to ban whisky, teach virtue, and punish sinners.

Until the New Deal there was no agreed definition of the word "slum" nor could there be, for there was still no agreement on what produced it. There were those who still blamed the inhabitants, saying that if they were given decent housing they would put coal in the

[2] (Edited by William D. Bliss) New York, Funk and Wagnalls, 1897, p. 1260.
[3] *Health Department v. Dassori,* 21 App. Div. 348, 47 N.Y.S. 641.

bathtubs. Others said the people were only the victims of their environment. The 1933 edition of the Webster *New International Dictionary* still included both definitions, calling the slum a "foul back street of a city, especially one with a slovenly and even vicious population," as well as a "low or squalid neighborhood."

In the ideology of the depression and New Deal, however, a more enlightened definition gained headway. The 15,000,000 unemployed suggested that society too might be to blame. In neither the preambles to the legislation nor in President Roosevelt's speeches were tenement-dwellers or Hoovervillagers blamed for their plight. The Real Property Inventory of 1934 laid emphasis upon the physical condition of a building and the absence of such things as running water, private toilets, heat, and bathtubs.

The period was marked by an inordinate number of vacancies in slums which made it possible to tear them down. The slum-dweller simply moved his meager belongings from one slum to another. Since an outstanding feature of the slum was its financial unsoundness, its social cost, disrepair, and general economic liability, society, it was felt, could best be served by slum removal.

In 1937 the definition of "slum" therefore rejected the older credos and reflected that of its own period and environment. The United States Housing Act of 1937 defined a slum as "any area where dwellings predominate which by reason of dilapidation, overcrowding, faulty arrangement or design, ventilation, light or sanitation facilities or any combination of these features are detrimental to safety, health or morals." The term slum was thus made to embrace the physical structures rather than an area inhabited by a low class of people. Slum clearance consequently had to be defined as the demolition and removal of the structures. To safeguard the new definition, in fact, the law required a slum dwelling to be eliminated for every dwelling unit built.

By World War II it had already become plain that the new definition was a blunder. The nation faced a housing shortage, not a surplus. Slum demolition meant bringing homelessness and overcrowding to the slum-dweller. We should have stopped tearing down houses and built more houses. But there is often an ideological lag between one stage of a reform program and the next. Slum clearance had acquired such political appeal and such irrepressible momentum that we simply could not stop tearing down slums.

Under the public housing program nearly 200,000 substandard dwelling units were eliminated by June 30, 1953; 77 per cent was accomplished through demolition, 17 per cent through compulsory repair, and 6 per cent by barring them to occupancy. Of the housing units built under the Housing Act of 1937, 89 per cent were on sites from which old structures had been removed and only 11 per cent on completely vacant land.

While we were in the process of tearing down buildings, the defense program intervened and we built as many "temporary" slums as had been torn down under the public housing program. On balance, we had simply torn down slums and put them back, in some cases substituting wooden slums for brick ones, public slums for private ones. With one hand the country was enforcing rent controls, on the assumption that a national housing emergency existed. Evictions were prohibited and rents fixed. But with another hand we were simultaneously evicting thousands of families as though one bureau of government was unconcerned with what any other was doing.[4]

If the public housing program did not increase the over-all housing supply for the underprivileged, it at least substituted good housing for bad. The urban redevelopment program provided no housing for them at all and deprived them of the housing they had.

It could of course be shown that not all urban redevelopment projects were aimed at evicting minorities. It could even be demonstrated that the presence of a larger percentage of nonwhites in the

[4] New York City, for example, was subject to an emergency rent control law. Yet in 1952 its Committee on Slum Clearance Plans proposed the eviction of 6000 low-income families from existing areas to make way for private urban redevelopment projects renting for upwards of $35 monthly per room, for which few if any of the evictees would be eligible. Simultaneously, the New York City Housing Authority proposed the eviction of another 25,000 families, making a total of more than 125,000 persons to be dispossessed. This is exclusive of evictions for public works. The justification for this oppression was that the people dispossessed somehow "always find places to live." No study had ever been made of where they go. In practice, when a slum area is designated, the residents are warned, cajoled, made fearful of imminent dispossession, and under duress find shelter of some sort. A few are lucky, 5 per cent or so may move into a project on the site, the bulk find less desirable quarters or double up.

slums was inevitable because of their low incomes, and that selection of so many Negro-occupied sites was at least partly coincidental. But the facts remain that: (1) overcrowding among nonwhites is four times greater than among whites, (2) nonwhites represent only 10 per cent of the population; yet (3) urban redevelopment evicted three times as many nonwhites as whites. Moreover, at a time when vacant or predominantly open land was available, occupied land has been almost exclusively selected for redevelopment—land occupied by those with the slimmest chances of finding other quarters.

It was all legal and proper. Wrecking a Negro's building no longer had to be done by a mob. Here was a way to do it constitutionally. The job of dislodging Negroes could be done according to Hoyle, not Hooligan; the law of the land could be substituted for the law of the jungle.

Distortion of the Enabling Legislation

The urban redevelopment statute had authorized four types of projects:

1. Slums or deteriorated areas, *or*
2. Deteriorated areas to be developed for predominantly residential purposes, *or*
3. Land predominantly open but obsoletely platted or in diverse ownership, *or*
4. Open land necessary for sound community growth to be developed for residential use.

The word "or" is in italics because the statute clearly intended the uses to be alternative. Administrator Raymond M. Foley of the Housing and Home Finance Agency took the position, however, that only slum clearance was authorized under the statute. After a series of wholesale evictions and under pressure from minority groups, he later modified his position so that open land might be used in connection with a slum project. But in practice the program continued to embrace only slum clearance operations. Foley's justification for not building on vacant land was that during the debate on the measure in Congress he had filed a letter stating that if the legislation was passed he would emphasize slum clearance. In line with this, Foley had also prepared local enabling legislation limiting urban redevelopment powers to slum operations. The result was that federal and local legislation which had been primarily designed to increase the housing supply during a housing shortage eventuated into a scheme to reduce the housing supply for minorities and evict them from their dwellings.

There were larger implications. The Supreme Court had held that where a law is clear on its face there is no necessity to find out what Congress meant.[5] Legislative history and other "extrinsic aids to construction" may be turned only " 'to solve, but not to create ambiguity. If the language is clear it is conclusive.' "[6]

The reason for this policy is evident. When a law says what it means, there should be no need to find out whether it means what it says. The Constitution in requiring three readings of an act in each house intended to insure that the listening legislators knew what they were voting on. Lawyers and their clients have a right thereafter to rely on the clear provisions of a statute without having to delve into the mental permutations of congressmen. When a bill is introduced and its meaning is clear, the rank and file who have read it and urged its enactment, the people affected by it, the press that supported it, and the President who signed it, all have a right to rely on its plain wording. Nor can it be assumed that every senator and representative read the record and knew about Foley's letter, or if they did know it intended to substitute its content for the plain words of the statute. If this were so we should be substituting the law of the letter for the letter of the law.

The fact is that throughout the Senate debate it had been stated that the urban redevelopment provisions were to include vacant land operations and that open land projects were necessary to enable "sucking the families out of the slums." In fairness to Foley it may be said that Senator Paul H. Douglas, who sponsored the measure, at first partly supported the Foley position when this writer raised the issue in an address to the National Housing Conference on May 6, 1952, to which Douglas replied:

I am quite certain that he [Mr. Abrams] is wrong both as regards the legislative interest in the Act, the intent of Congress, and the platform of the housing administration at the time the bill was passed. That was made manifest in debate after debate.

[5] *Ex Parte Collett,* 337 U.S. 55 (1949).
[6] *U. S. v. Shreveport Grain and El. Co.,* 287 U.S. 77, 83–84.

But then he added:

We recognized that it would be necessary to have something on the outskirts to take care of people who would be displaced by slum clearance—also, that we would reduce the pressure per acre within the slum areas, that the spillover would have to be taken care of elsewhere. Finally, we recognized also that some cleared slums would be used, not for residential, but for business and commercial purposes, or for residential purposes for upper-income groups. So we knew that there would have to be some building on the outskirts, that some public funds could be used either to take over raw land or decayed sub-divisions. But the primary purpose of this money was to clear, not to flee from, the slums.

Later, in a letter to the writer on June 23, 1952, Senator Douglas explained, "I meant that slum clearance funds could only be used for (a) actual slum clearance and (b) acquiring land on the outskirts to rehouse some of those displaced from the cleared slums."

This is certain—even if we assume that the act precluded developments on open or badly platted land except as part of a slum-clearance scheme and that the administration intended to use open-land projects for displaced families, not one such project had been authorized by 1953. What actually occurred was a widespread displacement of minorities with virtually no new housing built for them either on slum land or on unoccupied sites. In 1953, Albert M. Cole, Foley's successor, stated after assuming office that the primary objective of urban redevelopment was "the improvement of the housing conditions of American families" rather than slum elimination only, and this meant improving the housing conditions of displaced families as well. "Really persuasive evidence" of the rehousing of evictees in decent accommodations would be required, Cole said.[7] Whether this policy will be carried out remains to be seen.

The Stuyvesant Town Case

What made the urban redevelopment program doubly unfortunate was the attitude of the courts. When oppressive laws have been enacted against minorities, the courts have generally restored and reinforced the nation's moral standards. This was particularly true in racial discrimination issues, which the courts have viewed as one

[7] Address before the National Housing Conference, Washington, May 11, 1953.

of the great test areas of the democratic process. The issue decided in the Stuyvesant Town case,[8] justifying racial discrimination in urban redevelopment, therefore moves into ugly focus.

Stuyvesant Town is a housing development of 18 square city blocks in the heart of New York City's East Side, facing the East River between 14th and 20th Streets. It cost $110 million to build, houses some 25,000 persons. The idea was conceived and sponsored by New York City's dynamic Housing Coordinator Robert Moses as an alternative to public housing, and the enabling law was patterned to suit the insurance company's insistence upon freedom from public control. That it is a sound investment for its owner is due to a huge grant of tax exemption by the city, aggregating during the project's life more than $55 million. The city also turned over to the company public streets amounting to about 19 per cent of the area; these streets are now closed to the people and no one but the city comptroller may legally tread on them without the company's consent. The city also condemned the land, ousting some 10,000 low-income tenants from their homes, and tearing down a host of stores, churches, a school, and a limited dividend low-rent housing project. All this was possible because the enabling law endowed urban redevelopment with the novel power of "superior public use," meaning that it was superior to schools, housing projects, and playgrounds, which are legally only "ordinary" public uses.

There are no public playgrounds or schools inside Stuyvesant Town, for it was feared by Metropolitan's board chairman, Frederick H. Ecker, that "Negro children might attend." Negro tenants were to be barred, too, he said, because "Negroes and whites don't mix. A hundred years from now, maybe they will." The company openly admitted its intention to discriminate against Negroes before the contract was signed and defended its right to do so as a "constitutional privilege" after the project was built.

Urban redevelopment, of which Stuyvesant Town was the forerunner is, like FHA, another device entailing a liaison between government and private enterprise. Since the public benefit to be achieved is slum clearance, the plan provided for a government agency acquiring the slum land by condemnation, subsidizing the undertaking to make it attractive to the entrepreneur, and then

[8] *Dorsey v. Stuyvesant Town Corporation, op. cit.*

putting it in private hands without the restraints against abuse of constitutional protections to which the government itself is subject, i.e., to make no distinctions between black, brown, or white citizens in administering laws or dispensing public benefits.

The contribution of New York City in relation to Metropolitan's contribution was substantial. It had to be made, it was argued, because the land cost was too high and the city had to absorb some of it if Metropolitan was to become interested. Since Metropolitan paid only $17 million for the land and the tax-exemption granted by the city was worth $55 million, the city could have saved $38 million by presenting the land as a gift to Metropolitan in lieu of the tax grant. In addition to the tax grant, the city gave Metropolitan the use of its condemnation powers and street acreage worth at least $2 million. These grants were not made to benefit a low-income group, for there is no limit on the incomes of Stuyvesant Town tenants. Some earn as much as $50,000 a year,

The city expropriated the property from many hundreds of owners and tenants in the area. (When the city condemns property it need not pay the asking price but only the market price; nor need it pay for goodwill or usually compensate tenants for losing their occupancy.)

When the Metropolitan Life Insurance Company presented its contract for approval to the city's Board of Estimate, there was a public outcry against Ecker's statement that the new development would discriminate against Negroes. Not a single civic agency appeared in support of the contract, while more than 30 organizations opposed it. The contract, however, was finally approved after Mayor Fiorello LaGuardia had said he hoped Metropolitan would not discriminate against Negroes. This hope was futile. When the buildings went up and tenant applications were invited, the company made it clear that Negroes need not apply. A lawsuit was then brought by three Negro war veterans[9] who had been rejected because they were Negroes.

The case clearly posed for the first time the constitutional dilemma under the recent public-private joint venture in housing. Concededly private business may discriminate, but if the discrimination conflicts with the larger interests of society, the state may intervene. The

[9] *Dorsey v. Stuyvesant Town Corporation, op. cit.*

government, as keeper of the democratic morals, not only forbids the use of its own powers or subsidies to further discrimination but checks the private entrepreneur when he trespasses upon the community morals. The Fifth Amendment expressly bars discrimination by federal agencies and the Fourteenth Amendment bars discrimination by state or local agencies.

But suppose the government passes on its powers and subsidies to an individual or private corporation, as in the case of urban redevelopment, and the beneficiary elects to discriminate? Here the line is far from clear. Yet this is where the danger of subversion of minority rights is greatest.

Throughout America's history, rigid restrictions have been imposed upon the government's use of its powers, such as eminent domain, and the tax and police powers. These three powers constitute the working tools of any government, be it capitalist, fascist, or socialist. When abused, these are the powers that threaten life, liberty, and property. The manner of their exercise marks the difference between the democratic and the totalitarian society.

The power to regulate, for example, is also the power to regulate out of existence. The American system has always required that the courts stand guard to see that this power is exercised reasonably. The power of eminent domain is the power to take another man's property. It may therefore be exercised only for a public use and upon payment of just compensation. The power to tax carries with it the obligation to use the proceeds for public purposes and not for private or class use.

Under the American system, the determination of a public use is never entrusted to legislatures or Congress exclusively. The courts stand guard against abuse and have often struck down legislative authorization to condemn property when they felt the purposes were not public. The power to condemn land has been granted to railroads and public utilities, but only when the facilities were for public use. These utilities may not bar access to a customer, on account of race, creed, or color.[10]

Up to the New Deal there were few tests of discriminatory acts by private entrepreneurs using government funds or powers. With extension of the welfare power, the issues arose in *Steele v. Louisville &*

[10] 51 *Corpus Juris,* Brooklyn, N. Y., American Law Book Company, p. 7.

Nashville R. R.[11] when a Negro railroad employee sued to enjoin discrimination against him by a labor union which was the exclusive bargaining representative under the Railway Labor Act. The Supreme Court enjoined the union, describing it as "clothed with power not unlike a legislature which is subject to constitutional limitations on its power to deny, restrict, destroy or discriminate against the rights of those for whom it legislates and which is also under an affirmative constitutional duty to protect those rights."

There were a number of other cases in which the same issue arose and similar rulings were made. A political party was restrained from discriminating after it had adopted a resolution qualifying only white Democrats. Justice Cardozo ruled:[12]

The pith of the matter is simply this, that, when those agencies are invested with an authority independent of the will of the association in whose name they undertake to speak, they become to that extent the organs of the state itself, the repositories of official power. They are then the governmental instruments whereby parties are organized and regulated to the end that government itself may be established or continued. What they do in that relation, they must do in submission to the mandates of equality and liberty that bind officials everywhere. . . . The Fourteenth Amendment adopted as it was with special solicitude for the equal protection of members of the Negro race lays a duty upon the court to level by its judgment those barriers of color.

A privately endowed and privately run library, operating partly with public funds, was restrained from barring Negroes from its training school for librarians.[13] One of the most far-reaching cases imposing checks on private enclaves was *Marsh v. Alabama,*[14] involving a private company town outside Mobile, owned by the Gulf Shipbuilding Corporation. Describing the project, the Court said, "the property consists of residential buildings, streets, a system of sewers, a sewage disposal plant and a 'business block on which business places are situated' . . . in short the town and its public district are accessible to and freely used by the public in general and there is nothing to distinguish them from any other town and shopping center except the

[11] 323 U.S. 192 (1944).
[12] *Nixon v. Condon,* 286 U.S. 73; see also, *Smith v. Allwright,* 321 U.S. 649 (1944).
[13] *Kerr v. Enoch Pratt Free Library,* 149 Fed. 212 (Circuit Court of Appeals, 4th Cir., 1945), cert. den. 326 U.S. 721 (1945).
[14] 326 U.S. 501 (1946).

fact that the title to the property belongs to a private corporation." When a Jehovah's Witness was arrested for distributing religious literature in the wholly owned company town, the Court held for the accused:

> The State urges in effect that the corporation's right to control the inhabitants of Chickasaw is coextensive with the right of a homeowner to regulate the conduct of his guests. We cannot accept that contention. Ownership does not always mean absolute dominion. . . . Whether a corporation or a municipality owns or possesses the town the public in either case has an identical interest in the functioning of the community in such manner that the channels of communication remain free. As we have heretofore stated, the town of Chickasaw does not function differently from any other town. . . . Since these facilities are built and operated primarily to benefit the public and since their operation is essentially a public function, it is subject to state regulation.

These cases, at first blush, would seem to have established the principle that the Constitution sets limits to the activities of private organizations which exercise a governmental function or receive their power or funds from the state. But in the Stuyvesant Town case the New York Court of Appeals held otherwise, and the United States Supreme Court refused to disturb the decision.

It was not merely that minorities living in slums could now, with the help of city and state governments, be ousted from their homes to make way for private developments that would not accept minority people. Far more important was the fact that an ominous device for circumventing the constitutional safeguards against arbitrary government had received judicial sanction. Publicly sponsored enterprises aided by public funds and powers were held free to segregate, discriminate, and be above the law. Private corporations, the Court held, may now be lawfully handed these powers and funds of government and use them unhindered by constitutional restraint. What the government itself could not do constitutionally, it *could* do through an agent using its power and aid.

This surrender of public powers to nonrepresentative private groups —always in the name of social reform—is of course not a phenomenon entirely strange to the modern world, for it was one of the unique characteristics of the corporate states which have weighed like massive incubi on the prostrate body politic of Europe. It is new in America.

The judicial approval of Stuyvesant Town thus represents a dangerous relaxation of democratic controls in an era when reinforcement is called for. Its implications involve far more than the housing or civic improvements which were its ostensible purposes.

The Court of Appeals was divided 4 to 3. It is not difficult to see why dissenting Judge Stanley Fuld characterized the majority opinion as "perplexing," for where power is no longer limited, tyranny begins. The release of public power without check into private hands, which the Stuyvesant Town example presaged, opened a new chapter in American political theory.

It is impossible to balance the essence of democracy against fireproof buildings and well-kept lawns. . . . The Constitutions, Federal and State, forbid our putting the former into the judicial scales, just as they forbade the city officials from putting it upon the bargaining table . . . this undertaking is a governmentally conceived, governmentally aided, and governmentally regulated project. . . . Stuyvesant Town in its role as chosen instrument for this public purpose may not escape the obligations that accompany the privileges accorded to it.

The majority opinion of Judge Bruce Bromley justified the immunity from constitutional checks with these words:

The increasing and fruitful participation of government, both State and Federal, in the industrial and economic life of the nation—by subsidy and control analogous to that found in this case—suggests the grave and delicate problem in defining the scope of the constitutional inhibitions which would be posed if we were to characterize the rental policy of respondents [Stuyvesant Town] as governmental action.

The opinion went on to cite the merchant marine, air-carriers, and farmers as subsidy recipients not subject to racial restraints. It implied that what the state or federal government may not do directly, i.e., discriminate against minorities, may be passed over by contract to a private individual who may then violate constitutional inhibitions.

Of course we are far from embarking upon any conscious imitation of the fascist racist aberrations. But it is not the personal motives of politicians or businessmen which shape the relationship between the state and the individual. For political systems have an inherent dynamic of their own. Freedom is an ethic, but it is also the by-product of economic institutions. That it has flourished in America is due not only to the scheme of separation of powers but also to the separation of government from business. In the American system, up to now, enjoyment of both property and personal freedom have been inextricably linked. The bond survived the great shift from the free-hold economy to the modern corporate system when the great propertied and entrepreneurial classes continued to oppose government expansion so as to keep taxes low and regulation minimal.

With the release of the welfare and spending powers, however, the competition for government aid took a new turn. The insulation of business from government has ended. The government is now the main functionary in the economic milieu, and the driving forces of enterprise are focused on Washington. The trader and the tycoon strive to manipulate government policies for their own ends, to influence legislation and to harness the public official in the private interest. It is a natural by-product of shifting the source of profit from the marketplace to the political arena.

In consequence, the welfare state bids fair to be a far cry from the pure and simple dispensing of benefits to America's common man, as its initial sponsors had intended. Under the guidance of certain business pressure groups—as shortsighted as they are powerful—there is gradually emerging a business welfare state. The government is being called upon to pump the funds authorized under the newly expanded welfare programs into certain private pipelines. The common men are to become, as it were, the residual legatees instead of being the direct beneficiaries: their benefits will be enjoyed at a second or third remove.

In the name of such public purposes as defense contracts, housing betterment, encouragement of infant as well as senile industries, economic pump-priming during depressions, slums, protection of savings, home-ownership encouragement, and a growing list of other high-sounding goals, we are stumbling blindly in several directions, one of which is a subsidies-to-business economy. In the name of social reform the government is called upon also to loan to business at low rates, to socialize business losses when necessary, to remove risk from private enterprise by federal insurance. In the process, these protected enterprises insist, of course, upon the same immunity from regulation they enjoyed before they drew upon the government purse and the government's powers.

The dissenting opinion of Judge Fuld in the Stuyvesant Town case decries the lost principle and signals the danger:

> The construction and operation of Stuyvesant Town are not matters of "merely private concern." . . . Everywhere in evidence are the voice and authority of the State and City. . . . Stuyvesant is in no sense an ordinary private landlord. . . . The argument overlooks that the constitutional rights of American citizens are involved and that such rights may not be used as pawns in driving bargains. . . . The mandate that there be equal protection of the laws, designed as a basic safeguard for all, binds us and respondents as well to put an end to this discrimination.

In Stuyvesant Town the issue of private government versus the Constitution is thus clearly drawn. The crucial question is whether a 1789 constitution, devised for a private enterprise system and for a democratic government, can survive as a basis for a welfare state, be it general welfare or business welfare.

Awakening to the dangers of the program, minorities, civic associations, and libertarian groups have sought to accomplish by local legislation what had been denied by the courts. The public reaction to Metropolitan's policy was so intense that a city ordinance was unanimously enacted in 1944 barring racial discrimination in future projects benefiting from city aid. In 1950, a statewide law was passed banning discrimination and segregation in future publicly aided projects. After the Supreme Court had refused to review the state court's decision, the city enacted another ordinance which embraced Stuyvesant Town. The states with similar anti-discriminatory legislation include New Jersey, Indiana, Illinois, Minnesota, Massachusetts, Pennsylvania, Wisconsin and Connecticut; the cities include Los Angeles, San Francisco, Cincinnati, Cleveland, Toledo, and Hartford; the redevelopment authorities of St. Paul and Minneapolis have banned discrimination by resolution.

Despite these few gains, racial discrimination in urban redevelopment continues. Worst of all, it has contributed a precedent which may yet open the door to publicly backed racial discrimination. If it becomes the justification for further incursions, it may signal the reduction of a fundamental principle underlying the American system.

XIX

THE FALLACIES EXAMINED

The Quest for a Neighborhood

O NE of the questions troubling American families is: "Where and what kind of neighborhood shall we live in?" The problem is bound up not only with the family's investment in a home but with the type of school the children will attend and their playmates, the family friendships and associations, and a whole complex of desires, needs, and satisfactions connected with the environment of which the home is a part.

Fixity of neighborhood status has been possible in the static societies of Europe where succeeding generations of the same families have dwelt for hundreds of years and where land transfer has been the exception rather than the rule. In Germany even wholesale destruction of buildings has not altered the ingrained attachment to old sites that have been in family ownership for 300 years, and the rubble is being removed for another house over the same old wine cellar. Bombed-out families in Europe returned to the same streets and houses except where complete destruction had removed all semblance of the old environment.

But fixity of status is an illusion in most American areas. Industry is still on the move, settling freely where it wishes, drawing to the community the labor force it needs: skilled and menial, black and white, high-brow, medium-brow, and low-brow. Industry remains the ultimate arbiter of neighborhood destiny, for in the long run it is the call of jobs which determines the flow of populations and their general character, status, race, and color. Improved railroads and the automobile have made such migrations easier. One can no longer be sure that the folk envisioned for one's community when one moved into it will be the same ten years later. In fact, with the majority of American families moving once every five years, there is only one thing certain about the American community: the uncertainty of who will inhabit it a few years hence.

By 1940 there were almost 11.5 million foreign-born whites representing 8.6 per cent of the population, and 12.9 million Negroes representing another 9.7 per cent. There were also countless citizens— poor whites, backwoodsmen, hillbillies, Okies, Arkies, Communists, unskilled labor, menials, inebriates, homosexuals, and social and religious deviates of all sorts who might not qualify as candidates for the dream-world neighborhood. Under a more realistic definition, there are more minorities than many of us would care to admit and most of us could be classified as members of one minority or another. The "majority" in America is less a homogeneous composite than a minority aggregate.

The neighborhood of $30,000 houses might perhaps serve as its own effective fortification against invasion by the unwanted, for there are less folk who could afford to invade it. But for the FHA-sponsored economy house of 600 square feet or the two-bedroom Cape Codder in the typical subdivision, the newly advantaged groups stand as potential competitors. The 10 per cent down payment, the minimum specifications of the houses and their tendency toward early obsolescence, the disparate nature of the ownerships of small parcels in multiple hands, and the superior concern of each owner for his own financial welfare when the decision to sell must be made, all serve to preclude any long-term control of the type of neighbors in any given neighborhood.

So too, while the outsider may not relish the chilly glance of a resentful neighbor, competition for housing has built an inexorable logic. It has impelled minorities on the fringes of acceptability (and sometimes those outside the fringes) to risk intrusion. It is not boldness that inspires the step but desperation.

Every neighborhood is thus ultimately a candidate for infiltration. The infiltrators are not always the type imagined when the realtor promised a neighborhood of super-eminent, high-wrought, and selected neighbors plus a guarantee that their successors would be more of the same.

But logic and statistics do not always dissolve the stuff neighborhood dreams are made of. The dream of the stabilized neighborhood has survived. And with the dream has come the nightmare, with a stubborn refusal to face the dawn.

The fears that obsess the average homeowner today are three. They are widely held, deeply felt, and founded upon the sincere belief that minority infiltrations are a menace to his home, neighborhood, and security. The homeowner is afraid of losing (1) social status, (2) neighborhood associations, and (3) investment. These fears, long existent, have been intensified by the recent mass migrations.

Loss of Social Status. The social status of the American neighborhood is an item to be reckoned with by any homeowner, tenant or investor. Where a man lives indicates his station in life and is of marked significance to friends, potential friends, and business connections. It plays a part in finding "proper" playmates for the children and spotlights the daughter's status in her marriageable years. Class, race, and color play a part in measuring social position, and a neighborhood inhabited by a minority group implies a low social standard. Any neighborhood threatened by infiltration is viewed as subject to social contamination. Sometimes a single Mrs. Grundy in a neighborhood may unjustly inspire organized opposition to a minority neighbor, or precipitate an exodus by nervous owners. The departure of leading families is taken as the final judgment of the social arbiters. The section then becomes known as a less desirable part of town. In general, a freer out-movement by the majority takes place when dwellings are available, while resistance and violence may occur when dwellings are scarce and an alternative neighborhood difficult to find.

Loss of Neighborhood Associations. When neighbors depart, the established neighborhood associations suffer. The composition of the school changes, children lose their old friends, the bridge club breaks up, the old movie house is not what it used to be and neither is the church. The social pressure to move into a "better" section of town is then accelerated.

Of all the institutions in the neighborhood, the church is the most sensitive. Change of population may alter the faith or denominations of the new neighbors, and affect the solvency of an edifice built and maintained through laborious effort. Changes like these, however, are hardly the fault of the minorities but have occurred throughout American history. They were often the product of migrations by industries, the decline of outmoded enterprises and the rise of new ones. Just as a Catholic neighborhood may be depleted of its Catholics by an inflow of Baptist Negroes, so many Protestant neighborhoods were similarly affected during the Irish immigration by an influx of Irish Catholics. Often, the real cause of the dilemma is not the minority but a rundown neighborhood which affected the church's composition long before the arrival of the first Negro. In a few cases, officials of the local church, sometimes wearing its vestments, have led the fight against the incoming minority. But in other cases church leaders have checked hasty action, and brought about understanding between new-comers and older residents. By constructive leadership areas have been stabilized and panicky residents persuaded that the immigration is no signal for them to pack up and flee.

Loss of Investment. Loss of social status and neighborhood associations may precipitate a collapse in property prices. Mass exodus acts like a currency flight. Fears per se produce a condition which might have been avoided if fears had not arisen and the owners had stayed put. But the buying and selling of real estate have more epidemic characteristics than are found in other commodities. A panic sale of stock might be neutralized by shrewd security-holders buying in at the low price. The discrete nature of real estate and the inability to determine precise values at a given moment subject it more readily to a spiral of rumor, a sudden glut of offerings, a dwindling of buyers, a cessation of repairs, a decline in prices (often temporary), and subsequent purchase by the minority who may be the only buyers willing to meet the asking prices. Mortgagees may then insist upon payment of their mortgage principal or drastic reduction of their loans when due, and they will make no new loans in the neighborhood. It is this sequence which gives rise to the assertion that in-migration of a single minority member lowers the value of the real estate.

The fears wrought out of the competition for shelter flow from seven principal fallacies now current in our neighborhoods. Regardless of their errors, they exist, are believed, and play an important, if artificial, role in the determination of price and value. The fallacies are:

1. Negroes and whites do not mix.
2. Negroes (or other nonwhites) are dirty and will spoil the neighborhood.

3. Entry of minority families into a neighborhood hurts social status.
4. The minority always goes where it is not wanted.
5. Once the minority establishes a beachhead, many more will soon follow and displace the once dominant majority.
6. Values go down wherever a minority moves into a neighborhood.
7. Homogeneity stabilizes value.[1]

The Negro is not the only victim of these fallacies. Other targets are Jews, Catholics, Puerto Ricans, Mexicans, and Indians. But there is an initial difference between the docile stereotype, and the combative.[2]

The competition of the docile minority in business is not feared; in fact these people are often needed to do the less attractive chores so the dominant majority can function more conveniently. The competitive abilities of the combative group, however, are feared or envied— in enterprise as in skill. An eloquent example of shifting attitudes is the following rationalization made in 1879 when the Chinese were the problem:

In the "early days," when there were in what is now the heart of our city immense sand hills to level, the flat, low portions of the city to be raised, streets to grade, sewers to dig, railroads to be built, and a great deal of other laborious and unpleasant work to be done, the Chinaman filled a place and performed the labor which was not so agreeable to Anglo-Saxon masculinity. We were willing that they should do our drudgery, and glad to be rid of the necessity of doing it ourselves. Men would walk about the streets with their hands in their pockets for days, and sometimes for weeks, before they would condescend to do what they called "Chinamen's work." No complaints were made so long as the Mongolians confined themselves and their operations to this servile meniality, and left untouched the lighter and easier occupations. . . . But in later years, since our rough

[1] Chapter XX is devoted to a discussion of #6 and #7.
[2] The stereotyped Jew is of course not always consistent, as Lloyd George wrote in the London *Daily Chronicle* about the charges against Jews: "If they are rich, they are birds of prey; if they are poor, they are vermin; if they are in favor of war, that is because they want to exploit the bloody feuds of Gentiles to their own profit. If they are anxious for peace, they are either instinctive cowards or traitors. If they give generously—and there are no more liberal givers than the Jews—they are doing it for some selfish purpose of their own. If they don't give, then what would you expect of a Jew? If labor is opposed by great capital, the greed of the Jew is held responsible. If labor revolts against capital—as it did in Russia—the Jew is blamed for that also."

places have been made smooth, our mountains brought low, our deserts made to blossom as the rose, and the "Iron Horse" sent on his fiery track all over our coast, when this class of labor ceased to be a necessity, the Chinese began to make inroads on the lighter and better occupations which belong preeminently to white skilled labor.[3]

The docile minority may be excluded from a neighborhood because it is looked upon as a subordinate class. Its effort to attain parity challenges the social status of the majority, thereby challenging neighborhood relationships and property values. Exclusion of the combative minority, however, may be less involved with property values than with the effort of the dominant majority to bolster its social self-estimation by rejecting a group that is feared or envied. The docile minority today may become the combative one tomorrow as it moves up in the social scale.

The competition for dwellings has become a main factor in arousing common fears and insecurities.

Fallacy No. 1: *Negroes and Whites Do Not Mix.*   Whether Negroes (or other groups) do not mix involves a definition of a word which has vague and complex connotations. What "mix" means is not always clear to the user or his listeners. Generally it indicates resistance to or fear of a group seeking parity with his own, the dominant group. When Frederick H. Ecker of the Metropolitan Life Insurance Company said Negroes and whites do not "mix," he had no clear idea of what mixing would mean in a gigantic $110 million project (Stuyvesant Town). The few Negroes who might have become tenants would hardly have been noticed, much less mixed.[4]

There are, however, less sweeping definitions of the word "mix" which one confronts every day. The word may be used in:

a. A residential sense, i.e., the minority lives next door, down the block, or around the corner. They "bother nobody" or there is only a nodding acquaintance. They mix well or, being disinterested in their neighbors, don't mix at all.

b. An entrepreneurial sense, i.e., the neighbor is a good prospect for an insurance policy, a loan, a business investment.

[3] Jennett Blakeslee Frost, *California's Greatest Curse.* San Francisco, Joseph Winterburn & Co., 1879, pp. 15–17.
[4] Since some Negroes have moved in, they are in fact not being noticed and apartments in Stuyvesant Town are still at a premium.

c. A social sense, i.e., a good fellow to take a drink with, one with the proper *savoir-vivre:* my wife will like him and they'll make a nice couple for a gin game. There are of course different gradations of sociality. We might invite Levy when we entertain the intellectual or business crowd, but not when the boss or Mary's future father-in-law comes to dinner. While being seen with Jews may lower the host's status, if Levy is a man of status there may be a gain. Sociality may be achieved and ripen into confidence and a deep respect or dependency.

d. The civic sense, i.e., participating in community activities to keep the streets cleaner, the parks greener, the taxes leaner. Here the cooperation of the minority may be sought for the community good, with no further effort to advance the relationship.

e. The school-playground sense, i.e., the neighbor has two children the same age as ours, and they're nice kids.

f. A subordinate sense, i.e., the Negro, Chinese, Filipino, or Mexican may be one's servant, chauffeur, or superintendent and live in the same apartment building or block. As long as there is a recognized difference in status, the "mixing" may be close, frequent, and personal without fear of challenge.

g. A nuptial sense, i.e., our daughter is marriageable, so is Smith's son and I'd like to have them meet more often, so let's see something more of the Smiths. Or there is the other extreme: Smith is a Negro (Jew, Catholic, etc.)—I don't want my daughter to marry a Negro (Jew, Catholic, etc.).

h. A sexual sense, in which inhibition is collapsed into coition, or insulation into miscegenation.

Despite these variations, when one thinks of mixing with a Negro (or Chinese, Filipino, Japanese, etc.) he is apt to carry his thoughts from casual acquaintance right to sexual union in one kaleidoscopic sweep. He envisions the Negro through the stereotype (black, lazy, irresponsible, dirty) adjusted to the sexual stereotype (different, diseased, carnal) with whatever personalized connotations the stereotype may have for his wife, daughter, or mistress. No allowance is made for the intellectual Negro, the aged Negro, or the family man who offers no sexual threat. On the neighborhood competitive level, all become alike, all equally menacing. The invader automatically takes on the appearance of the neighborhood hippogriff.

In general, however, the sociality one expects from the neighbor is neither sexual attachment, intellectual affinity, nor spiritual agglutination. Acquaintance may be with many; intimacy limited to a few. The automobile, which has enlarged individual mobility, has also made each man less dependent on his neighbor. The proper function of the neighbor is to keep his garbage covered, his lawn trim, his children and radio quiet, his house painted, his troubles to himself. In the big cities a large percentage of residents do not even know their neighbors' names, though in suburban areas curtains are more transparent and gossip and rumor circulate more freely.

Fallacy No. 2: *Negroes (or Other Nonwhites) Are Dirty and Spoil the Neighborhood.* The plainspoken publican behind the well-stocked bar in Cicero, Illinois, was holding forth on why Harvey E. Clark, Jr., the Negro, simply had to be kept out of the apartment house. "Negroes are dirty," he said, eyeing the barricades manned by troops. "We are all Americans," he admitted in his thick Slavic accent, "but if we let them in, soon they filthy up the whole neighborhood. Look at Chicago." He was expressing what was said before the Detroit riots and what is taken for granted by laymen and even some experts.

The case of the Chinese is again in order. Never has a stereotype shifted with more permutations. When the Chinese first came and were needed, they were viewed as clean. They were hired as cooks; their restaurants were considered well kept, and were extensively patronized by gourmet and glutton.[5] "Their cleanliness, unobtrusiveness, and industry were often commented upon."[6] But in a few years they were considered "disgustingly filthy. . . . Nothing can exceed the noisome odors which exhale from their proximity . . . their streets and habitations filthy in the extreme . . . he will feed on the meanest kind of food including vermin . . . their presence in a particular quarter of a Caucasian city or town will deplete it in a short time of its white population. . . ."[7]

[5] Francis J. Brown and J. S. Roucek, eds., *One America.* New York, Prentice-Hall, Inc., rev. ed., 1945, p. 316.

[6] Mary Roberts Coolidge, *Chinese Immigration.* New York, Henry Holt and Co., 1909, p. 23.

[7] Hon. Edwin R. Meade, "The Chinese Question," a paper read at the Annual Meeting of the Social Science Association of America. New York, Arthur and Bonnell, 1877, pp. 8, 13, 14.

The stereotype is one generally associated with the slum-dweller who is blamed for the dirty condition. "If you gave them bathtubs they would put coal in them,"[8] a common argument used to oppose the public housing program, expresses the widely held notion of both the slum-dweller's ignorance and his filthy habits. As long as the Negro is the servant or cook, he or she could cook our food, make our beds, fondle our children, sleep in the same room with them. The picture of Aunt Jemima mixing pancakes does not hurt the sale of pancake flour and the portrayal of the Negro Pullman porter tidying up our berth is acceptable and even reassuring. But since the Negro has moved to the crowded city, he has stepped into the old immigrant's image. The slums are his fault. The failure of the city to collect garbage is translated into a vision of the Negro living in a house full of filth. The failure of the landlord to make repairs or to supply extermination services, causing the accumulation of rats and vermin in halls and cellars, is automatically imputed to the Negro's habits. No allowance is made for the fact that a newcomer from a backward region may need time for adjustment. There is no mitigation for the intense overcrowding that makes keeping a house in order all but impossible, nor for the fact that the Negro housewife is working away from home ten hours a day. The housing projects inhabited by Negroes are in fact outstanding for their neatness and spruceness, but this too does not alter the bias. The teeming slums have created a composite of an unkempt aggregation of mudlarks, and all members of the group are put into the same nest.

Fallacy No. 3: *Entry of Minority Families into a Neighborhood Hurts Social Status*. Here again a stereotype is constructed of the particular minority, this time in his new role of low-caste, despoiling invader. If he is a Negro he is now no longer lazy but brazen and meddlesome, going where he does not belong and is not wanted. If he is tolerated, all his kind will soon rush in and the neighborhood will degenerate. If he is a Jew, it will be laid to his aggressiveness.

Actually, one knows little about a neighbor's social status or wealth until evidence is given: an automobile, servants, jewelry, a blue mink, paintings, furniture, a listing in *Who's Who,* newspaper men-

[8] In the South the saying is that if you give the Negro a refrigerator he would put his feet in it, which suggests a kind of cute cunning and ignorance.

tion, gifts to charity. And even with these disclosures one is unsure, for much of the evidence may represent swagger, not swag.

Difference in financial status was more noticeable in an earlier day through identification with tenancy or ownership, or through the tangible symbols, such as the mansion or the cottage, the Rolls Royce or the Model T Ford. But with tenancy no longer a sign of ignominy, with the rise of intangible personalty that may never leave the vault, with stock houses as well as stock automobiles financed by installment buying, mortgages, and nominal down payments, and with boiler-makers now driving Cadillacs and debutantes Fords, identification of true status is much more difficult. Normally, this should be a sign of greater democratization of our society. It is not, because we have the increasing ascendancy of a *group* social status in place of the former *individualized* social status.

The growth of group status in neighborhoods has been accelerated by the tendency toward job stratification in the factories. Some-times it may be a socially leveling factor. But sometimes, frus-trated in their efforts to effect differentiation through their own talents or wealth, they have become more sensitive to attack upon their status as a social group. They function less like individuals than as an army. The same group of workers which accepts a Negro co-worker in a Detroit automobile plant and recognizes his equal vote at a union meeting is apt to be panic-stricken if that Negro moves into the group's suburb. The white worker has constructed two different identifica-tions with the two different groups of which he is a member. He may fight for his Negro co-worker in the plant, but at home with his wife and with his neighbors and their wives he will fight the same Negro co-worker with fire and dynamite when the Negro tries to move into his neighborhood.

What is the social status the white worker defends in his neighbor-hood? It may be only the idealized image of his own eminence raised to the level of his idealized neighbors. He is no longer an individual but part of a faction. The moment the stereotyped minority moves in, the group concept is under challenge and the pang is felt simultane-ously by the entire group—as though they were all an endless chain of Siamese twins. In this reaction, neighborhood becomes as much a stereotype as the intruder—the neighborhood as envisioned and as it threatens to become. Though the neighborhood may be deteriorating, the moment a minority enters, it is the "home and fireside," the refined cluster of homes that must be defended at all costs. The emotion stirred in the breast of the defender becomes a common cause. Any who support the minority may even be classed as Communists. Idealism soon functions in reverse, the Christian label is used to achieve the un-Christian purpose, and those who dare defend the nation's basic principles are marked as the nation's enemy.

The sequence illustrates how the current operation of racial stereotypy may have dangerous consequences. One stereotyped group spontaneously generates a counter-stereotype: the challenged group. When the imagined threat against the top group's property, prestige, or status becomes intense, members lose their sense of individualism and hate and fear as a group, sell their property as a group in panic, and may even resort to violence as a group.

The fact is that minorities do not often enter any communities except those which by age, initial shoddiness, or other factors are already on the economic as well as social downgrade. Environmental degeneration may start with occupancy of a new subdivision by home buyers of the same social and financial level. The houses are all alike, built to minimal standards, and quickly lose their pristine sheen.

Gas stations and other undesirable commercial ventures often intrude and as the section ages and declines in status, tenancy increases. Some houses may even be rented furnished to transients. With each decline in physical appearance or social status, some families leave. Each exodus helps to push values further down, opening housing opportunities to a lower income group—or to an ethnic group that can buy only in deteriorated sections.

By confusing cause and effect, the new ethnic or lower economic group is blamed as the cause of the social deterioration and economic decline. This confusion of cause with effect has been aided by the solemn pronouncements of the real estate appraisers and builders, and by the FHA, which after 1935 was responsible for the bulk of the subdivisions in America. FHA said:

The appeal of a residential neighborhood results from the general condition and attractiveness of the properties located therein; the kind and social status of the inhabitants. . . . The older district still remains desirable, but only to families whose social status or standards of living are lower than those of the families which have vacated the district. This process of change in occupancy by families of successively lower standards of living is accompanied by declines in desirability and value. . . .[9]

In the era of individualized status, when social differences between neighbors were plainly marked by the house and other evidence, neither pride nor property was injured if a Negro lived nearby. Today the presence of a single Negro is viewed as a more significant index of blight than the physical condition of the house. This does not hold true in areas where people decline to be frightened by Negroes. In Detroit, a once stylish area was losing its inhabitants to incoming Negroes. A group of white college teachers began to buy in the neighborhood, stemming the out-migration and reviving values. In Cambridge, Massachusetts, when Ralph Bunche had tentatively accepted a professorship at Harvard University, the Civic Unity Council found there would be no difficulty finding room for him in the most fashionable part of the city. There had been no mass influx of Negroes in Cambridge, and intellectual status outweighed racial status in the more expensive areas. Bunche's intellectual capacities were viewed as elevating rather than depressing local status. The situation might be different for Negro workers or students.

A similar tendency may be noted in cities where Negro superintendents live in exclusive apartment blocks with their wives and children. The Census tracts include many of these. Everybody accepts the pattern as satisfactory. But if any of these superintendents began paying rent there would be a shift from subordination to parity, the status of the residents would be challenged, and panic would set in. In Baltimore's pattern, the Negro long lived in the alleys back of the mansions, but today the mansion folk are fleeing to the suburbs because Negroes are living nearby. In the South there are many areas where the Negro lives on the same block with the whites without challenging their social dignity. In countless southern cities, Negroes not only reside on the same streets but some occupy fine homes they have purchased or once inherited from white masters. The fact that their houses are good and costly has raised no more challenge to the southern whites than has the presence of a few decrepit houses in genteel blocks. The dominant southern white feels secure in his dominance or at peace with his paternalism. It is only

[9] *Underwriting Manual.* Washington, Federal Housing Administration, 1935. §§315, 207(2).

when the Negro moves up in status, and asserts it, that a challenge is seen and tension is stirred.

In Washington, D. C., Negroes represent 35 per cent of the population and live in all parts of the city. But whites have been moving into Negro-occupied areas like Georgetown without sacrificing any prestige. In northern cities, mixed communities inhabited by a variety of social, racial, and religious groups were long typical. Before the mass influx of Negroes to the North after 1914, Negroes were represented in many fashionable sections without disturbing neighborhood status. In some parts of New England this is still the case.

The Virgin Islands in 1952 were inhabited by some 1000 whites and 30,000 Negroes. The whites are the same whites we see in the northern suburbs, the Negroes are the same color seen in Detroit, New York, and Chicago. The dominant Negroes are represented in the professions, politics, and enterprise. Yet whites are strongly attracted to the Virgin Islands. After this writer had been seen dining with a prominent Negro at the new $3,000,000 hotel built for the white tourist trade, he learned that some northern visitors had felt he must be a man of note or status to enjoy the company of this native. The Negroes on the Islands have not been visibly disturbed by the infiltration of the new white minority.

Although the attack upon social status may be baseless, snobbish, or the product of insecurity, it exists as a social concept and thus possesses a measure of validity. It will continue valid until the causes are removed or it is supplanted by a more dominant drive or value. The whole background of American development has demonstrated that it is not the mere presence of a minority that creates opposition but the rise of some challenge. The competition for housing and the social progress of minorities are spurring that challenge. The mass movement of minorities is intensifying it. Add to these factors the inherent tenuousness and insecurity of current neighborhoods and the encouragement of bias by real estate groups and government officials, and the picture becomes comprehensible. The most salutary way to change the pattern is to diminish the primary cause of trouble—the competition for housing—by building enough for everybody so that people can move where they please instead of where they must.

Fallacy No. 4: *The Minority Always Goes Where It Is not Wanted.* A housing shortage for the majority is a housing famine for the minority. The more the minority is excluded from land and dwellings, the more pressing becomes its need, the more likely becomes entry into areas it would normally avoid.

The fallacy that a minority always goes where it is not wanted is grounded on the mistaken notions that:

a. A person feels comfortable in places where he is not wanted.
b. He is willing to suffer loss of privileges and opportunities in a hostile community.
c. He will gamble his life's savings on a house in an unfriendly neighborhood.
d. He will submit his children to rebuffs and discomfitures.

The fact is, however, that it is often difficult to get minorities to go even where they *are* wanted. The public housing experience showed that Negroes applied only when the projects were in existing Negro areas, or where a sustained and reassuring effort was made to encourage occupancy of projects outside of Negro neighborhoods. Even where the housing need was intense and the rents low, Negroes were loath to apply. In Cleveland, Ernest J. Bohn, director of the housing authority, told this writer that though Negroes were free to apply for space in the outlying projects, none did so until after a long and concerted effort to relieve their anxieties.

During the depression of the 1930's vacancies were plentiful in most cities, particularly in white slum areas, and landlords were willing to rent to Negroes. Yet the minorities tended to remain in their old sections. In New York City's Lower East Side there were vacancies of 20 to 25 per cent. The Negroes refused to leave their overcrowded rookeries in Harlem and elsewhere.[10]

The 1630 dwelling units in the New York City Housing Authority's Williamsburg project were applied for only by whites, while the 577-unit Harlem River project got only Negro applications. The pattern persisted until the Authority made positive efforts to integrate the races within the projects. Even then the Negroes were reluctant to move away from established friends and institutions into

[10] Leo Grebler, *Housing Market Behavior in a Declining Area.* New York, Columbia University Press, 1952, p. 149.

predominantly white areas. This is a main reason why Puerto Ricans do not as yet move out of New York City in greater volume.

Once the minority is reassured and the way paved for their entry, mixed occupancy can readily be arranged.

New York City in 1953 had 86 projects with 100,000 mixed low-rent dwellings. No project owned by the Authority was all-white. Both the Negro and white populations have been educated in interracial living. The Negro knows he will not be a token black sheep in the project.

Queensview Houses, a nonprofit cooperative in Queens, New York City, is in a white neighborhood adjoining a public housing project. It receives tax-exemption on the improvements and houses 728 families with annual incomes up to $6990. The project, sponsored by eminent citizens including Harold C. Sheperd, president of the National City Bank, Howard S. Cullman, banker, Henry Morgenthau, Jr., Albert D. Lasker, and Louis H. Pink, was intended as a demonstration in interracial living. After the first announcement of the project in September, 1948, there were only 50 applicants. Some observers said the dearth of applications was caused by a nondiscrimination ordinance applicable to such projects. After an article in the New York *Post*[11] endorsing the project and mentioning its nondiscrimination policy, there was a rush for applications and a million dollars in apartments sold within a few days. Despite the statement that the project was nondiscriminating, only 12 Negro families applied. (Further promotion brought the final figure to 20, or less than 3 per cent of the total dwellings.)

The attitude of Negroes was well expressed by one of the applicants, a Negro leader, who told this writer about the conflicts he and his wife had to resolve before applying. They did not want their children to grow up in the Negro ghetto where they were living and where they would see only Negro children. After being assured that the project would be interracial and the family would not be guinea pigs, the man was ready to join. His wife held out, because she felt her children would be insecure in a predominantly white project. When assured there would be enough Negro families to provide a feeling of security, she yielded to her husband's preference.

[11] Charles Abrams, "$8,000,000 Cooperative Here a Challenging Venture," September 28, 1948, p. 8.

Other private projects have had similar experiences. Certainly, exclusion practices have played a part in keeping Negroes out of some areas. Equally, it is often the minority's own decision to stay out. For example, any Negro can now enter the most fashionable New York City restaurants, yet it is unusual to see many of the city's 800,000 Negroes in them. High prices are not the only reason. The fact is that most Negroes would still hesitate to go where they might feel uncomfortable. Similar considerations condition the Jew's attitude in clubs, resorts, schools, and homes. But as he moves up the social and cultural scale, he may not like confinement to all-Jewish places. He wants to meet people in all walks of life. But he will usually move only when and where he finds himself welcome. He will not gamble on embarrassing his family or risking his investment in an area where he knows he will be unwelcome or his wife and children feel discomfited. Though he may occasionally venture into non-Jewish areas, his general tendency is to stay with his own group until social strictures are eased or removed. This caution accounts for the feeling of many gentiles that Jews are clannish.

The restrictions against Jews in Baltimore have been so rigid that even educated Jews of the third and fourth generations, and of high economic and cultural standards, have moved into all-Jewish suburbs, and new Jewish and gentile neighborhoods are divided into distinct areas. One finds the same pattern in Westchester County, New York. This product of fear, social strictures, and exclusion practices offers a striking contrast to the pattern of San Francisco where similar anti-Jewish barriers have not existed.

Fallacy No. 5: *Once the Minority Establishes a Beachhead, Many More Will soon Follow and Displace the Once Dominant Majority.* This is true under some circumstances, but is fallacious as a generalization. While a minority will usually not enter an area unless there is a semblance of a sympathetic community which will give it security and companionship for the children, conflict will arise when economic opportunities draw a home-hungry minority into an area that offers few opportunities for housing compared with the minority's needs. The new arrivals will then seek shelter wherever they can, but they will still not deliberately challenge the existing setup. In fact, strangers ordinarily look for neighborhoods of their own people. Most Chinese, for example, will stay together even though it means intense overcrowding. Assimilated minorities have less need to live with their own group, but they too seldom venture elsewhere until they feel welcome. Minorities will venture into strange areas only when their hunger for shelter offers them no other choice. The decision is made not as a challenge but with trepidation and in desperation. The Negro presents the most difficult problem because of his numbers and visibility. The volume of Negro migration has been so great, his income so inadequate, and the housing restrictions so intense that he tends to live overcrowded within circumscribed borders. He cannot adequately compete with whites, for the latter are preferred as occupants and better able to pay the going market prices. The Negro usually looks for houses within the ghetto, or for substandard quarters elsewhere, which others will not have.

Since the housing famine, the Negro has sought to satisfy his housing needs in three types of areas:

1. White areas bordering on overcrowded nonwhite areas.
2. Obsolete or run-down areas.
3. Panic areas.

In the first the bulging Negro population, kept from diffusing into other parts of the city, presses upon the adjoining section. Normally, the proximity of Negro dwellings would offer no threat to the adjoining whites. But the Negro's anxiety to hold on to his new job and get a roof over his head may embolden him to eye buildings just over the line. Landlords, sensitive to the intense Negro demand, know they can get the same or higher rentals without making the necessary repairs. The block tends to run down and the sequence may be repeated on the next street.

Obsolete and run-down areas inhabited by whites are the most susceptible candidates for the sequence of desertion, infiltration, and influx by nonwhites. These sections are cheaper and their owners often more anxious to sell. But new developments are not immune. Houses recently built are often so flimsy that the owners find themselves on the treadmill of everlasting repairs. The underprivileged are often the only ones who will bail them out of their investments.

These substandard areas frequently include abandoned houses, untenantable hazards, garages, coops, sheds, shanties, houses fronting on smelly factories, hovels in sections unsuitable for normal living, and tenements or pretentious and obsolete houses that can be cut up into small units. These supply the initial beachhead.

The panic area suffers desertion the moment one or a few minority members move into it. If the residents would stay put, the section would settle in value and status,[12] but the spiral of rumor and fear takes a heavy toll. Offerings glut the market, vacancies appear, maintenance and upkeep are put off, and blight sets in. Panic areas exist, particularly in cities that have experienced large Negro in-migrations. Availability of alternative housing for the whites speeds the exodus. When shortage sets in, the exodus may be halted and the level of social status steadied.

A practice becoming more common is "blockbusting." Taking advantage of an owner's fear that Negroes may move into an area, a shrewd trader approaches an owner in an all-white block and persuades him to sell. Negroes are then moved into the house. The other owners offer their homes at bargain prices. The trader buys them and when he has acquired a sufficient number at low cost, sells them at mammoth profits to home-hungry Negroes. Oddly, experienced block-busters interviewed by the writer avoid buying houses in areas where there is no prospect of panic and quick purchases at declining prices. If all that can be gained is purchase of only one house while the remaining owners remain unaffected by the change and hold on to their properties, there is precious little money to be made by the blockbuster.

A responsible realtor can avert a selling panic. An incident several years ago in Schenectady illustrates the point. A Negro professional man answered an owner's advertisement of a house for sale in an upper middle-class neighborhood. Selling to a Negro was the last thing that would have occurred to the owner and his wife. But they liked the applicant personally and did not object to his color. News of the sale threw the neighbors into a state of sustained panic, only a few degrees short of hysteria. A woman realtor received no less than a dozen telephone calls from frightened men and women. Some

[12] East 95th Street, New York City, is an example. It lies only one block below the beginning of the intense East Harlem concentration. Yet while some infiltration has occurred, the houses (long inhabited by people of high social and financial standards) have been improved and there has been no mass exodus.

wanted to sell at once; others asked what they should do. "Don't do anything," each caller was advised. "Nothing is going to happen to you or to your property. If you like the neighborhood, stay where you are." The advice was taken. Nobody sold, and today the neighborhood is as sound as ever. There was an initial period of awkwardness when the new owner moved in. The Negro handled himself well. He kept the house and garden in perfect condition, responded cheerfully but casually when neighbors finally began to say, "Good morning," and before long he was swapping plants and vegetables and going to the neighborhood church.

The key factor in majority-minority tensions is the housing shortage. Failure of the home-building industry to provide enough houses creates an intense competition for dwellings and a real estate market which trades on fear, insecurity, rumor, and deception. The end-product is dangerous tension between groups which, but for the shelter shortage, might live in mutual respect.

XX

MINORITIES, HOMOGENEITY, AND "VALUE"

Homogeneity as a Neighborhood Concept

Any inquiry into the desirability of homogeneity requires definition. The most dissimilar people are in some respects homogeneous and those who appear most homogeneous to a realtor might have far more dissimilarities than the realtor might imagine. Few people will have counterparts in intelligence, outlook, background, estate, experience, and ambitions. They may be homogeneous in race, color, nationality, wealth, sex, or social status, but unalike in thoughts, aims, education, attitudes, aptitudes, and appetites. Place ten vice-presidents of the Chase National Bank on ten psychoanalysts' couches and they will reveal as wide a variety of backgrounds, biases, sexual inclinations, and general proclivities as might be found in a publican, a Republican, grocer's clerk, confectioner, biology teacher, butcher, lawyer, journalist, civil servant, and a writer on housing.

The homogeneity of interests so much esteemed by the realtor may be no community of interests but only a cultivated hatred for a different class. It may be little more than common fear of the people of a race or religion, fanned into a mistaken notion of one's own superiority. The humble state of others may provide the ladder on which we ascend to self-estimations that fall somewhat short of fact. In an age when it is easier to be against something than for it, the emphasis upon homogeneity serves the misguided troublemaker at home as it once served the master propagandist of the Third Reich.

Some homogeneity in neighborhoods may be a good thing. It is doubtless desirable to live in a neighborhood where there is a reasonable number of intelligent and interesting human beings. But this does not mean that a neighborhood is doomed unless all are so or that all must be Catholics, Jews, white Protestants, advertising men, white white-collar workers, or executives, all of the same age-group to boot. If all were drinking men or all devotees of Alcoholics Anonymous, the former would not be on hand to benefit from the latter's ministrations and the latter would have no one to minister to. With the standard living room now able to accommodate only a half-dozen couples at best, and with the increasing need for finding not only five good husbands with a common interest but an equivalent number of wives all tolerable to each other, the element of selectivity would seemingly function better in a neighborhood with variety than in one with unmitigated uniformity.

Assuming, however, that the homogeneity concept is sound, it seems hardly practical. A neighborhood requires a variety of people to make it function economically and socially. Without maids, delivery boys, dishwashers, laborers, window cleaners, plumbers' helpers, food dispensers, street cleaners, and garbage collectors, our cities and suburbs would soon go to the ghosts. Some of these jobs, lowly and menial, are filled by minorities, and it is practical that they live within convenient distance of their work. The man-made boundaries of cities may persist on paper, but they fade under the heels of those who make the community function.

In one city of 5000 inhabitants in northern Florida, most of the Negroes live outside the white residential area. They have no telephones or automobiles, and the white employer is obliged to call for his servant and take her home at the end of the day. Some of the white residents are sensibly urging that Negroes be permitted to live within walking distance. They contend that infiltration would increase values in their now homogeneous city.

The problem is not unique. Many suburbs are finding it increasingly difficult to carry on the daily chores while barring those who do the dirtier work. The problem is less troublesome, of course, if there is a city nearby where the minorities can live, but there is a limit to the flat or gently undulating land close to cities which the subdivider can use for his homogeneous homesites. The available land is also keenly sought for factory sites, golf courses, airports, shopping centers, and cemeteries.

As the suburbs push out to the more distant regions, partly in an effort to locate as far from minority areas as possible, they become less and less accessible to the workers who operate the civic machine. Simultaneously, cities have been offering better employment opportunities to the minorities. The length of the journey to work influences many to take jobs in the city rather than in the distant suburbs. At the same time, rising costs of new suburban homes have dictated elimination of the extra bedroom which once housed the sleep-in servant. Homogeneity and exclusion practices must ultimately be paid for with the drudgery of unnecessary housekeeping or the prohibitive cost of the reluctant servant.

The increasing tendency of cities to house an extraordinary proportion of minorities has in turn affected urban social and financial solvency. It has put an increased load on their social facilities, educational plant, relief agencies, and housing; it has started a trend toward minority homogeneity in many sections, forced an outmigration of groups better able to contribute to city upkeep, and thereby sharply affected municipal tax bases and budgets. The suburbanite may shut his eyes to the plight of the cities, but sooner or later his purse may have to be open to pay federal and state levies for city aid.

Homogeneous neighborhoods based on uniformity of youth or age create special problems. Where the hundreds of thousands of veterans' houses were built, age-grouping of children is loading some classrooms while others remain empty. The younger-age classrooms are jammed at the start, only to be unused as the neighborhood population matures. The same is true of tot-lots, playgrounds, and playfields.

A well-known appraiser who valued some extensive holdings in Detroit, leased to a large five-and-ten-cent chain store, advised his client to sell because he saw no future for the property—the residents were homogeneous in age and status.

The resident population tends more and more to be made up of older couples whose children are grown up. . . . This district is acquiring a type of homogeneity which is adverse to high retail land values. A more stable situation would be found where a better distribution of age groups, with a greater percent of young children, existed. However, where such a trend as is here found exists, that trend is seldom reversed.[1]

[1] From an unpublished appraisal for a client by a prominent appraisal firm.

The reasoning behind this appraisal is never found in the textbooks.

Suburban exclusion of the elderly, the by-product of the economy house and two-bedroom units, is depriving children as well as parents of the experience and counsel of the old—cutting off the most dependable supply of baby-sitters. Many older people have been forced into small urban hotels and furnished rooms, losing their important associations with youth and children. This situation accentuates the need for a national program to house the elderly in a manner that will bring them back into the life of communities.

Public housing projects, homogeneous because of rigid income limitations imposed by the pressure of the Washington real estate lobby, have caused both inconvenience and hardship to the occupants. The policy of restricting eligibility to a fixed maximum income has given an institutional character to the projects. The occupants are tagged as people who earn less than a specified income, so that a tenant feels more like the inmate of a poorhouse than a rent-payer. The daughter of a project tenant cannot withhold her father's income from a suitor long enough to be courted on her own merits. Concealment of salary rises and snooping by neighbors is encouraged. A rise in income due to increased earnings, which should be cause for joy, may result in a family's eviction. By indirectly curbing demands for wage increases which might render a tenant ineligible, public housing has tended in some cases to subsidize the employer. The policy of evicting those who do improve their status drives out the more exemplary tenants, leaving a less successful residuum. Income homogeneity has been a destructive force in the public housing program.

So too, concentration of tenants of uniform social status or income in private projects is bringing about a boring uniformity which must ultimately exert a financial and social impact upon the community. Agglomerations of people of a single class and temperament are dull. On the other hand, a sprinkling of poor artists or frustrated writers may be a tonic to a neighborhood of bank clerks or shopkeepers. The presence of a few restaurants with some good Chinese, Italian, or Negro cooks may promote more neighborhood vitality than all the restrictive covenants aimed at these chefs.

As they grow up, children suffer from the effort to impose social or economic uniformity. Their associations are limited—unless, of course, they escape to the cities for their opportunities, as many of them do. Having escaped, however, they are apt to marry and, under the current pattern, move to one-class suburbs again.

The most serious mischief of the homogeneous pattern is the group conflicts it engenders. The homeowners place undue emphasis on the importance of keeping minorities out, rather than on the real values which make a neighborhood sound. Bias is encouraged, violence often invited. Children cannot be happily raised where they are taught to hate or fear people who are different, vandalize their property, or fight them with stones or fire.

Where minorities are excluded, the psychological effects of the new homogeneity upon excluders and excluded are equally harmful. Where there is participation between groups, mutual understanding and respect are apt to evolve. "Two fiercely passive needs—property and sex—appear to be the final bastions of conservatism. In a life where mature adjustments in these regions are not worked out, and where anxiety dwells, there seems to be a higher probability of rigid, exclusive, suspicious character-formation."[2]

A poll of leading psychologists and sociologists, eliciting 272 replies from the psychologists and 96 from the sociologists, showed that 92 per cent felt that enforced segregation had detrimental effects on the segregated groups. Four per cent had no opinion and another 4 per cent did not answer the question. Eighty-three per cent of the respondents believed that enforced segregation had detrimental psychological effects on the group which enforces the segregation. Only 4 per cent thought it did not, 9 per cent had not formed an opinion, and 5 per cent did not answer the question. Factors which play a disruptive part, according to some of those polled, were feelings of guilt, deterioration of moral values, the requirement to act according to an irrational and inconsistent moral standard, impairment of the grasp of reality, the distortion of sound perceptions, the illusion of security, and the frustrations which reality brings.[3]

[2] Gordon W. Allport, "Prejudice: A Problem in Psychological and Social Causation," *The Journal of Social Issues,* Kurt Lewin Memorial Award Issue, Supplement Series, no. 4, November, 1950, p. 15.

[3] Max Deutcher and Isidor Chein, with the assistance of Natalie Sadigur, "The Psychological Effects of Enforced Segregation: A Survey of Social Science Opinion," *The Journal of Psychology,* vol. 26, second half, October, 1948.

At a White House Conference on Children and Youth, a fact-finding report on the effects of prejudice, discrimination, and segregation on the personality developments of children confirmed that the personality of all children, majority as well as minority, is damaged.[4] The minority children feel a sense of inferiority and humiliation, become confused about their personal worth, and are affected by a feeling of self-hatred and rejection by their own group. While different children react differently, depending on the stability and quality of their family relationships, their social and economic class, their parents' cultural and educational backgrounds, and their own personal qualities, many feel rejected and suffer serious loss of morale. All are encumbered in some ways by segregation and its concomitants.

The children of the majority, taught to learn the society's biases unrealistically, compare themselves to the minority group. They are apt to evaluate themselves not by standards of personal ability and achievement but in relation to a group they feel is weaker than themselves. Their attitude may be roughly, "I'm better than a dirty nigger." They often harbor guilt feelings and make unnatural rationalizations to justify what cannot be justified: their acquired fears and hates. Confusion, conflict, moral cynicism, and disrespect for authority are consequences, particularly when children are taught the moral and religious principles of brotherhood by the same adults who discriminate. Others develop a rigid and uncritical idealization of their parents and an admiration for the dynamic political leader. They despise the weak;[5] they conform to the demands of the strong, yet develop at the same time a subconscious hate for the strong.

Authority is ample to suggest that by distorting reality and blocking natural communication, segregation may lead ultimately to a social climate where racial tensions or outbreaks may be inevitable. These findings were confirmed in a report signed by 32 sociologists, anthropologists, psychologists, and psychiatrists, part of the brief filed as an appendix to the appellant's brief in the school segregation

[4] K. B. Clark, "Effect of Prejudice and Discrimination on Personality Development," *Fact Finding Report, Mid-Century White House Conference on Children and Youth*. Washington, Children's Bureau, Federal Security Agency, 1950 (mimeographed).

[5] T. W. Adorno, E. Frenkel-Brunswik, D. J. Levinson, R. N. Sanford, *The Authoritarian Personality*. New York, Harper & Brothers, 1950, pp. 384–387.

cases.[6] The report points out that if properly guided, desegregation can proceed without major problems and lead to a friendlier relation between the groups.[7]

These findings are in sharp contrast to those of the appraisal and realty groups. They put the question in issue. They are as much elements deserving consideration in assessing home and neighborhood value as the quality of the bricks and plumbing. A house in a neighborhood where guilt feelings may be generated, moral values disrupted, and irrational action made the norm should not be worth living in at any price. A house in such a community may still command a price but the environment may gnaw at the larger, long-term values of the property.

Minorities and Home Prices

Assume, however, that short-term price levels should be the sole criterion. Do the available facts support the facile conclusion that infiltration of an "antipathetic racial group" inevitably drives down prices? There are of course many cases where it does, but the evidence is that there are at least eight different price reactions to minority infiltration. Prices may remain constant or may rise as well as fall. These reactions are:

Status	*Price*
1. Original area	100
After infiltration	100−
After inundation	100+
2. Original area	100
After infiltration	100−
After inundation	100−
3. Original area	100
After infiltration	100+
After inundation	100+
4. Original area (already long occupied by minority)	100
After infiltration by majority	100+ or −
After inundation by majority	100+ or −

[6] *Brown v. Board of Education; Briggs v. Elliott; Davis v. School Board of Prince Edward County.* 347 U.S. 483.

[7] See *Minnesota Law Review,* May, 1953, for excerpts from the experts' report.

Status	Price
5. Original area	100
After infiltration	100−
Area stabilized, no inundation	100+ or −
6. Original area	100
After infiltration	100+
No inundation	——
7. Original area with originally mixed area settled in pattern	100
8. Original area (inhabited by minority)	100
Infiltration by another minority	100+ or −
After inundation	100+ or −

The existence of these variations has been confirmed by experience. The statement that one race or group inevitably affects price favorably and another unfavorably disregards the complex of factors which play a part, such as the social and economic status of a particular minority at a particular time; its numbers in relation to the numbers in the majority group; the latter's social and cultural level; the minority's capacity for social improvement and assimilation; the size of the city and the physical condition of its neighborhoods; the particular pattern of minority distribution; the nature of the then current minority stereotype; the type of social and educational leadership and maturity in the community; the social and economic role of the minority in the community; the relationship between the groups in employment, and a host of other factors.

The attitudes toward Poles, Irish, Jews, Puerto Ricans, Negroes, or Mexicans, moreover, will vary within each region. A Chinese can live anywhere in New York City, but not in San Francisco. Occupancy by Negroes may sometimes be more challenging than that of Poles, Mexicans, or Jews, because of the difference in their appearance and social or economic status. Negro occupancy may sometimes not disturb a community in one city while it might elsewhere. What may be true in Boston may not be true in adjoining Cambridge; what may be true in the North may be untrue in the South and Midwest.

Shortages may intensify competition for dwellings and push up values, while simultaneously intensifying antagonism between the competing groups. Whether values rise or fall may also depend upon the ability of the newcomers to bid up prices. Thus, no one can say that the influx of Jews to Miami, Long Island, or the Westchester suburbs has depressed values. One FHA insuring office observes that "the infiltration of Negro owner-occupants has tended to *appreciate* property values and neighborhood stability in contrast to its depreciating use by white families as a rental area."[8]

Nor do values automatically collapse because the minority happens to be of a lower economic status. A group may be of lower economic but higher social status, and vice versa. Even when there is both economic and social inferiority, the value of the area may not be affected. This is illustrated by the many sections where Negro, Chinese, or other nonwhite groups have occupied quarters near their social and financial betters for years without affecting neighborhood status or realty values.[9] The Chinese who first came to California were "not merely desired because of their invaluable service at this period, but respected for the picturesque and dignified element which they added to society,"[10] and though sentiment changed thereafter, values in Chinatown, San Francisco, today have risen sharply and have maintained themselves. That properties occupied by Negroes have frequently increased in value or remained unaffected both in new settlements and old is substantiated by a number of authorities and surveys.[11]

G. W. Beehler, Jr. states that "sections newly occupied by colored during the past two or three years . . . increased in value from 60% to 100% on the average." Belden Morgan cites properties which

[8] Rufus S. Lusk, *Washington Business Review,* annual number, 1948, Washington, D. C., pp. 17–19.

[9] Lloyd Rodwin, "The Theory of Residential Growth and Structure," *The Appraisal Journal,* July, 1950, p. 306.

[10] Mary Roberts Coolidge, *Chinese Immigration.* New York, Henry Holt and Co., 1909, p. 22.

[11] According to Oscar I. Stern, "Long Range Effect of Colored Occupancy," *The Review of the Society of Residential Appraisers,* January, 1946, p. 5: "It is a fact, the axiom that colored infiltration collapses the market is no longer true." Robert C. Weaver, *The Negro Ghetto,* New York, Harcourt, Brace & Company, 1948, ch. XV. According to George W. Beehler, Jr., "Neighborhood values in areas newly occupied by colored people have sharply increased and will continue to increase." ("Colored Occupancy Raises Values," *The Review of the Society of Residential Appraisers,* September, 1945, pp. 3–6, 12). Cf. also Rodwin, *op. cit.,* pp. 295–317. Compare also Negro proximity to fashionable houses in Georgetown, Washington, and in Baltimore.

increased in value by 8 per cent when Negroes moved in, while the general price index for the whole metropolitan area dropped by 13 percent. In another case, after a Negro "invasion," the prices of the Negro-owned property ran well ahead of the general market price index for the area. According to Morgan, "These cases are typical for this neighborhood. There are many others and they all tell the same story. Prices have advanced more here than in neighborhoods unaffected by population movements. Furthermore, this advance was evidenced during all three stages of the change—in the period of the threatening 'invasion,' during the early stages of transition and in the later stages of mutation."[12]

Clifton R. Jones of Morgan State College, writing on a home-buying situation in a section of Baltimore where the ratio of Negro-white occupancy is one to two, says: "In other words, these homes are now being sold to Negroes for as much as 150 per cent above the 1940 market value, and at least 75 per cent above the present market value. Real estate operators readily admit that they are buying homes now occupied by whites as rapidly as they become vacant to sell to Negro buyers at a much greater profit than they could obtain elsewhere."[13]

A careful San Francisco study in 1951[14] of a series of test areas into which nonwhites had moved and in comparable all-white areas shows that prices in neighborhoods undergoing change were not only not affected adversely but that prices in some cases were somewhat higher. The author summarized his data as follows:

The bulk of all sales in the test areas whether to whites or non-whites, brought prices slightly above those in control areas, except for two minor qualifications:

About 9 percent of the sales to white buyers took place at prices which were between 12 and 22 percent lower than those for comparable properties in control areas, whereas no sales to nonwhites fell in this range.

About 4 percent of the sales of nonwhite buyers took place at prices which were between 22 and 26 percent higher than those for comparable properties in control areas, whereas no sales to whites fell in this range.

[12] Belden Morgan, "Values in Transition Areas," *The Review of the Society of Residential Appraisers,* vol. 18, no. 3, March, 1952, pp. 9–10.

[13] Clifton R. Jones, "Invasion and Racial Attitudes: A Study of Housing in a Border City," *Social Forces,* March, 1949, p. 288.

[14] Luigi M. Laurenti, "Effects of Nonwhite Purchases on Market Prices of Residences," *The Appraisal Journal,* July, 1952.

These results do not show that any deterioration in market prices occurred following changes in the racial pattern.[15]

Belden Morgan, noting that panic selling sometimes follows early sales and that prices drop, points out that "after the first hysterical selling phase passes prices become stabilized, then gradually increase under pressure of Negro bidding. . . . It usually will be found that sales activity is greater in racially mixed areas, especially in low and moderate price ranges, and that the high effective demand among Negro buyers not only sustains price levels but often increases them."[16]

The experience of the public housing authorities having mixed occupancy policies is also enlightening. Negroes have been placed in the new projects in substantial numbers. Often there was no Negro occupancy whatever before construction of the project, yet values in the surrounding areas tended to rise after project occupancy. General Thomas F. Farrell, then chairman of the New York City Housing Authority, commented: "There has been no tendency for neighborhood people to move away because of the projects. . . . Business in the neighborhood improves."[17]

This is supported in a study by the New York City Housing Authority[18] on the effect of mixed projects on surrounding values. The projects studied included one in a densely occupied area and another on sparsely occupied land, surrounded mainly by one- and two-family houses. Mr. Fialkin writes:

In the instance of both types of projects, we found a definite increase in assessed valuations for a depth of about two blocks surrounding the project. The effect was most marked within a depth of one block surrounding the project where a good number of commercial establishments either had been opened or expanded because of the population introduced by the public housing project.

[15] *Ibid,* p. 327.

[16] *Op. cit.,* pp. 8–9.

[17] Thomas F. Farrell, "Object Lesson in Race Relations," The New York *Times Magazine,* February 12, 1950, p. 37.

[18] Cited in a letter of Harry N. Fialkin, chief of research of the New York City Housing Authority, to Fair Employment Practice Committee, Youngstown, Ohio, May 28, 1953. ("The Effect of Negro Occupancy in a Public Housing Project or Private Housing on the Value of Neighboring Residences," prepared by Richard B. Anliot, executive director, Fair Employment Practice Committee, Youngstown, Ohio, November 18, 1953, p. 5 [mimeographed]).

The increase in valuation was smaller in the second block and there was no change in the area beyond it. From observation, the same effects were noted in projects built on vacant land, and a Research Committee of the National Association of Housing Officials found that "the experience in New York City, as shown in the few studies we had made, had been duplicated in studies conducted in other cities."[19]

In Portland, Oregon, a study of price fluctuations around a public housing project of 400 units in which there were 20 nonwhite families, showed increases in the surrounding areas of from 45 to 96 per cent.[20] Building activity spurted around the racially integrated Tasker Homes in Philadelphia, and within a few years 200 houses representing more than $1 million of new investment had been built in the adjoining section.[21] In Atlanta, Georgia, the monthly rate of private construction in the vicinity of a Negro housing project showed a gain of 500 per cent, or eight times the gain for the city as a whole.[22] Numerous other authorities from various cities confirm these findings.[23] The land around Parkway Village in Jamaica, N. Y., trebled in value after this mixed project for United Nations personnel was built by 15 New York City savings banks.

While sectional deterioration may invite minority penetration, neighborhood reclamation or improvement by construction of public housing, or projects such as Queensview Houses in Queens, New York City, will raise values regardless of the presence of minorities. Mixed public housing projects are often built in an area to stabilize its racial patterns, and they do.

Although a wholesale withdrawal of white occupants from multiply-owned panic areas may lower prices at the beginning, it is not the influx of the minority that affects prices but the mass exodus. This gluts the market with houses for which there may be a demand

---

[19] *Ibid.,* 5–6.

[20] "The Effect of Public Housing on Adjoining Property Values in Portland, Oregon," from information assembled by the Citizens League for Better Homes, Portland, April, 1950.

[21] "How Does a Public Low-Rent Housing Project Built on Vacant Land Affect Private Construction and Property Values in the Neighborhood," The Philadelphia District of the Health and Welfare Council, Inc., July 5, 1950.

[22] "Racial Problems in Housing," *Bulletin no. 2,* New York National Urban League, Fall 1944.

[23] Fair Employment Practice Committee, Youngstown, Ohio, *op. cit.*

only by the home-hungry groups who enter the abnormal market. If the market is not suddenly deluged with senseless offerings, the prices will tend to stabilize. To a great extent the spiral of sales has the same damaging effect as a bank run. Warnings by government officials and realtors that minority infiltration hurts values often produce a temporary loss in value. Give a neighborhood a bad estimate and it will soon begin to live down to it.

The Youngstown Metropolitan Housing Authority asked the City Planning Commission to change the zone designation on a vacant site to permit construction of a racially integrated public housing project. The neighboring residents had objected that the project would lower real estate values in the surrounding area. Youngstown's mayor then asked the official Fair Employment Practice Committee to survey the facts. After examining the evidence, the Committee concluded:

1. The average Negro tenant takes as good care of his property as other tenants of the same economic status.

2. Racial discrimination and prejudice rather than race is the cause in most instances of Negroes living in substandard housing.

3. Rather than lowering property values, integrated public housing projects have had the effect of increasing the value of adjacent property and stimulating the construction of private homes.

4. There is no one universal effect of Negro occupancy upon property values.

5. There are numerous examples where residences in racially mixed neighborhoods have been sold to both white and Negro purchasers at prevailing market prices or better.

6. Too many homeowners trying to sell their houses at the same time is the primary cause of temporarily lowered property values after Negro entry into an all-white neighborhood.

7. Property values in a neighborhood of racially integrated occupancy can be maintained or increased when there is a sufficient number of buyers who can afford to and desire to buy the homes for sale.[24]

While undue emphasis has been placed by realtors on the presumed decline in value after minority infiltration, little is said of homogeneity's threat to values.

Levittown, Long Island, a community of some 35,000 inhabitants

[24] Anliot, *op. cit.*, p. 19.

about 50 minutes from New York City, houses no Negroes. Its business section must supply a good portion of the revenues required for the schools and other public services. But some of its businessmen have found it inconvenient to launch enterprises because of the lack of Negro labor. The president of a chain cleaning establishment told this writer in 1953 that he cancelled an agreement to lease land at $8000 a year when he found there was no Negro labor available. A large undertaking like the U. S. Steel plant at Morrisville, Pennsylvania, is feasible only because it is near Trenton and Philadelphia which provide Negro labor for the coke ovens and other tough jobs.

There are no fixed rules as to when minority neighbors raise or lower values; examples may be cited both ways and much study is still needed. But this is certain: a neighborhood limited to people of single social status, income, or color is more often socially and psychologically unsound than a mixed neighborhood. Its depreciation is accelerated by one or all of four factors—boredom, insecurity, fear, hate. In the long run it may prove financially unsound as well.

XXI

THE SUPREME COURT: SHIELD OR SANCTUARY?

T HE SUPREME COURT has always been the great national lexicon. In the course of hearing disputes between litigants, it defines and redefines the meanings of "due process," "equality," "privileges and immunities," "public use," "private property," and a number of other generalizations which run through the Constitution and mark the rights of citizens under it. Its definitions, if not always constant, are relatively conclusive; its judgments, if not infallible, are final. The power to define carries with it the power to construe or construct, oppress or protect, create or destroy. The Supreme Court is as close to being a national conscience as an institution can be. It holds the power to elevate the national ideals toward the nobler aspirations or depress them into rationalized desuetude.

In the wake of the Civil War the country had adopted the Thirteenth, Fourteenth, and Fifteenth Amendments and a series of laws to implement them. The aim was to assure the Negro minority the same rights and privileges enjoyed by other citizens. Under its power to define, however, the Court soon developed a series of doctrines which enfeebled those protections. Its rulings, rendered in a series of controversies over a period of six decades following the Civil War were:

1. No federal law may be passed barring private individuals or groups from discriminating and there is no constitutional civil right authorizing this. It is up to the states to protect (or not to protect) the minorities against private oppressions.

2. The "privileges and immunities" granted to citizens by the Fourteenth Amendment do not embrace the rights and privileges of Negroes or other minorities. They refer only to the limited privileges

and immunities of national citizenship (such as the right to move freely from one state to another). The privileges and immunities of minorities can be secured only through state law—again if the state so elects.

3. Federal protection exists only against violation of rights by the states, as when the state discriminates or denies equal access to public facilities or services to the minorities or lends its aid to private oppressions. But segregation is not discrimination. While "equality" must be afforded by the state in such facilities, equality is satisfied by equivalence. Enforced separation of Negroes and whites will not be interfered with by the Court so long as the facilities are more or less similar.

From 1868 to 1936, Negroes won three tests in peonage cases, but only 6 of 16 cases in which they had sought federal protection in the franchise or other rights of citizenship. They won 12 of 21 cases in which they had sought fair trials in criminal cases, but lost 12 out of 14 cases in which they sought use of the same facilities as whites in public places, transportation, schools, or housing.[1]

The Fourteenth Amendment, enacted primarily to protect Negroes, was used mainly to protect corporations. From 1868 to 1911, in fact, the Court handed down 604 decisions of which only 28 affected Negro rights, and of these, 22 were decided against the Negro interest. "It is not the negro, but accumulated and organized capital which now [1912] looks to the Fourteenth Amendment for protection from State activity."[2]

When Franklin D. Roosevelt took office in 1934 and launched his program to convert the old limited federal sovereignty to one of more general power, he found a Court deeply immersed in the old order. The states were still the source of the health and welfare power and any expansion of federal power in that direction would be frowned upon. So with any expansion of power in the direction of minority rights.

The subsequent effort to "pack" the Court was not concerned

[1] E. F. Waite, "The Negro in the Supreme Court," *Minnesota Law Review,* XXX (1946), pp. 219–304, cited in Morroe Berger, *Equality by Statute: Legal Controls Over Group Discrimination.* New York, Columbia University Press, 1952, p. 65.

[2] C. W. Collins, *The Fourteenth Amendment and the States.* Boston, Little, Brown and Company, 1912, pp. 46, 47.

with the racial or minority question but with the Court's position on the limited nature of federal sovereignty. The President feared that its decisions might upset his recovery measures. A Court which in the 1920's had blocked child labor legislation and minimum wages for women would hardly be disposed to expand the general welfare clause into a broad grant of federal authority. In fact, when the federal government in 1935 sought to condemn land in Louisville, Kentucky, for a public housing project, both the U. S. District Court and the Circuit Court of Appeals held this activity beyond federal power. The Attorney General refused to carry the case to the Supreme Court for fear that the whole series of New Deal measures would be ruled invalid in the process.[3]

As the Court changed in composition, important changes occurred in its thinking on the racial issue. Not only were the new judges of a more liberal bent, but a number of outside developments were pointing up the mischiefs of race and religious conflict which an enlightened Court could hardly ignore. Hitler's mass murders and his emphasis upon the "Master Race" highlighted the contrast with the American credo. With the war's end, the United Nations Charter and other documents sharpened the emphasis upon racial and religious equality. In the Truman administration racial egalitarianism was again spurred by the President's Committee on Civil Rights,[4] and there was courageous presidential opposition to southern standpatism.

But the old judicial decisions survived as precedents, and precedent had to be respected in principle. The old segregated patterns in schools and transportation lingered on. They could not be too suddenly shaken, mainly because of the "separate but equal" rulings. A clear statement of the principle of equality was needed, but equality had always proved one of the great abstractions in the American language. Its definition was not rendered easier by the multiple uses of the word, such as equality of economic opportunity—the right to seek a job, buy a home or farm, do business, or seek an education; equality before the law—to be equal in the rights, privileges, and immunities

[3] *U.S. v. Certain Lands in Louisville, Ky.*, 9 Fed. Sup. 137, Aff'd 78 F2d 684 (1938); *Dornan v. Philadelphia Housing Authority*, 331 Pa. 209, 200 Atl. 834 (1938); *New York City Housing Authority v. Muller*, 270 N.Y. 333; see also briefs in these cases by this writer and others.

[4] *To Secure These Rights.* Washington, U.S. Government Printing Office, 1947.

conferred under the law and in its duties and penalties; political
equality—the right to vote and to hold office without subordination
because of caste or color, breed, creed, or credo; social equality—to
enjoy access to social opportunities and status on one's merits.

Barring the great enigma of slavery, the American scheme had
never authorized legal stratifications by race, creed, or religion. Early
references to Christianity in the Constitution were omitted. Equality,
regardless of religion or race, was implicit in the natural rights credo
that preceded the constitutional amendments. The principle which
underscored the American faith was that men are identical when born.
But environment was regarded as submissive to manipulation and so
long as the force of law could not be mustered by one class against
another, access to opportunity could remain at least relatively free.

The Supreme Court, however, had shunned the same concepts of
equality that informed the Supreme Being, i.e., that "There is neither
Jew nor Greek, there is neither bond nor free, there is neither male nor
female: for ye are all one in Christ Jesus."

With the more recent movement of Negroes and other minorities
toward the cities, southern segregation patterns in education, transportation, and other areas now threatened to be carried to the North
and West. Southern whites who moved north were carrying their
biases with them. Segregation patterns began to appear practical and
even necessary in housing and neighborhoods.

Racial covenants kept the minorities confined to ghettos and
barred them from the space they needed. The racial character of
the new neighborhoods was in turn influencing the racial composition
of the schools and public facilities. If segregation in neighborhoods
received judicial approval, the compulsory ghetto threatened to become an accepted and permanent part of the American landscape—
north, east, and west as well as south.

The judicial interpretations of housing cases therefore loomed into
prime significance when the test cases were presented to the Court.
The decisions involving housing and land operations up to the time
the Eisenhower administration took office may be summarized as
follows.

1. Racial Zoning. In 1917 the pre-New Deal Court, while firmly
holding to the separate but equal doctrine, had rendered an important
opinion striking down municipal ordinances zoning residential areas

by color and race. It held that "such legislation must have its limitations" and that those limitations were being "exceeded."[5] The finding that there were "limitations" had thereby exposed to judicial scrutiny "excessive" applications of segregation. The fact that legalized separation in housing exceeded those limitations gave hope that a remedy existed to stem the trend toward organized segregation. The decision was not challenged in the three decades that followed and there is little question that statutory racial zoning—an effective device current in South Africa—would not be countenanced by the courts here, whether of conservative or liberal bent.

2. *Restrictive Covenants.* Although the Court had indicated in 1926 that it was not disposed to enjoin judicial enforcement of such covenants,[6] and refused several times afterwards to hear the issue, the new Court now accepted review and held that the covenants were not enforceable by state or federal courts, though valid as between parties making them. In the first of these decisions[7] the Court adhered to its classic doctrine that the Fourteenth Amendment prohibited discriminatory action by the state while granting no federal protection against discriminatory action by private individuals.[8]

Restrictive subterfuges, however, are made possible by the Court's holding that private agreements are legal as long as they do not invoke the use of public power to enforce them. The companion case to *Shelley v. Kraemer*[9] involved covenants written in the District of Columbia. Since the protection of the Fourteenth Amendment was available against state action only, it was technically inapplicable to the District. The Court, however, reached the same result by relying on the fragment of the Civil Rights Act[10] which provided that "all citizens of the United States shall have the same right in every state and territory as is enjoyed by white citizens thereof to inherit, purchase, lease, sell, hold and convey real and personal property." The court also invoked public policy as a basis for its decision.

[5] *Buchanan v. Warley,* 245 U.S. 60.
[6] *Corrigan v. Buckley,* 271 U.S. 323.
[7] *Shelley v. Kraemer,* 334 U.S. 1 (1948).
[8] A later decision—*Barrow v. Jackson,* 346 U.S. 249—involving damage suits for violation of the covenants followed the same rationale, with the Court barring any award of damages.
[9] *Hurd v. Hodge,* 334 U.S. 24.
[10] 8 U.S.C. §42.

3. Constitutional Restraints on Action of Federal Agencies. Reliance on the Civil Rights Act and public policy which formed the rationale of *Hurd v. Hodge* might, if the test were ever made, similarly invalidate discriminatory action by the Federal Housing Administration, the Veterans Administration, and any other arm of the federal government. The test would, however, be subject to the caution recently expressed by the new Court through Justice Frankfurter, that the Civil Rights Act should not be applied so as to upset the balance in the federal system. In *Stefanelli v. Minard*,[11] a criminal case involving the Fourth Amendment enjoining unreasonable search and seizure, Justice Frankfurter said "differences in application [of the Civil Rights Act] inhere in the attempt to construe the remaining fragments of a comprehensive enactment, dismembered by partial repeal and invalidity, loosely and blindly drafted in the first instance, and drawing on the whole constitution itself for its scope and meaning."

4. Alien Land Law. While the Supreme Court has upheld legislation denying aliens the right to own real property, it struck down state laws depriving citizens of the right to own because their parents were ineligible aliens (in this case Orientals). A statutory presumption that the property is being surreptitiously acquired for the alien parent's use was held unfair. The Court based its decision on the Fourteenth Amendment's guarantee of equal protection to all citizens regardless of race.[12]

5. Redevelopment. Supreme Court doctrine on race bias in redevelopment projects remained to be formulated. In 1950, the Court refused to hear the Stuyvesant Town case after having the matter under advisement for about eight months.[13]

By refusing review, the Court left minorities to the mercy of those

---

[11] 342 U.S. 117 (1951).

[12] *Oyama v. California*, 332 U.S. 633 (1948).

[13] Its refusal was handed down with its decisions in the cases extending the Negro's rights in transportation and education (*Henderson v. U. S.*, 339 U.S. 816; *Sweatt v. Painter*, 339 U.S. 629). A number of inferences may be drawn from its refusal: that the Court opposed extending the rights of the Negro to equal treatment in neighborhoods where public power was employed, but may have been unwilling to put an unfavorable decision on the lawbooks; that the issue was entirely too touchy to be handled at the time; or that in handing down the liberal decisions in transportation and education it was going as far as should be reasonably expected.

redevelopment authorities which saw the redevelopment program as a convenient device for getting Negroes out of areas where they were not wanted. Simultaneously, Negroes were denied the new accommodations on the sites from which they had been evicted.

The state decision holding that Stuyvesant Town could discriminate though enjoying the benefits of public condemnation, tax exemption, ceding of streets, and other special benefits, seemingly ignored Supreme Court doctrine in analogous fields.[14]

6. Segregation in Public Housing. Whether racial segregation in public housing projects offends the Constitution has never been passed upon by the Supreme Court. Opinions in the lower federal courts and in the state jurisdictions vary, with some authorities holding that the law requires only provision of separate but equal facilities, and others viewing segregation as invalid.[15]

In general the position of the Supreme Court up to May, 1954, was that equality is still equivalence, but equivalence has to be nearer equality than ever before. Thus, separate law schools for Negro and white students could not be equal no matter how equal the separate facilities,[16] and a state statute requiring segregation in interstate buses was invalid as constituting a burden on interstate commerce.[17]

On May 17, 1954, the Supreme Court, in an epochal decision involving segregation in public schools, all but buried the separate but equal doctrine.[18] Citing the social harm of segregation to children, the court concluded that "in the field of public education the doctrine of 'separate but equal' has no place. Separate educational facilities are inherently unequal."

Since the Court had primed the country for it in a series of prior

[14] *Smith v. Allwright,* 321 U.S. 649 (1944), recently reaff'd in *Terry v. Adams,* 345 U.S. 13 (1953); *Steele v. Louisville & Nashville Ry. Co.,* 323 U.S. 192, followed and extended in *Brotherhood of Railroad Trainmen v. Howard,* 343 U.S. 768 (1952).

[15] *Banks v. Housing Authority of San Francisco,* 260 Pac. 2d 668 (1953); Will Maslow and Joseph B. Robison, "Civil Rights Legislation and the Fight for Equality, 1862–1952," *Chicago Law Review,* vol. 20, no. 3, spring, 1953, pp. 363–413.

[16] *Sweatt v. Painter, op. cit.*

[17] *Morgan v. Virginia,* 328 U.S. 373 (1946); see also *Henderson v. U.S., op. cit.*

[18] *Brown v. Board of Education of Topeka* and companion cases, 347 U.S. 483.

decisions which had left little but the bare bones of the doctrine for burial, the decisions caused a rattle but no cataclysm.

A few days later the Court remanded three cases to the lower courts involving segregation in a university and a public theater with instructions to review them in light of the school decision, and in the same package of decisions refused to hear review on an appeal by the Housing Authority of San Francisco from a California decision striking down its policy of segregation.[19]

The Court's refusal to review the housing decision brought panic to the heart of Senator Burnet R. Maybank (D., S.C.) and other supporters of public housing. The decision, said Maybank, "makes it impossible for me, believing in local government, to support any public housing." The Senator had evidently mistakenly construed the meaning of a denial of certiorari as an affirmance, when, as the Court has repeatedly asserted, such a denial had no significance whatever.[20]

In face of the Court's older and more recent decisions, what protections can minorities expect from it?

Although judicial attitudes are far more sympathetic and the separate but equal doctrine has been discarded, complete or even major reliance on the Court would still appear to be unwarranted. The reasons are:

1. The constitutional generalizations which the Court has been able to reconstrue to favor minorities may ultimately be reconstrued against them should the membership of the Court or the temper of the country alter. Congress was more liberal on race relations than the Court after the Civil War, and today the Court is ahead of Congress. But there is no assurance it will always be so. Judges are not immortal, nor are their decisions. Moreover, as Justice Frankfurter noted (before he went on the bench) the judges "are not supermen" and hardly half a dozen have been "towering figures."[21] A judge can be a Harlan or a Byrnes in point of view, and the storehouse of precedent is so diverse that ample authority can be culled from its broad and conflicting inventory to support either view. What personalities happen to dominate the courts are as important and often more important than

[19] *Banks v. Housing Authority, op. cit.*

[20] *Maryland v. Baltimore Radio Show,* 338 U.S. 912 (1950).

[21] Felix Frankfurter, "Supreme Court, United States," *Encyclopaedia of the Social Sciences.* New York, The Macmillan Company, 1937, vol. XIV, p. 481.

the precedents. The Court's wide discretion in construing sociological evidence and in making fine distinctions from one case to another, or in ignoring an issue altogether, makes precedent only a limited refuge.

The attitudes of Congress, the Chief Executive, and the Attorney General still play a part, as does the state of public opinion and the reaction the Court thinks the public might have to a given decision. In recent arguments before the Court, in fact, the readiness of the community to accept equality in education was actually argued by counsel.

The forcefulness and prestige of the groups fighting an issue count materially in the measurement of that public opinion. The intervention of important racial and religious organizations may influence the Attorney General's decision to intervene on the side of the minority which in turn will influence the Court to consent to hearing the case. These groups and the support they muster to their side are controlling forces in helping the Court decide whether the issue is "ripe" or "important" and whether the progressive decision it may render will be accepted and enforced. The effectiveness of its rulings depends upon the prestige it maintains. The Supreme Court not only interprets law but reflects public opinion, and public attitudes may move up somewhat toward the higher levels after a progressive opinion, or the Court's rulings may move down toward the level of reactionary opinion.

2. Minority rights, though backed by public opinion and protected by the Court in normal periods, may be sacrificed during periods of stress or emergency when fear or prejudice may sway the most stable mind. The decisions involving the federal curfew and evacuation program after Pearl Harbor demonstrated this.[22] Most of the 110,000 Japanese subjected to the curfew order, banned from the Pacific Coast and detained in camps, were loyal citizens. Many were willing to fight for the United States and ultimately did. The Court, however, unanimously upheld the order because it feared danger to war production in their presence. Though citizens, wrote Chief Justice Stone, there was reasonable doubt as to their attachment to Japan. While recognizing that "distinctions between citizens solely because of their ancestry are by their very nature odious to a free people

[22] *Hirabayashi v. U.S.,* 320 U.S. 81 (1943); *Korematsu v. U.S.,* 323 U.S. 214 (1944).

whose institutions are founded upon the doctrine of equality," the Court nevertheless ominously observed that: "We cannot close our eyes to the fact, demonstrated by experience, that in time of war, residents having *ethnic affiliations* with an invading enemy may be a greater source of danger than those of a *different ancestry.*" (Italics supplied.) The concept that a group of one national extraction might be more dangerous than another "is not to be condemned merely because in other and in most circumstances racial distinctions are irrelevant."

If ancestry and race distinctions are relevant in war, they may be relevant in other "emergencies." Conceivably, the government might during emergencies jail those whose only fault is their "ethnic affiliation." Suppose, for example, Israel goes communist and allies itself with the Soviet Union. Might not all Jews be considered "dangerous" because of imputed ethnic affiliations with the Israeli? If it is claimed that the Jew is American and loyal, or at least diverse in sympathy, the answer is, so were the Nisei. And if ethnic loyalties are a criterion, why not religion? Might we not herd all Catholics into concentration camps should the Pope be on the side of a foreign power? Considerations like these, farfetched though they may sound in normal periods are less so today when many institutional protections and traditions have been contracted by Congress and by an ever-widening array of administrative agencies.[23]

3. There is also the fact that the Court may close its eyes to a violation of minority rights by refusing review, which it has done in a number of matters of great moment. While refusal to review is understandable, and while the Court has repeatedly emphasized that no implications are to be drawn from it,[24] the Court when it

---

[23] As the emergency eased, the Court ordered the release of a loyal Nisei evacuee, ruling that detention must be related to prevention of sabotage or espionage. (*Ex Parte Endo,* 323 U.S. 83.) When the war was over the Court became even more solicitous of the rights of Japanese citizens. (*Oyama v. California, op. cit.; Takahashi v. Fish and Game Commission,* 334 U.S. 410 [1948]).

[24] "It may be desirable to have different aspects of an issue further illumined by the lower courts. Wise adjudication has its own time for ripening. . . . If the Court is to do its work it would not be feasible to give reasons, however brief, for refusing to take these cases. The time that would be required is prohibitive, apart from the fact . . . that different reasons not infrequently move different members of the Court in concluding that a particular case at a particular time makes review undesirable." (*Maryland v. Baltimore Radio Show, op. cit.*)

refuses review need give no reason. If at least four of the judges feel on a superficial examination of the papers that the issue is not "ripe," it matters little how important the cause may be. The Court has thus conferred upon itself full right to evade an issue without granting a full hearing to the aggrieved party.

In the Stuyvesant Town case, the New York Court of Appeals, one of the most respected courts in the land, divided on the issue of racial discrimination by 4 to 3. The opinions on each side reflected the critical nature of the national issue involved. No technical reasons for refusing review existed, and Justices Black and Douglas dissented from the majority's refusal to hear the case. These dissents in themselves spotlighted the need for airing the issue and for inviting open argument by counsel and the raising of questions which counsel might have the opportunity to answer. The Supreme Court is not so omniscient that it can tell by a quick glance at a certiorari application whether the issue is important and "ripened" and what the case's implications are. More often, in fact, it is only after review is granted that the national implications become fully clear and the argument persuasive. This was demonstrated in the restrictive covenant issue.

Nor is Justice Frankfurter's explanation that the Court is too busy an adequate answer. Professor Fred Rodell of Yale studied the work done by the Court and concluded that it is doing less work than its predecessors.[25] An examination of the Court's decisions indicates that it has been accepting patent and contract claims, stockholders' suits, and a host of other issues far less important than constitutional rights.

The most serious implication of the Court's refusal to hear a case is its statement that "wise adjudication has its own time for ripening." If the new test of due process is to depend not solely on whether the Fourteenth Amendment has been violated but on whether the issue has ripened as well, then the Court has reconstructed the due process clause so that not only must the *process* be due but the *issue* must be due as well.

This is not to overlook the great moral leadership the Court has given the country in recent years or to underestimate its task in the civil rights field. It must often lead the country toward enlightenment on sensitive issues and tread cautiously lest it advance too far against the tide, hurt its own prestige, or render a decision which cannot be enforced. The point remains, however, that the very refusal to

[25] "Our Not So Supreme Court," *Look Magazine,* July 31, 1951, pp. 60–64.

review which today may be salutary, may in the hands of a less enlightened Court tomorrow represent the most flagrant and frustrating denial of justice.

Failure to hear a case at such a time can be one of the most irremediable denials of process. From an adverse decision by the Court, the aggrieved might have a remedy—the surge of a protesting public opinion or new legislation to correct the injustice. From the refusal to hear there is no protest and no appeal. The refusal often encourages continuation of the wrongs or oppressions from which the complainant sought relief.

And who will foot the bill for all the useless test suits before review is finally granted? The organizations making these tests have already found themselves harried by lack of funds, by accusations of radicalism when they seek to protect democratic rights, by the fear of citizens to join them in days when guilt is judged by association, by the frequent refusal of the Internal Revenue Department to grant tax-exemption on contributions to such organizations, by congressional attacks on foundations who aid them.

The costs of such tests today run high—$25,000–$50,000. With the Supreme Court repeatedly refusing to review important cases, the figure must be multiplied by the number of cases presented to the Court until the issue is finally accepted and heard. The hearing on racial covenant cases, for example, was turned down many times before the Court finally elected to review. In the Stuyvesant Town case the court fight lasted seven years before it finally came before the Supreme Court, only then to be met by a refusal to review.

4. Winning the case in law does not mean winning it in fact. Evasions of the Court's decision too often follow as a matter of course. The courts cannot police civil rights or enforce their orders easily. Ultimately, observance of those rights depends upon the cooperation of officials and the sympathy of the public. A favorable Court decision, while important in the total fight, may be an advance in principle only.

The greatest dangers to minority rights, moreover, lie in ever-widening areas which can no longer be effectively reached by the judicial process. Public officials today are often effecting discriminations through subtle administrative determinations and through official acts in which the discrimination cannot be identified and subjected to judicial scrutiny. Winning a case may only establish the illegality of a single administrative act which when repeated necessitates further tests, further outlays, further delays. When the issue is finally won it may be only of local significance or be held controlling only on the facts of the particular case.

Although the school decisions in 1954 gave civil rights advocates cause for rejoicing, it may be expected that some local officials may now speed up slum clearance, public works, and urban redevelopment projects which will displace minorities from an area within a public school district and thereby sidestep the Supreme Court's mandate. Not only creation of new all-white sections will be encouraged in order to maintain white schools but abolition of presently mixed areas may be anticipated as well. In the long run the fulfillment of equality in education as well as in housing will depend less on how the Supreme Court implements its order than on how public officials react.

To sum up, the Supreme Court today is a shield, not a sanctuary. The shield alone cannot afford full protection, but is only a single implement in the democratic armory. It offers no certain protections to minorities. Protection may be uncertain during emergencies. The dangers of violations also expand with the expansion of public power. A favorable public opinion is essential; so is education, citizen support, official support, and the use of all devices essential to create a proper climate of opinion. Only in such a climate and under such conditions can the Court become a greater protection, and its opinions emerge into the clear moral voice of the people and their institutions.

XXII

INTERRACIAL HOUSING

THE FEDERAL public housing program is of far greater significance to minorities than the dwellings it produced. Arriving at a time when every conceivable device was being employed to zone, clear, or blast minorities from their homes, this program inaugurated as an experiment in 1934 became a significant demonstration.

1. It was the first major effort to provide decent housing at rents families of underprivileged minorities and immigrants could afford.

2. It was the first program to establish by actual practice that Negroes and whites could be integrated into housing and communities without friction.

3. It helped to break the barriers which kept urban land from being used for the housing of minorities.

4. Because it built neighborhoods instead of small developments, it offered a practical method for integrating schools, playgrounds, and other public facilities.

5. Because housing projects consisted of large assembled parcels, it stabilized neighborhoods and property values in many areas. It helped ease fear that the presence of a few minority families would automatically be followed by an inundation of the minority.

6. It was a program in which the South demonstrated a sincere desire to improve substantially the housing conditions of its Negro citizens. Negroes received the largest proportion of the public housing built in southern areas.

7. It was the first program to supply a workable formula for financing housing for nonwhites which had theretofore been unavailable even when backed by federal insurance. Public housing bonds

issued through local housing authorities were sold at rates of about 2 to 3 per cent per annum.

8. It was the only program capable of providing alternative housing for minorities displaced by slum decay, slum clearance operations, urban redevelopment, or public works.

9. It helped to bring the accepted racial mythology into issue and to demonstrate that given a decent environment, Negroes and other minorities would pay their rent, make good neighbors, improve their health and living conditions, and react like other human beings to a favorable environment.

The program is not without faults.

It is a rental program only and makes no provision for home-ownership—in fact its operations often displaced poorer home-owners from slum areas and provided only tenancy as an alternative. Its principal emphasis is on slum clearance, thereby tending to keep the dwelling supply constant instead of adding to it. It emphasized slum clearance even when the shortage of housing grew desperate and the displaced slum-dwellers had nowhere else to go.

By dispossessing occupants whose incomes increase, it tends to homogenize the tenantry by income, render their occupancy uncertain, exact a penalty for ambition, and encourage misrepresentation of incomes.

Finally, its architecture, held to a minimum by statute, is too often vertical, rigid, and unimaginative.

These defects were not implicit in the original scheme. They are the products of defective legislation, the political pressures of opponents, and sometimes poor administration. The remarkable fact is that the program, in face of its obstacles, has succeeded at all; that large blocks of land were assembled under it; that 41 states enacted the necessary enabling legislation; that more than 1100 communities set up housing authorities and gave them tax exemption, and that hundreds of millions of dollars of private bonds were successfully sold for its financing. Despite its faults and limitations, it stands out as one of the most important demonstrations in the history of public operations.

Most significant among its many contributions was that it proved that whites and nonwhites can live in neighborly association. The tensions between these groups had been so common that early attempts at integration were viewed as a stargazer's dream. But when the federal government had to decentralize its program for legal reasons,[1] it passed down responsibility for public housing administration to local housing authorities. The authorities met the problem of minorities in diverse ways.

The patterns of tenant distribution in projects represented decisions by authority members and officials using courage, instinct, and common sense. The experiences of housing authorities with a successful integrated policy emboldened others to follow their example. The federal government laid down no rules except that projects were to follow "community patterns and trends." The race question was looked upon as a hot potato to be handled delicately if political fingers were not to be burned. A special race relations section in the federal public housing agency, in contrast to FHA, served as an information center and guide. As one project after another proved itself, it helped by its information and guidance to increase the number of integrated projects,[2] until today they are no longer experimental but are accepted practices from coast to coast.

The varying patterns created throughout the country are:

1. Complete segregation, i.e., an entire project is occupied exclusively by a racial minority group, or complete segregation by project sections, i.e., a project is programmed and developed so that dwellings for the minority tenants are segregated from those of other public housing tenants through the construction of separate sections in projects for each group.

2. Complete integration, i.e., families of all racial groups are housed in the same project solely on the basis of need, regardless of the location of their apartments.

3. Segregation by or within buildings, i.e., all families of a given racial group are housed in the same building or buildings within a bi-racial project or a project comprised of multifamily buildings in which there is a definite pattern of segregation such as concen-

---

[1] *U.S. v. Certain Lands in Louisville, Ky.,* 9 Fed Sup. 137, Aff'd 78 F2d 684 (1938).

[2] Robert C. Weaver, "Summary of Conference and Plans for Future," *Inventory of Research in Racial and Cultural Relations,* vol. 5, nos. 2–3, winter–spring, 1953, pp. 204–213.

tration around stairwells, specific corners of the buildings, or specific floors.

4. No pattern or a token pattern, i.e., a project in which Negro occupancy is a token number or too small to form a definable pattern.

In June, 1953, the racial patterns in public housing projects tenanted partially or totally by Negroes[3] was as follows:

By Projects:
1. Total number of projects occupied by Negroes   1101
2. Number of completely segregated dwellings occupied
   by Negroes   683
3. Number of projects jointly occupied by Negroes
   and whites   418
    A. Completely integrated   268
    B. Segregated by buildings and
       segregated within buildings   77
    C. No pattern or no pattern reported   73

By Dwelling Units:
1. Total number of dwellings occupied by Negroes   136,043
2. Number of completely segregated dwellings occupied
   by Negroes   102,988
3. Number of dwellings occupied by Negroes in
   mixed projects   33,055
    A. Completely integrated   26,984
    B. Segregated by buildings and
       segregated within buildings   4953
    C. No special pattern or no pattern reported   1118[4]

The significance of those figures is not in the 102,988 completely segregated dwellings. Most of them are in the South, where any other pattern is impractical for the time being. The figure to ponder is that of 33,055 dwellings occupied by Negroes in projects where white neighbors are usually next door or across the hall. These 33,055 families, one fourth of all the Negroes in the federal public housing program, are getting first-hand experience in interracial living. So are their white neighbors, who probably comprise a much greater number of families.

[3] Excluding veterans' re-use and defense housing projects for which data on occupancy patterns are not available. This information was furnished by Edward Rutledge, Racial Relations Adviser, New York Regional Office, Public Housing Administration.

[4] Includes 633 units in one project having a variety of occupancy patterns.

The lesson in interracial living is being learned by a far larger number than the statistics indicate. There are, in addition to the federal projects, a score of state- and city-aided integrated projects in New York, Connecticut, and elsewhere. About one fourth of all the families in the federal program move out each year. New tenants take their places and discover that it is perfectly feasible to live pleasantly with people of different skin color.

The proportions of minority representation in mixed projects vary from city to city and from project to project. There may be only a handful of Negro families, a considerable number, or, in Negro neighborhoods, an overwhelming proportion. Some housing authorities in northern cities have only recently adopted a policy of mixed occupancy, and they have cautiously proceeded to install a few selected Negro families in formerly all-white projects. The percentage of Negroes will probably be increased gradually.

The experience gained from these projects is not unseasoned, for many have been in operation 15 years or more. It would have been an important demonstration if it had succeeded in only one project. Considering the novelty of the approach and the complexities inherent in any effort to reshape a living pattern founded upon stubborn prejudices, the experience in so many is one of the most revealing in the history of the race relations enigma. Here is a rough summary of the experiences:

Isolation of races into separate areas of the same project has tended to emphasize a line of demarcation, i.e., a "place" each race is to respect. An unwritten rule soon insinuates itself under which Negroes are not to cross the line. This pattern accentuates the differentiation and generates jealousies and hostilities.

Projects under which the minority has only token representation are problem projects. Members of the token minority feel uncomfortable, for they stand out as the lonely exceptions. They are the "black sheep" in the school, the recreation center, and at community meetings. Parents worry about the gibes of white children and incidents which may make lasting impressions.

A New Jersey housing authority, for example, was told by the city's political boss to admit a Negro family to assuage the Negro community. The authority followed the instructions literally and a year later reported that it "wouldn't work." The Negro tenant "didn't take part in the community activities." The right method is to include a fair number of minority tenants to give them a feeling of security.

In projects where the minority accounts for more than half the tenants, the majority may feel like a minority. The white tenants may see a loss in social status. As vacancies occur in predominantly white projects elsewhere, they will request transfers. Soon the manager will note a tendency for his project to become all-Negro.

It is of course difficult to lay down a rule of precise ratio, for much depends on the proportion of Negroes in a city, the type of management, the site selected, and the community attitudes. A city like Minneapolis with a small proportion of Negroes scattered throughout the city would have less difficulty than a southern city in which neighborhood segregation may be the age-old practice. On the other hand, in some southern cities Negroes and whites live on the same blocks and the mixed pattern could be continued without fraying tempers. In some cities a 50-50 representation has gone well as long as the tenants feel they are making a demonstration of gallantry. But in the long run, the best project is one in which there are no striking or unusual disproportions.

Projects where Negro representation ranges from 6 to 30 per cent have been generally the successful ones. The minority has a sufficient representation to give it the security it needs in a new environment, the majority does not feel dominated by a group that is different, and the surrounding neighborhood accepts the project.

Should different types of tenants be selected by specific percentages? Normally this should be unnecessary. Where a minority is only 5 per cent of a city's population, the chances are that its proportion in the project will be 5 to 20 per cent, depending on housing need and income ranges. If the percentage rises disproportionately it is because the site may be near a minority area, because poor public relations policy has discouraged white applications, because income limits are so low that they abnormally favor nonwhite occupancy, or because minority pressure for housing is abnormally heavy. Where, despite authorities' efforts, project occupancy heads toward homogeneity—either majority or minority—an effort to keep the project in workable balance is desirable.

There may be some who would call this a "quota" system. But

it is far from that. A quota system is a device to exclude people, not include them; to effect segregation not to break it down. There would be no need to maintain a balance in any project if adequate housing were available for all, and there were no barriers. Until that has been attained the maintenance of workable communities during the development process is essential.[5]

In most cases, however, there should be no need for such a policy. Of all nonfarm families in the entire country, Negroes are 8 per cent. If tenants are selected on the basis of need without regard to color, the Negro representation should seldom exceed the 32 per cent average for Negro admissions throughout the United States in 1952. The ratio would be considerably less on sites selected in all-white areas, and more in Negro-occupied areas. Demand by the minorities will of course relax as more housing is provided for them.

Where a project is in an all-white neighborhood the housing authority may have to make a real effort to get Negro applicants. Negroes will hesitate to go where they might find hostility, or they may not like to be separated from their churches, friends, and associations in existing Negro areas. The same is true of other minorities. Most housing authorities have found it as important to educate minorities in interracial living as to rid the majority of its biases. In some cities, Negroes may be loath to apply because they would feel like the unwanted few in the projects, but in a city like New York, where the Negro now accepts the housing authority's long-standing interracial policy, there are applications for all projects, though Negro applications still tend to be heavier in projects built in established Negro areas.

Housing authorities often prefer sites in mixed areas for their initial ventures. The new projects improve the neighborhood and stabilize values in the surrounding sections, while not upsetting the neighborhood's prevailing racial pattern.

In the 1950's, some cities were faced with a sharp increase in the

[5] The quota system in universities can hardly be compared to the effort to maintain balanced communities, for the former is employed deliberately to bar minorities rather than as a gradualistic device to include them. The only possible basis on which a college quota might be justified would be if its aim were primarily to eliminate the quota, i.e., for all the discriminating schools to raise the quotas to such levels that there would actually be a free choice of schools by minorities so that the threat of mass influx would not occur and quotas would disappear.

number of Negroes. The private builders provided no homes for them. The entire burden for housing minorities was placed upon the housing authorities. In these cities, a large portion of the minority had a lower income than the majority's, and the housing shortage was simultaneously so intense that applications for public housing came predominantly from Negroes. The low-income limitations in the housing projects, coupled with the rising incomes of whites requested to leave the projects, headed the projects toward a predominant Negro occupancy. The solution was to increase the income limitations so the whites could remain, while simultaneously providing more projects for which Negroes would be eligible. The Negro group would therefore be represented dominantly in some projects but would be satisfactorily integrated in most. The most effective medium for easing housing in the long run is a larger program, more use of vacant land, curtailing the destruction of minority housing through slum clearance, and simultaneously increasing the private supply of housing for eligible minorities.

Whether projects are bi-racial, homogeneous, predominantly minority, or balanced in occupancy depends upon policy determinations and on how faithfully the policies are carried out. The sites selected, the size of projects, proper public relations, and education of majority and minority all affect the subsequent nature of the occupancy. Excessive clearance of sites occupied by minorities and income limitations for occupancy also play parts in determining what kind of tenants will be admitted. Of course the best-intentioned policies can fall in the hands of an incompetent or untrained staff.

It might be argued that partially permitting a large minority representation through selection of sites near minority-occupied areas will lead to ghetto life. The term "ghetto" has too often been subjected to misapplication. A voluntary ghetto has certain virtues, not the least of which is that a given minority may feel more comfortable living with people of its own kind, race, or tongue. It is as peremptory to forbid it as to compel it, and as absurd to insist upon compulsory assimilation as to insist upon compulsory segregation. In both instances a person is told where he *must* live. What we should insure is that ethnic composition is the product of voluntary action, that the opportunity for a free exodus as well as free entry exists, and that the process of social fluidity functions as well as it can be made to function.

In all cases, however, every man's choice must be free. Society has a duty to be color-blind in dispensing aid or power and in operating public projects. Society must keep any one group or groups from ganging up on a minority member and telling him where he must or must not live. It also has a duty to remove those elements of insecurity which encourage the minority to choose living in a ghetto because prevailing sanctions offer no alternative.

While it may sometimes be unavoidable to have projects occupied predominantly by a minority, these families must have the choice of any other projects where they might wish to live. In practice this means that all projects should aim for some minority representation, though some will have more than others. It requires a positive effort to keep every project from excluding any single group. This is precisely the pattern in the New York City public housing program. In Harlem there are projects almost exclusively for Negroes, but Negroes are nevertheless represented in every other project.

The integrated projects have demonstrated that if Negroes and whites live in self-contained communities without segregation, make daily contact with each other in the communal facilities, enjoy the same privileges and share the same responsibilities, initial tensions will tend to subside, differences become reconciled, and an unstrained cooperation ensue.[6]

The conclusion is supported by many reports from housing authorities that have ventured into mixed occupancy. Children are found playing together with no consciousness of their differences; community responsibilities are accepted by tenants without favoritism or discrimination. Project managers have overcome the initial objection of some of the white tenants by firmly explaining the policies of the housing authority. There have been few instances of tenants moving out even where comparable dwellings in other projects were offered them. The common use of recreational facilities has been an important factor in creating the environment for accord. The Negroes are members of tenant associations, participate in the cultural programs, and often lead in community activities. It is not unusual for white tenants, who had looked dubiously upon the prospect of sharing a project with Negroes, to say, "We were mistaken—they are as nice

[6] *Open Occupancy in Public Housing.* Public Housing Administration, Housing and Home Finance Agency, Washington, 1953.

and often nicer than other people." This has been confirmed by housing authorities in Philadelphia, Pittsburgh, Los Angeles, Chicago, New York, and scores of other communities.

The Philadelphia Housing Authority, which has effected mixed occupancy in some of its projects, concludes that "we have been able to operate housing projects with mixed occupancy without difficulty or untoward incidents." Pittsburgh has eight projects under its jurisdiction, all with successful mixed communities. The Los Angeles Housing Authority "points with pride to the harmony that has been achieved in its Aliso Village, an 802-unit slum-clearance development devoted temporarily to the housing of war workers among whom are large representations of various races, colors, religions, and nationalities." The Chicago Housing Authority found in a project of 586 dwellings, of which 117 were occupied by Negroes, that an adjustment was made "within a suprisingly short time despite the fact that many of the tenants in the project are living in Chicago for the first time and that many came from small communities where interracial living was unheard of."[7]

New York City's experience with mixed occupancy has been in progress since about 1935. In none of the projects are Negroes separated from the whites, and in none has there been friction. "The experiment," says the authority, "if you wish to term it an experiment, has been a very successful one in every way." Further:

The effect of housing projects on neighborhoods has been generally good. There has been no tendency for neighborhood people to move away because of the projects. The projects are well built and are well maintained. Business in the neighborhood improves. With rare exceptions the tenants are good neighbors. . . . Within the projects, the results have been solid and enduring. In the business of raising families, of children playing together, of lending a hand in emergencies, of living side by side in peace, much has been done. In caring for each other's children, helping in sickness, working together in tenants' organizations and social and athletic events; in practicing tolerance in the best sense of the word, the tenants have raised a little the iron curtain between the races.[8]

[7] *Experience in Public Housing Projects Jointly Occupied by Negro, White, and Other Tenants.* 1944 Annual Conference of Racial Relations Advisers, January 31, 1944 (mimeographed).

[8] Thomas F. Farrell, "Object Lesson in Race Relations," The New York *Times Magazine,* February 12, 1950.

There have been problems, managerial headaches, and disappointments. The infiltration of southern Negroes and southern whites into war production areas brought conflict in some cities. In a few cases, poor management and ignorance of how to proceed delayed proper integration. There were inadequate neighborhood facilities, and cases where the housing authority insisted upon segregation in these facilities. In other cases the authority vacillated instead of explaining the policy firmly in advance. In Philadelphia, Cleveland, and New York, where there were large movements of minority populations, most applications in the 1950's were from the minorities. These problems point up hurdles, but the hurdles are surmountable.

The demonstration would have been significant had it succeeded in only a single instance. That it succeeded as often as it did is of epochal importance, pointing up the baselessness of the mythology that still persists.

In a study of interracial housing, one of the conclusions was:

> The guide for behavior to the white housewife who lives in an integrated project is that of positive interracial association; the standard implicit in the segregated projects is that of avoidance, with the connotation that interracial association brings trouble or that it is socially degrading. . . . Our results indicate that the housewives are generally more friendly with each other . . . they do more things together, they like each other better, and they have more close friends within the project.[9]

Private and Quasi-private Housing

When building sites consist of small individual lots, the existing pattern of segregation is difficult to alter without inviting tensions. Infiltration of one or a few minority families into a neighborhood arouses fear of an inundation. But since 1935, the new approach to housing has been the larger, well-planned community that creates its own environment. Not only is the property kept from deteriorating in these cases by a unified ownership, but there is no tendency for occupants to vacate in panic at the first sign of minority occupancy.

After the successful demonstrations in public housing, private investors began to learn that Negroes or other minorities do not

[9] Morton Deutsch and Mary Evans Collins, "Interracial Housing," *The Journal of Housing,* January, March, April, 1950, subsequently published by the University of Minnesota Press, Minneapolis, 1951. The study was made at the Research Center for Human Relations, New York University, New York, N. Y.

threaten investments. There were no mass inundations, no decline in values, no friction between groups.

When New York City enacted an ordinance in 1944 barring discrimination in tax-exempt projects, critics predicted that no more urban redevelopment or limited dividend projects would be launched. Higher-income families, it was said, would not live with Negroes nor would private investors and mortgage-lenders advance building money. Pressure for repeal of the ordinance was unremitting.

But the critics were overpessimistic. Hundreds of millions in private as well as public funds have been invested in nondiscriminatory projects. By October, 1954, 75,000 families were living in New York City's mixed public housing projects, and another 20 projects were under construction with accommodations for about 17,000 families. All of the projects were actually mixed and integrated. In New York City's program for middle-income families, with rents at about $16 a month per room, successful racial integration was likewise achieved. These projects together involved an outlay of a billion dollars by 1954. Construction was financed through the sale of housing authority bonds to private investors at interest rates of about 3 per cent.[10]

New York City also had 11 limited dividend projects, subject to a nondiscrimination ordinance and open to Negroes. These projects represent an investment of about $30 million and additional projects are in process. Amalgamated Housing, a private cooperative which had been all-white, has three Negro families in its Lower East Side project. Stuyvesant Town, a $110 million redevelopment project which originally banned Negro occupancy, now has a few Negro families. Queensview Houses, a 728-unit cooperative project, has been nondiscriminatory from the start. Twenty Negro families made down payments of $600 a room for their cooperative investment. Though the project is mixed, the Mutual Life Insurance Company advanced $6 million at 4 per cent interest without hesitancy. The Bowery Savings Bank has made loans of more than $13 million to other nondiscriminating projects. Henry Bruère, Bowery's board chairman, wrote that the approach of the bank is now "pragmatic and not governed by prejudice or unawareness of new social habits."[11]

When Queensview Houses was first organized and cooperators

[10] New York City Housing Authority Department of Public Relations and Information, October 1954.

[11] Letter to this writer, May 6, 1949.

made their down payments, it was feared that not all of them knew of the nondiscrimination policy and that when they did learn of it, many would withdraw their deposits. A meeting of the first 250 cooperators was called. Five of those attending were Negroes. A white cooperator asked whether the project would accept Negroes. When Louis H. Pink, chairman of the board, said it would, there was a burst of applause. Only one prospective tenant pulled out. The project was over-subscribed, a new unit is being added, and a similar project in Brooklyn, to be called Kingsview Houses, is under way. After several years of operation there has been no friction. In fact, one of the Negro cooperators was made head of the tenants' organization in 1953. The action of hundreds of cooperators in putting their money into a nondiscriminatory project shows that progress is being made.

Parkway Village, the United Nations project in Jamaica, Queens, operates in a white area as a mixed undertaking, housing people of all races and colors at upwards of $25 a room, higher than the neighborhood average. Land values in the surrounding area have risen by more than 300 per cent since the project was built. The presence of U.N. personnel (Negro, Oriental, and white) has in fact attracted more than 150 white non-U.N. tenants who are willing to pay the higher rents because of the cultural benefits from living in this heterogeneous neighborhood.

It is significant that while New York City was forging ahead with private redevelopment subject to its nondiscrimination ordinance, not a single private project was being undertaken in upstate New York—where discrimination for a time could be freely practiced. One reason may be that financial institutions are more likely to invest where the issue is settled, but will hesitate to accept public aid for a dis-criminatory project when there may be a legal fight or public hostility. Public opinion may tolerate discrimination in wholly private under-takings, but when public money is involved, fair play often becomes the issue. Few lending institutions are willing to face the recriminations that were heaped upon the Metropolitan Life Insurance Company when it first barred Negroes from Stuyvesant Town.

By 1952, most informed mortgagees were convinced that inter-racial housing in large-scale projects was no longer an experiment. Neither the Wicks-Austin law barring discrimination in future publicly aided projects in New York State, nor the New York City anti-bias ordinance precipitated the flood of minority applications or the withdrawal of white occupancy which the skeptics had predicted. Investors have learned that in these large projects the spirit is considerably better and the fears that prevail in homogeneous projects are absent.

San Francisco had similar experiences after the passage of its anti-bias ordinance. It has had no difficulty with its urban redevelopment program or with private investors. In Chicago, a few private developers are offering some of their apartments in predominantly white developments to a few Negro tenants without fear of endangering their investments. In Washington, D. C., Negro owners are offering private mixed accommodations to whites. In fact, today there are hundreds of private investments throughout the country where Negro and white families live side by side. It is not the presence of the minority per se that arouses fears but fear of an impending minority homogeneity. In a stabilized area where there is no fear that a neighborhood will be overwhelmed by one group, there is no danger to investment or social prestige.

That these demonstrations can succeed in America distinguishes it from South Africa. That despite tension and violence, its principles could survive to make such experiments possible gives hope in a troubled world that it will yet set the great example.

XXIII

EDUCATION FOR DEMOCRATIC LIVING

THE NEIGHBORHOOD patterns created in the last twenty years and the propaganda which inspired them have done more to veer the public toward discrimination than all the court decisions, pamphlets, and preachings have done to promote tolerance.

Generalizations about loving one's neighbor will mean little to a family selling its home in panic to a block-busting syndicate. The rhetoric of court decisions will not temper the anxieties of homeowners pledged to keep a minority from competing en masse for their homes. The tolerance a child is taught in public school will be dissipated if in the home he is taught that Negro children are not proper playmates. As long as there is a wide gap between the teachings of Christ and the real estate texts, the covenant with one's God will not discourage the racial covenant with one's neighbors.

Manifestly, education must play an important role. But the word "education" has been used in connection with the racial problem so often and so loosely that it has lost definition. Often it is little more than a pretext for scuttling specific action and for doing nothing at all. "Time" and "education" will not solve the racial problem if in that time anti-racial propaganda is at work and neighborhood patterns are being formed which daily make the prospect of tolerance harder.

Constructive education is therefore important. It embraces a multitude of devices. It can mean public instruction or the education of public officials, press, minority groups, and others. It may entail the use of pulpit, cinema, newspaper, and civic group as media; it can embrace oral or visual means of communication, or it can mean training by example. The lines between education and propaganda are not easily drawn and often both are essentially interchangeable. Most often an effective program calls for the use of many techniques at once. Any planned program directed at segregation should (1) assess the obstacles, (2) aim to remove the causes, (3) be comprehensive in its approach, (4) be continuous, (5) be well timed, and (6) produce the actual demonstrations which prove the practicability of the proposals.

Assessing the Obstacles

Prejudice has persisted through the ages and may remain dormant, exhaust itself in harmless episodes, or be activated into discrimination and oppression. Activation is spurred when pride, prestige, status, or property are directly challenged.

Today, the most sensitive area of prejudice is the neighborhood and the dominating fear is not religious or mercantile competition but housing competition. Once prejudice has begun to operate in the area of housing it starts a vicious circuit. Discrimination in the building and sale of housing further intensifies the housing shortage; the greater the shortage the greater the antagonism which still further tightens the housing supply for minorities. Segregation increases— voluntary self-segregation for the discriminators and compulsory for those discriminated against. As discrimination spreads it becomes indiscriminate about its aims and its victims. It may be implemented by individual or collective action or by invoking political processes. Mixed public housing and all public and private housing become targets. Targets widen to include other minorities and to inspire newer devices.

Removal of Causes

To eradicate the causes, the educational process should be directed toward:

1. Expanding research in the causes of discrimination and prejudice in neighborhoods and in methods of remitting them.

2. Educating the real estate enterprise in the need for building enough homes for minorities and building socially solvent neighborhoods in which antagonisms and discriminatory practices can be mitigated.

3. Educating experts and public officials in those aspects of racial

and group frictions which tend to activate prejudice and discrimination.

4. Educating the press and other media of communication in their role and responsibilities.

5. Educating all kinds of citizens and citizen groups in the nature and causes of tensions, in the injustice of prejudice and discrimination, and in the opportunity for creating democratic environments.

6. Educating minorities in their rights and responsibilities, and encouraging more leadership among them.

Some aspects of the educational process can achieve multiple results and should receive special attention. For example, building houses in integrated neighborhoods will ease the housing shortage and at the same time provide a salutary demonstration to private builders, public officials, minorities, and the general public. Legislation or court rulings outlawing discrimination can do double duty as educational media and as checks on housing patterns which further spark prejudice and race fear.

Expansion of Research and Study

Many courses are given in the nation's colleges based on texts and teachings favoring segregation and discrimination. Thousands of practicing or prospective real estate men are annually trained in the gospel. Not a single text refutes the theory of "Gresham's Law of Neighborhoods,"[1] now accepted by the real estate men. The Golden Rule will not prevail unless we also understand the rule of the market.

The old dogmas must therefore be re-examined and brought into issue; the fruits of more authentic studies embodied in a new literature. The few studies made on isolated aspects are important, but represent hardly a start.[2]

An inventory is needed of the following unexplored areas of in-

[1] Chapter XIII.
[2] Robert C. Weaver, "Summary of Conference and Plans for Future," *Inventory of Research in Racial and Cultural Relations,* vol. 5, nos. 2–3, winter-spring, 1953; Morton Deutsch and Mary Evans Collins, "Interracial Housing," *op. cit.*; American Jewish Committee, *Studies in Prejudice Series,* New York, Harper & Brothers 1949–1950; Robert C. Weaver, *The Negro Ghetto.* New York, Harcourt, Brace & Company, 1948. For miscellaneous articles, see *Selected References on Housing of Minorities.* Washington, Housing and Home Finance Agency, Race Relations Service, September, 1951.

formation and a comprehensive study should be made to fit them into a coherent picture:

1. The rise of the all-white suburb and the practices of entrepreneurs who build one-class neighborhoods.

2. The causes of neighborhood prejudice, friction, and violence, and the means of counteracting them.

3. World trends toward homogeneity of all sorts (racial, national, ethnic, color, age, social, economic) and their implications.

4. The effect of infiltration and mixed neighborhoods on property value.

5. Varying effects of the presence of minorities ranging from token numbers to larger proportions.

6. Methods of improving the status and speeding the acceptance of special groups, particularly Negroes, Puerto Ricans, and Mexicans.

7. Further analysis of successful examples of integration and of those less successful.[3]

8. Methods to break the blockade against financing of homes for minority people.

9. Special public and private exclusion devices, such as racial zoning, covenanting, exclusive neighborhood clubs, and other practices.

10. The effect of existing civil rights legislation on neighborhoods and the role of new legislation as well as its limitations.

11. The character and effects of current instruction in real estate in colleges and secondary schools.

12. Exclusion practices in resorts and travel agencies.

13. Eviction and relocation practices in slum-clearance, public works, and urban redevelopment programs.

14. The effect of current public housing, urban redevelopment, and FHA practices on neighborhood composition and tensions.

15. The effect of various city planning and zoning techniques upon neighborhoods.

16. The techniques and the effectiveness of official and unofficial racial and intergroup commissions and organizations.

[3] *Integration of Racial Minorities in Public Housing Projects: A Guide for Local Housing Authorities on How to Do It,* prepared by Edward Rutledge, racial relations officer, New York Field Office, Public Housing Administration (mimeographed), May, 1951; *Open Occupancy in Public Housing.* Washington, Public Housing Administration, Housing and Home Finance Agency, 1953.

17. The effect of housing shortages or surpluses on neighborhood in-migrations and out-migrations.

18. Political, cultural, and financial effects of in-migration on the older cities and their neighborhoods.

19. The effect of population changes on religious institutions, the operations of religious groups in combating prejudice, and the directions expanded efforts might take.

20. The new role of status in the American scene.[4]

In all these areas, the interest of the sociologist, anthropologist, social psychologist, racial expert, city planner, public official, economist, industrialist, appraiser, and realtor should be enlisted. The expanding role of governments means an ever-growing involvement of government policies; a fresh look is needed at official programs and practices as they affect the racial problem.

Educating the Real Estate Enterprise

The financial stake of the federal, state, and local governments in neighborhoods now runs into billions; ownership of homes represents the principal investment of the little fellow in the economy. In the seven and a half years from the end of World War II through mid-1953, about 6.5 million private small homes were built. Including multifamily structures, total housing starts numbered 7.7 million. Virtually all of these houses were for whites. Simultaneously, migration of minorities has been worrying older residents in both city and suburb. The creation of segregated patterns is still in process, with houses in segregated neighborhoods being built at the rate of 1 million to 1.4 million annually.

The overwhelming majority of the men who are building, financing, insuring, managing, and selling these houses still subscribe to the doctrine of neighborhood segregation.

The success of a single integrated project will supply impetus for the building of others. The demonstration project will stand most chance of success if it is substantial in size, creates its own environment, and adopts the proper techniques.

Since most of the private housing built today is aided by the federal

[4] W. Lloyd Warner and others have made a good start here, but the information should be brought into the focus of housing and planning practices and programs. See W. Lloyd Warner, Marchia Meeker, Kenneth Eells, *Social Class in America*. Chicago, Science Research Associates, Inc., 1949.

government, federal officials should encourage real estate men and builders to undertake these ventures with the advice of a well-staffed Racial Relations Service of the Housing and Home Finance Agency. Priorities and special government aid should be given to entrepreneurs willing to build integrated projects. Simultaneously, integrated public housing operations should be expanded and where possible included in well-planned neighborhoods composed of public and private housing.

Educating the Educator and Specialist

A primary need is to educate and multiply the specialists in race relations. An area rife with troublemakers requires an appropriate number of trouble-shooters. Too many housing experts know little of the race problem, and too many racial experts are poorly informed on housing and neighborhood problems. Racial commissions are usually composed of sympathetic but inexperienced citizens.

Since there are few facilities for training, some may learn by doing. But primary mistakes set precedents which are not easily eradicated. Many local housing authorities have labored over belated integration where mixed occupancy could easily have been introduced at the start. Although the National Association of Intergroup Relations Officials attempts to obviate this situation by holding annual and frequent regional meetings of racial relations officers and issuing helpful literature, the general dearth of material, coupled with the absence of basic training and the lack of adequate machinery for developing and disseminating information and experience, saddle the interracial adviser with a heavy responsibility. There is no known pool of professionals for jobs; personnel is often chosen for political considerations rather than ability.

There is also imperative need for experts in other areas directly concerned with the race problem. These include:

1. Federal Agencies. Practically every federal agency needs an expert in race and minority relations. The Army, Navy, Air Force, and Marine Corps require a vast amount of information on integration and minority problems that are ignored at West Point and Annapolis.[5]

---

[5] Witness for example the racial policy pursued by the Marines during the occupation of Haiti, the record of American forces in England during World War II in teaching Britons to discriminate against Negroes or the Army's attitude on the Nisei in World War II.

Their defense and war housing programs muddled through with little or no expert guidance. Prejudice in the ranks has been tackled and progress made, but it has been far from eliminated. In 1945, for example, 1710 white enlisted men were asked how they would feel about inclusion of Negro platoons. Among the infantrymen where there was already a Negro platoon, 33 per cent said "they would rather not, but it would not matter too much," and only 7 per cent expressed positive dislike. But in units which did not have colored platoons, 27 per cent said it would not matter too much and 62 per cent expressed positive dislike.[6]

The State Department has special cause for concern about American race policy. Dean Acheson, then Acting Secretary of State, said on May 8, 1946:

. . . the existence of discrimination against minority groups in this country has an adverse effect upon our relations with other countries. . . . Frequently we find it next to impossible to formulate a satisfactory answer to our critics in other countries; the gap between the things we stand for in principle and the facts of a particular situation may be too wide to be bridged.   An atmosphere of suspicion and resentment in a country over the way a minority is being treated in the United States is a formidable obstacle to the development of mutual understanding and trust between the two countries. We will have better international relations when these reasons for suspicion and resentment have been removed.[7]

The United States could do a much better job of publicizing the honest progress we have made in race relations, but the State Department will need more qualified experts for that task.[8]

[6] *To Secure These Rights.* Washington, U.S. Government Printing Office, 1947, p. 86.

[7] *Ibid*, p. 146.

[8] In 1946, 1948, and 1950, while delivering talks in Europe on housing, this writer was repeatedly questioned about our attitudes toward Negroes. Often he sensed that the question was put not because the questioner sought information but because he saw another chance to bait an American on one of the country's most prominent contradictions. The gains we had made were usually underemphasized, forgotten, or distorted.

In 1946, during an address to a group of Danish architects at the American Embassy in Copenhagen, this writer gave the brighter as well as the darker side, citing the progress in New York where we had effected successful mixed occupancy in public housing projects. To his surprise, his talk was featured on the front pages of the Copenhagen press. The Embassy's press representative was startled. He asked whether this writer knew of any American Negro in Europe who could meet with him publicly. Having met a Negro minister in Stockholm, this writer cabled him to come to Copenhagen. The press officer

The Department of Labor should be concerned with the problem of minorities moving into cities to take jobs, the housing problems they face, and the neighborhood tensions they spark. Some of the difficulties confronting the Puerto Rican and Negro migrant can be traced in part to this agency's lack of interest in the problem of migrants.

The Department of Interior supervises American Indians ghettoized in their reservations. It should give more attention to discrimination against Indians in housing and neighborhoods.

The Department of Justice should vastly expand its Civil Rights Section. The Department of Agriculture could do more about rural housing and rural–urban intermigrations. The Executive Department should be more interested than it is in the evolution of those fundamental policies which influence minority migrations and infractions of minority rights. The Atomic Energy Commission, with its segregation policy in housing and schools, could especially benefit from some expert guidance.

The movement of minorities into the cities has created a maze of problems which the federal departments have not risen to meet or even begun to analyze. There will be no substantial progress until the departments are all supplied with experts trained to understand and handle the problems of minorities.

It is risky to leave all these responsibilities to the federal government simply because the states, counties, and cities are decades behind the times in this area. Responsibility for protections are as much the concern of Waukegan as Washington. But federal power has traditionally spread out to fill the vacuums in civil liberties and minority rights created by inaction at the local level. If there is danger in over-centralization—and most political scientists agree that there is—the real danger lies not in a more active protection of civil rights but in the general expansion of a federal power which ignores those rights or subverts them in the process of expansion.

2. *Housing, Planning, and Redevelopment Agencies.* The policies and determinations of these agencies critically affect the lives, living places, and livelihoods of minorities.

---

arranged a public luncheon where photographs of both were taken. Copenhagen newspapers seemed satisfied that in America we do not cage our Negroes nor lynch them regularly.

Anti-racial zoning devices are often the consequences of a planning official's ignorance if not his biases. The wholesale evictions of minorities for an urban redevelopment project may be the result of official ineptitude or a calculated aim to wipe out a neighborhood of Negroes in the name of slum clearance. The policies of FHA officials have too often reflected popular biases or the rules of the game as laid down by the entrepreneurs.

3. Large Industrial and Financial Enterprises. These employ thousands of members of minority groups with pressing problems in housing and neighborhood relations as well as employment. The United States Steel Corporation's establishment of a new plant at Morrisville, Pennsylvania, is an eloquent example of entrepreneurial irresponsibility and of the consequences for the surrounding community. The company entered the community with no thought about housing for the minorities to be employed. Instead, the company used modern public relations devices to suppress the issue that was created when an all-white community was built with its help and encouragement.

Without confronting the objections to company towns, modern industries could for example build cooperative nondiscriminatory housing for their workers. These projects could be financed through Section 213 of the National Housing Act, or other favorable schemes which require no capital except the temporary initial advances for land assemblage and blueprints. Upon completion, the multiple dwellings or single-family developments could be turned over to the worker-tenants for cooperative management. Racial integration in the projects would eliminate neighborhood tensions and materially improve morale in the plants.

4. Local and State Governments. Most states and cities are concerned about the effects of suburban expansion, minority in-migration, growing social budgets, group tensions, population flight, and overcrowding. Officials too often greet with alarm what could be met with dignity. Some cities have made sound starts through their local race relations agencies, but the major problems reach beyond city boundaries.

The housing problem in New York City, for example, cannot be solved solely by increasing housing appropriations. Consideration must be given to the Puerto Rican problem in the city and to opening up opportunities for these citizens in other areas of the country.

The effects of mass migrations into cities and of out-migrations of older city residents into suburbs involve policies which can often be mitigated by the federal and state governments. Yet propaganda is too often accepted as fact, and fact ignored as propaganda. When in 1949 Mayor Martin H. Kennelly of Chicago was disturbed about the effect of a proposed nondiscrimination ordinance on private investment in redevelopment projects, he journeyed to New York to consult with Mayor William O'Dwyer, who was equally uninformed, but who hazarded a few guesses.[9] Kennelly returned to Chicago and opposed the measure. The consequences are being felt in policy conflicts and tensions which have increasingly plagued his city.[10]

5. Labor Unions. The increasing number of minority members in labor unions has made expert advice indispensable. The service trades and garment unions can no more ignore the Puerto Rican problem in New York City than steelworkers can ignore the Negro problem in Bucks County, Pennsylvania. The National Maritime Union has successfully established integration in living quarters on ships, but no union has been able to do the same thing in neighborhoods. Men who have learned to work side by side at the machines should be able to live within a mile of one another in common neighborhoods. Unions have concentrated entirely on wages, working conditions, and pensions, giving no heed to neighborhood problems. Tensions within unions often stem from neighborhood tensions and it is no accident that white workers in tension areas are often the

[9] Kennelly also saw General Thomas F. Farrell, chairman of the New York City Housing Authority, who, he claimed, told him the New York City ordinance did not work. Farrell denied this, however. In the many communities which now have nondiscrimination ordinances applicable to urban redevelopment projects, private financing and investment have not been deterred in a single known instance. Much of that information could have been made available to Kennelly.

[10] A similar ordinance was proposed for San Francisco in May, 1949. The urban redevelopment director bitterly opposed it because he felt sure it would discourage private financing of the projects. The ordinance was approved after an off-the-record meeting at which this writer was asked "on his honor" whether private investment had been discouraged in New York. It is now safe to say that his honor was not violated. The ordinance has not deterred private investment in San Francisco, as it never did in New York City.

easiest bait for bigots. Yet with industry recruiting a growing number of minority workers and with housing offering the main obstacle, the unions must rise to their responsibilities.

The ever-mounting pension funds could be used to great advantage to finance nondiscriminating housing for workers and retired workers. Except for vigorous support of national housing legislation the unions have in general not moved toward the great opportunities that beckon. The exceptions are the projects of the Amalgamated Clothing Workers, the International Ladies' Garment Workers' Union, the International Brotherhood of Electrical Workers, in New York City, and the Philadelphia project of the American Federation of Hosiery Workers.

6. *Churches.* The movement of minorities into old neighborhoods and the mass exodus to the suburbs by older urban residents have affected the investments by churches and religious institutions. What should be the function of the church? How rationalize the conflicts of its members with its moral duties to the new neighbors? Though there be "neither Jew nor Greek" under Christ Jesus, what shall His ministers do when Jews or Greeks descend upon an area en masse? Shall the investments be liquidated at a sacrifice and a new church built in the suburbs? And will not the new church be ultimately threatened too?

These questions have hardly been explored. Some clergymen have openly opposed the newly arriving poor and a few have even spoken out against public housing projects. In other cases, leadership by an enlightened churchman has helped stem the senseless flight of his flock and brought about understanding between the old and new residents.

A Congregational Church in New York City's East Harlem moved directly into a changing section and took leadership in social work and in betterment of housing conditions. The work of the Quakers in Pennsylvania is outstanding. The National Council of the Churches of Christ in the U.S.A. has adopted a policy to sponsor "every sound and reasonable effort to put an end to the exclusion of any person on account of race, color, creed, or national origin or ancestry from equal opportunity to rent or purchase living accommodations. . . . Legislation and effective administrative procedures responsibly carried out by persons skilled in intergroup relations are necessary for the elimination of discrimination. . . ."[11] But how can a church which should be the guide and leader be expected to assume its appointed role when it lacks the expert information needed for sound decisions?

7. *The Schools.* The public school is where the vast proportion of the American public first learns the nature of our institutions. It is the soil which nurtures the seeds of either bias or tolerance. Teacher, pupils, and parents are conditioned by neighborhood stresses and tensions. An influx of minorities means a similar influx into the schools.

Under these circumstances, the enlightened teacher may find it difficult to maintain his moral equilibrium. He must cope with frictions between white children and the new darker ones and the fears, hates, and uncertainties they bring to the school from their tension-charged neighborhoods. Often he cannot speak the language of the new children nor they his. Local officials and citizens may reflect their antagonism to the shift in the school and neighborhood, to the over-crowding of the school by the new minority, to the higher social costs the migration has imposed upon the community.

With urban redevelopment and large-scale public and private housing undertakings, the school should be planned as part of the neighborhood instead of being built as an afterthought. A school in a stable neighborhood composed of people of all colors and religions will have a stabler student body than one subject to population flux and to the irrational attitudes of frustrated minorities or of students with a false sense of superiority.

When slum-clearance or urban redevelopment projects displace thousands of minority families, the effect of their enforced inundation of other areas and their schools must be grasped. Experts from the school systems should be involved from the start in the preparation of housing and redevelopment programs. Training of teachers should include instruction in neighborhood and minority problems. The successful experience in interracial occupancy should be publicized. Parent-teacher associations and other civic organizations should lend the moral leadership and support.

The effect of the court decisions banning school segregation needs

[11] "Statement on the Churches' Concern for Housing," Adopted by the General Board assembled in Washington, D. C., November 18, 1953.

careful watching, too. What may not be accomplished by direct segregation may now be sought to be done by neighborhood redevelopment, by placing schools where segregation is inevitable, by redistricting existing schools, and by other devices. The victory in law may be lost in fact.

The Role of the University

The universities have a signal opportunity to train the experts. But most universities have not seen their opportunity nor assumed their responsibility. Some have avoided the problem; others include the subject only in real estate courses which teach the wrong things; still others give it a passing nod in their urban sociology, anthropology, or social psychology courses, or treat only with that phase of the problem which touches upon the specialty of a given professor. The over-all approach that would deal with the problem as an entity is lacking. Nor is sufficient emphasis placed upon the racial aspects of the neighborhood scene in existing courses in sociology, social psychology, anthropology, real estate, and psychology. City-planning courses too might well include special training in intergroup relations, while schools of adult education can serve an important function by offering instruction for people in business, real estate, and social work.

A few pilot courses in the East, West, North, and South can point the way for others. The leadership should be assumed by those larger universities in which departments are already treating with some phases of the subject and which are in or near the cities where the racial problem can be studied first-hand. There will, of course, be interdepartmental conflicts. And there is always the danger that a professor will veer the subject toward his own horizons or limit its development to his own abilities. It is best therefore to draw into the department experts from the field. Grants from foundations should be sought to make these pilot courses possible. Qualified students should be enlisted and an ample number of scholarships offered. Negro students should be encouraged to take courses, and white students might well undertake studies in Negro colleges. The training of students drawn from the various minority groups is desirable because of their familiarity with the habits and problems of their own people and because they can provide the confidence which others might have difficulty in winning. In-service training in the cities' race relations departments would help considerably, too. Training should include special courses in the problems of particular minorities, emphasizing the practical approaches as well as the social and psychological aspects of environment.[12]

Educating the Media of Communication

Newspapers, magazines, radio, and television all have a potential for doing good or evil. A high proportion has proved indifferent to minority problems.

Newspapers realize the sensitiveness of the issue and are unwilling to risk the protests and pressures which a progressive stand might entail. Most newspapers do not know how to handle racial news and rather than become involved in a controversial issue, use the freedom of the press to print nothing—even when a major riot occurs. Some papers, like those in Chicago, have opposed nondiscrimination ordinances while professing sympathy for the minority's problems. Others charge that honest efforts by citizens are linked with communist troublemakers.

To their credit, some influential newspapers have defended the right of a Negro to buy in a white section where the residents were bitterly opposed. But it is almost unheard of for editorial writers or reporters to probe the causes of tensions and hammer away at the need for unsegregated housing. Newspapers have conducted full-dress crusades against practically every known evil from the black market in babies to the mulcting of cemetery plot buyers. Their crusading fervor flickers out on the subject of race relations.

The minority press of course does give wide coverage to the racial issue, but few members of the majority see the Pittsburgh *Courier* or the Baltimore *Afro-American*. Southern newspapers for years even refused to use "Mr." or "Mrs." before the name of any Negro and printed a minimum of news other than crime stories about Negroes. Happily, there has been a noticeable change in the policies of some southern newspapers. It is no longer a rarity to find "Mr." used before a Negro name. The New Orleans *Times-Picayune* and a few other papers have begun to report news of Negro progress. This trend may signal the ultimate reversal of a discriminatory policy.

[12] The ability to speak Spanish may be important because it is from Spanish-speaking lands that much of our new immigration and migrations may be expected.

The adverse or noncommittal attitudes of normally progressive or middle-of-the-road newspapers toward racial problems are often due to the failure of civic leaders or public officials to brief the editor or publisher. This is a vital area for educational work. The San Francisco *Chronicle's* editorial opposition to a nondiscrimination ordinance in urban redevelopment was attributed to the newspaper's misunderstanding of the issue. Once a newspaper has declared itself, it can hardly be expected to change its point of view the next day. But the *Chronicle,* after the Civic Unity Council had conferred with its publisher, agreed to give better news coverage to the antidiscrimination side and a few years later was in the vanguard of a crusade for race tolerance in a San Francisco suburb.

Until the press learns the implications of racial isues, civic associations can play a strategic role in their education. The most effective journalism is the campaign that continues until it has achieved its goal. But this requires the services of a specialist who knows his subject and who can also write—a rare combination. But while The New York *Times* and the New York *Post* tackled the sensitive Puerto Rican issue, the former in a few articles and the latter in an extended series, neither newspaper gave a complete picture.

Radio and television have generally shunned the racial problem as too touchy. The motion picture industry, after eschewing it for most of its life (except for the hardly helpful *Birth of a Nation*), in recent years made a few films characterized by fume and foam, instead of using the subtler, more perceptive approach found in the good novel or play.[13]

The home magazines, as already pointed out, foster the great American dream—the home in the serene and semi-bucolic neighborhood, pure, white, and unperturbed by the minorities pressing at its boundaries. Sometimes these publications subtly cater to anti-racial sentiment in both articles and advertisements. One may look in vain for the pioneering article that gives readers the facts.

Education and the Communist Issue

The communist issue in America has had a serious impact on the problem of neighborhood bias. Communists at first viewed neighborhood tensions in terms of headlines and support from well-meaning

[13] Elliot Cohen, "Letter to the Movie-Makers," *Commentary,* August, 1947.

people willing to aid any good cause. So they helped organize tenant groups, pushed their way into some progressive fights where liberal groups were asleep, and filtered into some branches of Negro organizations.

Though they fared well for a time and tried to assume leadership on the racial issue, they were more nuisance than help. Their charges were often reckless, their tactics unscrupulous, their sponsorship suspect. Less concerned with achieving a gain for the minority group than with advancing their own interests, their leaders favored striking out in all directions at once with no heed to the real strategy of racial progress. They antagonized friendly organizations, alienated support more often than they won it.

Despite the virtual elimination of the communists from the role of minority protagonist, the communist issue has persisted in the race and housing contests. It has been kept alive by groups equally irresponsible and dangerous who attack every liberal movement as communist-inspired. While vociferously the most anti-communist, in practice they are the best friends the communists ever had. By charging indiscriminately that communists are behind certain movements led by liberals, they also built up the ragged party's prestige, and often weakened the position of the genuine liberals holding the line in progressive causes. By diverting the fight from the facts the discriminators often put liberals on the defensive and sometimes win a cheap victory. The local newspaper is the most important medium for clearing the air, but too often remains aloof or joins the smearers.

In the Stuyvesant Town case, for example, the communists were successfully kept out of the fight by the aggressive leadership of the National Association for the Advancement of Colored People, the American Jewish Congress, and the American Civil Liberties Union which financed and fought the litigation.

Suspect groups did not become conspicuous in the fight until the case reached the New York State Court of Appeals and began to make the headlines. The American Labor Party entered the case by filing an *amicus curiae* brief, which is automatically accepted by the courts. A tenants' organization had been formed in Stuyvesant Town and, to the embarrassment of the lawyers in the case, flooded the press with releases which the press printed freely. Metropolitan's counsel, Judge Samuel Seabury, discovered in these activities the ammunition he needed to prop up his argument before the Court of Appeals in which he charged that the whole fight was communist-inspired and pleaded that Metropolitan's $110 million investment was being jeopardized by agitators. No one except the judges can say whether or not this argument was enough to sway one or two of the justices. But this is certain—such "support" is no way to win a lawsuit, and it did the case no good. Metropolitan won by a 4 to 3 decision.

When thereafter a local bill was introduced in the City Council by Earl Brown, a Negro Democrat, and Stanley M. Isaacs, the Republican minority leader, to outlaw discrimination in Stuyvesant Town, the New York *Daily News* and the New York *Daily Mirror* were handed a dossier of the left-wing clippings[14] by the insurance company's representative and published editorials attacking the bill as communist-inspired. The Communist Party thereupon wired every councilman to support the bill—as if this could help—and appeared officially to support it. Metropolitan's counsel, sitting in the first row of the Chamber, made way to give the Party representative his place at the rostrum. Fortunately, the noncommunist groups stuck to their guns, the local legislators saw through the ruse and said so, adopting the measure unanimously.

Left-wingers or outright communists are entitled to support any cause they choose. The trouble is that noncommunist groups fighting for good causes are often encumbered by unsolicited communist help and more often dogged by accusations of communist influence.

The only honest and fruitful course is to battle unceasingly, without being frightened by what the communists do or what other irresponsibles say.

Civic Associations

The most effective medium for neighborhood and civic education on the problems of minorities is a free association of citizens, formed to further the ideals of their members as distinguished from their self-interest.

These associations, always essential to protect the individual citizen against predatory and personal-interest groups at the political level,

---

[14] The New York *World-Telegram* also published the story of communist influence but changed its position in a subsequent story. The *Herald Tribune* and The New York *Times* took no position.

have become indispensable at a time when private pressure groups have achieved unprecedented power in the state and federal legislatures, and when local majorities have tended to become insensitive to the fundamental rights of local minorities.[15]

Citizens groups function both nationally and locally, for a variety of purposes. Some are semi-official, being composed partly or entirely of persons holding public office, as the United States Conference of Mayors, the National Association of Housing and Redevelopment Officials, or the American Society of Planning Officials. They are created primarily for the discussion or consideration of their own special problems. Issues affecting minorities, housing, and neighborhoods fall within their compass, but their activities are often limited by their semi-official character.

The National Association for the Advancement of Colored People, the American Civil Liberties Union, and the American Jewish Congress have done yeoman work in the courts and helped attain some important advances at the legislative and administrative levels. The Anti-Defamation League has fought bigotry in many localities and the National Urban League has interested civic leaders in Negro problems. The American Jewish Committee has sponsored important research projects and disseminated useful information, especially through its *Commentary* magazine and other media. The National Committee Against Discrimination in Housing, a recent organization, has brought about important changes in federal administrative policy in housing and urban redevelopment.

At the state and local levels, the New York State Committee on Discrimination in Housing has blazed a trail by organizing labor, church, welfare, and other groups throughout the Empire State. This relatively young organization persuaded the legislature to outlaw discrimination and segregation in publicly aided housing after the Stuyvesant Town decision. Its success influenced similar efforts in other cities. The Los Angeles County Conference on Community Relations, the Council for Civic Unity of San Francisco, and organizations in Philadelphia, Cambridge, Detroit, Youngstown, and Pittsburgh have all made similar contributions. The Hyde Park-Kenwood Com-

---

[15] How these organizations can be most effective is graphically described by Alexander L. Crosby in *The Citizen Association: How to Organize and Run It,* and *The Citizen Association: How to Win Civic Campaigns.* New York, National Municipal League, 1953.

munity Council in Chicago, the Germantown Human Relations Committee in Pennsylvania, and the Crown Heights Owners Association in Brooklyn, are all making commendable efforts to effect harmony in shifting sections. Many other organizations function collaterally on minority problems.[16]

Yet despite the fine work of these organizations, they have been beset by difficulties. They are supported by sporadic contributions which the Department of Internal Revenue often regards as not tax-exempt because they engage in legislative action. This ruling should be fought. The department should distinguish between the average lobby working for a financial stake in legislation and those organizations whose main aim is to preserve democratic values or ideals without self-interest.

Another obstacle is the tendency of wary citizens to shun public organizations—particularly those concerned with racial and civil rights issues—because of possible ties to communist groups.

While the national organizations have made considerable headway, little has been done at the local level. The vacuum has been filled by real estate pressure lobbies, hate groups, "neighborhood improvement" organizations, and pseudo-experts. Prejudice is more easily generated when property interests are at stake, and the absence of strong, constructive organizations in the cities has often meant easy enlistment of local officials on the side of the antiminority groups. Better organization at the local level would attract responsible community leaders, help raise the moral level, and strengthen the hands of enlightened public officials.

The great opportunity and the best hope for achieving progress in race relations lies with local organizations. Properly organized, they can perform at least some of the following vital functions. They can:

1. Investigate tension between groups and act before the situation reaches a climax.

2. Bring together the responsible leadership of the community to

[16] Among the more prominent are the American Council on Human Rights, the American Friends Service Committee, Congregational Christian Churches, National Congress of Industrial Organizations (Civil Rights and Housing committees), National Federation of Settlements, the American Association of Social Workers, National Council of Negro Women, the National Housing Conference, and the National Conference of Christians and Jews.

promote better understanding between groups and more citizen awareness of the problems.

3. Work with city agencies to get better law enforcement to provide for more equitable relocation of families, to select proper sites for housing projects, and to protect minorities against violence or oppression.

4. Keep in touch with national housing agencies on policies that affect minorities.

5. Bring pressure for remedial legislation to provide more housing, protect civil rights, and release public funds for construction when private money is unavailable.

6. Confer with mortgage-lenders, builders, real estate owners, cooperative organizations, and other interests to obtain the money not now available to build housing open to minorities.

7. Exert pressure to create more racial relations agencies and to improve the performance of existing agencies.

8. Confer with and keep newspaper editors abreast of local problems.

9. Use radio and television facilities to present important issues to the public.

10. Arrange public forums for bringing contending groups together to discuss grievances.

11. Arrange for film showings, photographic exhibits, and other public displays of visual media.

12. Assemble and disseminate information on disputed issues such as the practicability of integrated housing and the effect of minorities on real estate values, social status, and neighborhood relationships.

13. Help allay the fears of homeowners and tenants caused by neighborhood in-migrations.

14. Cooperate with church and industrial leaders in dealing with changes in the neighborhood's composition.

15. Organize "action programs" and neighborhood surveys.[17]

16. Help educate the minorities in their responsibilities and rights.

17. Sponsor legal actions when minority rights or liberties are infringed, or report infringements to appropriate national groups.

18. Encourage the preparation of articles, pamphlets, and texts on

[17] Alfred Marrow, *Living Without Hate*. New York, Harper & Brothers, 1951.

various aspects of neighborhood relations for publication in national magazines and periodicals as well as in the local press.

19. Stimulate schools and universities to give courses in community relations and help in the preparation of appropriate curricula.

20. Alert minority groups to the effect of incursions against other minorities and promote cooperation among all minority groups.

21. Keep in close touch with interested national organizations and report to them on local issues affecting minorities.

22. Solicit the aid of foundations and other donors for funds needed for research and other activities.

23. Induce qualified students to enter the field and persuade experts in related fields to embrace the areas of race relations, community tensions, and housing.

24. Keep a close check on professional bigots and troublemakers, expose their efforts, and alert public officials to any infringements of the rights of minorities.

25. Help educate labor unions and employers on neighborhood problems.

26. Help break the written and unwritten restrictions in neighborhoods which exclude minorities.

27. Bring influence to bear upon resort areas, hotels, and travel agencies which discriminate against minorities.

28. Stimulate public hearings or investigations where essential to bring unfair practices to public attention.

29. Help procure housing for homeless or overcrowded minorities and intervene to aid them when they are being deprived of their fair share of housing.

30. Bring to public attention conditions affecting the health and welfare of minorities, or of the community.

31. Question candidates for public office on important public issues, such as public housing, race relations, and unfair immigration laws and procedures.

Not all of these functions can be performed at once, nor is it expected that, with funds and personnel as limited as they are, they can all be accomplished. Proper timing and selection of the most important work to be done in a particular community is therefore important.

Local organizations will prove to be the most effective instruments for mass education and intelligent action. Advances will not come through local and state officeholders, who are always chary of taking a stand unless pressed and unless they are sure a policy has the backing of influential groups.

Although the whole movement for public education in the United States stemmed from the belief that loyalty to republican ideals and democratic equality could be advanced only through a general system of education at public expense,[18] that responsibility will not be assumed unless citizen associations insist on it.

Education of Minorities

No real efforts have been made to educate minorities in the problems they face in new and old neighborhoods. A program of instruction is needed in both rights and responsibilities.

After World War II, for example, a group of Nisei came to New York, smarting under the treatment they had received on the West Coast and fearful in their new environment. They did not know whether to herd together in one area or spread throughout the community and become part of it. On the advice of an *ad hoc* committee, they dispersed and have encountered no special minority problems.

So too, Jewish refugees from Hitler-dominated countries of Europe received the guidance of organizations such as the Hebrew Sheltering and Immigrant Aid Society (HIAS) and the United Service for New Americans, which helped arrange for housing and jobs. The Chinese help their own people individually and through their organizations. The Puerto Rican government maintains offices in New York and Chicago to guide its people and aid them in employment. The National Association for the Advancement of Colored People and the National Urban League work with Negro groups.

But most migrant minorities have had to face their problems alone. Little or no guidance is given by employers, unions, city officials, and civic organizations. The migrants are met by a wall of resistance and an atmosphere of animosity. They are looked upon as a social menace and a costly intruder. Members of their own

[18] I. L. Kandel, "Education," *Encyclopaedia of the Social Sciences.* New York, The Macmillan Company, 1937, vol. 5, p. 417.

race or class are sometimes unfriendly as well, for they sense competition and resent the re-stirring of old problems.

The in-migrants themselves, feeling the hostility, may react against the community strictures. These rebellions produce gang fights, resistance to public school teachers, and a breakdown of parental controls. When these things happen, the older residents, convinced that their fears and biases are justified, become more hostile than ever.

The sharp lines of residential segregation widen social cleavages. Sometimes homogeneity in neighborhoods is accelerated by the efforts of Jewish organizations to make their own people adhere to their own communities. Greater interest in general community problems of a nonsectarian nature could do much to bring the various groups into better association.

Leadership from the ranks of the minorities is indispensable. The Puerto Rican in New York has so far not shown that leadership. Only six and a half hours away from his homeland, he has not permitted himself to build up enough resistance to the jibes of the older residents he is displacing. He feels the pull of his homeland where, though conditions may be worse and opportunities not as plentiful, he can at least feel wanted. And if the atmosphere in New York, the most tolerant of cities, is so unfriendly, what should he expect of other cities where he would be a tiny minority, a stranger among the estranged? The Mexican migrant, too, is not permitted to sink roots in the cities. Unwelcome, he also feels the pull of his homeland, and has as yet failed to produce the needed leadership.

The ultimate and important need is for organizations at the local level that can tackle the neighborhood problems which directly concern the minority. Working together in citizen groups, old residents and new migrants can speed the process of assimilation and mutual understanding.

XXIV

A PROGRAM FOR ACTION

IN A PREAMBLE to the Housing Act of 1949, Congress declared the national policy as one aiming at "the realization as soon as feasible of the goal of a decent home and a suitable living environment for every American family. . . ." This declaration, while put into clear language for the first time, merely formulated what Congress and a growing number of federal agencies by a long series of acts, appropriations, and underwritings had already been trying to do. It stated expressly what was a fair implication from its many actions.

From 1934 to 1954, an intervention into housing originally intended as temporary and experimental had become permanent federal policy. In the depression years the federal government intervened in housing to promote recovery; in 1937 for the social purpose of rehousing "one-third of a nation"; in the 1940's to implement its defense program and later as part of the war program; thereafter to house returning war veterans, and in 1954 to avert a recession. While the emphasis might shift with each period, housing aid had become an accepted part of the federal function—by bipartisan declaration, by executive action, and by judicial sanction.

By investment, subsidy, or insurance, the federal government had become the largest stakeholder in the housing enterprise. Through FHA it was insuring mortgage risks on most private rental housing. It was building all the new housing (such as it is) for the lowest income group. It was the main factor in slum-clearance and urban redevelopment operations. Through one or another of its multiple agencies, most entrepreneurs and lenders had come to depend on its underwritings for finance capital. Its insurance system was enabling the purchase of a home with a nominal down payment. It not only approved home sites, the type of homes being built, and the terms of sale, but often the qualifications of the people who might occupy them.

On January 25, 1954, President Eisenhower in his message to Congress reaffirmed that:

> The development of conditions under which every American family can obtain good housing is a major objective of national policy. . . . The federal government must provide aggressive and positive leadership. . . . Millions of our people still live in slums. Millions more live in run-down, declining neighborhoods. The national interest demands the elimination of slum conditions and the rehabilitation of declining neighborhoods. . . .

He also recognized that the minority housing problem is one of the most pressing aspects of the over-all housing problem:

> It must be frankly and honestly acknowledged that many members of minority groups, regardless of their income or their economic status, have had the least opportunity of all our citizens to acquire good homes. . . . We shall take steps to insure that families of minority groups displaced by urban redevelopment operations have a fair opportunity to acquire adequate housing; we shall prevent the dislocation of such families through the misuse of slum clearance programs; and we shall encourage adequate mortgage financing for the construction of new housing for such families on good well-located sites.

This was supported by Albert M. Cole, administrator of the Housing and Home Finance Agency, who acknowledged that "at least two-thirds of the slum families in many of our major cities are minority families who, regardless of income, would find it extremely difficult to get other housing."[1]

These pronouncements were welcome acknowledgments of the problem and a reversal, at least on paper, of the outright discriminatory policies of 1935–1949. Statement of policy, however, is one thing, fulfillment another.

In 1954, neither Congress nor the Eisenhower administration was offering any program to meet the housing needs of minorities or to

---

[1] "What Is the Federal Government's Role in Housing?" address to the Economic Club of Detroit, February 8, 1954; see also The President's Advisory Committee on Government Housing Policies and Programs, *A Report to the President of the United States.* Washington, Government Printing Office, December, 1953, pp. 2–3, 255–276.

improve the critical conditions affecting the neighborhoods in which they lived. In fact, in many respects the administration program actually threatened to aggravate the problem. It proposed more favorable insurance terms for the home-buyer, builder, and lender but proffered none for minorities. The public housing appropriation from which a small pool of minorities and other low-income families were benefiting was all but scrapped.

A proposed mortgage insurance program for low-cost housing purchasable by families displaced by urban redevelopment with a nominal down payment could not be built in or near many larger cities into which minorities were pouring. Nor were many private builders likely to make it available to the tens of thousands being displaced.

Another provision authorized rehabilitation operations with liberal FHA insurance. But such operations would not only fail to provide additional dwellings for minorities but would dislocate many minority families now occupying the dwellings to be rehabilitated. The costs of rehabilitation would raise rents beyond the capacity of minorities to pay—even if the owners were prepared to offer them to minorities. Finally, the program provided more urban redevelopment (now called *urban renewal*) authorizations to local housing authorities which only presaged continued evictions as in the past without providing alternative accommodations. There was one bright spot and that was only a flicker. In 1954, Housing Administrator Albert M. Cole was making an earnest effort to encourage the homebuilders to program housing for Negroes and the National Association of Homebuilders was urging its members to do so—on a segregated basis, of course. Doubtless, some will now build—in the South, and perhaps in the North. But low Negro incomes, local biases, and lack of mortgage money will check any large-scale developments. Without adequate laws and adequate money there could be no adequate program. Apart from this slight concession to minority needs, all the signs pointed toward "Business as Usual."

If there were to be any constructive leadership and a well-intentioned effort to meet the problem, it could be evidenced only by a broad-gauged program which would have to encompass at least eleven specific aims:

First Aim: *A Comprehensive Long-range Housing Program for all groups.* Since a normal market must be created in which people can move or stay in their homes without fear by the minorities of exclusion, or fear by the majority of invasion, a publicly sponsored and publicly aided program should be sought to supplement private housing. Both kinds of housing should be available to all groups, a free commerce established in the housing market with adequate shelter for all at prices all can afford.

Essentially there can be no dual markets: for whites and blacks; blacks and reds; reds and yellows. A house has no lasting color-marks, race-marks, or use-marks. The house rented to a white family today may be occupied by a Negro tomorrow, or vice versa. The house built for sale may be offered for rent and the rented dwelling become owner-occupied. The one-family mansion may be turned into ten efficiency units or into furnished rooms. Easing neighborhood tensions and meeting minority requirements calls for an ample supply of housing of all types, in all places for all income groups, all colors and classes.

This does not mean that in the programming of housing or in the distribution of benefits the public agencies can ignore the groups who need housing most. Color-blindness by government does not mean complete blindness—and deafness as well. There is an obligation to meet needs where they are greatest, to program housing equitably, and to adjust policy, loans, subsidies, and other benefits so that the most pressing needs are met and to see that no one group is favored over another.

Group integration will be facilitated as the pressure for housing is eased. Conversely, competition for housing will be keener and fear and suspicion greater when the housing for any particular group is scarce. Four distinct steps are essential:

1. Estimating and programming housing need. Various estimates have been made from time to time on the extent of the housing need. In 1951, the Housing and Home Finance Agency estimated[2] that 14,386,000 additional dwellings would be required by 1960. This figure included 8,400,000 dwellings for replacement and rehabilitation and 5,986,000 for new families. Some two to three million units were required to meet farm needs, or a total of 16.4–

[2] *How Big is the Housing Job.* Washington, Housing and Home Finance Agency, October, 1951.

17.4 million dwelling units for the nation. This, said HHFA, meant an average annual quota of at least 1.4 million nonfarm dwellings alone.[3] Other estimates range from 1.5 million to 2 million units per year.[4] The National Housing Conference, in a carefully prepared estimate, computed a need for 2 million nonfarm units annually for 1955-60; 2.3 million in 1960-65, and 2.4 million in 1965-70.

While all these estimates gauge the over-all problem, they are unrealistic in terms of the minority problem. If, from the total programmed, minorities were to reap the same benefits as in the past, they would get little or nothing, and since such estimates also include provision for large-scale demolition of substandard housing, the plight of minorities would be worse than ever.

An estimate of national housing requirements is realistic only when related to needs and conditions not only of every community but of every group within the communities. It must include a reasonable vacancy rate in each locality and in each category to make possible the essential shift from one house to another as needs, standards, income, family size, and change of job situs require. The vacancy margin must exist in all areas and in all types of housing. A margin for higher income groups in one area or one type of housing may not draw occupants from others.

Manifestly, a new type of market analysis is needed to determine needs more accurately and relate programs to the ability of particular groups to participate in them. For Example, the lower incomes of nonwhites[5] require a greater emphasis on a subsidized program.

[3] Cf., the writer's estimate in 1946 of 18,600,000 units under a 10-year program; 21,300,000 units under a 15-year program, and 24,000,000 under a 20-year program (*The Future of Housing*. New York, Harper & Brothers, 1946, p. 70).

[4] These estimates are listed by William L. C. Wheaton in *American Housing Needs. 1955–1970, A Preliminary Estimate,* Reprinted from *The Housing Yearbook, 1954,* National Housing Conference, Inc., Washington, D. C., Table 7, p. 11.

[5] Census estimates of income distribution of nonfarm families for 1949 show about half of the nonwhite group had total money incomes of about $1700 or more; the other half below that figure. For whites the halfway mark was about twice as great. About 19 per cent of the nonwhite families, but 60 per cent of white families received $3000 and over; 9.3 per cent of whites had incomes between $4000 and $4499 against 3 per cent for nonwhites; 5.3 per cent of whites had incomes of $4500–$4999 against 1 per cent for nonwhites; 8.4 per cent of whites had incomes between $5000 and $5599 against 1.8 of the nonwhites (*Housing of the Nonwhite Population.* Washington, Housing and Home Finance Agency, July, 1952).

Though there is "a very substantial waiting market for Negro housing ranging from $40 to $90 in rents and from $6500 to $15,000 for sales housing, with a fair number of minority families able to enter the luxury housing market,"[6] an analysis must be made of the precise size of that market in all areas where these minorities live. Minority incomes being what they are, high-cost houses for them may find few takers.

There are definite indications that meeting the needs of the non-white minority is financially feasible and would entail no strain on the national land or materials supply. The Race Relations Service of the Housing and Home Finance Agency estimated that for the decade 1950–1960 some 2.5 million nonfarm dwelling units would be needed for nonwhites through new building, conversion, and rehabilitation.[7] The estimate was based on the following:

700,000 additional nonfarm units for new nonwhite family formation;

1,600,000 to replace dilapidated nonfarm or urban units lacking private bath or toilet.

40,000 nonfarm units occupied by nonwhites in April, 1950, which will be lost by 1960 through disaster, demolition, etc.

While this estimate fails to take into account the overcrowding that must be relieved and the pressure of new migrations, even a doubling or trebling of the estimate should not render fulfillment impossible. The entire number of nonwhites in the country is, after all, a minor fraction of the total population.

The main trouble is not the quantity of housing minorities require but that almost no housing is provided for them. As they seek access to any housing available, fear is sparked in the community they attempt to enter. Relieving the pressure even partly would be reflected almost at once in the stabilization of the challenged sections and the dissipation of fears.

The federal government should also assume responsibility for chart-

---

[6] Cole, *op. cit.*

[7] *How Big is the Housing Job Relating to Nonwhites in Nonfarm Areas?*, prepared by B. T. McGraw in consultation with E. E. Ashley III. Washington, Racial Relations Service, Housing and Home Finance Agency, January, 1954. This total (2,500,000) includes no allowance for any vacancy or undoubling in nonfarm units occupied by nonwhites, nor for their net in-migration to non-farm areas.

ing migratory movements by assessing industrial requirements for labor in specific areas, as it did during World War II. It makes little sense to legalize the entry of 200,000 Mexicans without simultaneously programming housing for them. Such programming involves not only the number of houses needed but the types, price ranges, and the public or private agencies which should build them. It should also take account of private housing capacity, cooperative housing, public housing, and urban redevelopment under an all-inclusive plan rather than under the sporadic and often conflicting programming by federal agencies.

2. *An extensive public housing program for the lowest income Group.* By 1954 the federal public housing program provided rental dwellings only for some lowest income families with little prospect of a comprehensive low-rental program. At its peak, the public housing program was little more than a demonstration effort, and though at one time it had the sponsorship of the late Senator Robert A. Taft, the Republican Party after his death elected to scuttle it.[8]

No longer can the private entrepreneur be depended upon to provide for the low-income migrant as did the entrepreneur of the 1890's and early 1900's. While the dwellings of the older immigrants were rude tenements, bandboxes, or huts, they were at least new and were supplied in quantity at prices the immigrants could afford. Suspicion of strangers, fear of anyone who is different, hostility to groups moving en masse created tensions before, but under the great leveling forces at work in the American scheme, the tensions soon subsided. But today instead of the great frontier, the locus of fear and competition is the suburb and city; instead of competition for land that is plentiful, the competition is for houses that are scarce. Housing standards and costs have risen; free land and materials are no longer available; the building operation has become specialized and can no longer be done by self-help. The dwelling supply for the current migrants is usually the leftovers; when they are filled doubling

[8] In an interview by this writer in January, 1948, Senator Taft said, "I believe there should be a comprehensive plan with the ultimate purpose of securing decent housing for all American families." He then said that he hoped public housing would take care of the needs of 10 per cent of the people and that "if I were sure we could solve the housing problem in this country and keep it solved by spending $400 million a year, I would favor doing it" (New York *Post,* January 27, 28, 1948).

up or homelessness is the alternative. A subsidized program is the only answer.

The size of such a program would depend on the needs and incomes not only of the minorities but of the entire low income group. Some 6.5 million families occupying substandard shelter had 1949 incomes of less than $3500. The average income of families in public housing projects was less than $2100 and the average income of those required to move from public housing was $3800. In 1950 there were about 5 million families with incomes of less than $2000 per year and more than 2 million families with incomes of $2000–$3000 who occupied substandard shelter. It is hardly beyond our means to provide for a long-range program of 500,000 dwellings per year for these families. A special effort should be made to make a quarter or a fifth of this available to minorities. At present Negro families (and a small proportion of other races) represent about 32 per cent of the total being admitted to public housing and 41 per cent of all families in such housing.[9] As of January, 1952, Negroes occupied 70,313 of the 186,886 permanent public housing dwelling units. This exemplifies both their low economic status and their inability to obtain decent private housing within their means. By emphasizing vacant sites, the over-all supply of housing could be increased and important breaches made in the present blockade. By simultaneously launching a program at low interest rates for an ownership program, still further breaches could be effected.

Of course the current public housing formula would need improvement. There is no reason for continued public ownership of all projects once they are built. Housing is not like a post office or a public school. The projects could be leased to nonprofit organizations or cooperatives and ultimately sold to them. Simultaneously, the housing authorities would be building the houses for sale as well as rental. A flexible mortgage interest rate, fixed for the first five years and reset no oftener than every three years thereafter, could adjust interest to income and relieve the owner of the ever-present fear of eviction. The interest rate would never exceed the market rate, and when it once reached that level, the mortgage or the senior portion could be

[9] The President's Advisory Committee on Government Housing Policies and Programs, *op. cit.,* p. 303.

disposed of to private mortgage institutions, thereby providing a revolving fund for other similar ventures.

Housing policy should no longer be dependent upon piecemeal development and random appropriation. If properly constituted local communities took the leadership in comprehensive neighborhood development, a master plan would become possible in cities and regions, and adequate shelter could be provided for all who need it. Land could be acquired and reserved for private, quasi-public, and public development.

The cost of a program as outlined above, while fluctuating, would be paltry compared to the social gains it would achieve, the employment it would encourage, the tensions it would dissolve, the prosperity it would spur.

3. A middle-income housing program for families not provided for by private or public housing operations. This group includes those earning $2800–$4400 a year, the income varying with each community and with the times. According to a report of the Senate Committee on Banking and Currency,[10] the group could pay rents ranging from $47 to $73 a month, or a median shelter rent of about $60 without utilities. In 1951, more than one half of the 35 million nonfarm families had incomes of less than $4000 at year.[11] This is the group whose housing requirements are not adequately met through FHA housing or by private builders.

While cash subsidies will not be needed for the majority of these families, favorable long-term financing is essential to maintain monthly costs at practical levels. This aid could be given through 40-year, 2.5 per cent mortgage loans. Under such terms, families in the higher cost areas earning $3800–$4100 and requiring larger homes, as well as smaller families with incomes as low as $3300, could be accommodated. In low-cost areas, families with incomes of $2900–$3200 and smaller families with incomes of $2500 could benefit. The program might be undertaken through private builders. If the response were unsatisfactory, it might be undertaken under a federally encouraged cooperative program.

[10] *Housing Act of 1950,* Report No. 1286. Washington, U. S. Government Printing Office, 1950, p. 52.

[11] U.S. Bureau of the Census, *U.S. Census of Population: 1950,* Vol. II, *Characteristics of the Population,* Part I, *U.S. Summary.* U.S. Government Printing Office, Washington, D.C., 1953, Table 57.

A formula for meeting the needs of these families was provided by the housing bill of 1950,[12] which failed to pass Congress. A national mortgage corporation should be empowered to make long-term low-interest loans to nonprofit or cooperative housing organizations constructing shelter for middle income families. Preliminary advances should be made to encourage formation of such nonprofit and cooperative corporations and to help them prepare plans.

Cooperatives up to now have failed in the United States for a variety of reasons: lack of leadership, lack of encouragement by the government, abuse of the cooperative name by private builders, poor management, lack of know-how, failure to obtain financing, and shortage of equity capital.[13] These obstacles could be removed if the federal government were to become more directly concerned. Cooperatives have been among the pioneers in establishing racial integration and nondiscrimination in housing projects. Queensview Houses, Amalgamated Houses, and other cooperatives in New York City have shown that the projects can be sound financially and socially. There is no fear in these projects that the racial minority will push out the majority. In communities where cooperatives do not function, nonprofit organizations should be set up to build for sale or rental.

4. Modification of practices in publicly aided private housing. Although the risk in housing built under the FHA and Veterans Administration programs is now carried by the government, the minorities have benefited little. The number of mixed FHA projects has been nominal.

The government today is equipped to break the boycott against minorities and to program housing in each locality on the basis of need by various groups. If some private builders treat minorities favorably, they should be favored with FHA and VA benefits. If other builders engage in unfair exclusion practices they should be barred from receiving federal benefits. More equitable appraisals by FHA and VA would be a helpful factor.

Another device would be favorable equity loans to nondiscriminating builders. Builders are often hard-pressed for capital to extend their operations and pay bonuses for front money and temporary loans.

---

[12] H.R. 6618, H.R. 6782, and S. 2246.
[13] Charles Abrams, "Another String to the Bow," *The Survey,* October, 1949.

Some have had to make private deals with officials of the savings and loan associations, turning over a share of the equity to them as an inducement for receiving favorable financing. Builders often feel they are being exploited. If temporary financing of land operations could be facilitated through federal loans, more of the smaller builders might build housing open to minorities.

The federal government should also help the minority groups to do more building themselves. There are some large-scale builders among Negroes, like W. H. Aiken of Atlanta, Georgia, but the number is all too small. Training programs in building, with a system of apprenticeships served under the more experienced builders, would help considerably. Until private lenders loosen up, liberal financial aid should be extended to them during the various stages of the building operation.

Second Aim: *Adequate Protection by Law of the Opportunity to Secure Shelter.* One of the most difficult questions to resolve is when and whether to seek the outlawing of discrimination by statute. The question poses a crucial choice of tactics in the fight for equality.

Enactment of laws to end discrimination in certain fields may be constructive and necessary. Positive gains have been scored by F.E.P.C. laws in private employment and by nondiscrimination laws in public places such as theaters, bowling alleys, hotels; laws to end discrimination in publicly aided housing are essential where resort to other devices has failed. Introduction of bills may sometimes also serve an educational function, as when they are combined with resolutions for investigations into discrimination.

Some well-intentioned pro-minority organizations, however, have made pressure for antidiscriminatory legislation their major task. The way to end discrimination, they contend, is to outlaw it. Hundreds of bills are introduced annually in state and federal legislatures, citizen support is mustered at great effort and cost, legislators are importuned to back or oppose the bills, and more than one legislator's career is made or broken in the outcome.[14]

One authority argued that law can not only eliminate group dis-

---

[14] Senator Paul H. Douglas told this writer that when he decided to vote against the Cain-Bricker amendment, friends and political advisers warned him it would end his political career.

crimination but modify human behavior, codify ideals, put the state's influence on the side of the minority, help minorities to defend themselves and improve their welfare. It can eliminate discrimination in housing, employment, and education, he says, and "help establish those fundamental conditions of social life which encourage free association of groups on a level of equality, and which discourage prejudicial attitudes."[15]

Law has a place in the fight to maintain democracy but it must be relegated to its proper role in the over-all fight and be carefully employed. Resort to antidiscrimination legislation as the main weapon may often open the way to subterfuges that destroy social legislation. Witness the antidiscrimination rider attached to the Housing Act of 1949 in an attempt by Senators Cain and Bricker to defeat public housing, a federal program which has done more to demonstrate the practicability of nondiscriminatory living than any antidiscrimination legislation ever enacted. The lobby committee reports later disclosed that the antidiscrimination amendment was conceived as a ruse by the real estate lobby to alienate the support of southern congressmen.[16] Yet the National Association for the Advancement of Colored People and other progressive organizations were induced to support it. Similarly, in 1943, an antidiscrimination amendment actually killed the aid-to-education bill.

Antidiscrimination laws can also be distracting. All too often civic groups press for these laws though they can have little practical effect. Interest is diverted from areas where real gains could be achieved.

Premature campaigns are another risk. Well-meaning groups often launch a bill before the public is ready for it. As a result, opposition to the law may be organized by inimical groups and a battle lost which might have been won at a later date.

Statute law should be regarded as one weapon in the democratic arsenal but not the only one. It should not be advocated as a pana-

[15] Morroe Berger, *Equality by Statute: Legal Controls Over Group Discrimination,* with a foreword by Robert M. MacIver. New York, Columbia University Press, 1952, p. 192. It is not always clear when the author includes judicial decisions as "law" but he seems to place heaviest reliance on statutes as a solution for discrimination.

[16] Hearings before the House Select Committee on Lobbying Activities, House of Representatives, Eighty-first Congress, Pursuant to H. Res. 298. Washington, U.S. Government Printing Office, 1950.

cea. It is a two-edged sword, and those who draw it have a responsibility to gauge its consequences and its risks; they must not only see that the groundwork is laid to make it work but be prepared to follow the legislation beyond enactment into every step of its administration and to guard it against perversion.

Some who resort to law as the primary weapon have adopted a cynical view, viz., "Laws can be enacted in response to the demands of a small minority or without the knowledge of the majority."[17] They cite the late Morris R. Cohen's quip, "That in a democracy the law is the will of the people is the statement not of fact but of an aspiration."

The argument weakens rather than strengthens the claims of minorities to equal treatment. Tyranny is as unjust when practiced by the minority in the enactment of laws in which the majority does not yet believe as it is when the majority imposes laws by which the minority is to be oppressed. If protection of civil rights must depend on authoritative procedures or laws passed by a few to gain their ends, it simply violates one important right to achieve another. It is a weak prop on which to rest the fight for minority rights.

Salvation of civil and political rights emanates not mainly from the will of a majority or from statute (though some new rights or penalties may be created by statute) but from the basic charter—whether it is called the Bill of Rights, or "unalienable rights" or "natural rights" or "public policy." These are all generalizations, and indeed they can be enhanced or diminished by interpretation. But they are the "authoritative" rights in the sense that statutes must conform to them.

To abandon the position that the basic rights are supreme and that the right to equality must be re-established through the painful and laborious if not impossible process of antidiscriminatory statutes (and against the will of the majority to boot!) would amount to fatal surrender of the principal supports that fortify the American scheme.

Violation of this fundamental law is checked in a number of ways. If violation is by states or municipalities they are enjoined through the courts under the state and federal constitutions. Violations by

[17] Berger, *op. cit.,* p. 3; see also Arnold M. Rose, "The Influence of Legislation on Prejudice," *Race Prejudice and Discrimination,* (Arnold M. Rose, ed.). New York, Alfred A. Knopf, Inc., 1948, p. 551.

private enterprise (when not acting as beneficiaries of public power or funds) may be enjoined by statute. It is in the private area that the new rights and duties of the individual may be continuously broadened by legislative enactment. An anti-discrimination law in housing is the familiar imposition of limitations upon rights. It is an effort to protect the right of people to live where they choose by limiting the right of others to live with whom they choose. The conflict is not always easy to resolve for it operates in the sensitive area of privacy. Its aim however is not primarily to protect a minority but to protect the general interest by maintaining freedom of access to one of life's essentials. And when enacted, it is not because the few write the laws for the many, but because the many either want those laws passed as representative of the fundamental ethic or because they are willing to acquiesce in their passage.

No statute should be needed, however, to outlaw racial discrimination by FHA, the Public Housing Administration, or other federal agencies. As agents of the government, they are assumed to be color blind in the dispensation of benefits. Nor is a statute essential to bar discrimination by a local housing authority or by a private company acting as an agent of the government or using its funds or powers. Seeking statutory protection in these cases, as so often happens, is an admission of the need for a special law and may be a retreat from rights already vested. Failure of passage may even suggest to the courts the nonexistence of the rights and the refusal of the legislature to recognize their existence.[18]

The barring of discrimination in publicly aided housing projects by administrative regulation would carry out the basic American principle that public funds belong to all the people without distinction. Resort to federal statute instead of to administrative pressure should be sought only after it appears clear that the administration refuses to conform or after the courts have ruled adversely, leaving statute as the only remedy. Outlawing discrimination in a new community, such as the Levittowns or similar developments which are aided or made possible by government, should be effected by executive order, or

[18] In *Dorsey v. Stuyvesant Town,* 299 N.Y. 512, 339 U.S. 981 the introduction of these nondiscrimination statutes and their failure to pass was cited by the courts as evidence that only statutes could assure nondiscrimination by the publicly-aided Stuyvesant Town Corporation.

thereafter by the courts. If these efforts fail, resort to statute may then be necessary.

Statutory enactments are also needed where private enterprise becomes affected with a public interest; where public morality is shocked into action by the exercise of unreasonable private power; where necessities of life or well-being are unjustly withheld from the free market and resort to administrative relief is impossible; where the interests of health, welfare, or safety require public action. Discrimination in employment and in restaurants, barber shops, and other public places are examples. In all instances, enactment will depend on whether the people are ready for the change.

Housing today has come within the broad sphere of public interest. It is no longer "private" in the nineteenth-century sense. It is drastically regulated by zoning and building ordinances; housing rents are controlled during shortages; moratoria on foreclosures are common during emergencies; public housing for the underprivileged is an accepted public purpose, and house building is being aided by federal insurance because it is felt to be in the public interest.[19]

In large cities the distinctions between hotels, furnished rooms, and apartment houses have gradually disappeared. The time is not far when the statutes barring racial discrimination in hotels will be extended to cover the many private rental undertakings as well.

Certain communities are prepared to accept further protection of minority rights in private housing, while for others it might be premature. Some will accept it in multiple dwellings but not in smaller houses. Outlawing discrimination in one- or two-family houses would probably be premature in most places and invite difficulties. But it might be ripe in large-scale private developments where the right of an owner to control the type of inhabitants is no longer considered co-extensive with the right of a homeowner to regulate the conduct of his guests.[20] In each case, determination must be made as to how the gain can best be achieved—by executive order, by demonstration, by court fight, by administrative ruling, or by federal or local statute. Reliance on statute alone or even mainly on statute can be as troublesome as it can be helpful. When legislation is decided upon

[19] "Housing is a necessity of life. All elements of public interest justifying some degree of public control are present." (*Block v. Hirsch*, 256 U.S. 135).

[20] *Marsh v. Alabama*, 326 U.S. 501. An ordinance barring discrimination in FHA rental projects was enacted in New York City in 1954.

as the appropriate remedy it should be sought in jurisdictions that are ripe for it and in which a successful administration of the statute can demonstrate its practicability for other areas of the country.

Proper strategy should also guide the bringing of test suits. A judicial decision in one jurisdiction serves as a precedent for others. A suit prematurely brought or argued without factual foundation and without adequate preparation may produce an adverse ruling creating precedents that become firmly imbedded as the law and which may impede progress for decades thereafter. Litigation is an important tool but should be properly timed and brought in jurisdictions where there is some chance of success.[21] Favorable judicial decisions can not only establish the rights of minorities on a wider basis than local statutes, but they may play an important educative role and serve to uphold the political morality of the community.

Third Aim: *An Executive Policy Prohibiting Discrimination by Those Dispensing Federal Funds or Benefiting from Public Power.* Though FHA's discriminatory provisions have been excised from its manual, its duties are still far from clear. No executive order exists which bans FHA from discriminating. Except for its sullen acceptance of a provision against insuring properties subject to newly placed racial covenants, there is no rule preventing it from discriminating in the field or from acquiescing in discrimination by its beneficiaries. Its actual performance for minorities remains a sorry contrast to the low-rent housing program of the Public Housing Administration.

---

[21] A good example is the decisions upholding the constitutionality of public housing legislation. After the federal courts in 1938 had enjoined the federal government from acquiring land for slum clearance, the New York City Housing Authority brought suit in New York State to test the public housing statutes (*New York City Authority v. Muller,* 270 N.Y. 233). The court upheld the Authority and in the course of the next few years the decision was followed in 22 other states. Later the Supreme Court held housing a proper federal purpose (*Federal Public Housing Authority v. Guckenberger,* 323 U.S. 329). A bad example is the action of the San Francisco Housing Authority in asking the Supreme Court to review the state court decision which held against its segregation policy in public housing projects (*Banks v. Housing Authority of San Francisco,* 260 Pac. 2d 668 [1953]). Did it expect the Court in 1954 to reaffirm *Plessy v. Ferguson* (163 U.S. 537) and its "separate but equal" holding and if the Court did, would the Authority have considered it a public service?

The question therefore gets down to the rights and duties of FHA. Thanks to the liberal terms of the FHA formula, home-builders today, while they need the front money for land and preparatory operations, no longer invest substantial equity money. Nor do they risk capital in rental housing, under the Section 213 cooperative housing scheme, or under the rental-housing formulas. The government assumes the risk in exchange for the assumed public benefits, while the entrepreneurs take the cash profit with little or no risk. Similarly mortgage-lenders need no longer take market risks, though benefiting from attractive interest rates.

FHA today can influence the flow of housing where needed as well as the racial patterns of American neighborhoods, and the agency has a duty to do precisely that. It is more than a private company concerned only with its stockholders. It is more than a tool for private builders. Mortgage insurance was designed to help veterans, homeowners, and hardship cases. FHA is in fact already required to prevent some kinds of discrimination, viz: "the mortgagor must certify that he will not discriminate against families with children." Violation of this requirement is a misdemeanor. Is it not logical that FHA should help those hardship cases caused by racial discrimination as well?

Under Section 207, FHA regulates not only charges, capital structure, and rate of return, but also "methods of operation." Should not its duty extend to methods of operation which ban housing to Negroes?

The FHA administrator may take shares of stock as part of the transaction in order to protect the interests of the United States and to make his regulations effective. In FHA-sponsored cooperatives, the administrator may take preferred stock ownership to protect the public interest. Is it not FHA's duty to see that its benefits are dispensed without bias?

FHA is indeed a creature of the public with an affirmative duty to protect the public interest. The full faith and credit of the United States remain behind every mortgage insurance contract. FHA has been accorded the same priorities in bankruptcy proceedings as are given to the United States. Its administrator is appointed by the President. It is answerable to the people—all the people, not merely the "homogeneous" citizens.

So too since FHA-insured mortgages are no longer wholly private risks, FHA has a duty to ban discrimination by lenders.

If FHA repossessed rental property it could not, as landlord, legally discriminate in the choice of tenants. FHA was confronted with precisely this situation when a Negro Air Force officer applied for an apartment in a repossessed rental project in Norfolk, Virginia. The local FHA representative, bewildered, asked for a ruling, and the embarrassing issue was relayed to the Washington office where FHA's attorneys ruled there was no way out but to admit him. The ruling, however, has not furthered integration in FHA-owned projects, for there is still a wide gap between what FHA lawyers say cannot be done and what FHA officials actually do. In 1954, FHA projects repossessed by the government were maintaining the old private discriminatory patterns. The agency intervened to ban discrimination by a private owner when a Philadelphia builder publicized his determination to discriminate in a large 608 rental project and social agencies threatened to make an issue of it. But this continues to be one of the prominent exceptions.

Yet FHA is by no means a passive insuring agency on the sidelines of the building venture. Its ownership of voting stock in private rental ventures imposes a duty upon it to speak up when a project bars a Negro, Chinese, or Jewish applicant. Its statutory obligation to protect families with children applies with no less force to Negro children than to whites. Its obligation to regulate project operations and to make rules binding on the operator implies the making of rules that will conform its operations to that of the federal Civil Rights Law granting minorities the same right to lease property as is given to whites.

The same logic applies to the Veterans Administration in the insurance of its mortgages and to the Federal National Mortgage Association, both of which are federal agencies operating under formulas which also place the risk on the federal government. VA ought not use its insurance powers to favor white veterans over Negroes, while FNMA, which became the federal dumping ground for billions of dollars of sour private mortgages, has a duty to dispense its lush benefits without turning away from minority-occupied property and taking mortgages only on the risky white-occupied parcels. The Urban Redevelopment Division has a similar duty.

It was a public aim not a federal money-making scheme that also inspired formation of the Home Loan Bank System and its complex complement of sub-agencies, the regional banks, their member institutions, and the Federal Savings and Loan Insurance Corporation. The affiliated regional banks and savings and loan associations, supervised by the Board, are a main factor in mortgage-lending today. By the end of 1952 these 4056 member institutions had estimated assets of $21,871,000,000.

The Home Loan Bank Board set up this system of home financing to meet the thrift and home-financing needs of the average American family; to equalize the distribution of home mortgage funds throughout the country; to promote sound lending practices; to enhance small-home ownership.[22] These are all public purposes. The regional banks lend the members the public's money against mortgages and may even buy shares of the associations, up to three times the subscription paid by private shareholders. To induce the public to buy association shares and make deposits the Federal Savings and Loan Insurance Corporation underwrites the security of depositors and shareholders.

The Board has broad powers of supervision over its members which include supervision of salaries of officers, expenses and budgets, dividend declarations, by-law amendments, and purchases and sale of investment securities. No institution may become a member if "the character of its management or its home financing policy is inconsistent with sound and economical home financing or with the purposes of this chapter." There is no reason why the Board should not also check oppressive or discriminatory practices. But nothing in the history of the Board or its members has indicated a concern for the "home financing needs" of Negroes or other minorities, or for "equalizing the distribution of home mortgage funds" so that minorities will get their share to "enhance small home ownership" by them. When its managers affirmatively bar loans to Negroes, the Board has shown even less inclination than FHA to interfere. Some of the Board's own officials in the past, as we have seen, have even advocated racial discrimination as sound policy. Though the aid dispensed by these federal agencies belongs to all the people, benefits have accrued least to those who need them most.

It is possible, of course, that in a proper court test these agencies

[22] *6th Annual Report.* Housing and Home Finance Agency. Washington, 1952, p. 165.

and their beneficiaries may be brought within the Constitution. But courts construe policies, not construct them. To rely primarily on the courts for relief ignores the fact that preventing discrimination in the use of federal funds or credit is primarily an executive responsibility. While it would be within the court's province to enjoin a federal agency or its beneficiary from discriminating, it is also within the power of the Chief Executive and his agencies to condition federal aid upon nondiscrimination. Manifestly, if the federal government felt itself obliged to indict New York City savings banks for conspiring to ban mortgage loans on Negro property, it should certainly be obliged to bring its own agencies into line with the democratic principle. An executive order providing that lenders benefiting from federal aid may not discriminate in the selection of risks on account of race or color would hardly be interfered with by the courts.

Such a requirement would not disrupt investment policy or management any more than similar injunctions have discouraged investment in hotels barred from discriminating. The area of managerial discretion would be unabridged except when policy is made on the basis of race, creed, or color. The same public interest which invokes public aid commands that the public aid be used without favoring one race or group over another.

Fourth Aim: *Curtailment of Slum-clearance Operations for the Duration of the Housing Emergency.* Slum clearance, begun when vacancies were ample, has little justification during housing famine, when a leaky roof is better than no roof. If slum clearance rather than decent housing were the only aim, it would best be accomplished by an earthquake. Until the housing supply is substantially increased, only the worst houses should be demolished.

The increase in population and the continued in-migration of minorities and other workers into cities have made overcrowding—not mere occupancy—of slums the most serious problem. A major building program is the only answer. But the public housing program popularized slum clearance to a point where the slum clearers no longer dared admit they were evicting families more effectively than they were housing them.

To take a single example: The New York City Housing Authority in 1953 had the largest housing program in the nation, entailing a capital investment of about a billion dollars. From the beginning the Authority concentrated on tearing down tenements and replacing them with new housing. The result has been only a nominal gain in the housing supply. Meanwhile, vacancies disappeared and with the influx of hundreds of thousands of Puerto Ricans, the housing shortage became a famine. In 1953 alone, 70,000 Puerto Ricans settled there, most of them low-income families whom the private builder could not serve. The Housing Authority, with a city, state, and federal program, was then providing an annual average of only 6500 new units, and many of these were replacements. Moreover, existing public housing, redevelopment, and public works programs called for the displacement of more than 150,000 persons.

Under the federal urban redevelopment program (urban renewal), the houses of minorities are being torn down throughout the country, and most of the displaced families are being excluded from the new housing built. To correct these flagrant distortions, the following modifications are essential:

1. The urban redevelopment program should no longer aim to shorten the supply of housing through one arm of the Housing and Home Finance Agency, i.e., the Urban Redevelopment Division, while other arms (FHA, VA, and the Home Loan Bank agencies) supply virtually no housing for the displaced families, and a third arm (Public Housing Administration) is incapacitated by Congress from giving the dispossessed any substantial help. If the effect of the urban redevelopment program must be displacement of a group that cannot be rehoused through alternative programs, clearance operations should be curtailed, at least until the PHA gets funds to build for evicted tenants.

2. The primary aim of the urban redevelopment and public housing programs should be to provide new shelter and more shelter than is being removed. Esthetic neighborhood improvement should be a collateral aim. Cities are not improved by ousting the occupants bodily from one neighborhood and jamming them into another. The public housing program should be restored to its main function as a home-producing instrumentality.

3. Both the public housing and urban redevelopment programs

should use much more vacant land for new projects. This is the only practical way for increasing the over-all supply.

4. Before slum-clearance or urban redevelopment projects are approved, a city should be required to produce a master plan that provides for relocation of the families displaced in housing of acceptable standards. Relocation should be handled by public agencies and accurate records kept of the places to which the evicted families move. There has been altogether too much generalization about "satisfactory" relocation being "accomplished" when all that has happened has been a wholesale displacement by intimidation and duress, lures of petty bonuses by the urban redevelopers, threats of ouster, condemnation, or demolition. Those forced to move have been considered "relocated," though driven into less satisfactory or more crowded quarters or herded into makeshifts. Since many of those displaced by the operations have been small homeowners, provision for relocation should include opportunity for home ownership as well as tenancy.

5. FHA, VA, FNMA, and the Home Loan Bank operations should be linked by effective administration to the slum-clearance and redevelopment programs. Urban redevelopment projects should not be approved in areas where builders who enjoy federal aid refuse to offer adequate housing to minorities displaced by such urban redevelopment projects. So, too, federal insurance aid and public housing on vacant sites should be stepped up where displacement is expected.

6. Where homes of minority homeowners are taken by eminent domain, "just compensation" should include an adequate solatium to enable purchase of other homes without out-of-pocket loss occasioned by legal fees, income taxes, and duress prices paid by the minorities. What is "fair compensation" for a white homeowner to whom the market for other dwellings is open may be only fractional compensation to a minority owner to whom the market is closed. Displaced tenants, too, should be compensated for moving expenses and other out-of-pocket losses.

Fifth Aim: *Adequate Land for Housing Open to Minorities.* Appropriation of funds for housing is meaningless when there is no land on which to build. Although there is more than enough building land for everyone in the United States,[23] little good land is available to minorities. Most of it is so far from transportation and utilities that it is unusable. A planned program of land acquisition is necessary. It should encompass 8 distinct steps:

1. Removal of restrictions that keep private land from minorities. Though the law makes buying, leasing, or selling real property a civil right, and racial covenants are unenforceable in the courts, the minorities still cannot buy good sites. Like the hydra of the Lernean marshes cutting off one form of restriction causes two more to sprout. Where practical, cauterization might be effected through legislation banning covenants or other devices which condition the sale or use of private land upon race, religion, or color. The prohibition should cover schemes requiring home-buyers to qualify for membership in a neighborhood "club." Such a law would not prevent the invention of additional exclusion devices but would help clear many titles and remove serious obstacles barring free access to homes. Such legislation should not be viewed as a panacea but as a supplement to other efforts.

2. Land acquisition under urban redevelopment programs. Since Title I of the National Housing Act of 1949 makes four types of land eligible for urban redevelopment (land in slum areas, land in deteriorated areas to be developed for residence, predominantly open but badly platted land, and open land), a new approach to the land-hunger problem is possible. Considerable land acquired under the program may be written down to use-value and resold, thereby enabling minorities to get building land at reasonable prices. Since this land would be acquired by public agencies, disposition could be conditioned upon its use for nondiscriminatory purposes.

3. Expansion of land acquisition under public and publicly aided housing programs. Through an expanded public housing program, housing authorities could acquire more land than they need for their projects, disposing of the excess for private and publicly aided housing operations. If these areas were planned as a unit, they would

[23] The entire population of the United States could be housed at a density of twelve families to the acre within a portion of a single state, or within view of the Pacific Ocean. The area actually occupied by all cities and villages covers only 10 million acres out of a total of 1903 million acres. There are enough empty lots in Chicago to provide for the entire Negro population, and enough in Cook County to care for many times the number in the whole state of Illinois. Though much of it is good, accessible land, the subdivider rarely makes it available to Negroes.

create their own environment, higher cost undertakings could be integrated with those of lower cost, the racial composition of the area would be better stabilized, and neighborhood fears would be dissipated.

4. *Acquisition of municipal reserve land for use of minorities and others.* The policy of accumulating land reserves has long been in effect in European cities. Stockholm owns some 47,000 acres, about half within the city limits. Its peripheral land is used for farming until required for development. Reserve land is also owned by cities in Finland, The Netherlands, Austria, Denmark, and Great Britain. In The Netherlands almost every city with a population of 20,000 or more has a land reserve policy and the book value of this land accounts for more than 12 per cent of the debt of these municipalities.[24] Copenhagen sells land when prices are low, thereby maintaining reasonable land-price levels and assuring an ample supply of acreage. New York State law already provides for this operation, though the power has not been used. A land reserve policy could benefit minorities by providing sites for nondiscriminatory uses during housing shortages. It would also facilitate not only more intelligent planning of transportation, schools, and public works but the coherent planning of whole areas from the start.

5. *Expansion of land beyond city boundaries.* One of the barriers to proper land development is the obsolete boundary line. Often land is entirely developed within city limits and expansion of housing accommodations is impossible. In the absence of some formula for rational expansion to meet growing needs, many cities have become paralyzed. A regional approach is needed. Five devices may be considered: *(a) Incorporation of the surrounding areas into the city.* This is not easily done, particularly where consolidation means higher tax rates and social costs. Nor can politicians in the smaller units be readily expected to surrender their holds. *(b) Intercity and interstate compacts.* These agreements might help rationalize transportation and other jurisdictional obstacles, but official minds are not apt to meet on the question of housing, particularly when the compact entails the housing of minorities. *(c) Granting the city control over land within a*

[24] For further details see Charles Abrams, "Urban Land Problems and Policies," *Urban Land Problems and Policies, Housing and Town and Country Planning, Bulletin No. 7,* New York, United Nations, 1953, pp. 3–58.

designated distance from its borders. The City of London has built a number of housing developments outside its boundaries and a few cities in the United States have similar powers. But political and tax considerations make any extensive program unlikely. *(d) Grant of land-buying powers to state and county authorities.* This could help in cases where the state or county includes jurisdiction over land lying beyond a city's outskirts. *(e) Regional land authorities.* The creation of agencies with power to make land purchases within a prescribed region could accomplish a great deal. Land would be bought, then sold or leased to private or public agencies receiving aid for urban redevelopment or housing. Enabling legislation would of course be needed, and resistance to this can be expected in many quarters.

Because the situation may vary from area to area, each of these schemes must be considered in the light of practicality. But the key to rationalization of land boundaries in all cases is held by the federal government. If the Housing and Home Finance Agency ruled that areas were not eligible for FHA, VA, and urban redevelopment benefits without prior submission of a master plan making sense from a regional and national point of view, coordination between local government units would be spurred. There is, of course, the stock objection that federal intrusion imposes upon local prerogative. The answer is that the boundaries are archaic, unrealistic, costly, and obstruct proper development. Present metropolitan areas, moreover, often cross state lines making rationalization possible only through federal intercession.

Another reason for more positive federal action is that the federal government has acquired the largest financial stake in housing and redevelopment and therefore is concerned with the proper use of funds. This only follows the accepted practice of the Department of Agriculture which conditions rural aid upon compliance with prescribed requirements. No area need cooperate, but if it wanted federal aid it would be obliged to do so. Localities would retain the right to select sites within the approved master plan, make building regulations, and generally retain the main duties and responsibilities for initiating programs within the approved framework. The federal government would concern itself mainly with the integration of plans between areas now hamstrung by conflicting jurisdictional limitations.

6. Acquisition by eminent domain where suitable land cannot be had voluntarily. Because most landowners will not sell to minorities, provision for compulsory acquisition is essential. Far-reaching extension of eminent domain is now authorized by state legislation allowing compulsory acquisition and resale of land to private developers. Acquisition of land by a public authority to facilitate settlement by squatters, subsistence farmers, and others needing land has been upheld.[25] Acquisition even by federal agencies would today be authorized under the broad war powers to decentralize cities and preserve citizens, black and white, from atomic annihilation. Acquiring land for those without living space would be authorized within this general legal framework and would bring into circulation that relatively small but vital portion of land required to meet minority and other housing needs. Not only would landowners receive full compensation but the policy would inure to the benefit of taxpayers as a whole by easing population pressures, checking population flight, stabilizing employment and home ownership, steadying property values, and fulfilling the clear obligations of government to its citizens.

7. New towns. The development of new towns offers another frontier. Unlike "dormitory towns" lying on the fringe of industrial cities, these towns supply within their borders most of the work opportunities, homes, services, and amenities. They afford relief from the congested patterns of the larger cities, tend to siphon off people and economic activities from them, and build coherent self-supporting units. The idea received impetus from the earlier garden cities movement.

In the United States, new towns have been built in connection with dam developments such as the Tennessee Valley Authority and Boulder City. During and after World War II, several new towns were built including the atomic energy towns of Oak Ridge, Tennessee, Los Alamos, N. M., and Hanford, Washington. But federal policy has countenanced and encouraged segregation. Oak Ridge's 2000 Negroes live in a segregated area, and schools are segregated as well. Before

---

[25] *People of Puerto Rico v. Eastern Sugar Associates,* 156 F. 2d 316, cert. den. 329 U.S. 772 (1946); see also Ira S. Robbins and Marian P. Yankauer, "Eminent Domain in Acquiring Subdivision and Open Land in Redevelopment Programs: A Question of Public Use," *Urban Redevelopment Problems and Practices* (Coleman Woodbury, ed.). Chicago, University of Chicago Press, 1953, pp. 463-513.

a separate high school was built for them, Negro children had to travel 25 miles to Knoxville to attend classes.[26]

The new role of government in housing, city development, and defense makes planning of new towns feasible. But, the enslavement of planning concepts to homogeneity and the failure to integrate groups into a workable social pattern are two obstacles which should be faced and overcome. If Negroes and other minorities were accepted from the start, there would be no trouble. In Levittown, N. Y., nearly all owners concede this, and a typical comment is "I'll admit it wouldn't have made a damn bit of difference to me originally."[27]

Public housing projects within the old cities have demonstrated that racial integration can work.

Sixth Aim: *Adequate Financing.* Mortgage funds are of course a primary factor. The private mortgage agencies cannot be relied on to meet any great portion of the need. New federal financing sources must be set up until private money shows more enthusiasm. Moreover, low interest rates and long-term amortization are essential due to the lower incomes of a large portion of the minority groups.

Loans would be made at various rates of interest, and for those in the lowest income groups, rates might vary from zero to the going government rate. Simultaneously, the Federal National Mortgage Association should make more of its direct loan facilities available to cooperatives with open occupancy policies. FHA should also encourage formation of "Approved Mortgagees" who would lend directly to borrowers able to pay the market rates. These agencies now function within limited jurisdictions prescribed by FHA mostly to place FHA-insured mortgages for whites or resell mortgage paper to lenders. They should be set up on a nationwide basis to help finance housing open to minorities. Lenders have said that the reason they make few or no loans for minority housing is that they are inexperienced in dealing with minority families, and that satisfactory servicing facilities do not exist. Setting up local servicing facilities through these approved mortgagees would help meet their objections. Approved mortgagees would each require an initial capital of at least $5 million to achieve

---

[26] The New York *Times,* December 23, 1953.

[27] Harry Henderson, "Rugged American Collectivism," *Harper's Magazine,* December, 1953, p. 85.

volume operations, and subscriptions by the federal government would be necessary at least at the start. As the agency became self-supporting the stock purchased by the federal government could be retired. At the same time, the government might encourage local banks and loan associations to service loans made at the low federal rates.

Federal aid would of course not preclude states from making loans for nondiscriminatory housing. Loans for middle-income housing are authorized by the New York State constitution, and state credit has already been used in other states, including Pennsylvania, Connecticut, and Massachusetts.[28] New York City also has a public housing program for middle-income families with rents of about $16 monthly per room. Housing is rented to whites and Negroes and the projects are well integrated and successful. Connecticut's program, initiated by former Governor Chester A. Bowles, provides low-interest loans for private builders. The state borrows the funds at short-term rate and lends them at a somewhat higher rate than cost. The houses are sold to individual buyers, and Negroes as well as whites have benefited. In New York City and Connecticut the feasibility of integrated projects has been proved, but the quantitative need is still far from met.

Although a few savings and loan associations make loans for minority housing, their operations are minor. Establishing lending associations to serve this specific purpose would help. Stock would have to be purchased at first by the federal government and held until it could be retired. Liberal facilities for discounting mortgages through the Home Loan Bank System would be desirable.

Building and loan associations should be set up with power not only to accept savings and make loans but to build housing, as they were originally meant to do. Resumption of building by these agencies would be a healthy development and would help minorities in particular.

Seventh Aim: *An Effective Program for the Repair and Improvement of Existing Housing and Maintenance of Adequate Occupancy Standards.* Repair of existing housing is no remedy in itself. But the fact remains that the current supply will be the main source of

[28] Harold Robinson and John I. Robinson, "State Aid for Housing," *Wisconsin Law Review,* May, 1949.

shelter for minorities for a long time to come. A good portion of these dwellings could be salvaged and improved.

One of the best known efforts is the so-called "Baltimore Plan," a well-meant attempt to get better law enforcement through a coordination of health, housing, sanitation, building, and fire and zoning agencies on a block-by-block basis, with violation orders enforced through a special housing court. As a limited effort, and as a supplement to a new housing program, it was good enough. But real estate interests adopted it as a cure-all for housing problems, touted its virtues throughout the land, and embarrassed its sponsors who found themselves holding a bull—an ordinary bull sold as a prize bull—by the tail. The plan became known as a substitute for new public housing.

A single block was fixed up as an example. Then a thousand houses, most of them in fair structural condition, were selected in a 27-block area. Filth and trash were removed, laws enforced. The latter venture took two years and ended some of the more flagrant violations. But the old row and street patterns, the nonconforming uses, the need for more play space, schools, and better planning remained. Businessmen in Baltimore arranged a "Fight Blight Fund" and some commercial loans for owners were made as a demonstration. The demonstration added up to no more than that; in fact it pointed up absence of funds for repair as a main problem.

The plan has brought greater inspiration and efficiency to law enforcement. It has worked best in houses and neighborhoods that were structurally sound, and showed once again that the worst slums can be more cheaply razed and replaced than renovated. The plan has demonstrated that rehabilitation, law enforcement, and education can do a small part of the over-all job—and no more than that. Rehabilitation belongs in any housing program, particularly during a shortage. The requirements for a rehabilitation campaign, however, are:

1. A sound enforcement agency. There are too many overlapping units in large cities with conflicting inspections made by building, health, fire, and other departments. Inspection and violation functions should be under a central agency.

2. Planned rehabilitation. Since piecemeal rehabilitation may defeat sectional replanning and make public housing or urban redevelopment too costly, the city's master plan should indicate which houses in an area are worth saving and which are not. A neighborhood of structurally sound houses which cannot be rehabilitated under individual ownership could be acquired by eminent domain. The worst houses would be torn down, others repaired, space and air opened, streets replanned, park space and other amenities supplied. The property could then be either rented or resold. A relocation program should take care of the tenants to be displaced. A public agency should be authorized to do the acquiring and actual rehabilitation where it involves a large-scale effort.

One of the pitfalls in a rehabilitation program is that frequently the cost of rehabilitation exceeds the cost of new construction.[29] Cost should be carefully considered in any plan. Too often the result may be hardly worth the expenditure. Where substantial rehabilitation is effected, moreover, the new rents are far higher than the old residents can afford.

3. Sound enabling legislation.   Bringing an owner to court for failure to repair is usually a tedious process. Many owners cannot afford to make improvements; others pay fines rather than comply; still others are from the minority groups themselves operating on a shoestring. Frequently properties are sold during the proceedings, compelling the city to track down the new owners or start over again. No city has enough inspectors to check bad housing and keep after the owners. Finally, the owner may threaten to close up his building rather than comply, and that might make the occupants homeless.

In 1937, New York City sought to overcome these obstacles by assuming power to make repairs where the owner refused. Since most properties were heavily mortgaged, the city made its outlay a prior lien on the property, collectable as an assessment. The original bill, as prepared by the housing authority, provided ample notice to the mortgagee and granted him an opportunity to demand compliance by the owner before the city did any work. Unfortunately, Mayor Fiorello H. LaGuardia, in a careless moment, struck out the notice and protective provisions as surplusage and the bill was subsequently held unconstitutional.[30]

A properly drawn bill would probably be upheld. It would be a

[29] *Housing Shortage Investigation.* Report by New York City Housing Authority, January 25, 1937.
[30] *Central Savings Bank v. City of New York,* 279 N.Y. 266 (1938).

much-needed spur to law enforcement and neighborhood rehabilitation. It would not be unfair to owner or mortgagee, for the property would benefit from the repair and compliance with the law. To aid the owner, repayment of the outlay might be allowed in installments over a ten-year period.

4. Adequate financing.   Funds should be appropriated to finance minor and major repairs, sectional rehabilitation, purchase of homes that should be torn down, and public improvements to round out a neighborhood improvement. Federal loans would be needed to supplement aids by the city and state. Improvements would be encouraged by coordinating financing with law enforcement, preferably through a single local agency.

5. Occupancy standards.   A major obstacle to rehabilitation is the occupancy of existing one-family houses by two and three families with some rooms occupied by as many as ten persons. Cooking may be done on a coal or oil stove by several families, with no provision for fire retarding or safety. In other cases, cellars and sub-cellars are used for living purposes. Illegal occupancy is often winked at or even legalized by the public authority. The choice lies between evicting the occupants or tolerating conditions dangerous to life and health. No absolute rule can or should be made. In some cases the fire hazards are so serious that certain eviction is preferable to likely incineration.

The break-up of good houses in sound neighborhoods into cubbyholes that prevent future restoration can and should be stopped. Proper codes can prescribe the number of persons allowed in a given space, prevent good homes from being turned into hot-bed dormitories, and establish adequate safety requirements. When houses are rehabilitated with public funds, similar requirements should be laid down.

The difficulties underline the fact that there is no easy solution for overcrowding. Rehabilitation is a limited and all too often a stop-gap remedy. The only real solution is a comprehensive housing program that will sharply increase the supply for all groups.

Eighth Aim: *Housing for Migratory Labor.*   The mounting number of transient migrants roving from one area to another are the great unclaimed—neither claimed by the community, nor claiming it. "As crops ripen, farmers anxiously await their coming; as the harvest closes, the community, with equal anxiety, awaits their going."[31]

Housing for most farm labor is crudely substandard. The program authorized by the Housing Act of 1949 was little more than a token, and a large-scale effort has been long overdue. But the worst conditions are those of the million migratory workers whose camps, barracks, tents, trailers, and shacks have been officially described as "the most deplorable in the Nation."[32] "Good" housing for a family of four to six persons is an unpainted cabin, 9' x 12', usually without running water. But most shelter is "bad," and for Wetbacks there may be no housing at all.

Housing and job are part of a package. The unorganized workers hundreds of miles from their homes in the South or Southwest are in no position to bargain. Proper inspection and regulation are responsibilities avoided by the states and opposed by most employers.

Since migrants are not considered year-round residents, local housing authorities are not inspired to spend their limited funds on them. But when minimum housing was supplied by the few Farm Security Administration projects, many of the migrants found permanent work and became year-round residents. Housing and absorption into a community are essentials if horizontal mobility is to become socially and economically vertical.

Proper schooling and a decent family life cannot be created in a transient life pattern. Absorption into the community's economy is the only satisfactory solution. This objective would of course require a new approach to the rural migration as well as the Wetback problem, with priority for work extended to citizen or resident labor. But conditions could be materially improved until a long-range program is devised. Health services, child and adult guidance programs, and recreation facilities would make a big difference. So would government action to provide decent shelter. Minimum wages should be paid, particularly for the benefit of migrant citizen-labor which cannot now compete with alien and illegal labor working for a pittance.

Various reforms have been advocated by the President's Commission on Migratory Labor,[33] but not even the surface of the problem has been scratched. The U. S. Employment Service should condition

[31] *Migratory Labor in American Agriculture:* Report of the President's Commission on Migratory Labor. Washington, U.S. Printing Office, 1951, p. 13.
[32] *Ibid,* p. 144.
[33] *Ibid.*

recruitment and referral of agricultural labor and the Immigration Service should condition importation of foreign workers upon the provision of housing of minimum standard. Properly constituted state agencies should enforce standards conforming to federally prescribed minima. Adequate camps should be built for seasonal workers with the aid of federal subsidies. County housing authorities should help do the job and where these are nonexistent, a federal building program should be instituted. Camp sites should have basic facilities for water, showers, sanitation, laundry, cooking, and recreation.

The Department of Agriculture, with the aid of the Housing and Home Finance Agency, can extend credit to enable migratory workers to build permanent homes in areas where workers are needed. Public housing should be built through an adequate rural nonfarm program to shelter migrants at their home bases. Above all, an attitude and a policy are needed under which these workers will be viewed as a part of the nation and of the communities in which they choose to settle.

Ninth Aim: *Local, State, and Federal Racial Commissions.* Racial commissions can do much or little, depending on the caliber of the membership and the support they receive. In 1953, Philadelphia's commission, under George Schermer, supplied an example of the best, while New York City afforded an example of one that hardly functions. Fortunately for New York, civic and racial organizations do much of the work.

The racial commission is still in swaddling clothes. Appropriations are small, techniques undeveloped, employees few, and experienced staff executives rare. The well-meaning citizens who sit on the commissions are frequently required by political pressures to hold down minority protests instead of holding up minority rights.

With minorities pouring into cities by the millions and older residents pouring out, a local agency's jurisdiction is limited to the boundary of the city when the problem may be complicated by the exclusion practices of an adjoining suburb. A state commission would be able to deal with these cases, particularly because it would be further removed from local pressures.

A successful local commission must have an adequate staff, adequate appropriations, adequate authority, and freedom from political influence. Both state and local commissions should have power to investigate and hold hearings on racial problems not only in housing but also in employment, recreation, education, and civil rights. They should be able to cope with tensions, as when minorities move into public housing projects. To improve group relations, they should educate the public in racial integration and recruit the support of influential citizens. Misuses of power by public officials should be scrutinized. Pressure should be directed against discriminators, and civil rights cases should be supported in the courts. Establishing and maintaining the high moral level of communities is paramount.

Because the maintenance of civil rights is the concern of all three levels of government, a federal commission is also needed. It should impose affirmative responsibility for improving racial understanding on the federal government and its agencies. It should work closely with racial relations services of the various federal departments, help disseminate information among federal agencies, and keep local and state racial commissions abreast of research and effective techniques. It should intervene in areas of tension and recommend intercession by appropriate federal agencies where needed. The federal commission should study various aspects of racial problems, as did the President's Committee on Civil Rights, but as a continuing function.

In short, the federal commission should raise the sights of federal agencies to the level of constitutional ethics. The agencies must be taught color-blindness and educated in the differences between public and private responsibility.

Tenth Aim: *A More Effective Federal Civil Rights Section.* The Civil Rights Section of the Attorney General's office should be made a more effective arm of the federal government. The section occasionally prosecutes sheriffs, policemen, or local judges who misuse their power. But enforcement occurs only in the most flagrant cases and wavers with the interest of the particular Attorney General. An alert, impartial interest can hardly be expected from an Attorney General appointed for his political contributions to the Presidency, and one who has recently emerged from a campaign ridden with political compromises and deals. Nor has the racial section ever been properly supported by Congress or been adequately helped by the Federal Bureau of Investigation. Yet there has never been a time when perversion of official power has played a more prominent part in the subversion of minority rights. The failure of the Civil Rights Section to intervene in the long series of riots in Chicago's Trumbull Park housing project is inexcusable. Its firm intervention would blast the position of bigots who use the currently popular Communist issue as a pretext for inspiring race hate, violence, and arson.

Constitutional compliance would be better assured by a separate, well-staffed, well-supported civil rights division alert to violations of minority rights by local officials and cooperating closely with a federal racial commission and the various racial relations services.

A budget commensurate with its responsibilities is imperative. The section should have full division status in the Department of Justice, with regional offices set up, as recommended by President Truman's Committee on Civil Rights. The regional officers should have the status of assistant U.S. attorneys to avoid their becoming political subordinates of the local U.S. attorneys. Their staffs should be part of a well-trained special unit of investigators. Investigation of infringements should be initiated by the division itself without waiting for complaints or actual violence.

If simultaneously a standing committee of Congress were set up to provide a medium for consideration of proposed legislation, Congress would be enabled to keep in touch with violations of minority rights, give continued study to the subject, and become expert in legislative needs.[34]

Prosecutions by the Attorney General of conspiracies to violate civil rights laws should be pressed more effectively. Real estate boards, banks, and loan associations which boycott minorities should be brought before the bar by civil or criminal proceedings.

Prosecution for conspiracy to violate the anti-trust laws presents an important ground on which to break up the various devices which have succeeded the racial covenant. Real estate operations are thought to be local and therefore beyond the scope of interstate commerce. But there are many aspects of real estate and building operations today which enter the interstate sphere. Examples are: the acceptance by Congress of housing as a national problem; the interstate nature of large building operations; the interstate aspect of local jurisdictional

[34] *To Secure These Rights.* Washington, U.S. Government Printing Office, 1947, p. 155.

boundaries and exclusion practices; the interstate migrations of millions of members of minority groups; the restraints on home financing by large institutional lenders operating between states; the nation-wide influence and operation of the National Association of Real Estate Boards, the home-building lobby, the United States Savings and Loan League, and other private agencies using federal aid; the impact of artificially limited construction activity on the minority group, and the importance of minority labor to the national economy and national defense. All these factors point to the need for a new approach by the Attorney General. Federal action should of course be supplemented by damage suits by injured individuals and by prosecutions under state anti-trust statutes where possible.[35]

Eleventh Aim: *Expansion of Racial Relations Services in Housing and other Related Departments.* The federal Racial Relations Service in the Housing and Home Finance Agency has been one of the most promising aspects of government policy to date. A special assistant to the administrator helps formulate and execute basic policies and procedures to assure a more equitable participation of minority groups in all phases of the housing program. He sits in at staff meetings and his specialized staff, carefully built up ever since Nathan Straus introduced the service in the U.S. Housing Authority, has helped evaluate operations, implemented a nondiscriminatory employment policy in housing, assembled and disseminated experience on the housing of minorities, and in general tried to reflect the minority point of view to agency personnel.[36]

In field offices the service's personnel analyzes the local market; reviews selection of sites to prevent unjust ouster of minorities; evaluates employment practices in federally aided projects; assists in the relocation of families displaced by slum clearance and urban redevelopment; advises with local officials, builders, and community leaders on racial problems connected with the program; tries to achieve revisions of agency policies and procedures; anticipates racial con-

[35] See unpublished brief of Peter Weiss, *Anti-Trust Action against Discrimination in Housing.* Yale Law School, New Haven, February, 1952; Melvin Stein, "Application of the Sherman Act to Housing Segregation, *Yale Law Journal,* June, 1954.

[36] *The Role of the Racial Relations Service in the Administration of Housing Programs of the Federal Government.* Washington, HHFA, December, 1952 (mimeographed).

flicts, and helps overcome obstacles to an equitable distribution of housing.

As a result of its selection of top-flight men, the service has developed an extensive body of knowledge and techniques on minority problems and racial integration. FHA, beset by the influence of realtors, has occasionally had to call on its racial relations experts for advice. So have the Urban Redevelopment Division, and other housing agencies. Even in the South, local housing officials are relying upon the HHFA service for guidance while some knowledgable private builders are turning to it as well.

Unfortunately, political pressures intervene too often to keep the service from doing its proper job. These political pressures intervened in 1953 when an effort was made to replace Frank S. Horne, the service's pioneer director, with a political appointee. Thereafter important members of his staff were harried by baseless charges. If the service is to do its job properly, the following are imperatives. It should have:

1. A professional staff free from political pressures;
2. Assurance of continuity in operations;
3. An unequivocal policy giving all racial groups equitable participation in publicly aided housing programs;
4. A service which can operate as an integrated part of the top administrative office of the Housing and Home Finance Agency, with participation in staff discussions when policies are formulated, and with access to field reports which evaluate all agency operations affecting racial relations;
5. Field representatives empowered to work with housing officials in the field and to appraise and advise on operations at the local scene;
6. Freedom to work closely with national and local industry, civic and consumer organizations;
7. Sufficient funds for doing a good job.

The Racial Relations Service has made a creditable demonstration of what could be done if there is a will to do it. But there is always the temptation by federal office-holders to avoid the tougher aspects of minority problems, to let local biases take their course, and to yield to the pressures of builders and discriminating local officials.

The service needs expansion and reinforcement, not contraction.

Above all, the formula should be extended to other branches of government so that a professional instead of a partisan approach can be made in all the social, economic, and political areas where race and minority issues arise.

Twelfth Aim: *Planned Integration of Minorities into Neighborhoods*. Techniques for integrating racial, religious, or ethnic groups into neighborhoods will vary with a city's composition, its size, its particular patterns of minority distribution, its public attitudes, and the nature of the public leadership. In no case ought there be a policy —direct or indirect—which restrains an individual's choice of living space or the free movement of populations. A minority family may wish to live with its own group or live outside it. The choice is its own and it must be a free choice. Within a free market, integration policies can be evolved which might help reverse the current trend toward segregation and race friction.

In general, cities fall into the following categories:

1. Southern cities with large minority aggregations. Patterns vary. There are neighborhoods in which the Negro population is substantial and those where they are smaller. Patterns of distribution differ too, including those with Negro populations distributed throughout the city and those with small scatterings. In still other cases segregated groupings may be found.

Because the South is popularly the main focus of social discrimination there is much misunderstanding about southern attitudes and policies in housing. Discrimination in housing is not solely segregation. The principal forms of housing discrimination include: (1) providing no private or FHA-aided housing; (2) providing no public housing; (3) displacing minorities from housing they now occupy; (4) enforcing segregation in housing. Providing no housing (as is the case under the FHA program) is the most flagrant and most serious aspect of discrimination.

The South is far out in front in providing public housing for its nonwhites. Its neighborhood patterns in the private sectors are often mixed rather than segregated. Though private housing for Negroes is small proportionately, Negro builders are more active and some are large-scale operators. There is segregation in public housing as there is in many parts of the North, but the displacement through demolition is no worse than elsewhere. There is also a greater feeling of citizen responsibility for housing in the South than there is in the North.

This is not to underestimate the dangers: urban redevelopment, public housing, and public works may be increasingly employed as devices for separating the races and thereby achieving in practice the school segregation which the courts have now proscribed. But it is also true that with proper handling of the problem considerable gains may be attained. The basic principles arrived at on December 13, 1946, by a committee of southern and northern housing officials headed by Catherine Bauer Wurster[37] still represents a constructive approach, i.e., more land and living area available to minorities, enough houses fairly distributed, maximum progress toward non-segregation, balanced neighborhoods rather than geographical standardization by class or race. That these principles could be adopted is an indication of how progress can be achieved through statesmanship.

In general, where Negroes live in the same areas with whites the patterns should not be disturbed by superimposing a homogeneous federally aided development. There should be no retreat from gains already made. The practice of rooting out Negroes from their established sections, disrupting their associations and institutions, and confining them to isolated districts is bound to prove troublesome in the long run. Where, because of long-standing regional biases, communities insist upon segregating Negroes within public housing projects, the segregation within a single neighborhood while undesirable is less harmful than complete isolation in separate districts. It might at least permit use of the same schools, institutions, and facilities.

In southern areas where neighborhood segregation already exists, inclusion of Negro families in all new project areas can be effected if done strategically by qualified people. Proximity has proved to have healing qualities. It is best that leadership be enlisted from the South itself where an enlightened interest has frequently been demonstrated, and that compulsive measures be sought only after other

[37] "Race Relations in Housing Policy: Basic Principles and Program," National Public Housing Conference, Committee on Race Relations, Catherine Bauer (Wurster), chairman, Washington, February 24, 1947 (mimeographed).

means have failed. Those measures when taken should have nation-wide application and northern as well as southern discrimination embraced.

2. Cities with a small minority population which is widely distributed. Minneapolis is an example. Here the Negro population is less than 2 per cent and distributed throughout the city. This is a healthy pattern and should remain that way. FHA and VA should not encourage housing projects which disrupt it. Suburban development should follow a similar pattern; urban redevelopment or slum-clearance projects should not aim to oust the minority or force it into ghettos elsewhere. Where areas are cleared, the new projects should aim to include the mixed groupings already within the rebuilt sections. Where the Negro population is about 5 per cent, as in Cambridge, Massachusetts, segregation of minorities in public or in private housing is unnecessary. In such a city, the two large universities can assume a primary educational role. They might, for example, refuse to recommend living places for students where the owners discriminate against Negroes or Orientals.

3. Cities with a small but isolated minority population. In areas where the minority population is small, no valid reason exists for enforced segregation. Opening more areas to the minority would distribute the small population into other sections of the city and ease pressures upon existing sections should the minority population expand.

4. Cities with no minority population or with only a token representation. Such cities include those with compulsory exclusion practices such as Dearborn, Michigan, Cicero and Berwyn, Illinois, and the two Levittowns. In all such areas, as previously noted, it would have been simpler to include minorities from the very beginning, for it is more difficult to effect integration when all the dwellings are occupied and the all-white pattern "built-in." It is difficult for the existing residents as well as for the first minorities who are later admitted. It has been accomplished successfully, however, in a number of large public projects despite the obstacles.[38]

[38] Edward Rutledge, *Integration of Racial Minorities in Public Housing Projects: A Guide for Local Housing Authorities on How to Do It.* Washington, Public Housing Administration (mimeographed), May, 1951; *Open Occupancy in Public Housing.* Public Housing Administration, Housing and Home Finance Agency, Washington, 1953.

A planned program of education should be launched under the auspices of a sympathetic leadership carefully developed within the area. Fears of a mass influx or of a decline in values should be met by circulating relevant information. Cooperation of FHA and state and city officials is essential, and where a city bans minorities, federal housing agencies should withhold federal benefits. Illegal subletting to minorities surreptitiously undertaken to break down exclusion may often lose public sympathy for a just cause. Emphasis should be placed upon the unethical aspects of exclusion and a well-timed campaign worked out in collaboration with national organizations.

5. *Cities with a large proportion* (*upwards of 15 per cent*) *concentrated in one or a number of sections.* Baltimore, Cleveland, and Philadelphia are examples. In Philadelphia, where Negroes represent 22 per cent of the population, the program is being partly met by Negro movements into a wider number of in-lying areas. But this alone is no solution, for new subdivisions and more open land must be made available to these families so that pressure upon central areas can be eased. A regional approach to their housing problem is indispensable. FHA and HHFA should take steps to make housing available throughout the area. The same approach should be taken in Baltimore and Cleveland.

New York City's problems are in many respects more difficult than those of other cities. Its large Negro population is concentrated in a few areas, notably Central and East Harlem, the Bedford-Stuyvesant section of Brooklyn, the lower Bronx, and scatterings in other sections. Simultaneously, its Puerto Rican influx has put a heavy burden on its housing, while accessible land for building is becoming scarce.

Despite the handicaps, its housing policy has been exemplary and its tolerance level high. Some of its public housing projects in the established Negro areas are virtually all-Negro, but there is not a single project where Negroes are not substantially represented, including those located in all-white areas. Cooperative and urban redevelopment projects are following the principle of mixed occupancy —the old bogies that the whites would flee or that the section would inevitably go down in value have disappeared. Though some minorities have moved toward outlying areas, the freedom to move is, as in other cities, limited.

New York City's main problem, however, is not solely one of housing but is involved with the whole social and economic problem of Puerto Rico. Inadequate attention is given to this subject by its understaffed racial commission while its city officials "study the problem" by making periodic junkets to the island for a week or two. Not only is a new look at the migration required by the Puerto Rican government but by the American government as well.

Puerto Ricans deserve to be treated as part of the American labor pool and accorded its protections. They should enjoy equal participation in industrial employment and at least equality with, if not preference over, alien labor in agriculture. The U.S. Employment Service, instead of subordinating opportunities of Puerto Ricans, should encourage the hiring of this citizen labor throughout the country.

Puerto Ricans should be free to compete for rural labor without waiting upon certification by state officials. The United States government must assume the same responsibility for its Puerto Rican citizens as for those on the mainland. Both the United States and the Commonwealth should undertake a national survey of labor opportunities and train migration leaders to conduct groups of settlers to promising areas. The practice of waiting for actual job offerings to turn up before Puerto Rican labor is dispatched to the area should be modified to encourage settlement wherever there are fair probabilities of future jobs or the prospect of labor turnover.

Settlement groups in outlying areas should include both men and women. The current practice of omitting provisions for family life and permanent settlement is shortsighted and unrealistic. A survey should be made of the number of Puerto Ricans compelled to return to the island, the reasons ascertained, the facts stated. An educational campaign in Puerto Rico should present those facts to the Islanders and encourage them to migrate where work is available. Airlanes from Puerto Rico to as many large cities as possible should be opened at reasonable rates. More intensive education in the English langauge would facilitate settlement and assimilation.

All these measures will do little unless we are prepared to see the Puerto Rican problem as a problem and discuss it candidly, not merely in terms of political or sectional considerations but with a higher regard for the human values involved. The main objective should be not less migration from Puerto Rico but more. It should be directed not only toward New York City but to every area of opportunity throughout the country.

It is difficult of course to lay down uniform formulas for all cities. Much will depend on how far the local citizenry is prepared for the task and how much headway fears and rumors have already made in shaping attitudes. Firm policy, frank disclosure, sound public relations, support of the local press and of public interest groups, and a wholehearted interest in the program are important factors.

Integration cannot be achieved overnight. It is particularly difficult during a housing shortage. But it is remarkable how a single successful venture sparks widespread interest, inspires further examples, and in a relatively short time becomes the accepted pattern in a widening number of areas.

Less than 20 years ago, integration in public housing projects was thought impossible. Today it is a fact in hundreds of projects throughout the country. It was unthinkable in private projects. Today it is being accepted as workable in a growing number. False fears can be dissipated as quickly as they were aroused by proving them false and restoring neighborhood confidence.

In 1940, when a housing policy that might have been culled from Hitler's Nuremberg Laws was the government's formula for the nation's neighborhoods, the prospects for fulfilling a program such as the one outlined would have appeared hopeless. But the succeeding years have demonstrated the powerful reserves that underlie the American system and the irrepressible forces at work here for a leveling of social and economic differences.

The expanding economy with its demand for labor and the private enterprise system with its continued emphasis on profit and skill rather than color or caste have both continued to favor minorities. As in Lincoln's day, the penniless beginner is still able to enter the stream of labor and begin his upward move on the economic scale under a system that gives hope to all, and consequent energy and progress and improvement of condition to all.

Opportunities once available to the newcomer from Europe are now being grasped by the newer migrants. There are more Negroes today who are foremen and clerical, professional, and technical workers than ever before. Nonwhite average income has trebled since 1940 and while wage levels are still far below average, the prospects for equalization in the long run are favorable.

Simultaneously, strong social forces are working toward a social equalization. Though the color problem makes assimilation more difficult, it is not insurmountable particularly where equal opportunities are extended. Though schools are often segregated, Negro college enrollment by 1950 was up 2500 per cent over 1930, with more than 132,000 Negroes enrolled in colleges and universities.

The breakdown of segregation in the armed forces, its diminution in transportation facilities, in northern restaurants, hotels, and in the nation's capital are also helping to reduce social barriers. Decisions of the Supreme Court and statements by Presidents Roosevelt, Truman, and Eisenhower on racial equality, though not translated into neighborhood equality have helped to shore up the general level of morality. America's international role has influenced incorporation of democratic principles into charters and pronouncements and is keeping these principles in the foreground.

The important gains won in social and economic areas are being matched in the political sphere. With expansion of federal activities, minorities have been alerted to the danger that invasion of one minority's rights may mean invasion of another's, bringing a greater solidarity of effort. Minority concentrations have increased the political influence of minorities—the South had more than a million registered voters in the 1950's compared to 300,000 in 1938. In a growing number of areas, discrimination is now viewed as a political liability. The strength of the minorities in the cities has been demonstrated by the number of statutes outlawing racial discrimination in public places and by the state or local laws banning discrimination in employment. In a number of states racial segregation or discrimination in public housing and urban redevelopment is banned as well.

In the South, the Negro's northward move has been accompanied by a growing enlightenment among southern leaders. It is best illustrated in the improvement of educational facilities—in 1910 there were 42 public high schools for Negroes; by 1950 there were 2500.[39] Whites and Negroes are working side by side more than ever. Southern legislators have been among the leading advocates of public hous-

[39] See Harry S. Ashmore, *The Negro and the Schools*. Chapel Hill, University of North Carolina Press, 1954.

ing, and though the new housing is segregated, it is a step toward improving living conditions and effecting social rapprochement.

Despite the political, social, and economic obstacles which have long kept Negro citizens from moving toward the areas of economic opportunity, their move has now been ventured, the initial challenges made, the footholds established from which they cannot be easily displaced. The improved economic and social conditions of minorities must sooner or later exert themselves in an effective demand for better living conditions in neighborhoods as well. Even FHA now recognizes this.

Yet there is an element in the situation which not only menaces the gains in other areas but threatens the democratic structure which has made them possible. The right of a family to shelter is now more than ever a function of government and the entrepreneur has become dependent upon its decisions, policies, loans, and subsidies. Government policies, moreover, are made in response to majority pressures and the majority may not always be ready to subordinate its own interests in a neighborhood to those of the minority. Already minorities are being brought into conflict with local majorities upon whose whims the right to live where one chooses depends. No longer price or the profit motive controls the choice of a place to live, but the decisions of local homeowners, local police, local housing officials. With the vast expansion of federal aid in housing, one of the crucial issues is whether the federal government will tacitly support or actively oppose local oppressions; whether it will assume its guiding role in the emerging ethical contest or conceal itself behind the screen of local autonomy; whether it will continue to permit social reforms and new political devices to become perverted into new instruments for effecting discrimination.

As long as housing discrimination prevails, fundamental rights will be violated—the right to a home, to work, to privacy, to temporary shelter, to the equal protection and privileges of the laws, to due process, to freedom from fear, to security in one's home and possessions. The right to move, the right to leisure, recreation, life, and health will all be impaired as long as racial laws limit free movement. However the courts may strike at segregation in schools, such segregation will continue when there is segregation in neighborhoods—in fact the latter may even become the new vehicle for achieving indirectly the school segregation which the courts have outlawed directly. The right to freedom from fear and to security in one's possessions does not exist as long as minorities are burned out of their homes by mobs or confined to ghettos by law.

In every part of the world there is emerging a similarity of symptoms affecting neighborhoods—slums, migration of the underprivileged to the cities, overcrowding, a growing disparity between wages and rents, squatting, social disruption of family life, and increasing insecurity of tenure. The most recent phase of the industrial revolution is marked by a movement of nonwhites in Asia, Africa, America, and even in some parts of Europe. Simultaneously there has appeared an increasing emphasis upon discrimination and homogeneity in neighborhoods. These symptoms are exhibiting themselves in developed and in underdeveloped countries alike. To meet problems of industrialization and housing famine, an extensive expansion has also occurred in the role of government. With housing one of the key issues on the world's political stage, there are forces working toward a democratic dispensation of the benefits of public power and subsidies. But with a rising fear of people from the hinterlands who are different, other forces are simultaneously seeking to harness public power on the side of segregation and racial, social, or religious discrimination. Even a country as liberal as England is being pressed toward an exclusion policy because no more than 70,000 nonwhites had immigrated from its colonies in recent years.

America has often been singled out for blame on the race issue and there has been little disposition to concede that discrimination today exists not there alone but wherever the challenge of race and color is making itself felt. That the United States has functioned for more than 150 years as the haven for the oppressed from countries everywhere is overlooked and that it has made remarkable strides, against great odds, toward extending equal privileges to its alien and non-white citizens is forgotten.

If, therefore, America can demonstrate that under its new welfare economy the lengthening arm of government will now be employed to secure a decent family life in neighborhoods which afford equal access to all regardless of race, creed, or color, that demonstration will circuit the world as once did its proclamation of freedom, right, and justice. It will awaken all minorities who now suspect the West to a new faith in the democratic principle. It will demonstrate that freedom of opportunity can be secured in American urban frontiers as it was secured on its rural frontier—for the darker people as it was for the lighter people. The world is ripe for such a demonstration and there are real signs that America is posed to make it.

INDEX

Chein, Isidor, 283 fn.
Chicago, 21, 103 ff., 182 ff., 188 ff.
  Negroes, 21
  neighborhood associations, 183 f.,
    188 f.
  violence, 103 ff., 182
Chicago Citizens Association, 114
Chicago City Council, 112
Chicago Commission on Human Re-
  lations, 111, 116 f., 186 fn., 189
Chicago Commission on Race Rela-
  tions, 21 fn., 182 fn.
Chicago Council Against Racial and
  Religious Discrimination, 106,
    107 fn.
Chicago Housing Authority, 110 f.,
  118, 315
Chicago *Sun-Times,* 114
Chicago *Tribune,* 114
Chickasaw, Ala., 101, 256
Chinatown, 34, 35, 287
  San Francisco, 34, 287
  New York, 35
Chinese, 11, 29 ff., 267, 287
  and property values, 287
  demonstration against, 31 f.
  sentiment against, 11, 30 ff.
  stereotype, 267
  violence against, 31
Churchill, Winston, 192
Cicero, Ill., 102 ff., 382
  anti-Negro violence, 102 ff.
CIO, *see* Congress of Industrial Or-
  ganizations
Cities, minority problems of, 380 ff.
City College of New York, xi
City planning, 212 ff.
Civic associations, 110, 336 ff.
Civic Unity Council, 271
Civil rights, enforcement of, 376 ff.
Civil rights acts, 5, 157, 206, 297,
  298
Civil Rights Bill of 1875, 20
Civil Rights Law of 1866, 105
Civil rights laws, 191
Civil War, 4, 293
Clark, Harvey E., Jr., 103 ff., 267
Clark, K. B., 284 fn.
Clark, Tom C., 220 fn.
Class structure, 164 ff.
Clein, Ervin, 124
Cleveland, Ohio, 172, 383
"Clinton Court," 23
Closed city, 9, 101 f.
Club, the, 179 f.
Club membership requirement, 224
Cobo, Albert, 97 f., 99

"Code of Ethics," 156, 157
Cohen, Elliot, 334 fn.
Cohen, Morris R., 355
Cole, Albert M., 172, 242, 251, 344,
  345, 348 fn.
Collins, C. W., 294 fn.
Collins, Mary Evans, 316 fn., 322 fn.
Colonialism, 55
Columbians, 85
Columbus, Ohio, 20 f.
Commentary, xi, 337
Committee on Slum Clearance Plans
  (New York City), 248 fn.
Communication media, 333 f.
Communist issue and education,
  334 ff.
Communist Party, 336
Community Builders' Handbook, 183
Competition, from Japanese, 36 f., 39,
  41 f.
Conant Gardens, 94
Concord (N.H.) *Monitor,* 199
Congregational Christian Churches of
  the United States, 220 f., 338 fn.
Congress of Industrial Organizations,
  97
Coolidge, Mary Roberts, 30 fn.,
  32 fn., 33 fn., 208 fn., 267 fn.
  287 fn.
Cooperatives, housing, 352
Corpus Juris, 254 fn.
Corrigan v. Buckley, 219 fn., 297 fn.
Cortwright, Frank W., 169 fn.
Costs of housing program, 350 f.
Coughlin, Charles, 13, 91, 97
Council for Civic Unity of San Fran-
  cisco, 337
Cox, James M., 123
The Crisis, 82 fn., 109 fn.
Crosby, Alexander L., x, 337 fn.
Crown Heights Owners Association,
  338
Cullman, Howard S., 274
Cutmore, Harry S., 166 fn.

Dade County Property Owners' Asso-
  ciation, 126
Daily Calumet, 118, 119
Darrow, Clarence, 93
Dean, John P., 72 fn., 140 fn., 218 fn.
Dearborn, Mich., 99 ff., 382
  anti-Negro sentiment in, 100 f.
"Democracy stinks," 154
Democratic pattern, threats to, 8 f.
Density, population, 177
DeRose, Mrs., 126
Deterioration, social, 139

Date Due